HISTORICAL ATLAS OF ANCIENT ROME

HISTORICAL ATLAS OF ANCIENT ROME

NICK CONSTABLE

Checkmark Books™
An imprint of Facts On File, Inc.

HISTORICAL ATLAS OF ANCIENT ROME

Checkmark Books
An imprint of Facts On File, Inc.
132 West 31st Street
New York, NY 10001

For Library of Congress Cataloging-in-Publication data, please contact
Checkmark Books. Control Number 12803030.
ISBN 0-8160-5331-6

For Thalamus Publishing
Project editor: Warren Lapworth
Maps and design: Roger Kean
Illustrations: Oliver Frey
Four-color separation: Proskanz, Ludlow, England

Printed and bound in Italy

10 9 8 7 6 5 4 3 2 1
This book is printed on acid-free paper

PICTURE CREDITS

Paul Almasy/CORBIS: 33, 123 (bottom), 143 (bottom); Archivo Iconografico, S.A./CORBIS: 1, 6–7, 14, 15 (top), 16, 18, 20, 40–41, 62 (top), 69, 70, 76, 83, 92 (top), 94 (bottom), 95, 103 (top), 104 (right), 114, 123 (top), 124 (top right), 124 (bottom), 134 (top right), 139 (top), 139 (bottom), 147 (bottom), 148 (left), 155 (bottom), 156, 165 (bottom), 166 (top left), 166 (bottom), 167 (center), 179; Arte & Immagini srl/CORBIS: 98; Dave Bartruff/CORBIS: 110; Morton Beebe/CORBIS: 99 (top); Bettman/CORBIS: 26, 82, 146; Burstein Collection/CORBIS: 92 (bottom); Christie's Images/CORBIS: 19; Elio Ciol/CORBIS: 150; Gianni dagli Orti/CORBIS: 24, 30, 38, 116; ESA/PLI/CORBIS: 2–3; MacduffEverton/CORBIS: 29, 127; Muzzi Fabio/CORBIS: 60 (bottom); Oliver Frey/Thalamus Studios: 12 , 13, 22–23, 25, 28, 37, 39, 41 (all), 42 (all), 44 , 45 (top), 46 (all), 48 (top), 51, 55 (inset), 57 (top), 57 (bottom right), 60 (top), 62 (bottom), 63 (both), 66, 67 (top), 71 (bottom), 72, 74 (top), 80–81, 85 (bottom), 102, 104 (left), 107, 108–109 (all), 111 (top), 121 (center), 122, 124 (top left), 126 (left), 129, 132 (bottom), 134 (top left), 134 (bottom), 135 (bottom), 141 (bottom both), 142 (top left), 142 (bottom left), 142 (bottom right), 143 (top), 145 (bottom), 147 (top), 154 (all), 158, 159 (top), 164 (both), 165 (top right), 166 (top right), 167 (top), 167 (bottom), 168 (top), 169 (bottom), 170 (inset), 171 (both), 172–173 (all), 174, 178 (bottom); Jason Hawkes/CORBIS: 175; Chris Hellier/CORBIS: 117 (right), 169 (top); John Heseltine/CORBIS: 45 (bottom), 118 (left), 135 (top); Angelo Hornak/CORBIS: 178 (top); Hanan Isachar/CORBIS: 157; Mimmo Jodice/CORBIS: 72–73, 120 (center), 132 (top right), 133 (left), 133 (right); Steve Kaufman/CORBIS: 111 (bottom); David Lees/CORBIS: 17; Charles & Josette Lenars/CORBIS: 36, 84; Massimo Listri/CORBIS: 148 (right); Araldo de Luca/CORBIS: 10 , 11, 32, 77, 85 (top), 87 (top), 87 (bottom), 89 (bottom), 94 (top), 105, 120 (top), 121 (top), 126 (right), 138, 142 (top right), 142 (center); Massimo Mastrorillo/CORBIS: 86; John & Lisa Merrill/CORBIS: 131 (right); Richard T. Nowitz/CORBIS: 151, 176; Thalamus Publishing: 89 (top), 103 (bottom), 118 (right), 118–119 (top), 119 , 125 , 130 (right), 131 (left), 152,153 (both), 161 (bottom); Vittoriano Rastelli/CORBIS: 130 (left); Carmen Redondo/CORBIS: 79, 117 (left), 149, 160;
Roger Ressmeyer/CORBIS: 120 (bottom); Benjamin Rondel/CORBIS: 155 (top); ML Sinibaldi/CORBIS: 106;
Gustavo Tomisch/CORBIS: 57 (bottom left); Ruggero Vanni/CORBIS: 68, 71 (top), 99 (bottom); Gian Berto Vanni/CORBIS: 161, 180 (left), 180 (right); Vanni Archive/CORBIS: 48 (bottom), 56, 74 (bottom), 88, 91 (bottom), 115, 140, 159 (bottom), 165 (top left), 168 (bottom), 173; Sandro Vannini/CORBIS: 78; Roger Wood/CORBIS: 40, 47, 49 , 118–119 (bottom), 121 (bottom), 132 (top left), 141 (top), 145 (top), 170; Adam Woolfitt/CORBIS: 54, 67 (bottom), 100, 177; Michael S. Yamashita/CORBIS: 90

Page 1: The history of ancient Rome is not all about architectural grandeur and clashing legions—there was also ordinary life. Bas-relief depicting a Roman butcher cutting pork in his shop, dating from the 2nd century AD.

Frontispiece: Europe seen from Earth orbit, shows the principal western regions of the Roman empire.

CONTENTS

Rome's Diverse History

The Roman empire encompassed a broad sweep of history, at times enlightened, at times barbarous, involving territories euphemistically known as the civilized world. From tribal beginnings, Rome exerted influence over the Italian peninsula, then southern Europe, North Africa, and the Levant. Thus the Romans were not one race but the product of many, living in numerous countries during a period of some 1,100 years.

To discuss the Roman empire in general terms is implausibly difficult. Its borders perpetually extended (and shrank), its enemies changed identity, as did its allies. Most of its citizens were paupers, although some were richer than kings.

Even the lifestyles of an artisan living in Rome and his brother manning a far-flung outpost were starkly diverse. While the first might have indulged in the political machinations that bubbled under the surface of cosmopolitan city life, the other would have only a passing glance at the official ruler of the day, being in the thrall of a charismatic commander in the field. Each would have a very different story to tell about the Roman empire.

During this swathe of history, technology advanced, changing the face of everyday living. From the Romans we got arrow-straight roads and cubic town planning. But the Romans were receptive to ideas from elsewhere, as their faith and culture reveals. Greek ideas, culture, and religion seeped through Roman society, before and after conquest of Greece.

We know much about the Roman empire due to a massive body of literature centered on its civilization. It includes the writings of an army of historians at work during antiquity, including such luminaries as Cassius Dio, Polybius, Josephus, and Tacitus. From them we get detailed accounts of life in ancient Rome.

Alas, they were often writing about events hundreds of years after they happened. While oral tradition was strong, there must remain a shadow of doubt over the veracity of some stories. Likewise, all had a different agenda and most were imbued with patriotic fervor, or at least toed the official line, skewing their

perspective on events.

It is desirable, but not always possible, to back up the words of the ancients with archaeological discoveries. Many artifacts have been unearthed—most spectacularly those at Pompeii, the Roman city swallowed whole by volcanic ash and preserved for centuries, like a hidden diorama. It is one of the few clues that tell us what life was like for the ordinary Roman citizen, for ancient historians focused on the glories of Rome, its leaders, generals, and accomplishments.

This book charts the story of a city and its huge sphere of influence, its climb to greatness and fall from grace. It offers a framework on which to place dizzying tales of heroism, drama, murder, mayhem, exploration, adventure, strategy, science, faith, and fortune. On every page it underscores the relevance of the Romans, who did so much to shape and order the world that we live in today.

The Roman genius for civil engineering is never better exemplified than by Pont du Gard aqueduct, which spans the River Gard, and once carried water between Uzes and Nimes, France.

CHAPTER 1

ROME AND ITALY

Peeling back the centuries is a task best undertaken with a wedge of ancient manuscripts and a wealth of archaeological artifacts at hand. Contrasting the evidence thrown up by both helps to illustrate what went on years ago. Alas, these options are not available to the student of old Rome. Not the Rome of twisted emperors like Nero, or the one known by the ambitious general Julius Caesar. Not even the Rome that Hannibal of Carthage had in his sights when he transported men, horses, and elephants on a demanding trek over the Alps. These periods are relatively well known.

The Rome we want to know more about began life as a humble village and, through a set of happy circumstances, rose to greatness. There is precious little with which to gain insight into what occurred to herald the glories of Rome. The remaining nuggets of information handed down from generation to generation have been transformed into fables that have delighted but bear limited credence. Today it is impossible to extricate truth from fiction.

Yet without these muddied myths the history of Rome has no personalities to ponder, no characters to champion. Perhaps it is as well to people the backdrop by putting them in the context of semi-legend. One feature of early Roman life that is certain is the existence of clans that evolved into renowned families, which dominated early political life and has parallels in dynasties and elite circles of the later republic and empire.

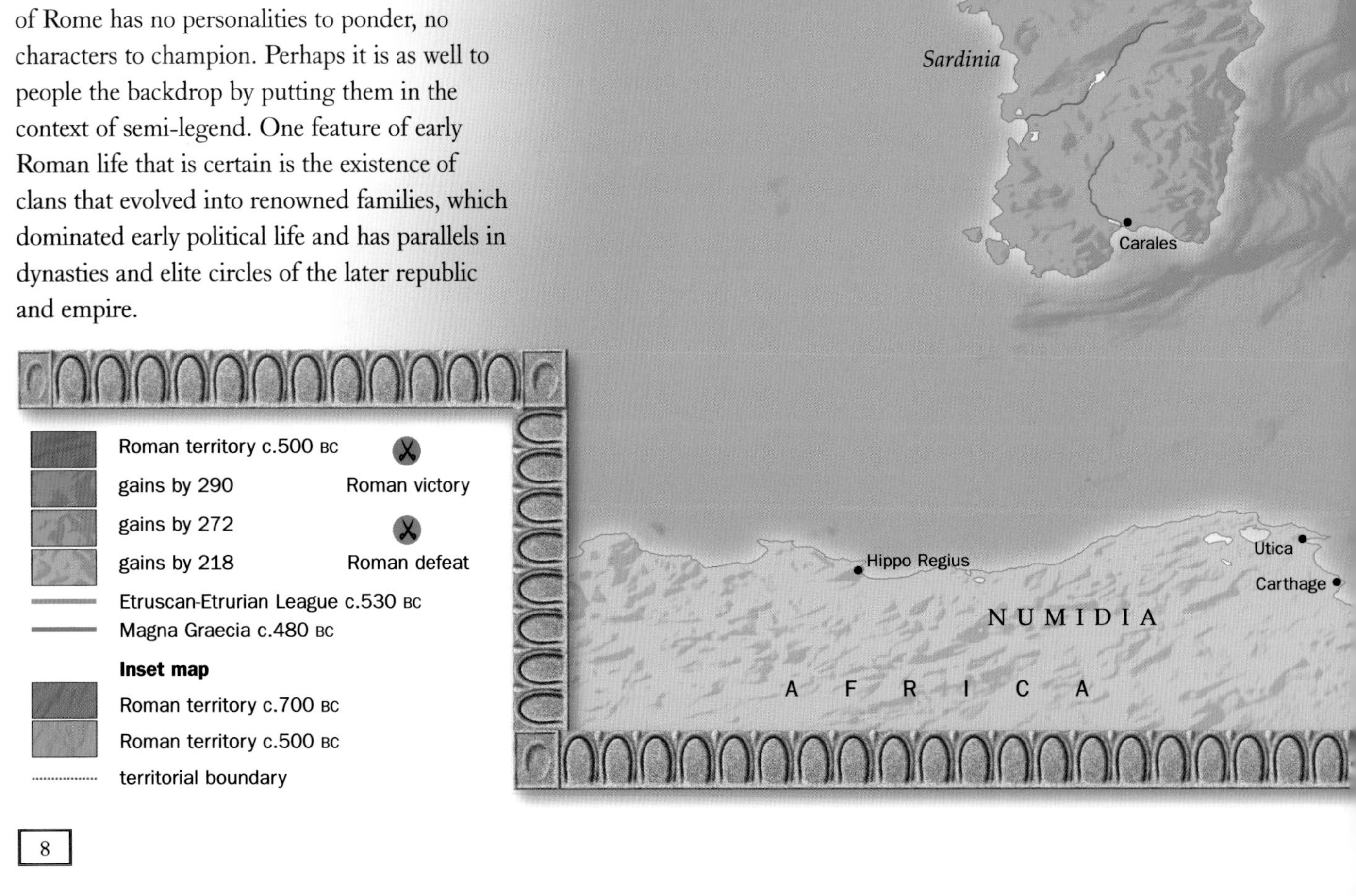

Sardinia
Carales
Roman territory c.500 BC
gains by 290
gains by 272
gains by 218
Roman victory
Roman defeat
Etruscan-Eturian League c.530 BC
Magna Graecia c.480 BC
Inset map
Roman territory c.700 BC
Roman territory c.500 BC
territorial boundary
Hippo Regius
Utica
Carthage
NUMIDIA
A F R I C A

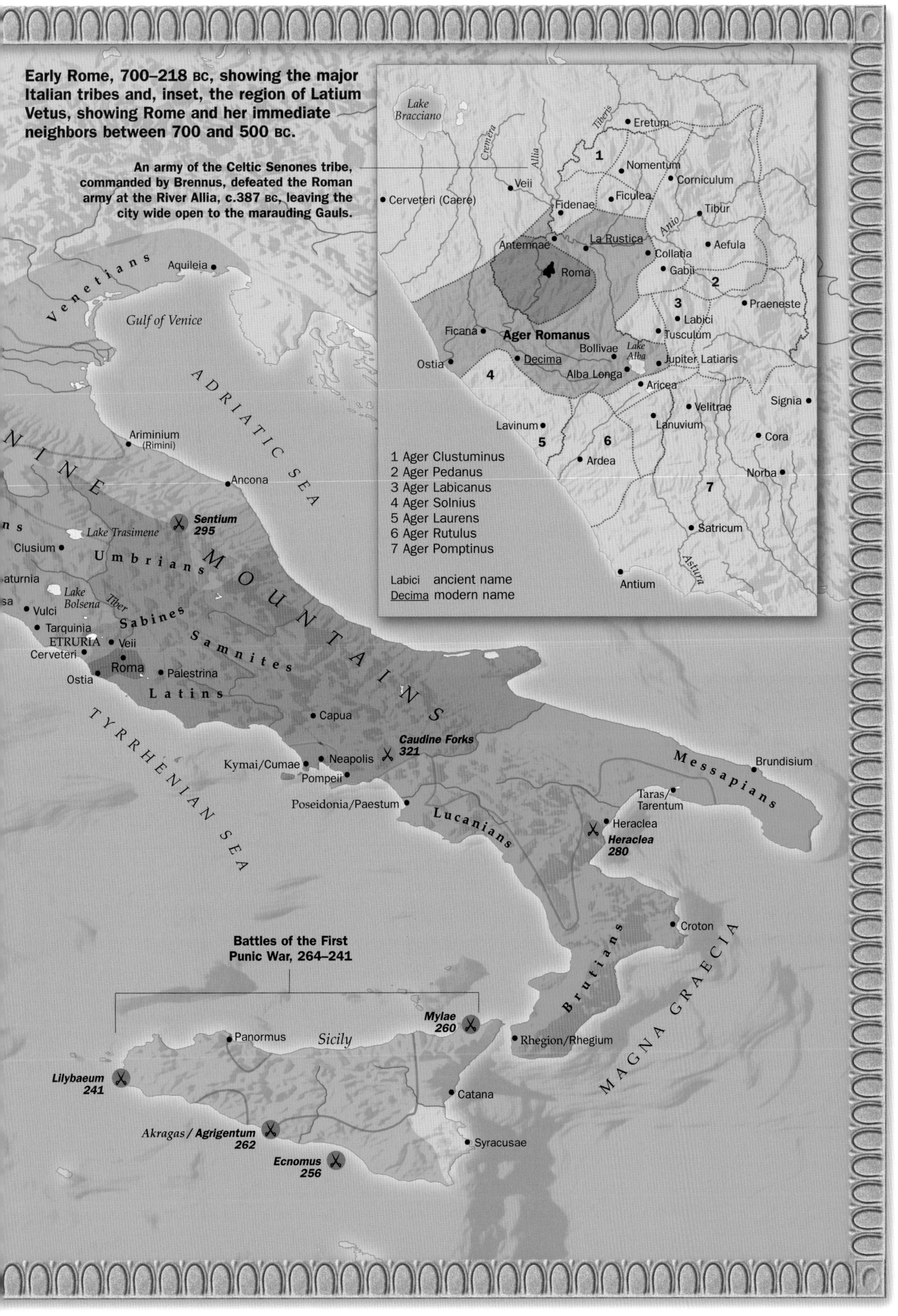
Early Rome, 700–218 BC, showing the major Italian tribes and, inset, the region of Latium Vetus, showing Rome and her immediate neighbors between 700 and 500 BC.
An army of the Celtic Senones tribe, commanded by Brennus, defeated the Roman army at the River Allia, c.387 BC, leaving the city wide open to the marauding Gauls.
Lake Bracciano
Cremera
Allia
Tiberis
Eretum
Nomentum
Corniculum
Veii
Cerveteri (Caere)
Fidenae
Ficulea
Tibur
Anio
Antemnae
La Rustica
Aefula
Collatia
Roma
Gabii
Praeneste
Labici
Ficana
Ager Romanus
Tusculum
Bollivae
Lake Alba
Ostia
Decima
Jupiter Latiaris
Alba Longa
Aricea
Velitrae
Signia
Lavinum
Lanuvium
Cora
Ardea
Norba
Satricum
Astura
Antium
1 Ager Clustuminus
2 Ager Pedanus
3 Ager Labicanus
4 Ager Solnius
5 Ager Laurens
6 Ager Rutulus
7 Ager Pomptinus
Labici ancient name
Decima modern name
Venetians
Aquileia
Gulf of Venice
ADRIATIC SEA
Ariminium (Rimini)
Ancona
Sentium 295
Lake Trasimene
Clusium
Umbrians
MOUNTAINS
Lake Bolsena
Tiber
Vulci
Tarquinia
Sabines
ETRURIA
Veii
Cerveteri
Samnites
Roma
Palestrina
Ostia
Latins
TYRRHENIAN SEA
Capua
Caudine Forks 321
Kymai/Cumae
Neapolis
Pompeii
Poseidonia/Paestum
Messapians
Brundisium
Taras/Tarentum
Lucanians
Heraclea
Heraclea 280
Croton
Brutians
MAGNA GRAECIA
Battles of the First Punic War, 264–241
Mylae 260
Panormus
Sicily
Rhegion/Rhegium
Lilybaeum 241
Catana
Akragas / Agrigentum 262
Syracusae
Ecnomus 256

Foundation and Legend

A legend attached to the founding of Rome provides a date, as well as a pen portrait of the man who named the city. The seven hills undoubtedly sheltered one or more communities before Romulus, but the story still has resonance.

Below: The Capitoline she-wolf, from the early 5th century BC. Early Greek historians attributed the foundation of Rome to Trojan hero Aeneas. Later, Romans linked this story to that of Romulus and Remus—suckled by a she-wolf—who were said to be Aeneas's descendants.

Myths have a habit of growing, like a beanstalk from a kernel of truth. Unlikely as it may appear today, it is worth recounting the story of Rome's twins, still the most famous legend linked with the city.

After being raped by Mars, the god of war (the Roman version of the god Ares in Greek legend), the beautiful princess Rhea Silvia gave birth to twin sons named Romulus and Remus. Her father had recently been toppled from the throne by his ambitious brother. Fearful that the babes would inherit the realm, their great uncle cast them into the River Tiber in a wooden chest.

They were rescued by a she-wolf who suckled them until a shepherd adopted them. They lived a kind of Robin Hood existence as adults, attacking robbers and dividing the spoils among their close community, which lived among the hills on the right (east) bank of the Tiber. Eventually they deposed the usurper and replaced their grandfather on the throne. It was here that the twins founded new settlements. They chose different hills on which to build their fortresses, but when Remus mocked Romulus, his angry brother slaughtered him. King Romulus established his settlement on April 21, 753 BC* and gave it his name.

Romulus gathered around him outcasts and exiles and became concerned that there were insufficient women to ensure the survival of the fledgling state. Accordingly, he arranged a feast for the neighboring Sabines, settled on Quirinal, the most northerly of the seven hills. After the Sabine men were thoroughly inebriated, Romulus and his supporters seized the Sabine

* Third-century Roman writer Fabius Pictor gave the founding date as 748 BC, but other dates (728, 751, 753) were favored by later Republican writers. It was the scholar M. Terentius Varro who set the official date of 753 in stone at the end of the republican period.

women. Fortunately, the women fell in love with their captors and ultimately brokered a peace between Romans and Sabines. Romulus was either murdered by colleagues outraged at his delusions of grandeur or he vanished in a storm, *en route* for celestial greatness. Romans later worshipped him as the god Quirinus.

Healthful hills

This account is an approximate reflection of that given by different Roman historians, including Livy, although some put other personalities into the frame of the legend. Some go further, linking the brothers' descent to the family of Aeneas, the Trojan hero.

Mythology loomed large for Romans, even in empire days. There were obvious incentives to link the founder of Rome with potent gods. However, the custom to tailor a legend in order to explain the naming of a place belongs to the Greeks and the story of Romulus and Remus may reflect an early Greek influence in the Roman world.

This particular legend was currency from the fourth century BC and was committed to the written word soon afterward. Those propagating the story did not have access to the information we have now, that the area we know today as Rome was settled centuries before the era supposedly belonging to Romulus. The remains of rectangular wattle and daub huts on the Palatine hill are proof of it.

The seven hills of Rome on the east bank of the Tiber in the Archaic period

1–2 Possible first sites for Roman settlement under the legendary Romulus and Remus
3 Sabine settlement
4 site of Forum Romananum
5 temple of Jupiter Capitolinus
6 Arx
7 Forum Boarium
8 Pons Sublicanus (Sublician Bridge), thought to be constructed under the half-legendary King Ancus Marcius (ruled c.640–14)

Quirinal
Viminal
Campus Martius (Field of Mars)
Tiberis (Tiber)
Capitoline
Subura
Esquiline
Janiculum
Velian Slope
Palatine
Caelian
Aventine
N
Local route that will form the basis for the via Appia
Local route that will form the basis for the via Aurelia
0 500 1000 yards
0 500 1000 meters

But perhaps the important factor is not who founded Rome but why. As Livy put it in his *History of Rome*: "Not without good reason did gods and men select this place for founding a city: these most healthful hills; a commodious river, by means of which the produce of the soil may be conveyed from the inland countries, by which maritime supplies may be obtained; close enough to the sea for all purposes of convenience, and not exposed by too much proximity to the dangers of foreign fleets."

Once populated, there was little to distinguish Rome from a number of other settlements around Italy. Indeed, many boasted a culture and a history that far exceeded that of the infant Rome.

Left: A hut-urn to contain ashes of the dead. Before the Law of the Twelve Tables (451 BC) forbade burial within the limits of human habitation, villagers used parts of the Palatine and Esquiline hills, and the Forum, as cemeteries. Interrments included cremation and inhumation (burial). In the case of cremation, the ashes were first placed inside urns like this, designed in imitation of the dwellings common on the Roman hills. The urn was then placed in a pottery jar with a stone lid and placed in a deep, circular pit.

AGE OF MONARCHY

Rome began as a monarchy. While there is a body of legend describing the early kings, there is little archaeological evidence and no contemporary written record. The archaic era was hardly a model in wise government, and excess ultimately brought forth the great days of the republic.

Below: Reconstruction of an early Roman settlement on the Palatine. The huts are plastered mud, with thatched roofs. In the background, people can be seen fording the Tiber long before the construction of the Sublician bridge.

Romulus is credited with creating three voting tribes, each split into ten smaller units (*curiae*), who selected an assembly from among themselves (*comitia curiata*) to act as a curb on the king's powers. And it may have been Romulus or his successor, the Sabine Numa Pompilius (r.715–673 BC)*, who formed the advisory body of a hundred chosen "fathers" known as the Senate.

Kingship in Rome was not hereditary. On the king's death, government was continued by the senators, each one holding office for five days, with the title of *interrex* (between king), until a suitable successor was found. In this way, the young settlement chose Numa, who is credited with being a sage and peaceful ruler. It was said that his wisdom came from the goddess Egeria, who he met on a nightly basis just outside the settlement walls. Thanks to this deity, he learned the dubious art of foretelling the future from the intestines of cows. In consequence, Pompilius oversaw the creation of major religious institutions and the first calendar, which outlined the days on which religious festivities should occur.

His Latin successor, Tullus Hostilius (r.673–41), was troubled by border disputes throughout his reign. The more culturally advanced Etruscans of Veii and Fidenae were his most pressing enemies, but Tullus also fought a campaign against Rome's mother city of Alba Longa. Allies of Rome, the Albans were not reliable. When one Alban king held back troops during a clash between Rome and Fidenae so he could pitch in on the winning side, the victorious Romans tied him between two horse-drawn chariots. As the horses were whipped into action the king was torn in two, viciously symbolizing the dilemma of indecision.

The Sabine Ancus Marcius (r.640–14) survived a string of conflicts with nearby settlements. He enlarged the city by overwhelming neighboring villages and relocating their populations to Rome. According to Livy, it was Ancus Marcius who created the post of *pontifex maximus*, or chief priest. His role was to organize the religious calendar and it became a title hotly sought after in later generations. Intriguingly, *pontifex maximus* translates to "great bridge builder," leading to speculation that Ancus Marcius was responsible for the first bridge across the Tiber. If he indeed constructed a walkway between the riverbanks, he surely boosted the city's economy considerably.

Confidant or conqueror?

The next ruler of Rome was of Etruscan extraction. Yet Tarquinius Priscus (r.617–579), or Tarquin I, was not an invader but an elected king. Legend tells how Tarquinius and his wife traveled to Rome in search of a fresh start. As they perched on the Janiculum to survey the

* Dates given for the kings are traditional, not necessarily historical.

city, an eagle flew down and snatched the hat from his head. The bird circled overhead for a few moments before diving down to replace the hat. Tarquinius took this as an omen that he was to be crowned king of Rome. The eagle, along with the she-wolf who saved Romulus and Remus, remained a symbol of Rome.

The story goes on to tell how Tarquinius became a popular and trusted member of Ancus Marcius's court and succeeded to the throne on the latter's death. There is always the possibility this tale was woven to obliterate an unpalatable truth, that a hostile force sent by the superior Etruscans occupied Rome.

His successor, Servius Tullius (r.579–34), was a slave-turned-ruler who reorganized the Roman army along Greek lines, introducing phalanxes. The Servian Wall, which surrounded the seven hills, was named after him, but is more likely to have been constructed during the republic in the fourth century BC. Servius also created the *comitia centuriata*, a new assembly in which citizens were distributed in voting units, called centuries, according to the property and weapons they owned. It operated alongside the *comitia curiata* but eventually replaced it.

Servius, who claimed a special relationship with the goddess Fortuna, built her a temple in the Forum Boarium, and excavations have uncovered the foundations of a temple from this period, the mid-sixth century BC.

Servius was murdered, to be replaced without election by his son-in-law Tarquinius Superbus (the Proud), or Tarquin II. In that he seized the throne without the consent of either senators or the *comitia curiata*, it is clear that the later monarchy had changed its character. Tarquin II appears to have wanted complete control, and launched an all-out attack on the aristocracy, ignored the advice of the senators, and went so far as to have leading members of the Senate put to death. Similarly to his Greek counterparts, Tarquin II was a tyrant.

Tarquin was finally overthrown by a group of senators in a rebellion inspired when his son Sextus raped a noble woman in 509 BC. With his removal, Etruscan influence in Rome was brought to an end, and the city was now ruled by a two-consul system, probably devised while the kings were still in power.

Below: Known as the Lapis Niger, this fragment of stone was found under paving in the Forum. It is Rome's earliest known public document, probably from the early sixth century BC. The archaic Latin text cannot be fully understood, but is thought to be a ritual inscription for religious perfomance or the maintenance of a sanctuary.

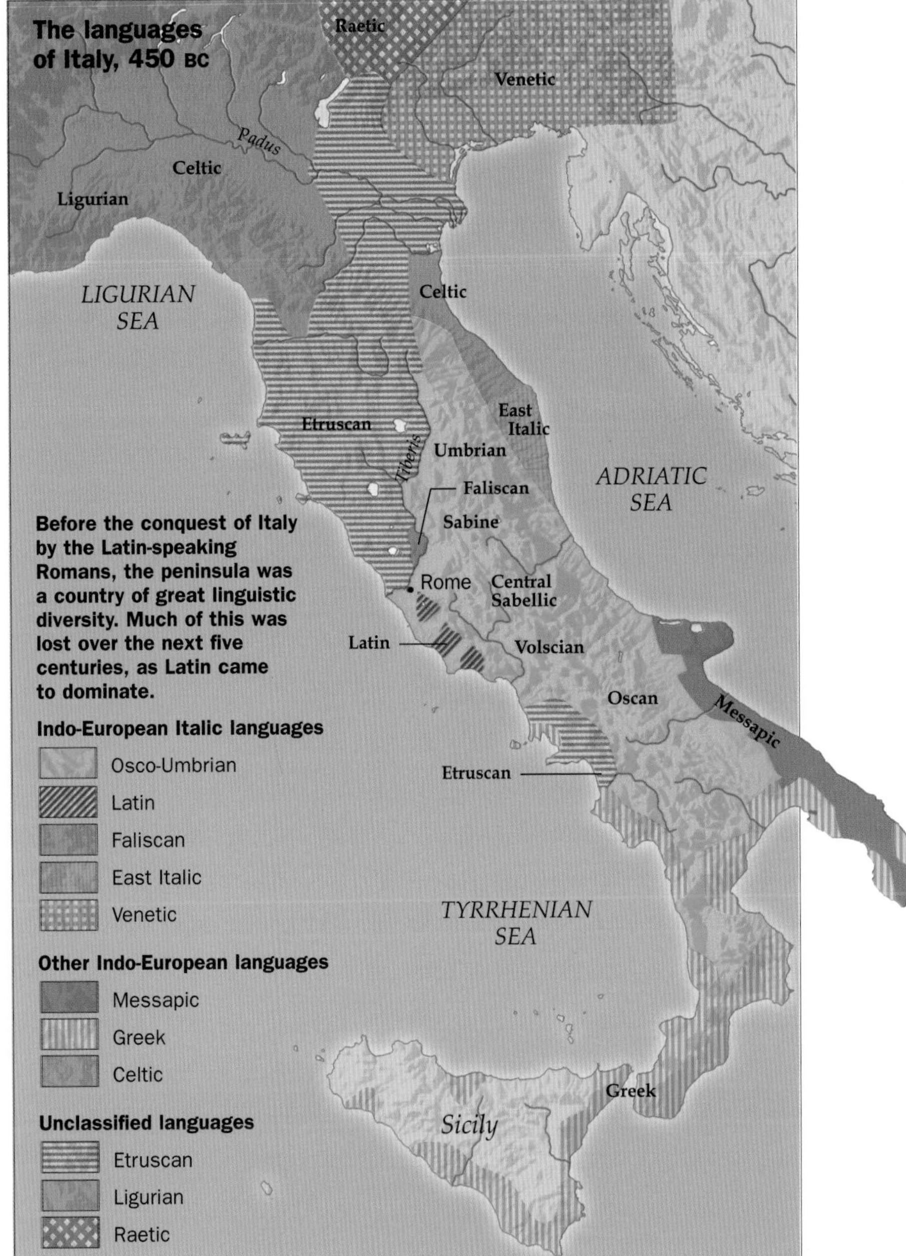

The languages of Italy, 450 BC
Raetic
Venetic
Padus
Celtic
Ligurian
LIGURIAN SEA
Celtic
Etruscan
East Italic
Umbrian
Tiberis
Faliscan
ADRIATIC SEA
Sabine
Rome
Central Sabellic
Latin
Volscian
Oscan
Messapic
Etruscan
TYRRHENIAN SEA
Greek
Sicily
Before the conquest of Italy by the Latin-speaking Romans, the peninsula was a country of great linguistic diversity. Much of this was lost over the next five centuries, as Latin came to dominate.
Indo-European Italic languages
Osco-Umbrian
Latin
Faliscan
East Italic
Venetic
Other Indo-European languages
Messapic
Greek
Celtic
Unclassified languages
Etruscan
Ligurian
Raetic

ETRUSCAN CIVILIZATION

The dearth of Etruscan buildings and written records has forced historians to seek clues to this enigmatic culture. Many of these were unearthed in Tuscany during the 19th century. Although landowners were quick to sell treasures, the surviving wall paintings reveal a fascinating story.

Facing: Etruscan sarcophagus of a married couple, c.520 BC.

Some of the more important murals (painted on stone) and frescoes (painted on plaster) have emerged at Tarquinia. Here, in the fifth-century BC Tomb of the Leopards, scenes of men and women banqueting, dancing, and pipe-playing, suggest that Etruscan funerals were upbeat affairs. The nearby Tomb of the Augurs, perhaps half a century older, depicts two men wrestling in front of a referee, an indication that the dead were expected to spend their days in paradise engaged in contests of strength or athleticism. A pile of metal dishes—presumably the winner's prize—can also be seen in the picture.

Above: Detail of the wrestlers, wall painting in the Tomb of the Augurs, Tarquinia.

In the later cemeteries more depressing images of death are revealed, perhaps reflecting the general downturn in Etruscan fortunes. The gory battle scenes portrayed on the walls of the François tomb at Vulci and the mythical monsters of the second-century BC Tomb of the Ogre at Tarquinia are among the best examples.

Several graves provide creature comforts for their dead occupants. At Cerveteri the third-century BC Tomb of the Reliefs (*see following page*) includes carved couches, while the Tomb of the Alcove tries to recreate the decor of a typical nobleman's house with sculptured ceiling rafters and fluted pillars. There is even a bedroom furnished with a stone bed and pillow. As in all Etruscan tombs, these chambers would have contained decorated terracotta or clay utensils and probably some fine bronzes (the Etruscans were accomplished metalworkers).

Because buildings were made of perishable brick and wood, it is difficult to judge the range of architectural styles found in Etruria. However, we know from ceramic models that temples were designed with a four-pillared entrance leading to three parallel alcoves, the abode of the main gods. Roman historians believed the Etruscan deities Tinis, Uni, and Menrva represented members of their own pantheon, Jupiter, Juno, and Minerva. There also seems to have been a higher spiritual plane occupied by Fate and certain figures from the Greek underworld.

Law and insight

Divination was a cornerstone of Etruscan religion and priests deployed an array of imaginative techniques. These included

predictions based on the outpouring of entrails from a freshly sacrificed animal, the position and frequency of lightning strikes, and the direction in which flocks of birds flew around a particular city. These practices were detailed in a religious manual known as the *Etrusca Disciplina*, which also laid down laws and moral standards.

Unlocking the Etruscan language has been a painfully slow process but we now know that it was based on early Greek and eventually distilled to an alphabet of 20 letters. Meanings have been teased out using a standard code-breaking technique that compares particular words with their setting. This process received a boost with the discovery of a 1,200-word Etruscan book detailing religious festivals and ritual practice, which was found in the Zagreb Archaeological Museum. It was written on linen cloth and had been recycled as the binding for an Egyptian mummy.

Equally useful was the recovery of three golden tablets from Pyrgi, the harbor of Cerveteri, written by one Thefarie Valianus in praise of the goddess Uni. Two of these were in Etruscan but the third provided a Phoenician translation, allowing morphologists to make crucial deductions about language structure. Alas, the Etruscans seem to have been masters of brevity. Often the writing in tombs simply names the occupant.

The might of the Etruscan navy reflects the importance of the region's sea-trade links. There was brisk business with the Phoenicians from the eighth century BC, with the Etruscans exchanging metal, wood, and animal hides for decorated pottery. The Greeks were enthusiastic buyers of bronzes and by the Iron Age Etruscan merchants were regular visitors to Spain's southeast coast, northern Gaul, and perhaps the tin mines of southwest Britain. Disruption of this sea trade by rival city-states was usually the driving force behind alliances—and a pretext for war.

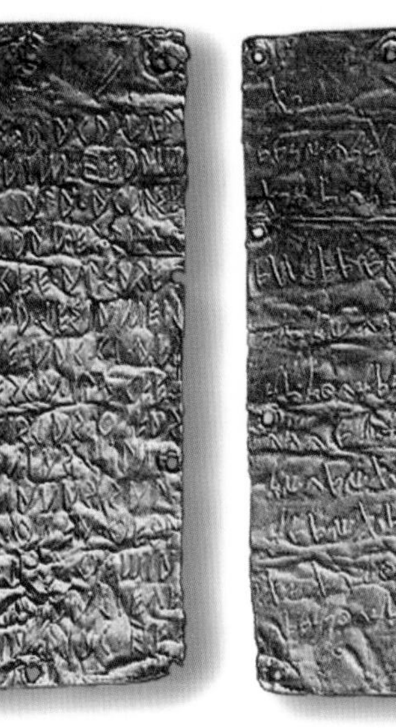

Above: Two gold sheets bear a dedication by a sixth-century ruler of Cerveteri. The text is Etruscan, with a shorter version in Phoenician, indicating a link to Carthage.

Rome and Etruria

The origin of the Etruscans was a hot debating point among Roman and Greek historians. Whether the peoples of this powerful maritime state were indigenous to the Italian peninsula or arrived from Lydia (modern western Turkey) remains uncertain.

The Etruscans were known as Etrusci to the Romans, a name that gradually became shortened to Tusci and survives today as the Italian region of Tuscany. Their first villages were built in the boggy coastal lowlands north of Rome and by the eighth century BC some of the aristocracy had amassed great wealth. Excavations of early tombs have logged imported gems from North Africa, Egypt, and western Asia, as well as locally sourced silver, gold, and amber.

Over the next 400 years Etruscan warlords established a group of influential city-states, such as Cerveteri, Veii, and Tarquinia, which themselves began colonizing new territories and sealing alliances. It is likely that the partly mythical early rulers of Rome, Lucius Tarquinius Superbus and his father Lucius Tarquinius Priscus, were Etruscan and their ancestors would have laid the city's foundations, drained the swamps, and cleared nomadic sheep-herders off the Palatine hill.

While Etruscan cities shared a common heritage they were far from a unified state. There was some economic and trading ties, joint military ventures, and occasional conferences to discuss political or religious matters. One of these summits was held annually at the shrine of the god Voltumna, above Lake Bolsena, but it seems to have contributed little in the way of joint strategies—in times of trouble, each

Below: Wall niches for couches in the Tomb of the Reliefs, Necropolis of Banditaccia, Cerveteri, 4th–3rd centuries BC.

Etruscan city looked after its own.

Trouble was inevitable. The Greeks regarded the Etruscans as immoral and accused them of piracy. Such a charge could equally have been leveled at any Greek city-state with half a navy, and the rhetoric was more about a struggle for control of the central Mediterranean than enforcement of law on the high seas.

No citizenship

In 474 BC the Greek-founded cities of Syracuse in Sicily and Cumae (Kymai in Greek) inflicted a major naval defeat on their rivals, marking the beginning of a slow decline in Etruscan influence. By the early fourth century Rome had conquered the city of Veii and was busy shoring up its crucial trading links across Etruscan territory to the north. Within a century the cities of Caere, Vulci, and Tarquinia were Roman client-kingdoms, forced to give up lands and pay tribute. Infighting among the ruling elite and social turmoil among the working classes resulted in more and more Etruscan cities seeking alliances with Rome.

During the first century BC this uneasy peace was backed by a general offer of Roman citizenship. Unfortunately for the Etruscans it coincided with the Roman civil war of 88–86, in which they backed the wrong side—Gaius Marius's middle class *populares* party. As soon as the victor and subsequent dictator Lucius Cornelius Sulla was assured of victory, he began a vengeful ethnic cleansing campaign against Etruria, burning cities, looting goods, confiscating property, and imposing draconian restrictions on freedom. It would be another century before the Etruscans became full members of the Roman family through re-colonization by the first emperor, Augustus.

One of the great problems with Etruscan history is that so few records survive. We are forced to rely heavily on a Roman view, summarized acidly by D.H. Lawrence in his *Etruscan Places*: "Those pure, clean-living, sweet-souled Romans, who smashed nation after nation and crushed the free soul in people after people... they said the Etruscans were vicious."

Be that as it may, Rome thrived on the habits of its neighbor. Its army was organized in Etruscan fashion, with legions answering the call of the tuba (originally an Etruscan instrument). The soldiers' temporary camps were raised on a north-south grid, just as sacred Etruscan laws specified. And right up to the early imperial years it was fashionable for Roman patricians to send their sons to Etruscan schools for a grounding in the moral code *Etrusca Disciplina*.

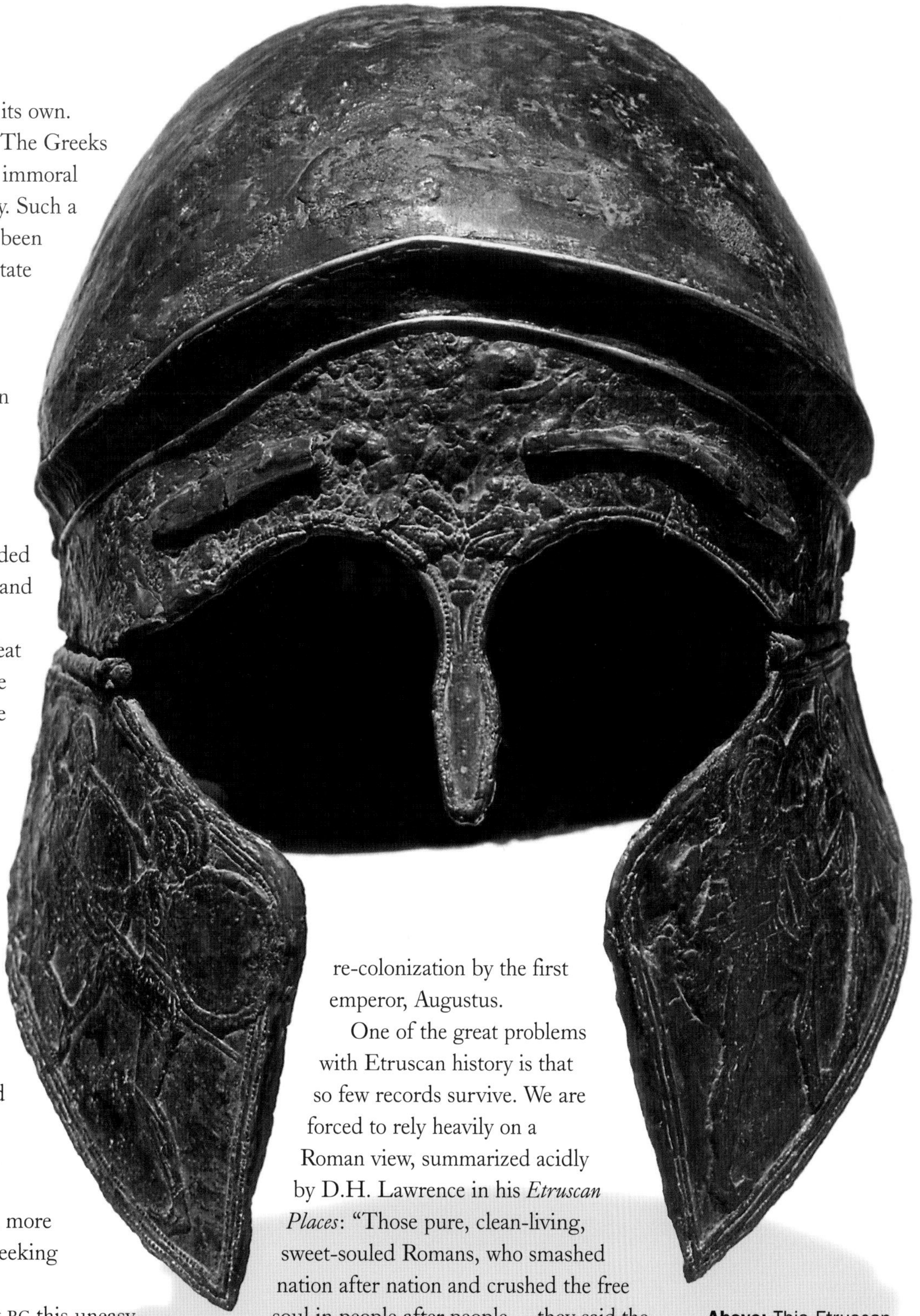

Above: This Etruscan helmet has cheek guards decorated with scenes of fighting men carrying round shields.

Hostile Neighbors

Rome was a collection of villages that joined together to become a town, lying in the region known as Latium Vetus. Many other culturally and linguistically different settlements dotted the peninsula, including in the south colonies of Greek city-states and in the north the migrating Celtic tribes of Gaul.

Above: This round vessel of c.450 BC is decorated with six snake heads and incised scenes of warriors, mounted and on foot, carrying spears and circular shields. The warlike—although largely agrarian—Celts of northern Europe sought the rich agricultural lands along the Po valley and came into conflict with expanding Rome.

Greek presence was so strong in southern Italy that it was known among Romans as Magna Graecia or Great Greece. The Greek-speaking states included Neapolis, Cumae, Heraclea, Thurii, Paestum, and Tarentum. There were other settlements, clustered in the same region as Rome and almost certainly sharing similar languages and faiths, who banded together in times of trouble to form the Latin League. Rome joined the Latin League in 493 BC; although burgeoning in size and importance, it was still competing with towns like Tibur, Praeneste, and Tusculum.

The most eminent Latin city was Alba Longa, some 12 miles from Rome, apparently founded in 1152 BC and probably the mother city of the Roman settlement. It led the Latin League until its defeat by Rome during the reign of Tullus Hostilius. Rome was emboldened by its successes in border skirmishes, and when Etruscan influence ebbed in the region it appeared ready to step into the void.

Convention dictated that Rome would not make war on her neighbors without due declaration or just cause. Hostilities began when a "magic" spear was thrown into enemy territory. Later, when Rome's boundaries were extended, the spear was symbolically thrown in a piece of consecrated ground outside one of the city's temples.

The precise movements of Roman forces in the fifth century BC are unknown. However, there was a war with Fidenae between 437 and 426, in which Rome triumphed. There were perpetual skirmishes between the Romans and the Sabines to the north, the Aequi in the northeast, and most significant of all, the Volsci, southeast of Rome. By the turn of the century, Rome appears to have got the measure of its opponents and secured its borders.

Celtic invaders

Following a series of disputes over control of a Tiber crossing point and nearby salt flats, Rome moved against the Etruscan city of Veii in 405, beginning a decade-long siege. The victory ultimately secured by Rome gave a hint of the military greatness to come. It was the proud possessor of a mighty haul of loot and had doubled its size. One tenth of the loot was dispatched to Delphi in Greece, as a thanksgiving to the god Apollo. In real terms, this was national bragging, alerting neighbors to Roman aspirations. Unfortunately, the victory was marred by the Roman general Furius Camillus, who allowed his troops to murder Veii's population. The few survivors were sold into slavery.

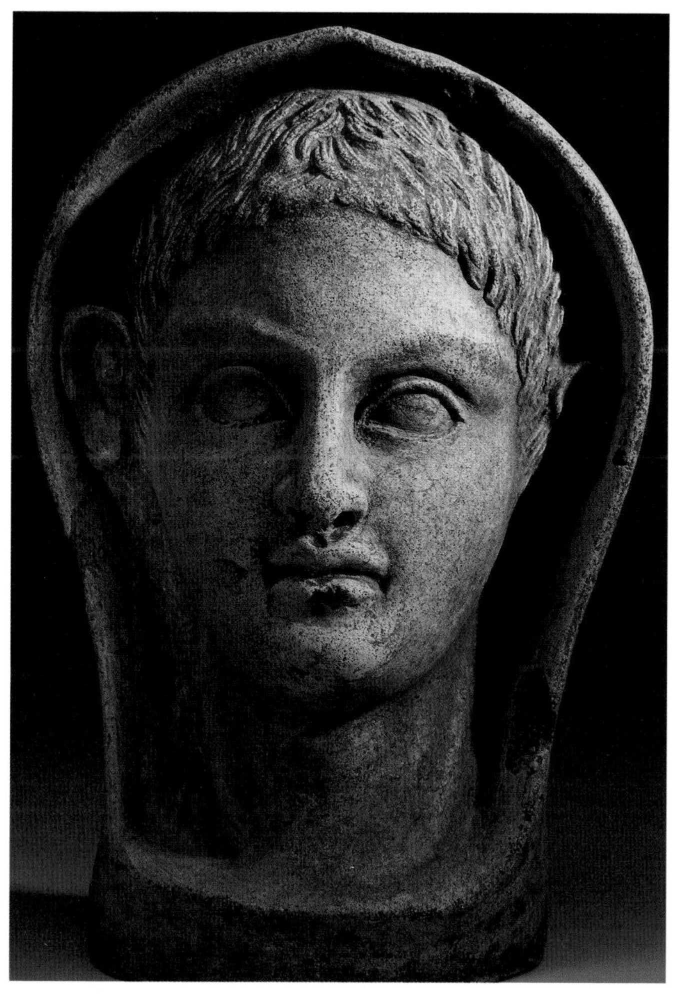

Those who began farming in northern Italy were threatened by further influxes from Gaul.

An army of marauding Senones came within ten miles of Rome in 387. When the outnumbered Romans engaged them in battle, they found their spears ill-matched against the Gallic long swords. Thereafter, the Battle of the Allia was remembered as a black day for Rome. The Celts marched on Rome, and the city folk withdrew to the Capitol. The Romans capitulated after a seven-month siege. Satisfied with a healthy ransom of gold and the plunder gathered from the city's temples and homes, the Celts withdrew without enslaving the population.

The sorry incident has given birth to numerous legends, including that of the sacred geese of Juno squawking when they detected a stealthy enemy raiding party, so that snoozing defenders were alerted and managed to beat off the attack. Elderly Roman senators, showing stoic contempt for the barbarians, apparently sat motionless on their ivory seats as Celts pillaged the city streets; all were massacred.

Left: An Etruscan terracotta votive male head dating from between the fourth and third centuries BC. The Etruscans also suffered during the Celtic invasion of northern Italy. Called Gauli (Gauls) by the Romans, after the land from which they came, the Celtic tribes of Insubres defeated the Etruscans near Milan, and the Senones marched south to attack Rome.

Any sense of superiority enjoyed by the Romans was quickly dispelled when the Celts invaded. They came in waves, heading over the Alps into northern Italy, with various tribes migrating to different regions and overwhelming the disparate settlements they encountered.

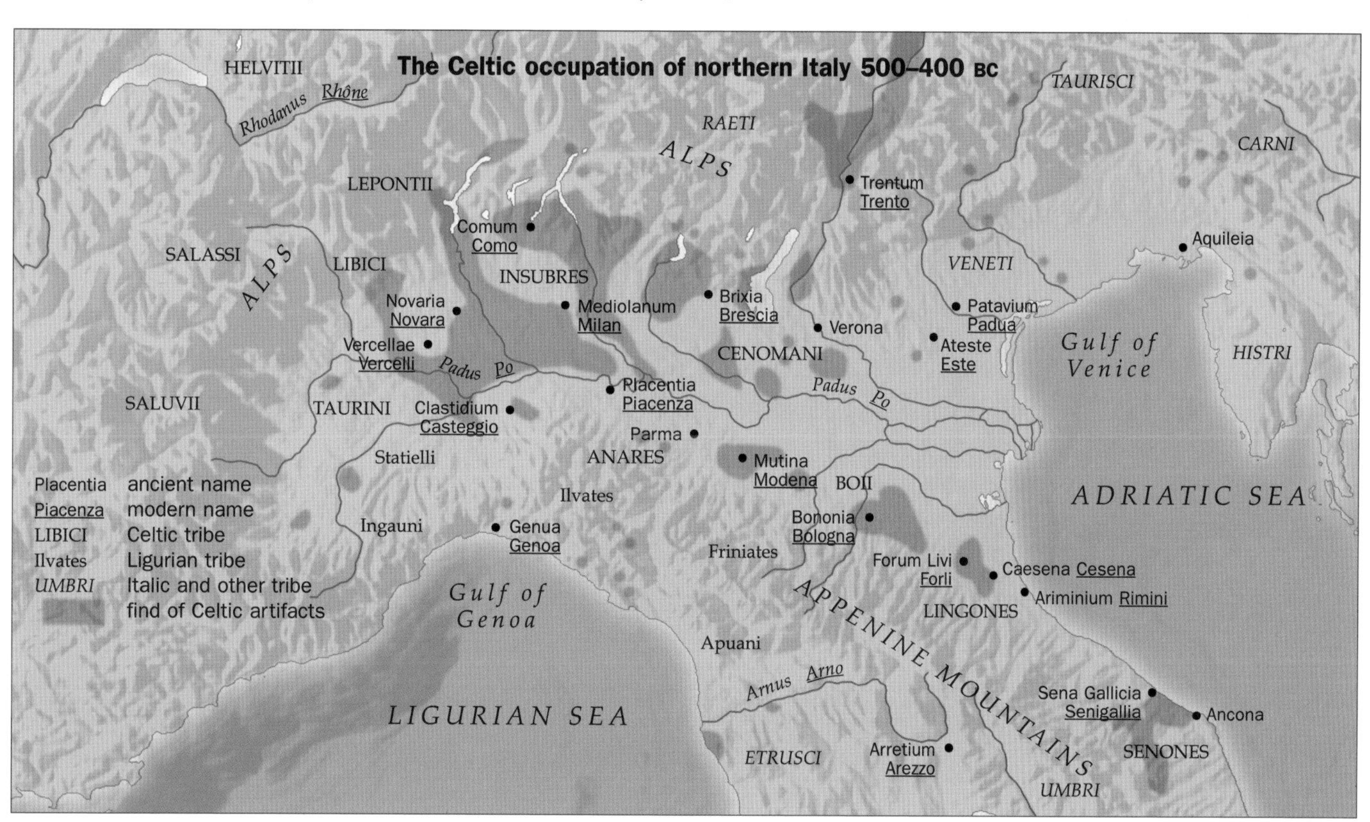
The Celtic occupation of northern Italy 500–400 BC
HELVITII
Rhodanus Rhône
TAURISCI
RAETI
ALPS
CARNI
LEPONTII
Trentum Trento
Comum Como
SALASSI
ALPS
LIBICI
INSUBRES
VENETI
Aquileia
Novaria Novara
Mediolanum Milan
Brixia Brescia
Verona
Patavium Padua
Vercellae Vercelli
Padus Po
CENOMANI
Ateste Este
Gulf of Venice
HISTRI
Placentia Piacenza
Padus Po
SALUVII
TAURINI
Clastidium Casteggio
Parma
Statielli
ANARES
Mutina Modena
BOII
ADRIATIC SEA
Ilvates
Bononia Bologna
Ingauni
Genua Genoa
Friniates
Forum Livi Forli
Caesena Cesena
Ariminium Rimini
Gulf of Genoa
APPENINE MOUNTAINS
LINGONES
Apuani
Arnus Arno
Sena Gallicia Senigallia
Ancona
LIGURIAN SEA
ETRUSCI
Arretium Arezzo
SENONES
UMBRI
Placentia ancient name
Piacenza modern name
LIBICI Celtic tribe
Ilvates Ligurian tribe
UMBRI Italic and other tribe
find of Celtic artifacts

UNIFICATION OF ITALY

Following the departure of the Celts, Romans had to forge a future from the bare bones of their past. Opportunist neighbors were poised to exploit newly revealed weaknesses in republican Rome, notably the Samnites and their allies, a thorn for almost 50 years.

Below: A wall painting of the fourth century BC depicts Samnite soldiers.

In ensuing decades of domestic disturbances, the Romans repelled numerous incursions in order to consolidate the territory it had won before the Celtic invasion. Initial hesitancy among Romans to take on an enemy following defeat by the Senones was ultimately overcome and they won a series of small-scale victories. Such was Rome's success that it finally imposed a treaty on the Latin League in 358 BC. A period of colonization began. Rome had already founded colonies on its borders, now it founded colonies in enemy territory—a process that would be continual.

The pressure driving Rome was the need to satisfy land-hunger. By drawing in the populations of conquered towns, it had to supply more food than ever before. Yet the area that Rome controlled was still relatively small and there were plenty of enemies on its borders. Sometimes Rome ushered in problems for itself, as with the First Samnite War.

In 354 Rome signed a treaty with the Oscan-speaking Samnites, rural people who dwelt on the slopes of the Appennines. Just 11 years later, Rome broke the treaty when it intervened in a dispute between the Samnites and the town of Capua. A Roman army first liberated Capua then garrisoned it. But the difficulty of maintaining discipline and lines of supply resulted in a negotiated peace with Samnium.

Manpower for safety

Sometimes trouble came looking for the Romans. Hawkish members of the Latin League took Rome's signature on successive peace processes as a sign of weakness and formulated an attack. The Latin War lasted for two years, won by Rome in 338. But although it dissolved the Latin League, Rome refrained from imposing harsh penalties on the vanquished. Many towns were incorporated into the Roman state and their inhabitants given Roman citizenship. Others were pardoned and allowed to remain independent as allies of Rome, which meant they had to pay taxes and provide military assistance in times of conflict, but were also entitled to protection and trading rights (*commercium*) with Roman citizens. They were not, however, allowed to exercise these rights among themselves or have political associations with one another.

1152 BC	c.1100 BC	753 BC	c.750 BC	715–673 BC	673–41 BC	640–14 BC	579–34 BC
Alba Longa is established, possible source of Rome's settlement	Etruscans begin to establish themselves in northern Italy	Traditionally, April 21 of this year is the date Romulus founded Rome	Byzantium is founded	Reign of the Sabine Numa Pompilius, successor to Romulus	Etruscans from the cities of Veii and Fidenae trouble the reign of Tullus Hostilius	Ancus Marcius expands Rome's population with the peoples of conquered cities	Servius Tullius reorganizes the Roman army and creates the Comitia Centuriata

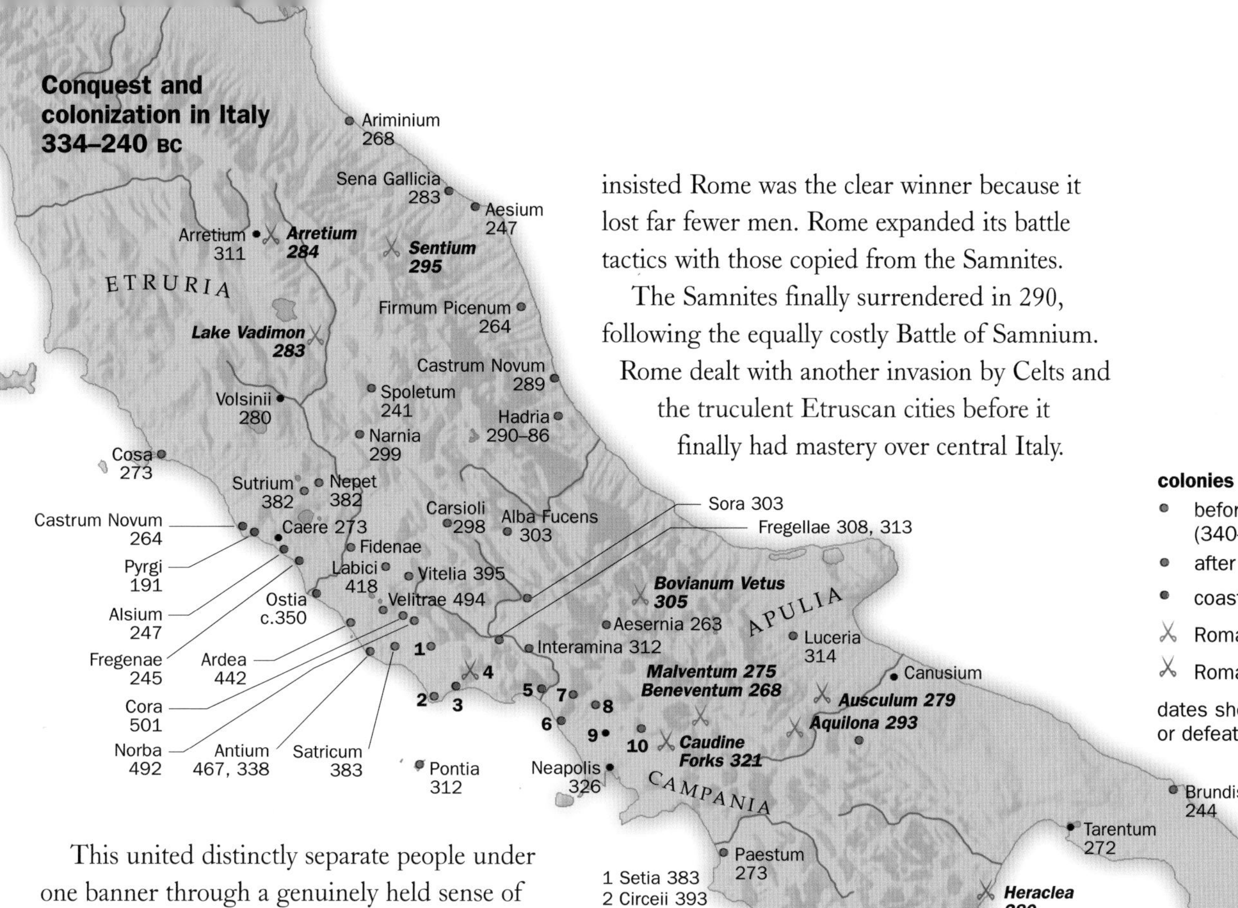

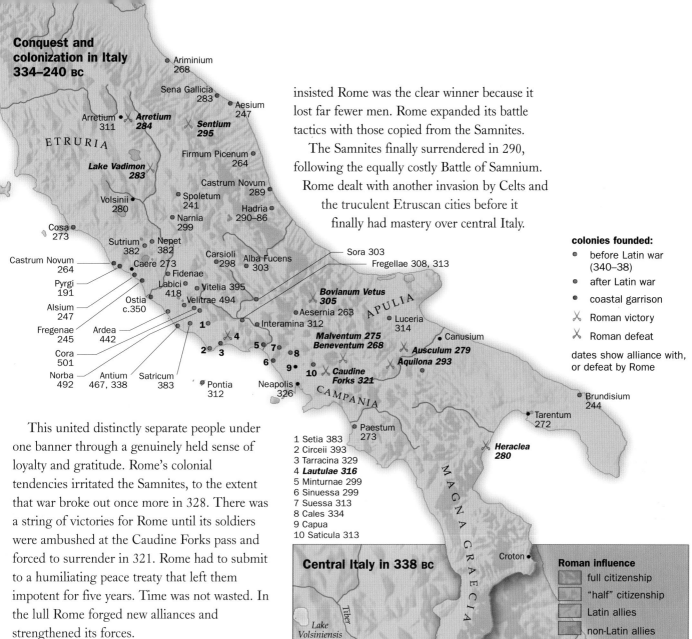

Conquest and colonization in Italy 334–240 BC
Ariminium 268
Sena Gallicia 283
Aesium 247
Arretium 311
Arretium 284
Sentium 295
ETRURIA
Firmum Picenum 264
Lake Vadimon 283
Castrum Novum 289
Volsinii 280
Spoletum 241
Hadria 290–86
Narnia 299
Cosa 273
Sutrium 382
Nepet 382
Castrum Novum 264
Caere 273
Carsioli 298
Alba Fucens 303
Sora 303
Fregellae 308, 313
Fidenae
Pyrgi 191
Labici 418
Vitelia 395
Ostia c.350
Velitrae 494
Bovianum Vetus 305
Alsium 247
Aesernia 263
APULIA
Luceria 314
Interamina 312
Fregenae 245
Ardea 442
Canusium
Malventum 275
Beneventum 268
Ausculum 279
Cora 501
Aquilona 293
Caudine Forks 321
Norba 492
Antium 467, 338
Satricum 383
Pontia 312
Neapolis 326
CAMPANIA
Brundisium 244
Tarentum 272
Paestum 273
Heraclea 280
MAGNA GRAECIA
Croton
Rhegium
1 Setia 383
2 Circeii 393
3 Tarracina 329
4 Lautulae 316
5 Minturnae 299
6 Sinuessa 299
7 Suessa 313
8 Cales 334
9 Capua
10 Saticula 313
colonies founded:
before Latin war (340–38)
after Latin war
coastal garrison
Roman victory
Roman defeat
dates show alliance with, or defeat by Rome

This united distinctly separate people under one banner through a genuinely held sense of loyalty and gratitude. Rome's colonial tendencies irritated the Samnites, to the extent that war broke out once more in 328. There was a string of victories for Rome until its soldiers were ambushed at the Caudine Forks pass and forced to surrender in 321. Rome had to submit to a humiliating peace treaty that left them impotent for five years. Time was not wasted. In the lull Rome forged new alliances and strengthened its forces.

Pre-empting further Roman expansion, the Samnites attacked in 316 and won the first round in battle at Lautulae. The following year, the tide turned in Rome's favor, but fighting continued for 11 years until, after a string of Roman victories, the Samnites were ready to bid for peace in 304. As the new century began, Rome was in control of Latium, the Apennines, and most of Campania.

The array of lands and associated power was sufficient to bind the Samnites, Celts, Umbrians, and some Etruscan cities together in an attempt to bring Rome to its knees. The result was the Third Samnite War and, specifically, the Battle of Sentium in 295, the biggest ever staged in Italy. Both sides lost thousands of soldiers, although later historians insisted Rome was the clear winner because it lost far fewer men. Rome expanded its battle tactics with those copied from the Samnites.

The Samnites finally surrendered in 290, following the equally costly Battle of Samnium. Rome dealt with another invasion by Celts and the truculent Etruscan cities before it finally had mastery over central Italy.

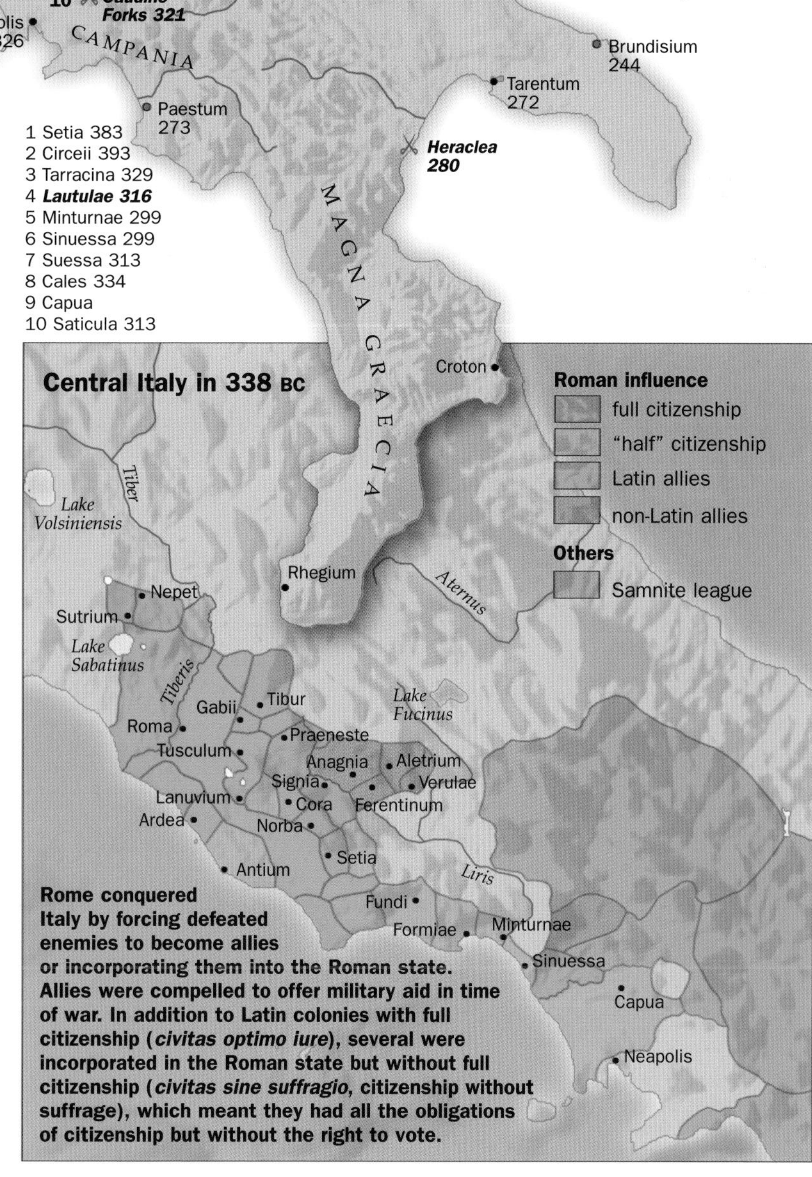

Central Italy in 338 BC
Roman influence
full citizenship
"half" citizenship
Latin allies
non-Latin allies
Others
Samnite league
Tiber
Lake Volsiniensis
Nepet
Sutrium
Lake Sabatinus
Tiberis
Aternus
Gabii
Tibur
Lake Fucinus
Roma
Praeneste
Tusculum
Anagnia
Aletrium
Signia
Verulae
Lanuvium
Cora
Ferentinum
Ardea
Norba
Setia
Antium
Liris
Fundi
Formiae
Minturnae
Sinuessa
Capua
Neapolis

Rome conquered Italy by forcing defeated enemies to become allies or incorporating them into the Roman state. Allies were compelled to offer military aid in time of war. In addition to Latin colonies with full citizenship (*civitas optimo iure*), several were incorporated in the Roman state but without full citizenship (*civitas sine suffragio*, citizenship without suffrage), which meant they had all the obligations of citizenship but without the right to vote.

c.540 BC	509 BC	499 BC	494 BC	493 BC	450 BC	437–26 BC	c.400 BC
Etruscans allied with Carthaginians defeat Greeks and increase naval power	Etruscan influence ends when Tarquin II is overthrown; beginning of the Roman Republic	Romans defeat rival neighbors at Lake Regillus	Magistrates and tribunes are appointed to care for the city of Rome	Rome joins the Latin League, an alliance of Italian cities	The Roman laws of the Twelve Tables are on public display as engraved tablets	Rome wins a war against Fidenae	Rome secures its borders, conquers Veii, and extends trade through Etruscan territory

CHAPTER 2

THE EARLY REPUBLIC

1
2
3
4
5
6
8
11
12
13

Reconstruction of Rome at the end of the monarchy and first decades of the republic. The Servian Wall was erected at a later date in the early republic, but probably followed the route of the archaic wall shown here, which may have been built by King Servius Tullius.

Having shed its monarchy, Rome was nimble in pursuit of power in the Italian peninsula. In the wars with neighboring states that followed, the settlement imposed upon losers set a pattern for the future development of Rome. Defeated Latin cities (*municipia*) were incorporated in the Roman state with full citizenship (*civitas optimo iure*), retaining their own identities and governing themselves. Non-Latin peoples were given the status of "half" citizenship, the *civitas sine suffragio*, which meant fulfilling all the military and tax obligations of full citizenship, but without the right to vote or hold office at Rome.

Ten city-states were prepared to enlist as allies of Rome, rather than risk all in battle.

15
16
17
21
19
18
14
9
20
10
21
Art based on a model in the Museo della Civiltá Romana, Rome

1 Sublican bridge
2 Portus (harbor)
3 Forum Boarium
4 Circus Maximus
5 Tarpeian Rock
6 Capitol/Jupiter Optimus Maximus
7 Arx/Juno Moneta
8 Palatine hill
9 Forum Romanum
10 Caelian hill
11 Aventine hill
12 via Albana (Appian)
13 Lake Camenarum
14 Subura
15 Campus Martius
16 cemetery
17 Quirinal hill
18 Viminal hill
19 Esquiline hill
20 Oppian hill
21 Servian Wall

The advantage for compliant states was the promise of extra security and the possibility of citizenship, which became more valuable as the decades went by. It was the start of a dependency culture that served Rome's imperial ambitions well. Tranches of Italian territory were soon gratefully assimilated.

But if negotiation failed, Rome was swift to act. There was growing evidence of militarism in society. Fighting wars became a way of life for the Romans, who were expert at finding just cause for conflict. The extension of Roman boundaries was a focus of its existence. By the end of the third century BC, Rome was in a position to rival the other great Mediterranean powers: Carthage, Egypt, Syria, and Macedonia.

Patricians and Plebeians

No one knows exactly when Roman society was divided between the patricians and the plebeians; this class system emerged before observers committed explanation to the written word. Yet together these groups became the dynamism behind the republic, one acting as a counterweight to the other.

Perhaps when the distinction between patricians and plebeians (*plebs*) was first made, it was acidly clear who belonged to which class. Inevitably, as time went by, the lines of definition began to blur, defying cut-and-dried description. There is much traditional and anecdotal evidence about patricians and plebeians but little sound material to go on, so discussion about them revolves around general themes.

Broadly speaking, the patriciate was comprised of a select group of families who were blessed with political and economical advantages, and who initially held a monopoly of power. Their political party became known as the *optimates*.

The *plebs* were underprivileged and sought emancipation, but they were not always without power, nor was the situation feudal. As early as 494 BC, the plebeians had the right to take part in a tribune formed to protect their interests. Soon the *plebs* began to flex their political muscle to assure themselves of a role in government. This became especially noticeable with the growth of a middle class, neither rich nor poor, yet with a vested interest in the political life of the state. Their political grouping was soon identified as the *populares*.

There were probably other groups in early Rome who distinguished themselves differently again, but the identity of these has been lost, leaving us a somewhat stark choice between patrician and plebeian. The tug of law between the two groups continued for two centuries, becoming known as the Conflict of the Orders. During this time the *plebs* did not pursue mob violence but a union-style bargaining process, probably led by the merchants (of Greek extraction) but fully backed by agricultural workers.

Earning dual government

Tax was not a mighty issue in republican Rome. Indeed, Romans were exempt from tax for many years, the reward for foreign conquests. The plebeian trump card was army recruitment. As Roman citizens, they were sorely needed to fill

Right: With increasing control of central Italy, Rome developed from being a parochial settlement to the urban heart of an expanding Latin empire. The Patrician class, growing wealthy from conquest, began to demand the finer things of life, and artisans were happy to oblige them. This bronze cista, found at Praeneste (ancient Palestrina), indicates that Rome was a major center for the production of high-quality goods by the last decades of the fourth century BC. Two inscriptions are engraved on its surface: "Dinidia Lacolnia geve this to her daughter," and "Novius Plautius made me in Rome."

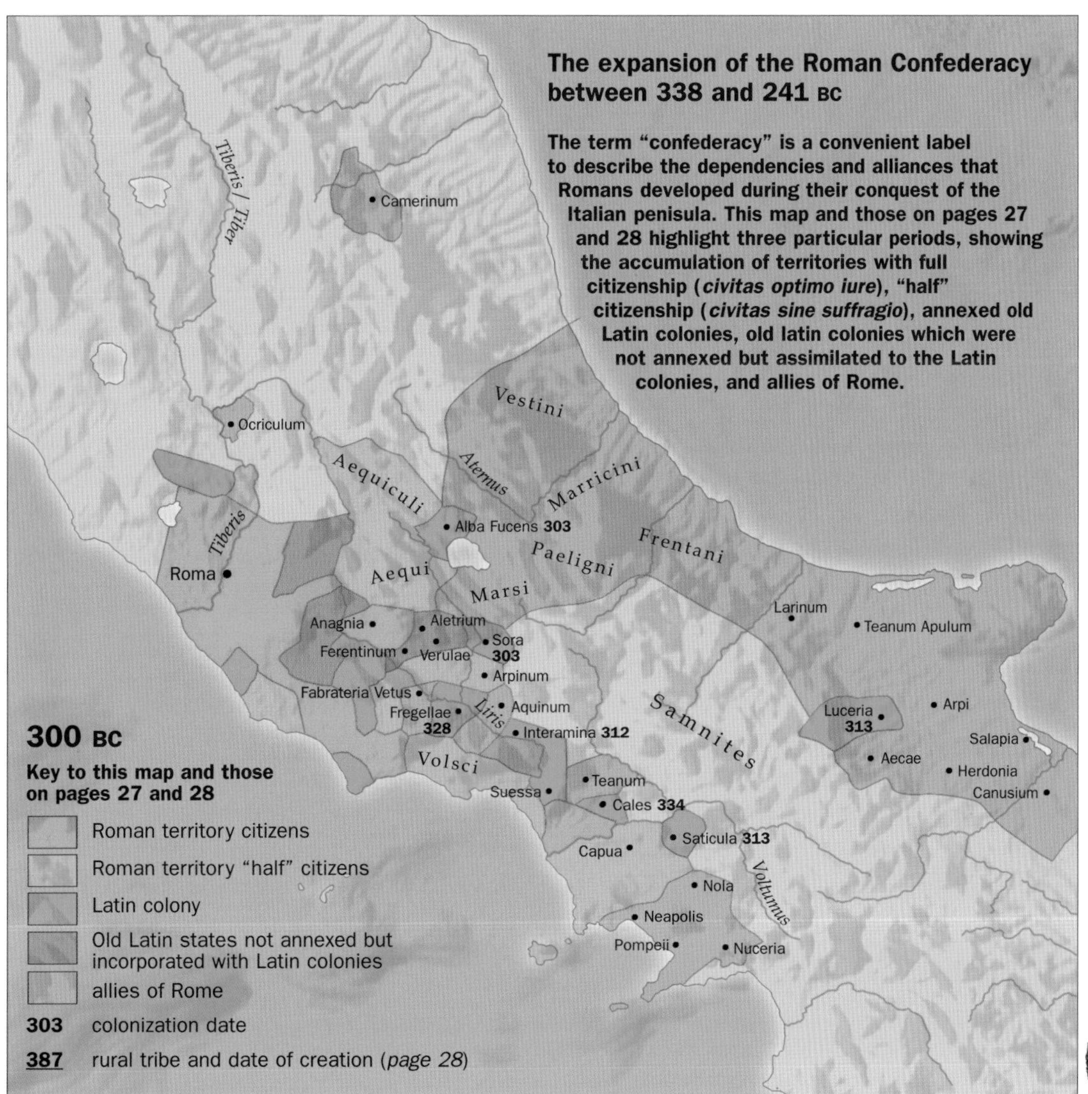
Tiberis / Tiber
Camerinum
Ocriculum
Vestini
Aequiculi
Aternus
Marrucini
Tiberis
Alba Fucens 303
Paeligni
Frentani
Roma
Aequi
Marsi
Larinum
Teanum Apulum
Anagnia
Aletrium
Sora
303
Ferentinum
Verulae
Arpinum
Fabrateria Vetus
Fregellae
328
Liris
Aquinum
Interamina 312
Samnites
Luceria
313
Arpi
Salapia
Aecae
Herdonia
Canusium
Volsci
Suessa
Teanum
Cales 334
Saticula 313
Capua
Volturnus
Nola
Neapolis
Pompeii
Nuceria
300 BC
Key to this map and those on pages 27 and 28
Roman territory citizens
Roman territory "half" citizens
Latin colony
Old Latin states not annexed but incorporated with Latin colonies
allies of Rome
303 colonization date
387 rural tribe and date of creation (page 28)

The expansion of the Roman Confederacy between 338 and 241 BC

The term "confederacy" is a convenient label to describe the dependencies and alliances that Romans developed during their conquest of the Italian penisula. This map and those on pages 27 and 28 highlight three particular periods, showing the accumulation of territories with full citizenship (*civitas optimo iure*), "half" citizenship (*civitas sine suffragio*), annexed old Latin colonies, old latin colonies which were not annexed but assimilated to the Latin colonies, and allies of Rome.

the ranks of the army and without them the state was vulnerable.

To prove their point, *plebs* were known to take part in general strikes, although the number of those that occurred in the fifth and fourth centuries BC probably amounted to no more than a handful. But in about 445, after a plebeian refusal to fight invading Aequians, the patriciate granted consular powers to the military tribunes. However, this did not mean there was parity between patrician consuls and plebeian consular tribunes. The latter were barred from staging a triumph at the conclusion of a successful military campaign. Nor were they subject to automatic elevation to the senate. This was changed by the Licinio-Sextian laws of 376, which made provision for plebeians to be admitted to the consulship; and L. Sextius became the first plebeian consul in 366.

Now both patricians and *plebs* were finely poised to balance the political system. Both were entitled to make laws, albeit by different routes, that would go to the *comitia centuriata*, the assembly above the senate. Those who sat on it were patrician but were painfully aware of the possible consequences of overturning plebeian proposals.

In a bid to control growing plebeian power, a mixed patrician-plebeian assembly was formed in 366, called the *comitia tributa*, which was allowed to pass laws with senate approval from 339. It meant the potential hurdle of the ancient *comitia centuriata* was removed, but plebeian politicians still pressed for more.

Finally, in 287, plebeian ambitions were realized when the law changed to enable both the plebeian *concilium plebis tributa* (formed c.494) and the *comitia tributa* to pass laws independently of the senate. There were now two branches of government which, surprisingly, tended toward co-operation, thus keeping a kind of peace in the Roman republican regimes.

Above: Bronze statuette of a *lictor*, third century BC. The *fasces* (ax and rods) he carries were an Etruscan regal legacy and a symbol of a magistrate's *auctoritas* (authority). Twelve lictors were official attendants of the consuls.

THE GROWTH OF GOVERNMENT

Early republican Rome remains a shadowy place, with history and legend intermixed. However, available information indicates a surprisingly sophisticated form of government came into being.

Below: Personal glory combined with civic duty to benefit Romans in many ways. One of the most spectacular of the period was the nine-mile-long Aqua Appia, or Appian Aqueduct, built by Appius Claudius c.310 BC. While it brought fresh water ito Rome, he also began construction of the Appian Way, the first major road that would take Romans out to the provinces.

Kings gave way to magistrates (*magistratus*, or one empowered to make laws and enforce them), who became known as consuls. In outward appearance they were similar to kings, donning regalia and purloining rights commonly associated with the monarchy. In common with some kings, they were elected by the Roman populous.

However, their tenure was restricted to a year and two occupied the post at the same time, one to counterbalance the other with rights of veto, the supposed safeguard against tyranny. Duty done, the consuls entered the senate as life members. Terms of office for consuls varied; in times of crisis, the consul might remain in post for an agreed period until the dilemma had passed, but after 434 BC the term was fixed at 18 months.

As the key figures in Roman government, when they were away at war or visiting the provinces crucial domestic matters had to be put to one side. Soon the need for more participating politicians was apparent and other offices were created. *Quaestors* were charged with treasury duty, *praetors* looked after the administration of justice, while censors took charge of tax collection, public buildings, and public morals. *Aediles* (the equivalent of a modern magistrate) were created in 494 at the same time as plebeian tribunes, to care for the city of Rome, govern weights and measures, and organize public games.

Setting out the tables

The Twelve Tables, the codification of Roman laws, were probably the most significant development of government during the early republican period. From 450 the Tables were engraved on copper tablets and displayed in the Forum. This meant that for the first time everyone from the mightiest patrician to the lowliest plebeian had access to the law and could learn the penalty for any misdemeanor that might be committed.

The Twelve Tables were drawn up by a committee of patricians but were the result of

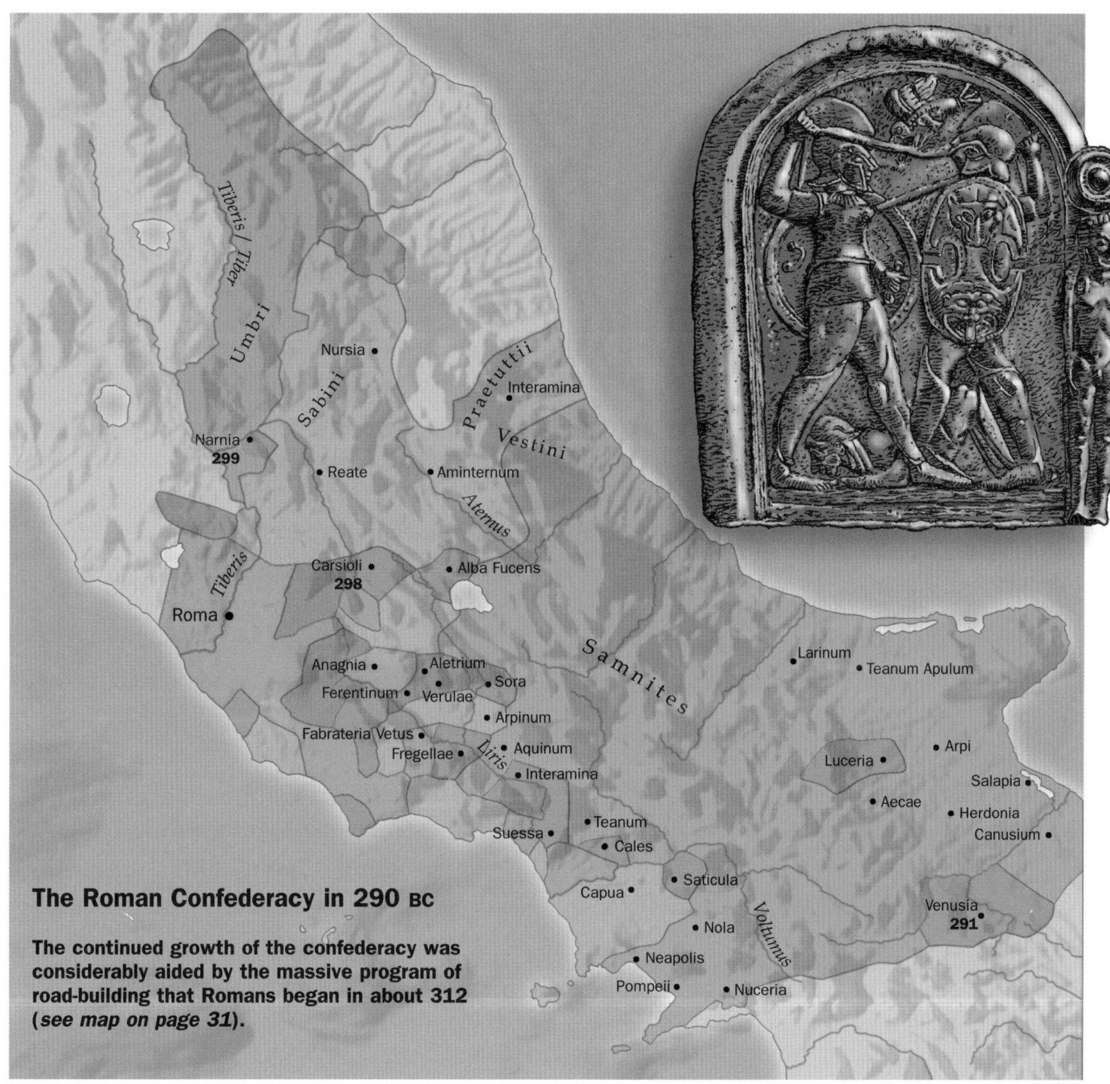
Tiberis / Tiber
Umbri
Nursia
Sabini
Praetuttii
Interamina
Vestini
Narnia
299
Reate
Aminternum
Aternus
Tiberis
Carsioli
298
Alba Fucens
Roma
Samnites
Anagnia
Aletrium
Sora
Ferentinum
Verulae
Arpinum
Fabrateria Vetus
Fregellae
Aquinum
Liris
Interamina
Larinum
Teanum Apulum
Arpi
Luceria
Salapia
Aecae
Herdonia
Canusium
Teanum
Suessa
Cales
Saticula
Capua
Volturnus
Nola
Neapolis
Pompeii
Nuceria
Venusia
291

The Roman Confederacy in 290 BC

The continued growth of the confederacy was considerably aided by the massive program of road-building that Romans began in about 312 (*see map on page 31*).

Left: Armor and weapons of the soldiers of early Rome were no doubt heavily influenced by the Etruscans, two of whose warriors are depicted in this bronze fitting on a war chariot.

sustained pressure from the *plebs*. The tables contained merits and deficiencies. People were now safe from arbitrary judicial sentences and could appeal legal decisions. At the same time, marriage between members of the patrician class and plebeian class was banned, closing the door on movement into the aristocracy. This archaic statute was superceded within five years, although in practice marriage between the orders was rare.

In the main, the Twelve Tables encompassed a progressive outlook for the era, befitting an up-and-coming world power. Indeed, some of its provisions remained in force for eight hundred years, until the end of the western empire. One of the keys to its success was its inclusivity. Freed men became Roman citizens, thus forever strengthening and rejuvenating the population and, more importantly, the army. Citizenship was a necessary qualification for army entry.

With citizenship came the right to vote—but Rome was far from being a modern democracy. Only magistrates could summon and address the various *comitia*, and citizens had no right to debate or amend proposals. Neither did Roman citizenry encompass all. Women and slaves could never be citizens, and often foreigners and provincials were ruled out. Mostly it was men who bore arms who were franchised.

Further, to cast a vote meant a trip to Rome. Since only a select few in the rural tribes could afford to do so, the urban plebeian was better placed in the democratic process than the country-dweller. Nevertheless, Rome's concept of government can be traced into today's world.

Rome was not immune from vigor of charismatic leaders. One such man was Appius Claudius, credited with building the Appian Way and the nine-mile aqueduct known as the Aqua Appia, c.310. While he was censor, he commissioned these projects without consulting the senate. He refused to give up the post of censor and even tampered with the composition of the senate, earning the enmity of aristocrats but the undying loyalty of *plebs*. From the established Claudii family, it is believed Appius went against his class loyalties to preserve an old order that he saw being threatened by a new plebeian nobility. He was perhaps the first political personality to galvanize all Rome.

Pyrrhic Invasion

When the prosperous Greek city of Tarentum decided to resist Rome's expansion, an alliance was made with the ambitious King Pyrrhus of Epirus. Romans suddenly found themselves engaged in a war against an overseas invader.

After centuries of internecine warfare, the fortunes of the once-flourishing Greek city-states in the heel of Italy were waning as Rome's star rose. The exception was Tarentum, which alone prospered. In common with other city-states owing allegiance to Sparta, Tarentum was well defended by effective phalanxes. These had secured many victories in the region and held Roman expansionism at bay until a treaty was negotiated in 303 BC.

The uneasy peace came to an end in 280, when Roman warships sailed into the Bay of Tarentum in response to a request from nearby Thurii, which itself was under attack from the Greek Lucanians. The Tarentines sunk four of the ten Roman ships and the dispute swiftly spiraled into war.

To counter Rome's military might, the Tarentines bought and paid for an army led by Pyrrhus of Epirus. Pyrrhus was recognized as a brilliant strategist. His shortcomings lay in an apparent inability to strike the final hammer blow against an enemy, consequently his campaigns were drawn-out. The attrition

Ariminium 268
Pisaurum
Fanum Fortunae
Sena Gallicia
Ancona
Sarsina
Faesulae
Pisae
Arretium
Volaterrae
Iguvium
Potentia
Perusia
Camerinum
Firmum Picenum 264
Populonia
Clusium
Asisium
Vetulonia
Asculum
Rusellae
Volsinii
Tuder
Spoletium 241
Castrum Novum
Hadria 289–3
Narnia
Vulci
Cosa 273
Tarquinia
Falerii
Roma
Qurinia 241
Sabatina 387
Stellatina 387
Arniensis 387
Tromentia 387
Maecia 332
Aniensis 299
Scaptia 332
Poblilia 358
Pomptina 358
Oufentina 318
Velina 241
Terentina 299
Falerina 318
Larinum
Teanum Apulum
Aesernia 263
Arpi
Salapia
Herdonia
Teanum
Asculum 279
Beneventum 268
275
Canusium
Barium
Aeclanum
Venusia
Abellinum
Salernum
Brundisium 244
Genusia
Tarentum 272
Metapontum
Paestum 273
Grumentum
Heraclea 280
Velia
Thurii
Consentia
Petelia
Croton
region affected by the Pyrrhic wars
Vibo Valentia
Caulonia
Locri
Rhegium

The Roman Confederacy in 241 BC

As Rome extended full citizenship to more people, a series of new rural tribes was created along the original Romulan lines (*see page 12*), shown here, which functioned as voting units in political comitia.

Pyrrhus of Epirus (c.318–272 BC)

Above: The via Appia (Appian Way) outside Rome. The characteristic straightness of Roman roads echoes the single-minded drive of early republican Roman ambition. This first section between Rome and Capua, started in 312 BC, indicated what was to come, as Roman engineers constructed a web of military roads the length of the Italian peninsula (*see map on following page*). The ability to move men and armament gave Rome an advantage over would-be invaders like Pyrrhus. The original surface is paved with modern materials.

Pyrrhus inflicted on his enemies proved equally damaging to his own forces.

When he arrived in Tarentum in 280, Pyrrhus brought a 25,000-strong army supported by 3,000 cavalry and 20 elephants. These powerful creatures had been incorporated into the Greek armies following the victories against Persian king Darius during the campaigns of Alexander the Great, when their worth was amply demonstrated. The two forces, which met near Heraclea, were evenly weighted until Pyrrhus pitched the elephants into the equation. Roman horses, panicked in the face of the giants, charged through the Roman infantry, which lay at the mercy of Pyrrhus's cavalry. The Romans were driven from the field.

A utopian agreement

The defeat was sufficiently substantial for the Roman senate to contemplate peace terms tossed to them by Pyrrhus. A stirring speech made by the blind, frail Appius Claudius repaired their resolve. An architect of previous conflicts that had secured territory in Italy, Appius was unwilling to see his achievements forfeited.

So the war continued, although Plutarch tells a delightful tale in the first century about how Pyrrhus and the Roman envoy Gaius Fabricus became friends, treating one another with the utmost honesty and respect. Set against this bond, the Romans revealed to Pyrrhus an assassination plot by a treacherous doctor. In return, all Roman prisoners were freed, then Rome freed all Greek prisoners, imbuing the era with honor and integrity. Plutarch was writing hundreds of years after the event, so the accuracy of his account may be doubtful. Indeed, there is little first-hand knowledge regarding Pyrrhus.

In the following year, a second battle took place at Asculum, in which the elephants once again caused destruction. Roman casualties numbered almost twice as many as the Greeks, but this proved cold comfort to Pyrrhus, who was wounded in action. Dispirited, he surveyed the battlefield and uttered, "Another such victory and I am lost." Afterward his name was lent to the term for a hollow or costly triumph—a Pyrrhic victory.

The sentiment reflects how disillusioned Pyrrhus had become regarding Italian conquest against a well organized enemy with far more resources than he had at his disposal. When he received a missive from Greek cities in Sicily in 278, pleading for help in the face of a threat from Carthage, he withdrew his armies to assist his Sicilian kinsmen, leaving Tarentum to bear the brunt of Rome's hostility.

Within three years, Pyrrhus was once more called to their aid, after Romans laid siege to Tarentum. The two sides met at Malventum in 275, where Roman warriors got the better of the elephant brigade and won the fight. Leaving a small garrison at Tarentum, Pyrrhus headed home. Before his death in 272, Pyrrhus recalled the troops, and Tarentum fell to the Roman army in the same year. Now the entire Italian peninsula south of a line through Pisa to Rimini was under Roman domination.

THE SENATE

Formed to advise the king, the senate survived the transition from monarchy to republic and thrived. As its role evolved, the senate gained sufficient strength to endure rule by dictator and ultimately emperor.

Below: A relief of senators standing on a sarcophagus lid dates from AD 282.

At first there were a hundred members of the senate, all drawn from the patriciate. One of the kings apparently increased the size to 300 to reflect the inclusion of new tribes, although its observance of inherited privileges remained the same. Sulla the dictator tried to place abiding power in the hands of the (conservative) senate by increasing its number. Unfortunately, he failed to also maintain the quality of senators, dooming his plan to failure.

By Julius Caesar's time, the senate's membership had soared to nearly 800, but it was packed with his own supporters. It took provincial candidates a long time to make their way into the senate, so the French, Spanish, North African, and Asian peoples were without a voice. In short, there were few moments in Roman history where the senate could claim to be representative of the people.

Initially, it was the task of the senate to choose the consuls from senior political figures. When the consular term was completed, the consuls joined the senate's ranks. This ensured that power remained in the hands of the elite for a considerable period. The senate's nature changed after the Licinio-Sextian laws of 367 through the increasing admission of men from the leading plebeian families. The law made provision for one of the two consuls to be drawn from the *plebs*. In turn, this led to a new elite, the patricio-plebeian nobility (*nobiles*), who regarded the senior magistracies as their own preserve.

Despite the replenishment of senatorial ranks from new families, brought in through the plebeian consulships, senators remained insular and aggressively defended their rights above those of the common man, or even of the republic. And there was always an elite among the patrician families who developed the knack of imposing their will on the remainder.

Unpaid for the hours they invested in the job, senators were mostly devoted to carving out a power base for themselves, their patrons, or their close relations. Ultimately, this beckoned an era of corruption during which the senators served themselves and their class before the needs of the people.

The role of the senate later included the preparation of legislation, administration of finances, foreign affairs, and the supervision of state religions. Senators legitimately expected to be consulted on pending laws, given the Roman convention of consultation and debate. Further, they could invalidate laws introduced by consuls if they deemed them harmful to the republic.

S.P.Q.R.

In theory, the senate could meet at any public place within the sacred *pomerium* (perimeter) of Rome. In practice the meetings generally took place on a daily basis at the *Curia Hostilia*, in the northwest corner of the Forum. After 194 BC senators had the right to sit in the *orchestra* in theaters and amphitheaters, thus getting the best seats in the house. Senators wore tunics woven with a broad purple stripe and boots distinguished by the letter "c," presumably linked to *centum* (one hundred), the original number of senators.

The senate gave able orators a platform on which to perform. Their eloquent rhetoric was often sufficient to sway the sentiments of fellow senators or indeed the whole population of Rome. Its importance is underlined by the initials S.P.Q.R., often imprinted on Roman regalia. The letters stand for *Senatus Populusque Romanus*, meaning "the senate and the people of Rome." However, as the republican empire expanded, so the two-consul system operating in tandem with the senate and other *comitia* came under enormous strain. Senators lost power to the successful generals (*imperator*), who seized control of political events in Rome.

Today, Rome's hierarchical system appears fraught with problems and has little to recommend it, despite its code of conduct. Indeed, one man, Cornelius Rufinius, who had twice been consul, was expelled from the senate in 275 BC for possessing ten pounds of silver vessels, revealing an indulgence in luxury deemed inappropriate among the ruling classes.

Although the senate miraculously survived the centuries of empire, its *raison d'être* was severely challenged. For a while it served the purposes of emperors wishing to illustrate their observance of an old custom. It was the duty of high-ranking Romans to seek advice on difficult issues; their decisions had no credence if they did not. But the most autocratic emperors used intimidation to secure the advice or backing they sought. Senatorial purges occurred to eradicate opposition when the empire's politics became warped.

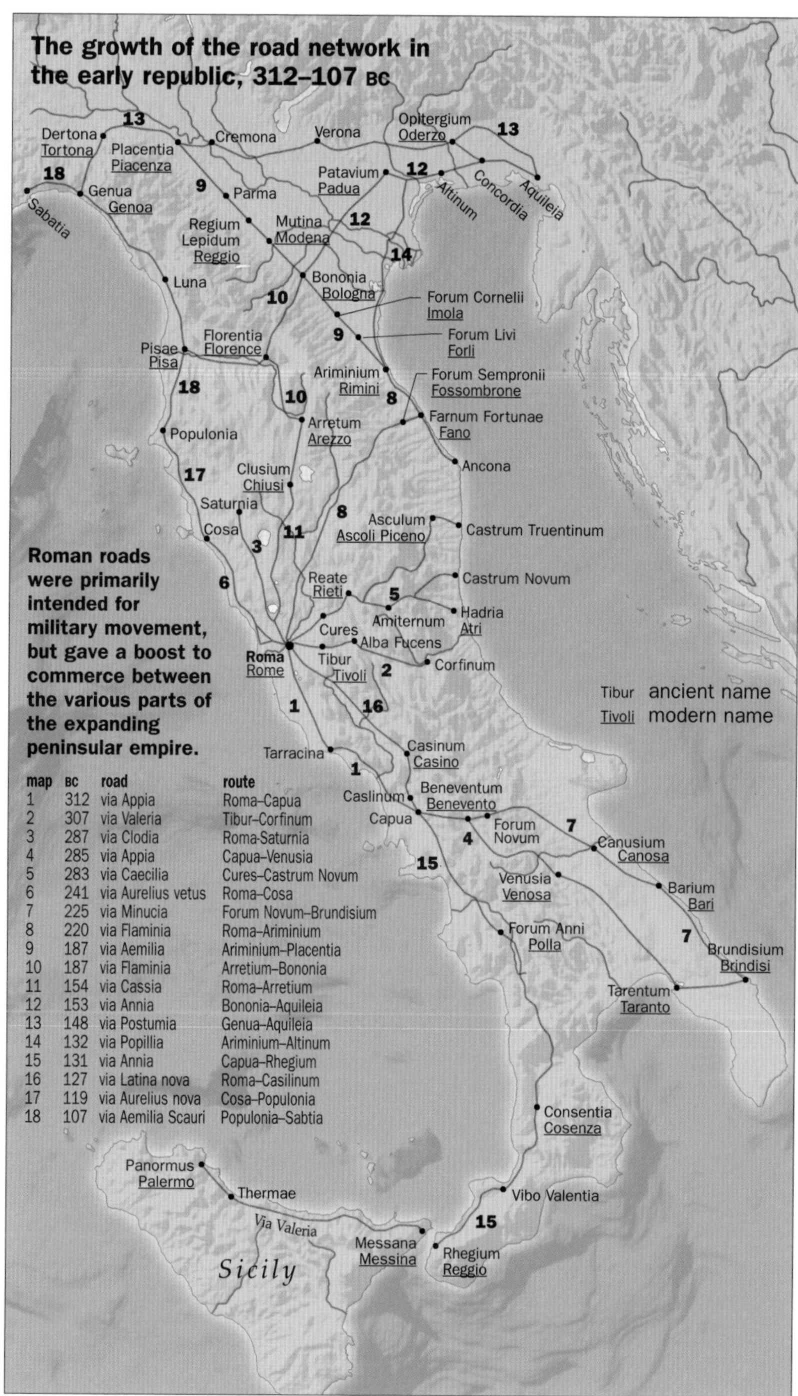
The growth of the road network in the early republic, 312–107 BC
Roman roads were primarily intended for military movement, but gave a boost to commerce between the various parts of the expanding peninsular empire.
Dertona
Tortona
Placentia
Piacenza
Cremona
Verona
Opitergium
Oderzo
Genua
Genoa
Parma
Patavium
Padua
Altinum
Concordia
Aquileia
Sabatia
Regium Lepidum
Reggio
Mutina
Modena
Luna
Bononia
Bologna
Forum Cornelii
Imola
Florentia
Florence
Forum Livi
Forli
Pisae
Pisa
Ariminium
Rimini
Forum Sempronii
Fossombrone
Farnum Fortunae
Fano
Arretum
Arezzo
Populonia
Ancona
Clusium
Chiusi
Saturnia
Cosa
Asculum
Ascoli Piceno
Castrum Truentinum
Reate
Rieti
Castrum Novum
Amiternum
Hadria
Atri
Cures
Alba Fucens
Roma
Rome
Tibur
Tivoli
Corfinum
Tibur ancient name
Tivoli modern name
Tarracina
Casinum
Casino
Caslinum
Beneventum
Benevento
Capua
Forum Novum
Canusium
Canosa
Venusia
Venosa
Barium
Bari
Forum Anni
Polla
Brundisium
Brindisi
Tarentum
Taranto
Consentia
Cosenza
Panormus
Palermo
Thermae
Via Valeria
Sicily
Vibo Valentia
Messana
Messina
Rhegium
Reggio

map	BC	road	route
1	312	via Appia	Roma–Capua
2	307	via Valeria	Tibur–Corfinum
3	287	via Clodia	Roma-Saturnia
4	285	via Appia	Capua–Venusia
5	283	via Caecilia	Cures–Castrum Novum
6	241	via Aurelius vetus	Roma–Cosa
7	225	via Minucia	Forum Novum–Brundisium
8	220	via Flaminia	Roma–Ariminium
9	187	via Aemilia	Ariminium–Placentia
10	187	via Flaminia	Arretium–Bononia
11	154	via Cassia	Roma–Arretium
12	153	via Annia	Bononia–Aquileia
13	148	via Postumia	Genua–Aquileia
14	132	via Popillia	Ariminium–Altinum
15	131	via Annia	Capua–Rhegium
16	127	via Latina nova	Roma–Casilinum
17	119	via Aurelius nova	Cosa–Populonia
18	107	via Aemilia Scauri	Populonia–Sabtia

Early Roman Religion

Like most civilizations throughout history, Romans looked to their gods for deliverance from enemies, hunger, illness, and other disasters. Their faith was a blend of ritual and superstition, which was frequently tailored to individual needs.

Right: Statue of a Vestal Virgin, Rome, third century AD. The institution of the Vestals proved to be one of ancient Rome's most enduring religious colleges. Their chastity was Rome's luck, a quality appropriated by the state. When rare scandal rocked the Vestal Virgins, the unchaste Vestal was tried in a special court and her lover in a separate court. If convicted, she was condemned to be sealed into an underground chamber and left to die. Her lover was executed in a more usual fashion.

To Romans, their religion was a framework that provided comfort and security in the face of the unknown. From a range of deities adopted from the Greeks and Etruscans, Romans altered the gods' identities but left their characters unchanged. Thus the chief Greek god, Zeus, became Jupiter—father, protector, and ruler. The temple of Jupiter on the Capitoline in Rome, dedicated in 509 BC, was the largest of the early temples. His consort was Juno, the equivalent of the Greek Hera. There were many gods outside the reinterpreted Greek pantheon. One could be born at any time, given that Roman gods were as prone to sexual liaisons as their Greek counterparts. However, some assumed greater significance than others.

Rationality was absent in the religious Roman outlook. Military triumphs were a sign of the celestial rewards, regardless of the comparative strength of the armies involved. Defeats were an example of divine retribution and an indication that certain gods demanded to be appeased. The role of ancestors was vital in Roman religion and they were reverentially treated. Here was a society ripe for exploitation by cults and most were allowed to continue unhindered, unless the patrician class believed them to be evil or immoral.

In the home, religious rites were performed by the head of the family, while elected priests and priestesses conducted religious ceremonies on behalf of the state. The Romans had *sacra*, rites by which their faith was honored, and *auspicia*, predictions by augers who might look for signs in animal entrails, or the manner in which rain fell, or animals moved. The interpretation of signs became a full-time occupation for many. Despite the random nature of an auger's work, they were revered in a society desperate for an opportunity to parley with the gods.

396 BC	387 BC	c.380 BC	c.350 BC	343 BC	340–38 BC	328–21 BC	316–04 BC
At the end of a ten-year siege, Romans take the Etruscan city of Veii	Gauls defeat Romans at Allia; after a siege they plunder Rome then depart	Defensive fortifications are built around the Seven Hills of Rome	Legend of Romulus and Remus is accepted	Rome breaks a treaty with Samnites to liberate Capua; First Samnite War	Rome dissolves the Latin League after defeating its members in the Latin War	Rome agrees a treaty to end the Second Samnite War, caused by Roman expansion	Rome enters Samnite territory and gains Latium, the Apennines, and Campania

College of Virgins

The auger's profession was helped incalculably in 249 BC by the actions of Publius Claudius Pulcher, son of the man credited with building the via Appia, who became increasingly infuriated with the refusal of the sacred chickens to peck, so that assembled soothsayers might know from the fall of the grain from their beaks what would occur in a forthcoming battle with the Carthaginians. "If they will not eat, let them drink," he raged, as he tossed the unfortunate birds into the sea. The military disaster that followed was ascribed entirely to his hotheaded response. He was found guilty of treason and heavily fined.

King Numa is credited with establishing the college of Vestal Virgins, six priestesses who steered the cult of Vesta, goddess of the hearth. The Vestal Virgins became an integral part of Roman religious observance and remained in a privileged, although at times precarious position. They were chosen for the task by the chief priest and drawn between the ages of six and ten from among the daughters of freeborn men to serve for 30 years. Other qualifications were that they had no physical or mental deformities and both parents were alive. If they were chosen they were removed from their family and their father's jurisdiction.

The role of the Vestal Virgins included keeping the sacred temple fire alight, fetching water from a religiously significant spring, preparing ritual food, housing wills, and leading public worship during the celebrations associated with Vesta. Of course, much depended on chastity, and any that succumbed to temptation were buried alive by way of punishment. Although their duties came to an official end after 30 years, at the age of 40, few married, for they were supposedly blighted with bad luck.

Left: Beside the Tiber in the Forum Boarium stand two of Rome's oldest surviving republican period temples. The round Temple of Hercules Invictus (Hercules Undefeated), pictured here, used to be wrongly identified with Vesta. It was probably the work of the Greek Hermodorus of Salamis and built between 146 and 102 BC (*see also page 58*). He may have been associated with the second, the rectangular Temple of Portunus, under which have been found the foundations of an archaic temple to Fortuna, probably built by King Servius Tullius in the mid-sixth century (*page 13*). The survival of both temples in such good condition is largely down to the fact that they were consecrated as Christian churches in medieval times.

312 BC	c.310 BC	303 BC	c.300 BC	290 BC	287 BC	280 BC	279 BC
The first military road, the Appian Way, is begun	The Aqua Appia aqueduct is built, under the direction of Appius Claudius	A peace treaty with the prosperous Greek city-state of Tarentum breaks down into war	Cities including Caere, Vulci, and Tarquinia are client-kingdoms	Rome defeats Samnites (Third Samnite War), and gain mastery of central Italy	Plebians finally gain equality; their committees can make laws without senate approval	Pyrrhus of Epirus, hired by Tarentum to counter Rome's ambitions wins the Battle of Hercalea	A Treaty of Friendship is drawn up between Rome and Carthage

CHAPTER 3

HANNIBAL AT THE GATES

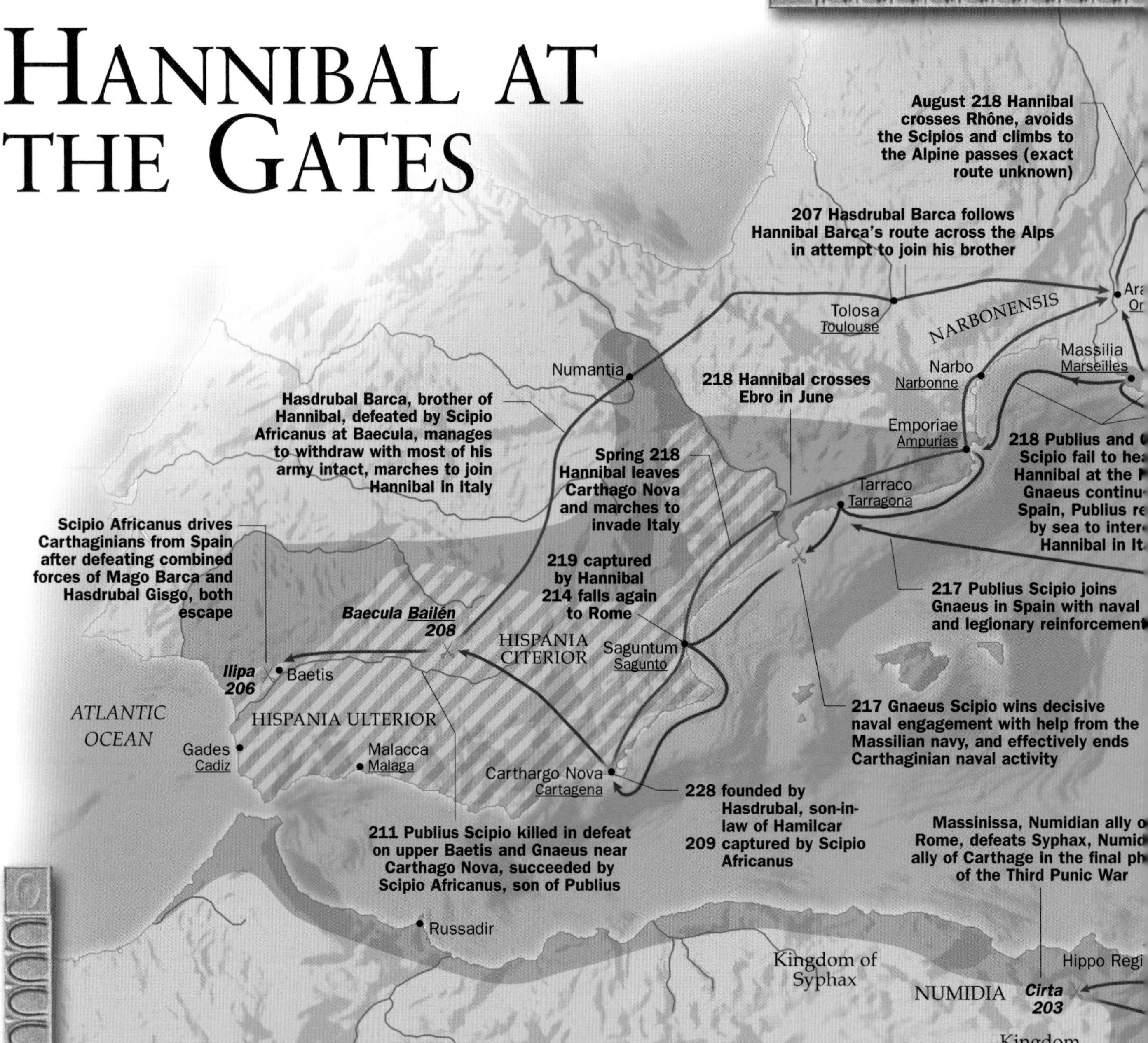

August 218 Hannibal crosses Rhône, avoids the Scipios and climbs to the Alpine passes (exact route unknown)

207 Hasdrubal Barca follows Hannibal Barca's route across the Alps in attempt to join his brother

Tolosa
Toulouse

NARBONENSIS

Massilia
Marseilles

Narbo
Narbonne

Numantia

218 Hannibal crosses Ebro in June

Hasdrubal Barca, brother of Hannibal, defeated by Scipio Africanus at Baecula, manages to withdraw with most of his army intact, marches to join Hannibal in Italy

Emporiae
Ampurias

Spring 218 Hannibal leaves Carthago Nova and marches to invade Italy

Tarraco
Tarragona

Scipio Africanus drives Carthaginians from Spain after defeating combined forces of Mago Barca and Hasdrubal Gisgo, both escape

219 captured by Hannibal
214 falls again to Rome

217 Publius Scipio joins Gnaeus in Spain with naval and legionary reinforcements

Baecula Bailén 208

HISPANIA CITERIOR

Saguntum
Sagunto

Ilipa 206

Baetis

217 Gnaeus Scipio wins decisive naval engagement with help from the Massilian navy, and effectively ends Carthaginian naval activity

ATLANTIC OCEAN

HISPANIA ULTERIOR

Gades
Cadiz

Malacca
Malaga

Carthargo Nova
Cartagena

228 founded by Hasdrubal, son-in-law of Hamilcar
209 captured by Scipio Africanus

211 Publius Scipio killed in defeat on upper Baetis and Gnaeus near Carthago Nova, succeeded by Scipio Africanus, son of Publius

Russadir

Kingdom of Syphax

NUMIDIA

Cirta 203

Kingdom of Massinissa

From our vantage point in the 21st century, Carthage appears to be a poor relation to Greece and Rome. But this is a distortion of the world as it was. To the victor go the spoils… and the history. In 146 BC Rome obliterated Carthage, and it was as if the once-mighty empire had never existed. There was no Carthaginian culture to recall, and no art or architecture survived to tell the story.

And yet, for a considerable period of time Carthage was a mighty Mediterranean power, the equal of expanding Rome and declining Greece. Its dynamic was different to that of Rome but Carthage was hugely successful—indeed, Rome lagged behind, taking time to appreciate the value of long-distance commerce.

Carthage had its fair share of inspired leadership, too. As Cicero later pointed out: "Carthage could not have maintained her pre-eminent position for six hundred years had she not been governed with wisdom and statesmanship." From Carthage came one of the world's greatest military minds. Hannibal defeated impossible odds in pursuit of his aims and had he triumphed, it might have been the end of republican Rome and the age of the emperors would never have dawned.

For a while, the Romans underestimated the military and mercantile power of Carthage. In doing so it nearly paid the ultimate price. To understand how the Roman empire evolved at this pivotal time, it is crucial not do that same.

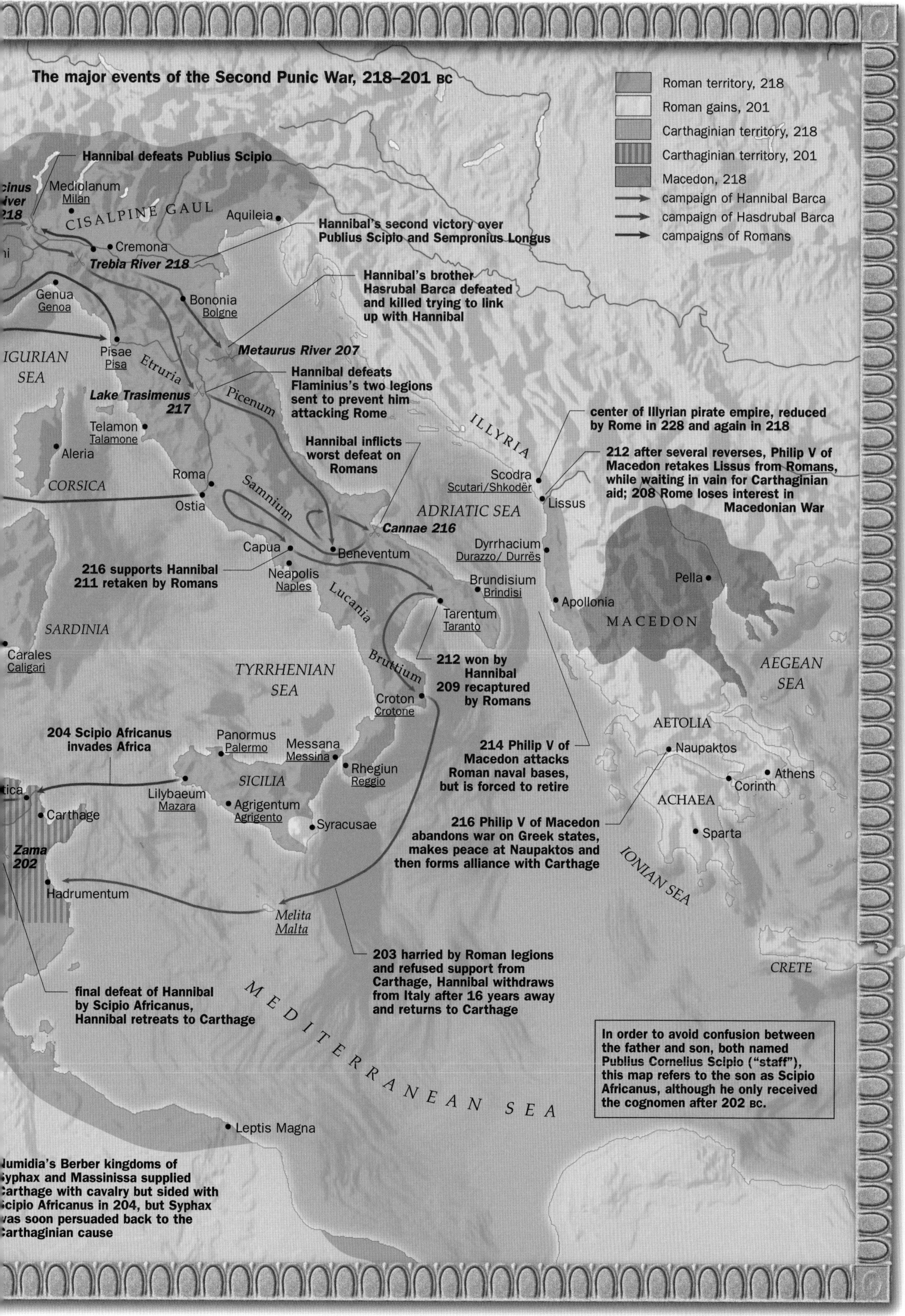

The major events of the Second Punic War, 218–201 BC
Roman territory, 218
Roman gains, 201
Carthaginian territory, 218
Carthaginian territory, 201
Macedon, 218
campaign of Hannibal Barca
campaign of Hasdrubal Barca
campaigns of Romans
Hannibal defeats Publius Scipio
Mediolanum
Milan
CISALPINE GAUL
Aquileia
Hannibal's second victory over Publius Scipio and Sempronius Longus
Cremona
Trebia River 218
Hannibal's brother Hasrubal Barca defeated and killed trying to link up with Hannibal
Genua
Genoa
Bononia
Bolgne
Metaurus River 207
IGURIAN SEA
Pisae
Pisa
Etruria
Hannibal defeats Flaminius's two legions sent to prevent him attacking Rome
Lake Trasimenus 217
Picenum
Telamon
Talamone
Aleria
Hannibal inflicts worst defeat on Romans
ILLYRIA
center of Illyrian pirate empire, reduced by Rome in 228 and again in 218
212 after several reverses, Philip V of Macedon retakes Lissus from Romans, while waiting in vain for Carthaginian aid; 208 Rome loses interest in Macedonian War
Roma
CORSICA
Ostia
Samnium
Scodra
Scutari/Shkodër
Lissus
ADRIATIC SEA
Cannae 216
Capua
Beneventum
Dyrrhacium
Durazzo/ Durrës
216 supports Hannibal
211 retaken by Romans
Neapolis
Naples
Brundisium
Brindisi
Pella
Lucania
Apollonia
Tarentum
Taranto
MACEDON
SARDINIA
Carales
Caligari
TYRRHENIAN SEA
Bruttium
212 won by Hannibal
209 recaptured by Romans
AEGEAN SEA
Croton
Crotone
AETOLIA
204 Scipio Africanus invades Africa
Panormus
Palermo
Messana
Messina
214 Philip V of Macedon attacks Roman naval bases, but is forced to retire
Naupaktos
Rhegiun
Reggio
SICILIA
Athens
Corinth
Lilybaeum
Mazara
Agrigentum
Agrigento
ACHAEA
Carthage
Syracusae
216 Philip V of Macedon abandons war on Greek states, makes peace at Naupaktos and then forms alliance with Carthage
Sparta
Zama 202
IONIAN SEA
Hadrumentum
Melita
Malta
203 harried by Roman legions and refused support from Carthage, Hannibal withdraws from Italy after 16 years away and returns to Carthage
CRETE
final defeat of Hannibal by Scipio Africanus, Hannibal retreats to Carthage
MEDITERRANEAN SEA
In order to avoid confusion between the father and son, both named Publius Cornelius Scipio ("staff"), this map refers to the son as Scipio Africanus, although he only received the cognomen after 202 BC.
Leptis Magna

THE POWER OF CARTHAGE

In every classical city, at each busy port, Carthaginian merchants were once a familiar sight. By bartering, buying, and selling, they funneled wealth back to their home city of Carthage, a prosperous metropolis that dominated the North African coast.

Below: The tomb of infants sacrificed in the 5th century BC stands in the Sanctuary of Tanit and Baal Hammon in Carthage, Tunisia.

Carthage was one of several outposts founded by the Phoenicians, adventurers from Lebanon who are best remembered as creators of the alphabet. One legend tells how Princess Dido fled from her brother, King Pygmalion of Tyre, with ships and treasure to found the city. Nothing is known for certain about the early years of the settlement, which now forms a suburb of the modern capital Tunis. Archaeological excavation indicates that nothing earlier than the last quarter of the eighth century BC existed on the site.

The burgeoning Carthage had potential, with its protected anchorage and plentiful supplies of fish. A busy population thrived in the region, eventually becoming noted as excellent furniture makers. Underpinning the community was wealth culled from silver, tin, and iron mining in the locale.

This wealth helped Carthage to spread its influence around the region at a time when Rome had no territories overseas. Some of its sons were keen explorers, Hanno for example, who is credited with colonizing Morocco during the fifth century BC. At its height the Carthaginian empire included the north coast of Africa, Corsica, Sardinia, about half of Sicily, and the lower half of what is now Spain. Its influence spread further, with maintained contacts to its Mediterranean mother-city of Tyre to the east, and as far west and north as the Cornish coast of Britain.

At heart, Carthaginians were traders, and not unreasonably, sought to profit from their transactions. This inherent respect for money was reflected in its system of government. Positions of power could be purchased and bribery was rife. Romans, on the other hand, were preoccupied with notions of virtuous nobility. Places in high government supposedly went to the worthiest or most popular candidates.

In Rome, merchants and trade were considered unsavory, and Carthaginians were bracketed accordingly.

There were religious differences, too. Carthaginians were said to placate their gods with the flesh of newly slaughtered children, although no one knows how frequently this practice occurred. Carthage was not the only culture of the era to indulge in such cruelty, but Romans—though equally superstitious—were less brutal before their deities.

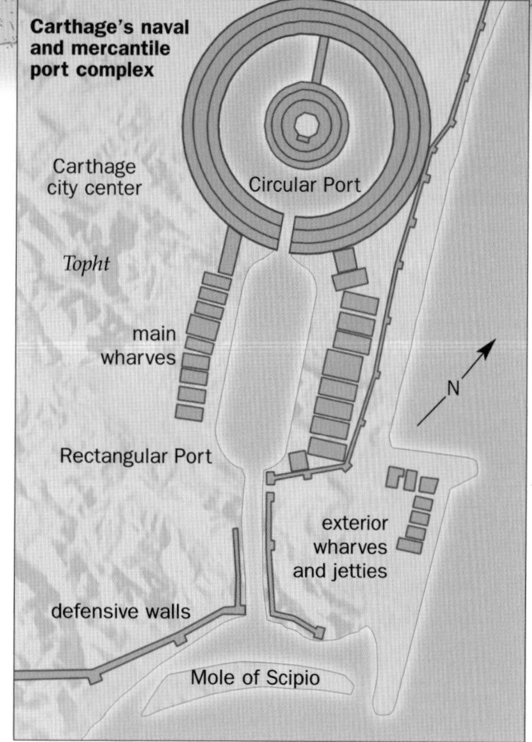

Carthage's naval and mercantile port complex
Carthage city center
Circular Port
Topht
main wharves
N
Rectangular Port
exterior wharves and jetties
defensive walls
Mole of Scipio

Above: The harbor of Carthage was one of the wonders of the Roman age and an inspiration for later port construction by the Romans themselves. The massive inner circular port may well have been in Trajan's mind when he ordered a new harbor at Rome's major port of Ostia.

Expanding into conflict

Rome and Carthage had survived peaceably alongside one another for many years before hostilities broke out. Romans referred to the Carthaginians as *Poeni*, meaning Phoenicians, from which the name "Punic" was derived. War between the two never seemed inevitable. Indeed, diplomacy and negotiation might have sidestepped the bloody conflict altogether or curbed it once it was underway. Roman ambition, however, was overweening.

History is rich in detail about the long-running series of conflicts, thanks to the work of Polybius (c.200–120 BC), a Greek captured by the Romans during the conquest of Macedonia in 168 BC. He became servant then friend to the influential Scipio family.

Although Polybius's knowledge of the first two Punic Wars is a matter of hearsay, he was well acquainted with the issues involved and witnessed the final sack of Carthage. The accounts were recorded in his *Universal History*, 40 books of informed comment, of which five survived. Impressed by the effectiveness of the Roman way, nonetheless he retained a degree of impartiality in his observations. These have been merged with other accounts, as well as modern academic study, to give a comprehensive picture of wars fought more than 2,000 years ago.

Carthage was chiefly concerned with trading opportunities and Rome, with its burgeoning wealth, was a vital outlet. It welcomed the Third Treaty of Friendship drawn up between Rome and Carthage in 279 BC that tied them to a policy of mutual support, and guaranteed Rome's exclusion from the Sicilian sphere. But when war came, it was sparked off by a petty squabble that involved Sicily, and the two powers were set on a collision course.

FIRST PUNIC WAR

Greeks colonized Sicily between the eighth and sixth centuries BC before coming into conflict with Phoenician invaders from Carthage in the sixth and fifth centuries. By the mid-third century, Carthage controlled Sicily's western end, while Syracuse, the chief Greek city-state, dominated in the east.

In 264 BC the city of Messana (Messina), which overlooked the vital strait between Sicily and Italy and through which all Mediterranean sea traffic passed, was in the hands of Mammertines. These Oscan-speaking mercenaries had come from Campania in Italy in 289 to fight for Syracuse, but then occupied Messana after a coup against its Greek authorities. Hieron, the *strategos* of Syracuse, had aided the Romans when they suppressed a ten-year long revolt of Campanians at Rhegium, aided by their Mammertine colleagues in Messana in 270. Now elected Tyrant as Hieron II (r.265–216 BC), he determined to regain Messana and attacked in 264.

Above: Front view of a gilt Roman cuirass, 3rd–2nd centuries BC. The wearer would have worn an almost identical design, but with flatter relief, on his back.

The Mammertines' choice for allies lay between Carthage—ancient enemies of Greeks—and Rome, which might accept the appeal from former Italians. Although the latter option was the preferred one, the Roman senate hesitated and Carthaginians arrived first and garrisoned the city, having first made an alliance with Hieron. However, a further appeal from Messana and a powerful Roman lobby with designs on Sicily combined to decide the issue. Still reluctant to break the treaty of 279, the senate passed the decision to the *comitia tributa*, who elected to send an expeditionary force to rescue Messana.

Appius Claudius Caudex ("the log") was given command and he moved his army swiftly across the strait from Rhegium and took Messana. Claudius permitted the Carthaginian garrison to leave in shame. Their leader, the admiral Hanno (no relation to the explorer), was later executed as a penalty for his inaction. Hieron, faced with the inevitable and anyway preferring the domination of Rome to that of Carthage, made a treaty with Claudius and withdrew to Syracuse.

Carthage, united with Syracuse, declared war on Rome. The outcome was by no means a foregone conclusion. Roman infantrymen were far more effective than the mercenaries employed by Carthage, but the Carthaginian navy had undisputed control of the seas. The Romans swiftly remedied this weakness by developing new ships (*see following page*). Now the odds were stacked in their favor and they duly won the war for Messana, although Carthage retained a Sicilian base.

The Romans pressed on to North Africa, regardless of the risks. In 256 BC Carthage's attempts to repel the Roman fleet failed, although the battle was costly to both sides. Inevitably Africa was a step too far for the Romans, whose supply lines were stretched to the limit. Carthaginians, fighting on home ground with Greek reinforcements, beat off the invaders.

A bloody stalemate

Carthage had been given new impetus by the leadership of Spartan general Xanthipus, who helped reorganize the troops. Elephants charging at the front and the skillful Numidian cavalry coming in from behind reduced the Roman force from 15,000 to just 2,000. Among the 500 prisoners taken was the Roman general Marcus Atilius Regulus.

However, Carthage failed to act strategically and did not hound or harry the Roman survivors, who were later rescued off the African coast. The success of that mission was radically diminished by the ravages of a summer storm that cost the lives of an estimated 100,000 men. Rome and Carthage pulled back from the conflict to lick their wounds.

Within a matter of months, Rome was ready

to go on the offensive once more. This time sights were set firmly on Sicily. Following a violent assault on Panormus (Palermo), the Romans installed themselves in this wealthy city set in a natural harbor. Yet the sum of their further attempts to gain Sicily amounted to little. There was a siege here, a naval battle there, but the rivals were locked in stalemate. Carthaginian commitment was weakened by uprisings back in Africa, and their defensive efforts ensured it became a war of attrition.

One victim was Hasdrubal, son of the admiral Hanno. After two years on Sicily he lost the advantage to the Romans and was, like his father, summarily executed for his failures. By comparison, deficient Roman leaders were merely fined and publicly disgraced.

A final Roman naval victory at the Aegates Islands (March 10, 241 BC) persuaded the Carthaginians to surrender. Their commander, the able Hamilcar Barca (d.228 BC), relinquished after losing 50 ships without hope of reinforcements. This victory, by giving the Romans undisputed command of the sea, made certain the fall of the Punic strongholds in Sicily. Rome had won its first overseas possession.

The First Punic War was concluded by treaty in 241. Carthage was permitted to withdraw the army from Sicily, but had to pay a heavy indemnity of 3,200 talents over ten years.

Above: Obverse of Syracusan coin showing the head of Hieron II. In this period portraits of people rarely featured on Roman coins.

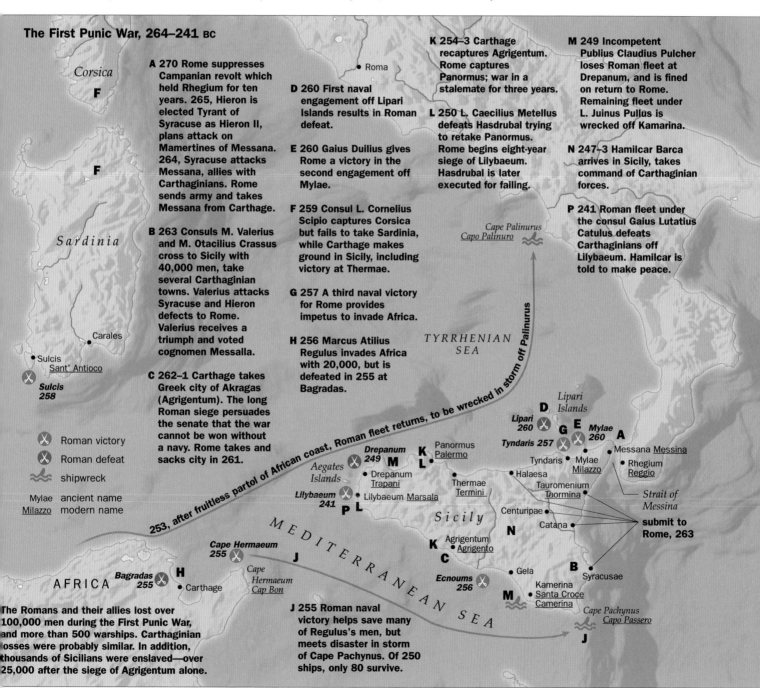

The First Punic War, 264–241 BC

A 270 Rome suppresses Campanian revolt which held Rhegium for ten years. 265, Hieron is elected Tyrant of Syracuse as Hieron II, plans attack on Mamertines of Messana. 264, Syracuse attacks Messana, allies with Carthaginians. Rome sends army and takes Messana from Carthage.

B 263 Consuls M. Valerius and M. Otacilius Crassus cross to Sicily with 40,000 men, take several Carthaginian towns. Valerius attacks Syracuse and Hieron defects to Rome. Valerius receives a triumph and voted cognomen Messalla.

C 262–1 Carthage takes Greek city of Akragas (Agrigentum). The long Roman siege persuades the senate that the war cannot be won without a navy. Rome takes and sacks city in 261.

D 260 First naval engagement off Lipari Islands results in Roman defeat.

E 260 Gaius Duilius gives Rome a victory in the second engagement off Mylae.

F 259 Consul L. Cornelius Scipio captures Corsica but fails to take Sardinia, while Carthage makes ground in Sicily, including victory at Thermae.

G 257 A third naval victory for Rome provides impetus to invade Africa.

H 256 Marcus Atilius Regulus invades Africa with 20,000, but is defeated in 255 at Bagradas.

J 255 Roman naval victory helps save many of Regulus's men, but meets disaster in storm of Cape Pachynus. Of 250 ships, only 80 survive.

K 254–3 Carthage recaptures Agrigentum. Rome captures Panormus; war in a stalemate for three years.

L 250 L. Caecilius Metellus defeats Hasdrubal trying to retake Panormus. Rome begins eight-year siege of Lilybaeum. Hasdrubal is later executed for failing.

M 249 Incompetent Publius Claudius Pulcher loses Roman fleet at Drepanum, and is fined on return to Rome. Remaining fleet under L. Juinus Pullus is wrecked off Kamarina.

N 247–3 Hamilcar Barca arrives in Sicily, takes command of Carthaginian forces.

P 241 Roman fleet under the consul Gaius Lutatius Catulus defeats Carthaginians off Lilybaeum. Hamilcar is told to make peace.

Roman victory
Roman defeat
shipwreck
Mylae ancient name
Milazzo modern name

Corsica
Sardinia
Carales
Sulcis
Sant' Antioco
Sulcis 258
Roma
Cape Palinurus
Capo Palinuro
TYRRHENIAN SEA
253, after fruitless partol of African coast, Roman fleet returns, to be wrecked in storm off Palinurus
Lipari Islands
Lipari 260
Mylae 260
Tyndaris 257
Messana Messina
Tyndaris
Mylae Milazzo
Rhegium Reggio
Panormus Palermo
Drepanum 249
Aegates Islands
Drepanum Trapani
Halaesa
Thermae Termini
Tauromenium Taormina
Strait of Messina
Lilybaeum 241
Lilybaeum Marsala
Sicily
Centuripae
Catana
submit to Rome, 263
Agrigentum Agrigento
MEDITERRANEAN SEA
Cape Hermaeum 255
Cape Hermaeum Cap Bon
AFRICA
Bagradas 255
Carthage
Ecnomus 256
Gela
Syracusae
Kamerina Santa Croce Camerina
Cape Pachynus Capo Passero

The Romans and their allies lost over 100,000 men during the First Punic War, and more than 500 warships. Carthaginian losses were probably similar. In addition, thousands of Sicilians were enslaved—over 25,000 after the siege of Agrigentum alone.

Ancient Galleys

Carthage was the supreme Mediterranean naval force of the period. The Punic War changed that, as Rome applied effort and ingenuity to create a navy and shifted the balance of power in its favor.

Carthage's ships not only acted in a military capacity but also sank rival trading vessels. Its fleet had three types of vessels: large cargo ship-cum-troop carriers, fast warships, and small, nimble boats that played important supporting roles in times of conflict.

In contrast, Rome—hitherto more wedded to land conquest—had neglected its maritime potential. The treaty of 279 BC had seemed to make a grand navy redudant. But tension between the two superpowers made the Roman patriciate aware of their vulnerability to attack from the sea. When a Carthaginian vessel ran aground on Roman territory it was taken apart so engineers could learn Punic shipbuilding from scratch.

Above: This clay votive model of a *cuirassed*, or armored, Roman galley was recovered from the sea near Cape Haleas. It dates from the first decade of the 1st century AD. The ship's beak, used for ramming enemy ships at the waterline, is clearly seen at the vessel's bow.

Roman ship designers sacrificed maneuverability to make their vessels stable and solid. The standard Roman warship was the quinquereme, a galley powered by five banks of oars and manned by about 300 men. This had tremendous speed, although ships with fewer banks of oars were more agile. In less than two years an entire navy was at sea.

This feat required acres of timber, thousands of men, and the training of ranks of sailors. It was a tribute to Roman doggedness that the new navy put to sea, although at first the more experienced Carthaginians subdued the fleet at the Lipari Islands in 260 BC.

On each ship the Romans installed a pillar of wood that supported a boarding bridge on a rope pulley. At the end of the bridge was a penetrating anchor-like spike called a *corvus*, named for its resemblance to a raven's sharp beak. The device hitched one ship to the next, enabling Romans to swarm aboard enemy ships after coming alongside.

The new invention was put to the test in the same year off the northern coast of Sicily at Mylae. In revenge for Lipari, the Roman fleet enjoyed an overwhelming victory through man-to-man combat, which had hardly been seen at sea before. Nearly half of a 130-strong Carthaginian fleet was lost, primarily because the Punic sailors were wrong-footed at the sight and action of the *corvus*, and were not prepared for fighting aboard ship. The consul in command of the new fleet, Gaius Duilius, returned home a hero and Rome celebrated its first naval triumph. To commemorate the victory, a monument was raised at one end of the rostra in the Forum, the Columna Rostrata.

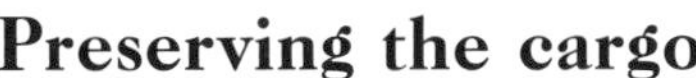

Preserving the cargo

An age of close-quarter fighting at sea began, replacing the old naval technique of ship ramming. Once again the Romans had reversed the strategic situation to dictate the terms of engagement, playing to their strengths.

Rome still suffered setbacks at sea. The heaviest losses were inflicted by vicious storms that sank hosts of ships on several occasions (*see map on previous page*). Roman designers came to realize that the advantage of

Right: A carving in stone depicts a 3rd-century BC Roman quinquereme.

the *corvus* was countered by the fact it made ships top-heavy and unstable. Soon after it was eradicated from the fleet.

To offer some idea about the importance placed on shipbuilding during the first Punic War, the senate responded to the loss of an estimated 270 ships off Sicily in bad weather by ordering a new fleet. Within three months 200 were launched and ready for action.

Roman soldiers powered the ships. The suggestion that slaves were made to row, certainly in the republican era, has never been adequately proved, although large numbers of slaves were certainly transported aboard ships between markets. Meanwhile, Carthage was dependent on mercenaries, who were far more likely to take flight in battle.

Ship-building assumed great importance during peacetime too, as merchant ships plied the Mediterranean, catering for an increasingly sophisticated Roman palate. The contents of Roman ships have been documented via marine archaeologists, thanks to the humble amphora, an all-purpose clay jar and forerunner to the wooden barrel. With a high neck, two handles, and a pointed bottom, the amphora was designed for easy portage and easy pouring. Amphorae contained every essential food item, including olives, olive oil, pickled fish, and wine. Archaeologists probing a wreck in 1950 established that a Roman cargo carrier operating in the first century BC possibly carried as many as 10,000 amphorae on one trip.

Below: A Roman quinquereme of the type that won the naval battles of the Punic Wars. It is fitted with a *corvus*, used for boarding enemy ships, and seen here in action.

Left: Roman merchant shipping and military transports tended to hug the shoreline and use oars. However, unlike warships, they relied more on sail to make speedier trips.

Below: The Greek bireme and trireme vessels were so named because they used two or three tiers of oarsmen. The Roman quinquereme did not have five banks, but three tiers manned by five (*quinque*) rowers, as shown here.

THE RISE OF HANNIBAL

Hamilcar Barca, out of power since his capitulation in Sicily, remained determined to avenge the defeat. But first he had an array of domestic difficulties to resolve. Lack of resources meant new regions had to be exploited, and Carthage's attention focused on Spain.

At the end of the war in Sicily returning mercenaries found their wages unexpectedly severed by a Carthaginian government short of funds. When discontent spilled over into conflict, Hanno was compelled to raise a new army, with the tacit approval of Rome. However, his lack of success in quelling the rebellion brought Hamilcar back to favor, and the two united to secure Carthaginian territory. In doing so, Hamilcar won unequivocal command in 238 BC. His antipathy toward Rome was well known. The senate sensed an ominous threat and executed a swift about-turn in its lenient policy toward Carthage.

Coins found in Spain show the heads of Hamilcar Barca (above), his son-in-law Hasdrubal (below), and son Hannibal (right), whose name means "the grace of Baal," the principal Phoenician deity.

In a precautionary move, Rome seized Sardinia in the same year and tightened its hold in Corsica. With Sicily, Sardinia, and Corsica gone, attention now turned to Spain, already partly settled along the coast by Carthaginians. In 237, Hamilcar, his son-in-law Hasdrubal, and nine-year-old son Hannibal crossed into Spain and set up headquarters in the Punic city of Gades (Cadiz). From here, he conquered the disparate Celtiberian tribes in the south and east, capitalizing on the regions' wealthy resources—silver and copper soon refilled Carthage's empty treasury. If suspicions arose over Hamilcar's actions, he had the perfect excuse to offer concerned Romans: he was ensuring that Carthage could meet the indemnity levied after the Punic War. In any case, Rome had its hands full elsewhere (*see panel*).

In 228, while withdrawing from a siege of Helice (Eleche), Hamilcar was drowned and his troops chose Hasdrubal to succeed him, later ratified by Carthage. Hasdrubal continued the conquest of Iberia but agreed with Rome in 226 not to cross the Ebro. Five years later, he lay dead at the hands of an aggrieved Celt and Hamilcar's 25-year-old son Hannibal (247–c.183 BC) took his place.

Call of vengeance

According to Polybius, Hamilcar had made the young boy swear an oath of eternal loathing against Rome, and it was this abiding animosity that both marked and marred a remarkable career. Hannibal also made remarkable conquests to the north before investing the city of Saguntum in 220. Although it lay south of the Ebro, it was ostensibly under Roman protection, and when Hannibal took it in 219, after an eight-month siege, Rome declared war.

With its mastery of the sea, Rome expected to dictate where the Second Punic War would take place: Spain and Africa. Hannibal had other views. He knew Rome's power could only be smashed by destroying her Italian confederacy. He determined to fight in Italy, and wasted no time. The ambitious plan called for the movement of (according to Polybius) 90,000 infantry, 12,000 cavalry, and many elephants north from the Ebro, across the Pyrenees, then a dash across the Rhône valley to the Alpine passes into Italy. The gamble was that he could achieve this before the fall closed the high passes and condemned his troops to a lingering death in the snow and ice.

At first, his luck held out. Two Roman legions under the consul P. Cornelius Scipio should have headed for Spain and would have met him at the Rhône, but were delayed by a Celtic uprising around the new Latin colonies of Cremona and Placentia. Scipio raised two more legions and reached the Rhône in August, only to find he had missed Hannibal by days. Contemplating Hannibal's folly in marching into the Alps, Scipio decided to send the legions toward Spain under his brother Gnaeus, while

he returned to Italy to gather the other two legions and await Hannibal south of the Alps.

As the Punic columns continued up remote paths toward Alpine summits, they were vulnerable to attack from hostile tribes and also severe weather. Countless men and animals died when they lost their footings on icy tracks. One of the routes identified as that likely to have been taken by Hannibal and his men reaches as high as 9,000 feet above sea level.

Despite the number of casualties and the extreme conditions, Hannibal reached the Italian peninsula in just 15 days, but with only 26,000 men. Despite the perils of the crossing, there was no insurgency among the motley troops, a telling tribute to Hannibal's charisma and leadership skills. However, his enemy had been equally swift. When he stormed the chief town of the Taurini (Turin), he discovered that the legions in northern Italy were commanded by Scipio, who had traveled nearly 1,000 miles in a month.

Distractions

Rome's attention was distracted from events in Spain by two other conflicts; one with the Celtic Gauls across the Arno and another across the Adriatic with Illyrian pirates. Gallic unrest was partly sparked by the distribution of land in the *ager Gallicus* to Roman citizens in 232 BC, which led to evictions of the sitting tenants. In 225 a Gallic army was defeated at Telamon, and the Romans advanced into the Po plain, capturing Mediolanum (Milan) in 222. Colonies were established at Placentia (Piacenza) and Cremona in 218, and were barely established when the Second Punic War broke out.

During the First Punic War, an Illyrian chieftan named Argon had built a considerable empire along the Adriatic coast from Dalmatia down to the Gulf of Corinth. The principal activity of this empire was piracy. While it only worried Greek shipping, Rome remained unconcerned, but when the Illyrians attacked southern Italy, Rome went to war in 299, with a fleet and 22,000 troops. The outcome was inevitable, and Illyria surrendered the following year. The significance of this event lies in that Rome's wandering eye had turned toward the Greek sphere for the first time.

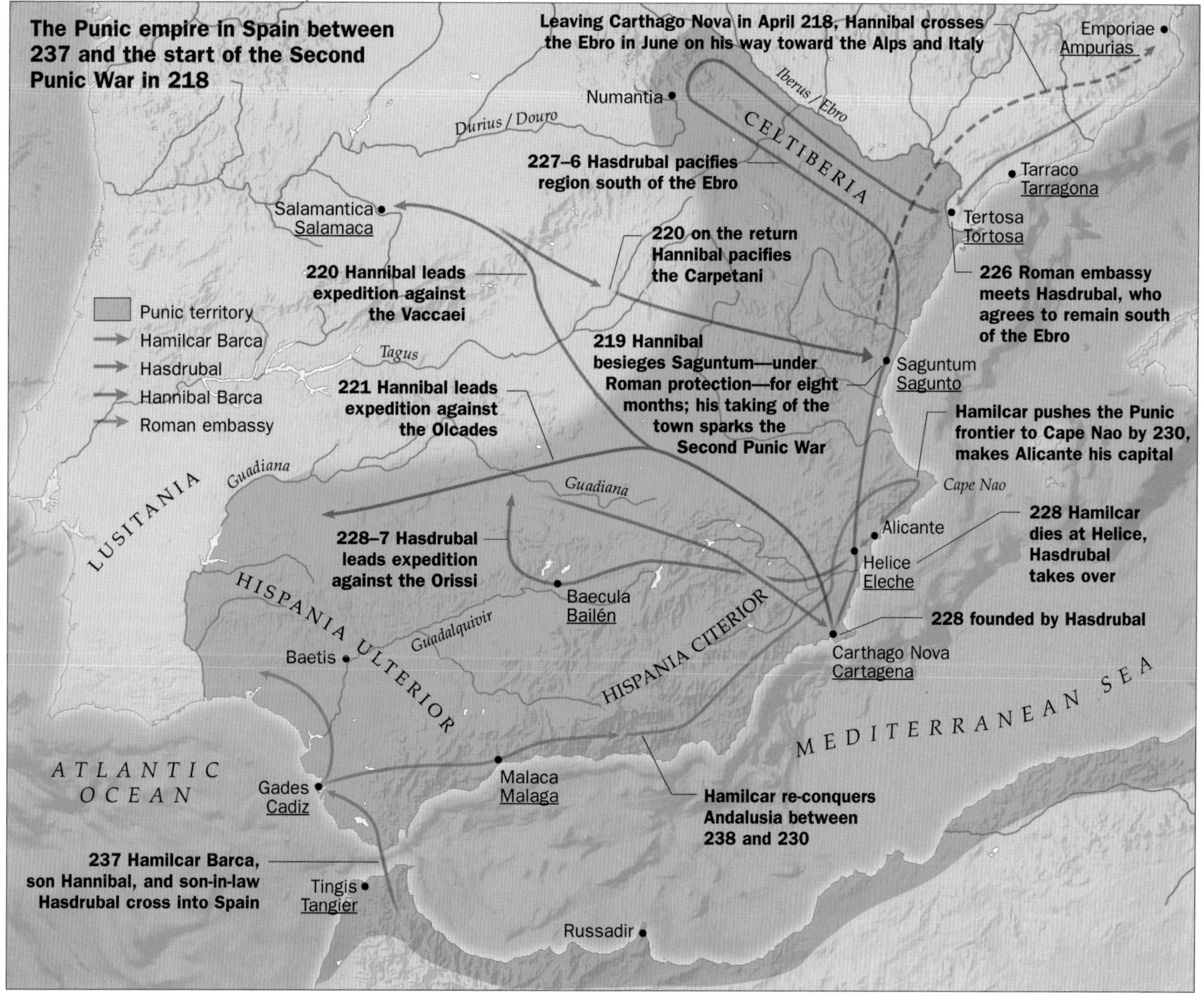
The Punic empire in Spain between 237 and the start of the Second Punic War in 218
Punic territory
Hamilcar Barca
Hasdrubal
Hannibal Barca
Roman embassy
Leaving Carthago Nova in April 218, Hannibal crosses the Ebro in June on his way toward the Alps and Italy
Emporiae
Ampurias
Numantia
Durius / Douro
Iberus / Ebro
CELTIBERIA
227–6 Hasdrubal pacifies region south of the Ebro
Tarraco
Tarragona
Tertosa
Tortosa
Salamantica
Salamaca
220 on the return Hannibal pacifies the Carpetani
220 Hannibal leads expedition against the Vaccaei
226 Roman embassy meets Hasdrubal, who agrees to remain south of the Ebro
Tagus
219 Hannibal besieges Saguntum—under Roman protection—for eight months; his taking of the town sparks the Second Punic War
Saguntum
Sagunto
221 Hannibal leads expedition against the Olcades
Hamilcar pushes the Punic frontier to Cape Nao by 230, makes Alicante his capital
Cape Nao
Guadiana
Guadiana
LUSITANIA
Alicante
228–7 Hasdrubal leads expedition against the Orissi
228 Hamilcar dies at Helice, Hasdrubal takes over
Helice
Eleche
HISPANIA ULTERIOR
Baecula
Bailén
Guadalquivir
HISPANIA CITERIOR
228 founded by Hasdrubal
Carthago Nova
Cartagena
Baetis
MEDITERRANEAN SEA
ATLANTIC OCEAN
Gades
Cadiz
Malaca
Malaga
Hamilcar re-conquers Andalusia between 238 and 230
237 Hamilcar Barca, son Hannibal, and son-in-law Hasdrubal cross into Spain
Tingis
Tangier
Russadir

Victory in Italy

For Hannibal the arduous business of war was just beginning. Although he was blessed with military acumen, his army was far from home and perpetually outnumbered. Nevertheless, Hannibal carved a route around the Italian peninsula that would remain etched on the Roman psyche for years.

Cannae was Rome's worst defeat. Hannibal, pictured right, proved to be a master tactician in defeating a larger Roman force. He masked the main army by placing light slingers and spear-men in the front rank. The Roman *velites* in front fell back to let the heavy infantry engage Hannibal's center. His light infantry also fell back and formed at the rear and sides. The legions did the usual, plowing on into Hannibal's crescent, which began to give way on purpose, drawing the Romans deeper in, not noticing the enemy skirmishers on their flanks. Hannibal's heavy cavalry pushed the light Roman horses back, then dashed across the field to fall on the rear of the allies' cavalry, before attacking the Roman rear. The trap closed.

When Hannibal arrived in Italy, it caused shockwaves in a Rome that had become complacent about the threat of invasion. But what was his purpose? Hannibal could not hope to colonize Rome and the Italian peninsula. He was vastly outnumbered and isolated from reinforcements and supplies. The senate expected swift retribution.

Scipio crossed the Po at Placentia and marched along the north bank to the Ticinus, hoping to catch Hannibal before his forces had recovered for the rigors of the Alpine crossing. Here, he met Hannibal's advance guard in October 218 BC, but was beaten back and was wounded. His life was saved by his son, who would one day become Hannibal's nemesis. Scipio retired to the Trebia, south of Placentia to wait for his consular colleague, T. Sempronius Longus, who had been recalled from the smaller African invasion force mobilizing in Sicily.

When they joined forces in late November, an enthusiastic Sempronius overruled the cautious Scipio and together they mounted a charge across the Trebia at Hannibal. Carthaginian forces emerged from hiding to scythe through the flank and the rear of the Roman army. An estimated 30,000 Romans died in the ill-conceived attack. The victory gave a massive boost for Hannibal's personal standing among vacillating tribes around the region.

Scipio was not blamed for the failure, and kept his command, but in the elections the *plebs*

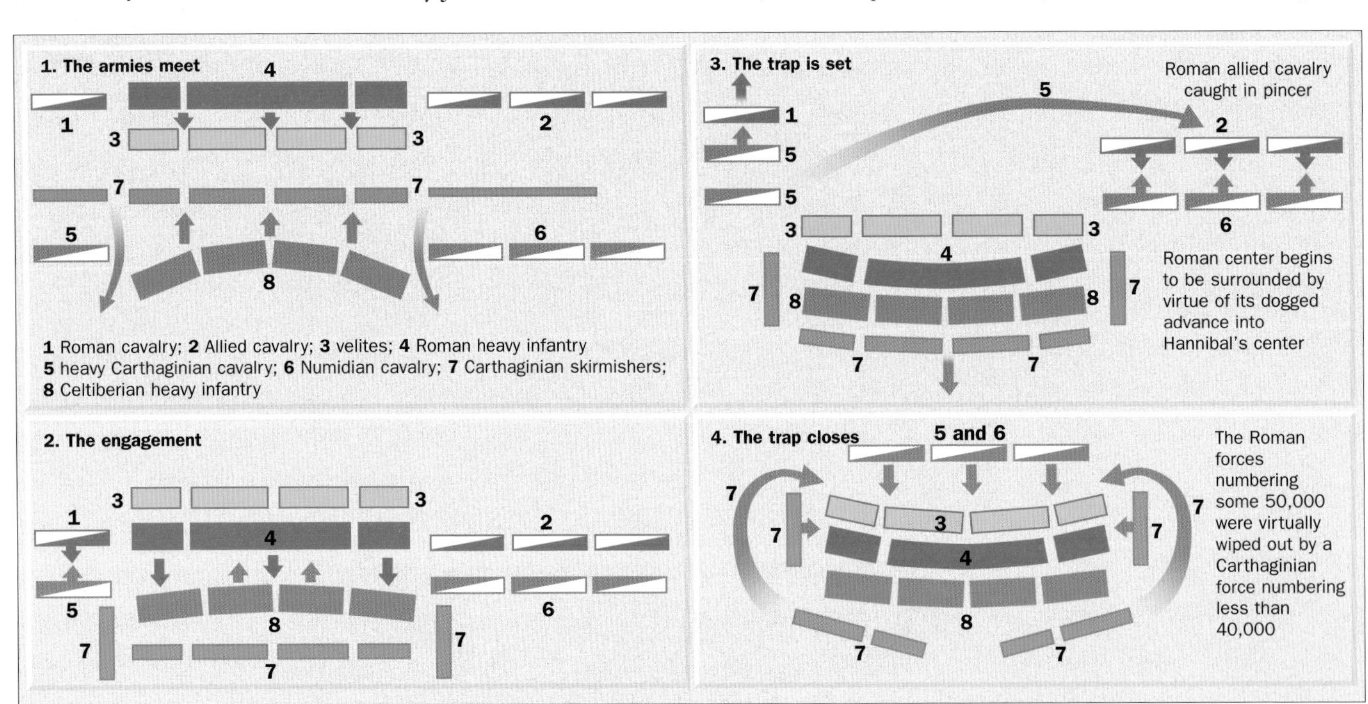
1. The armies meet
1 Roman cavalry; 2 Allied cavalry; 3 velites; 4 Roman heavy infantry
5 heavy Carthaginian cavalry; 6 Numidian cavalry; 7 Carthaginian skirmishers;
8 Celtiberian heavy infantry
2. The engagement
3. The trap is set
Roman allied cavalry caught in pincer
Roman center begins to be surrounded by virtue of its dogged advance into Hannibal's center
4. The trap closes
5 and 6
The Roman forces numbering some 50,000 were virtually wiped out by a Carthaginian force numbering less than 40,000

showed their discontent with the senate's conduct of the war by electing the popular leader Gaius Flaminius as one of the consuls. He moved north in spring 217, and met Hannibal at Lake Trasimenus. Showing elegant military ingenuity, Hannibal drew Roman forces into a perfectly executed ambush. Legionaries found themselves hemmed in between Carthaginians and the lake. Once more, the Roman army suffered many casualties—including the death of Flaminius—as a result of poor or non-existent reconnaissance.

Fabian tactics

Now the glories of Rome lay ahead of Hannibal, apparently within his reach. Yet at first he chose not to head for the capital, convinced it was still too secure to capture. Instead he went in search of support among the southern Italian states of the confederacy. However, he found few willing to lend outright support, despite Rome's lack of success to date.

In Rome, panic ensued. With one consul dead, the *comitia tributa* elected Fabius Maximus as dictator, the first for 30 years. Instead of confronting Hannibal, Maximus pursued a cautious policy of shadowing his army around Italy. The trailing tactics angered some Roman observers, who dubbed Maximus "Hannibal's lackey." It is more likely that his patience saved Rome from effective Carthaginian conquest. When over-caution allowed Hannibal to slip back across the Appenines, Maximus was replaced by the consuls Lucius Aemilius Paullus and Gaius Terentius Varro. Lack of caution drew their legions into another Carthaginian trap at Cannae in 216, where the Romans were completely surrounded and cut down in their thousands.

Polybius underscores the importance of Hannibal's achievements: "But I must make it clear from the facts themselves how great were the resources which Hannibal dared to attack and how great was the power which he boldly confronted; despite this, he came so close to his aim as to inflict major disasters on the Romans."

Hannibal now advanced on Rome itself, but again, to the surprise of all observers on either side, he turned aside only miles from the walls, and returned to the south. There had been another benefit to the Cannae victory. States so far wavering but remaining loyal to Rome changed sides in their droves, and declared common cause with the Carthaginians. Livy noted the Atellani, some Apulians, the Calatini, Hirpini, all the Samnites (except the Pentri), the Brutii, Lucanians, Uzentini, nearly all the Greek coastal settlements, and all the Gauls on the Italian side of the Alps. Since the biggest concentration of new friends lay in the heel of Italy, it is probable that Hannibal felt safer in that region, and would be able to recruit new forces more easily there, so he left the city alone. However, Rome's position now looked precarious. Not only had it lost too many legions, but the senate's ability to recruit from the southern colonies and "allies" was curtailed.

Above: Quintus Fabius Maximus Verrocus (c.275–203 BC) was nicknamed *Cunctator* (Fabius the Delayer). His defensive war against Hannibal after the third decisive defeat of Roman legions on Italian soil at Lake Trasimene was criticized and led to his recall. After the disaster at Cannae in 216, his tactics were vindicated and the strategy resumed. He was consul for the fifth time in 209, when he captured Tarento.

Left: Lake Trasimene (Trasimenus) today presents a peaceful picture, but in 217 what is now organized agricultural land was a series of treacherous marshes. As his force descended from the Appenines (in the background), Hannibal was able to trap the legions of Flaminius in the boggy ground and destroy them.

Scipio Africanus

Although the soldiers of Rome and Carthage were matched in skill and courage, Rome's weakness lay in poor military leadership. When a general of genius finally emerged to fill the void, Rome and Carthage battled on even terms.

In the late summer of 218 Gnaeus Scipio with two legions landed in Spain, where the war had begun. His brother Publius had demonstrated his understanding of how vital it was to deny the wealth of resources and manpower to Hannibal in Italy and his colleague in Spain, another Hasdrubal (son of Gisgo). With his limited force, Scipio advanced south from Emporiae (Ampurias) as far as the Ebro, where his tiny fleet destroyed a larger Punic naval force in 217. Later in the year, Publius Scipio brought reinforcements, and together they drove the Carthaginians back.

Carthage also reinforced Spain, with armies under Hannibal's brothers Mago and Hasdrubal. With three armies in the field, the smaller Roman legions were eventually cornered and both Scipios' forces were destroyed in 211. Their loss was not in vain, for it had prevented reinforcements reaching Hannibal. Further, the three Carthaginian generals failed to follow up the victories by co-operating with each other, preferring to exploit success on their own.

Above: Publius Cornelius Scipio (c.185–129 BC), later "Africanus," was the decisive general Rome needed. His war in Spain (209–6) against Hannibal's brothers Hasdrubal (**top right**) and Mago (**bottom right**) pushed the Carthaginians from the peninsula and helped weaken the city's alliance with Philip V of Macedon (**center right**).

In Italy, Rome's fortunes sank lower with news, shortly after the battle of Cannae, that two legions had been cut to pieces in Cisalpine Gaul. The policy now was to keep as many troops in the field as possible, harassing Hannibal and wearing him down, rather than risking direct confrontation. Before a pitched battle could be fought, a general of military genius was needed. And in a time of Rome's greatest need, the right man for the job was found.

Forsaking home for abroad

Who better to avenge the deaths of the Scipio brothers in Spain than the son of Publius? Aged 25, the young Publius Scipio arrived in Spain in 209 BC. Responding to a temporary withdrawal of Carthaginian troops, Scipio made a dash for New Carthage, seizing the city with a combined land and sea assault. In the following year, he took the fight into the hinterland and defeated Hasdrubal Barca at Baecula (Bailén) in 208. By 206, Scipio had driven the Carthaginians from Spain. Hasdrubal, however, made a masterly retreat from Baecula, and slipped away north to cross the Pyrenees to join Hannibal in Italy.

Initially, copying his brother by using the Alpine passes appeared inspired. Hasdrubal marched through the Alps without coming under attack, but communications broke down when he reached the Italian peninsula. The Romans fielded four legions against him to prevent any link up with Hannibal, and Hasdrubal died in 207 in battle at the River Metaurus. Hannibal remained impotent in the heel of Italy, an irritant rather than a threat to Rome. He was a long way from home and support. Appeals to Carthage fell on deaf ears—the city elders feared his adventurism would result in worse retaliation; there were even some who said this was Hannibal's war, not theirs.

Publius Scipio returned from Spain in 205 and was made consul. He now vowed to take the conflict to the Carthaginian heartland of North Africa. At first the senate was unwilling to reduce domestic defenses at a time when Hannibal still roamed the peninsula, but this changed in 203, when Hannibal was recalled to the defense of Carthage. Discouraged by his future chances, Hannibal embarked his force and left Italy.

Scipio reached North Africa in 204 with an expeditionary force and, with the help of Massinissa, a Numidian ally who had been harrying Carthaginian interests for some time, put Carthaginian forces to flight on several occasions. Hannibal squared up to Scipio in the Battle of Zama in 202, hoping his elephant corps would wreak havoc. In fact it was the legionaries and the Numidian cavalry whose presence really counted. Hannibal was comprehensively outflanked and surrounded, and sued for peace.

By 201 Carthage was heavily fined, stripped of its defenses, and permitted to keep just ten ships in its navy. Publius Scipio was lauded for his achievements, winning the honorific "Africanus." In the wings, Philip V of Macedonia waited and watched. Had he intervened more promptly on the side of the Carthaginians it might have altered the course of the war. As it happened, Philip was himself beaten by Rome three years after Hannibal.

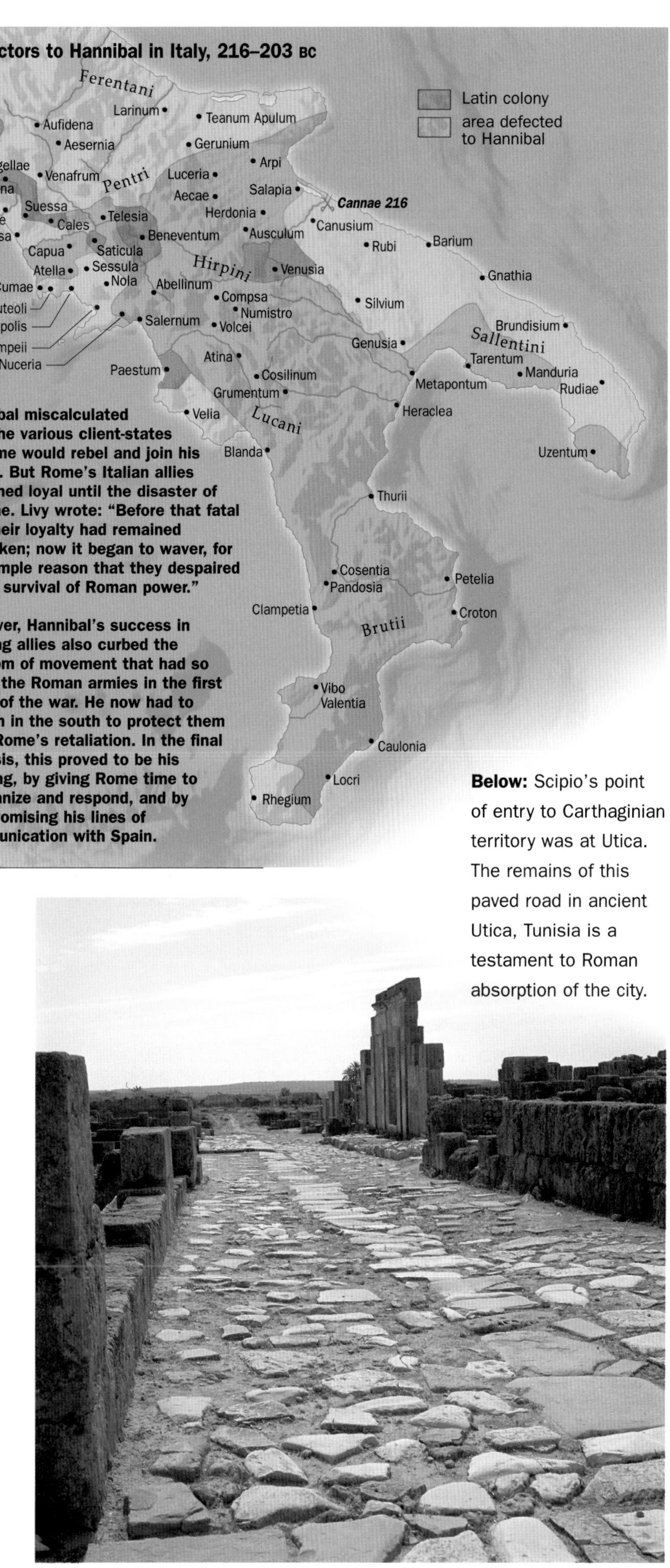
Defectors to Hannibal in Italy, 216–203 BC
Latin colony
area defected to Hannibal
Ferentani
Larinum
Teanum Apulum
Sora
Aufidena
Aesernia
Gerunium
Fregellae
Arpi
Venafrum
Pentri
Luceria
Interamina
Salapia
Aecae
Cannae 216
Suessa
Minturnae
Telesia
Herdonia
Cales
Sinuessa
Beneventum
Ausculum
Canusium
Capua
Saticula
Rubi
Barium
Atella
Sessula
Hirpini
Venusia
Nola
Gnathia
Cumae
Abellinum
Puteoli
Compsa
Silvium
Neapolis
Numistro
Salernum
Volcei
Brundisium
Pompeii
Sallentini
Nuceria
Genusia
Atina
Tarentum
Paestum
Cosilinum
Manduria
Metapontum
Grumentum
Rudiae
Heraclea
Velia
Lucani
Blanda
Uzentum
Thurii
Cosentia
Pandosia
Petelia
Clampetia
Croton
Brutii
Vibo
Valentia
Caulonia
Locri
Rhegium

Hannibal miscalculated that the various client-states of Rome would rebel and join his cause. But Rome's Italian allies remained loyal until the disaster of Cannae. Livy wrote: "Before that fatal day their loyalty had remained unshaken; now it began to waver, for the simple reason that they despaired of the survival of Roman power."

However, Hannibal's success in winning allies also curbed the freedom of movement that had so upset the Roman armies in the first years of the war. He now had to remain in the south to protect them from Rome's retaliation. In the final analysis, this proved to be his undoing, by giving Rome time to reorganize and respond, and by compromising his lines of communication with Spain.

Below: Scipio's point of entry to Carthaginian territory was at Utica. The remains of this paved road in ancient Utica, Tunisia is a testament to Roman absorption of the city.

CARTHAGE DESTROYED

In Rome distrust of Carthage thrived although it adhered to the terms of the treaty. An excuse to pick a fight was needed, and Massinissa supplied it. Despite making a heroic last stand, Carthage was quickly condemned to history.

Right: A coin struck by the cunning King Massinissa bears his profile. Having been a supplier of cavalry to Carthage, he was one of several rulers of the time who saw Rome's star rising, and became an ally.

Industrious Carthaginians helped restore the wealth of their home city, with some measure of success. At first Hannibal remained there, turning his considerable talents to administration. His fiscal reforms helped Carthage clear its indemnity debt to Rome in just a few years, but Roman distrust prevailed. In 195 BC he fled after Rome demanded that Carthage surrender him. Rumors were rife that he was consorting with Antiochus III of Syria, aiming to confront Rome once more. Scipio Africanus proved an unlikely ally by speaking for him in Rome but was unable to prevent the witch-hunt.

Hannibal found himself a Roman quarry once more when the republic defeated his Syrian hosts. This time he went to Crete, before retreating to the Turkish coast. During a naval clash with Pergamum, he was thought to be behind the Bithynian trick of catapulting clay jars packed with poisonous snakes onto ships. Afterward the Romans were on his trail again. This time Hannibal evaded them once and for all by committing suicide.

For its part, Rome was distracted by confrontations with the Gauls, Greeks, and Celtiberians. It had already resolved to finish a job begun before the outbreak of the Second Punic War—the subjugation of the Po valley—and in doing so Roman leaders developed a taste for overland expeditions.

The outlook was also bleak for those Italian communities that had sided with Hannibal. None was permitted into the ranks of the army, except as common soldiers. Their land was taken over by the state and the rights of

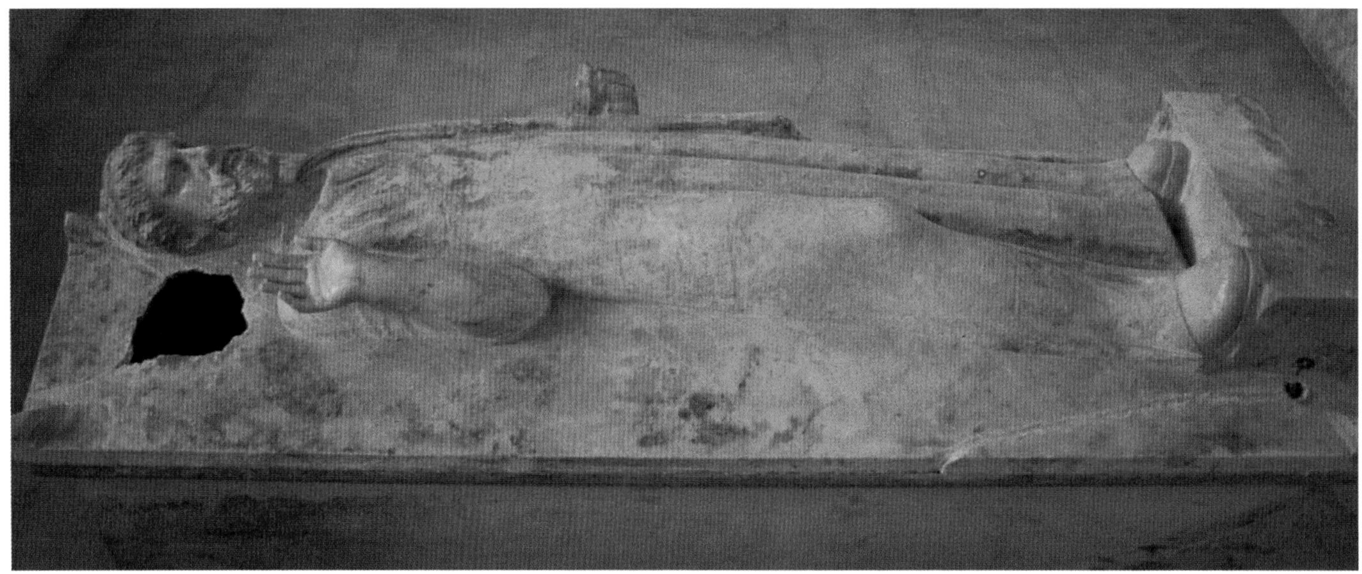

Below: A sarcophagus from the period of the Punic Wars is carved with a likeness of the Carthaginian nobleman who was entombed in it.

278 BC	275 BC	264 BC	260 BC	241 BC	237 BC	225 BC	218 BC
After hard-won victories, Pyrrhus abandons war with Rome to support Greeks in Sicily	Pyrrhus again fights for Tarentum against Rome, but is defeated at Malventum	First Punic War starts after Rome and Carthage clash responding to help Messana	With use of the *corvus* boarding device, Rome wins its second naval engagement	Rome's navy wins the First Punic War and adds Sicily to its territory	Hamilcar Barca gains Spanish territory for Carthage	Rome defeats Celts at Telamon, northern Italy	Hannibal crosses the Alps into Italy as the Second Punic War starts

citizenship suspended.

For another 50 years, Carthage remained chained by its treaty, but to many vocal patricians in Rome—most notably Cato the Censor (*see pages 56–7*)—it was an unsatisfactory situation. For those who agreed with him that Carthage "should cease to exist," it was convenient that the now elderly but still vigorous Numidian Massinissa provided them with an excuse to start a third war. Appreciating that Carthage was hidebound by its punitive peace treaty, Massinissa made repeated inroads into Carthaginian territory in North Africa. When Rome repeatedly ignored calls from Carthage to curb his ambitions, the city declared war on him in 150 BC. It was a thin excuse, but in attacking an ally of Rome, Carthage had broken the treaty.

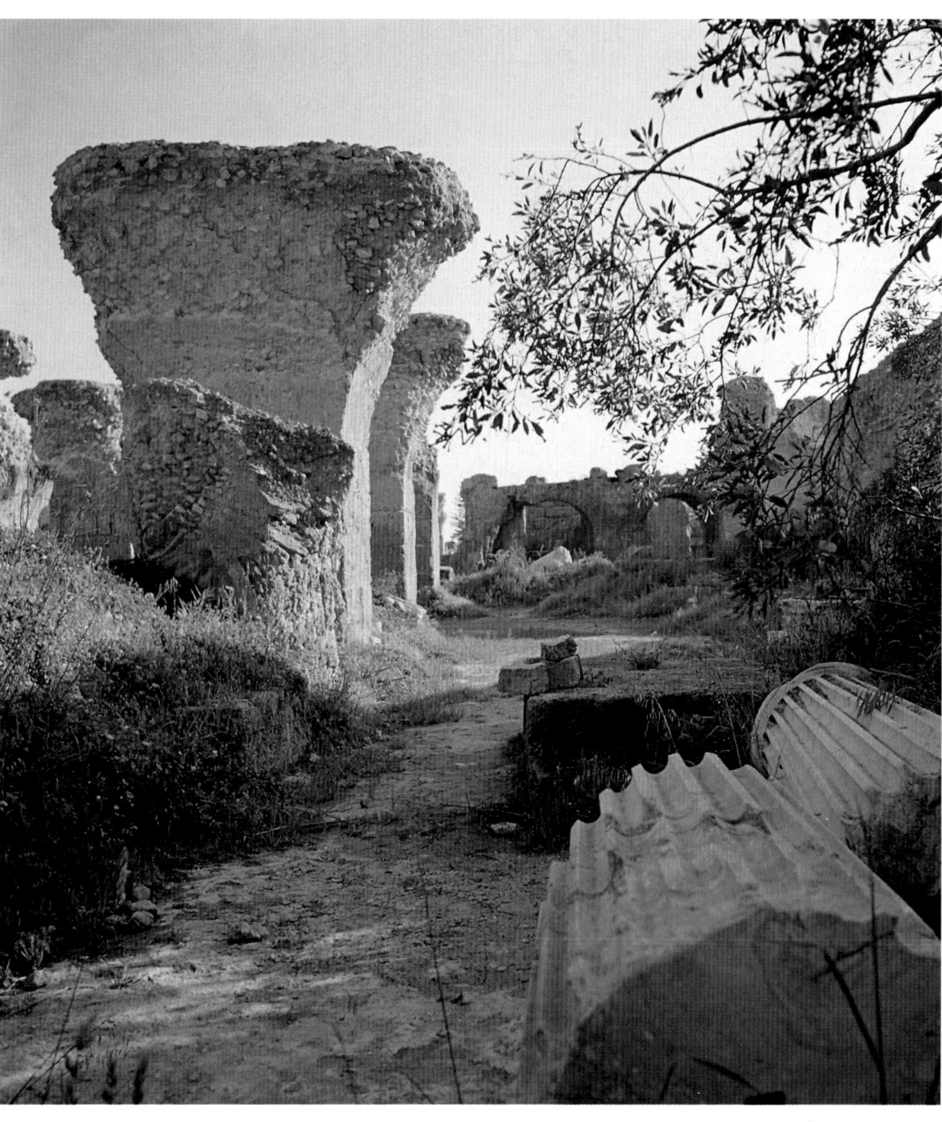

Carthage razed

The Cathaginian elders entreated for peace and Rome responded by raising the tribute demands and ordering its people to move from the city to settle where they liked, provided it was at least ten miles from the sea. At this second request the Carthaginians balked. At heart a sea-faring people, they determined to stay and fight. The Third Punic War (149–46 BC) had started.

Armed forces were rallied at speed and installed for a siege. This meant Rome was deprived of the swift victory its consuls had doubtless anticipated. For three years Roman forces chipped away at Carthaginian defenses. Carthage performed surprisingly well under pressure, although the lack of support from fellow Phoenicians along the seaboard was a severe blow.

The arrival of Cornelius Scipio Aemilianus, son of a distinguished military commander and adopted grandson of Scipio Africanus, finally galvanized the troops into a last, bloody push. Thousands of Carthaginians perished in street-to-street fighting. The rest were sold into slavery and Carthage was leveled, the centuries-old empire eradicated. Rome now possessed a new province. Human habitation of Carthage was forbidden and it became part of the Roman province of Africa, with surviving residents heading for Numidia. The site was redeveloped after 122 and the remains visible today belong to that Roman settlement.

Carthage was not the only city to be razed in 146 BC. Further to the east, one of the gems of Greek culture, the city of Corinth, was reduced to rubble at the conclusion of a long series of conflicts in the region that had taken place in the gap between the Second and Third Punic Wars.

Above: Fallen columns lie in the Roman Antonine Thermae (baths) in Carthage. Rome laid Carthage to waste at the end of the Third Punic War. For a period, the senate forbade any building to be raised on the site, but after 122 BC, a colony was founded and Roman Carthage rose from the rubble, in time to dissolve into ruin itself.

217 BC	**216 BC**	**214–205 BC**	**211 BC**	**209–6 BC**	**221 BC**	**204 BC**	**202 BC**
Hannibal defeats two Roman legions at Lake Trasimenus	Success at Cannae gives Hannibal control of southern Italy	The Achaean League seeks help from Rome in the First Macedonian War	Starved of resources in Italy, Hannibal is held in a stalemate	Publius Scipio (Africanus) conquers Carthaginian territory in Spain	Hasdrubal dies at River Metaurus; Hannibal inherits his territory and army	Scipio Africanus targets Carthage's forces in North Africa	Africanus defeats Hannibal at Zama, Carthage, ending the Second Punic War

THE EARLY REPUBLICAN ARMY

The Second Punic War proved to be a crucial turning point in Rome's history. Under the genius of Scipio Africanus's generalship, Roman legions became the most powerful army the world had seen. Discipline and organization were the keys to Roman success.

Before the military reforms of Marius (*see page 62*), the Roman army was organized along traditional lines that had evolved from the earliest times of the original settlement. The early republican army is sometimes referred to as the Servian army, since King Servius Tullius is credited with its formulation. At the beginning of each year, two consuls were elected, and their first task was to appoint their tribunes (staff officers). It was the tribunes' job to enrol sufficient recruits to keep the legions up to strength. This was done by specifying a day on which all property-owning Roman citizens between the ages of 17 and 46 had to assemble on the Capitoline.

The tribunes then took turns to have first choice, a method that ensured an even distribution of experience and ability throughout the legions. When the choosing was complete, the recruits swore an oath of obedience, but in typically efficient Roman style, this was sworn in full by only one recruit, with the others saying *Idem in me* (the same for me) after him.

In theory, a legion was the smallest unit capable of fighting a war in that it was complete in terms of manpower and equipment. However, a single legion was rarely called on to fight alone. The republican army of the Punic Wars period was comprised of four different types of legionary. Soldiers in the prime of life were called *hastati* and *principes*. The *hastati* stood in

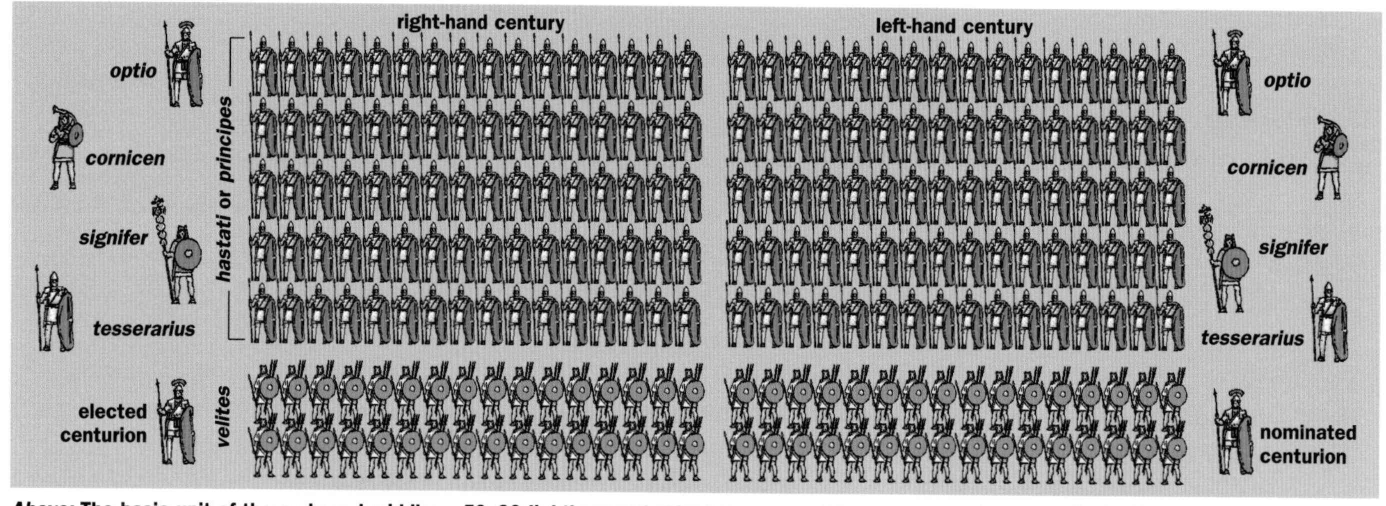
right-hand century
left-hand century
optio
cornicen
signifer
tesserarius
elected centurion
hastati or principes
velites
optio
cornicen
signifer
tesserarius
nominated centurion

Above: The basic unit of the early and middle republican army was the maniple. Maniples of the *hastati* and *principes* consisted of 120–150 heavily armed javelineers and 50–60 lightly armed skirmishers, or *velites* in the front ranks. The whole unit was organized into two centuries, each commanded by a centurion. One of these centurions was elected by the army as a whole, the second nominated by the elected centurion. Each centurion selected four men to be his other officers.

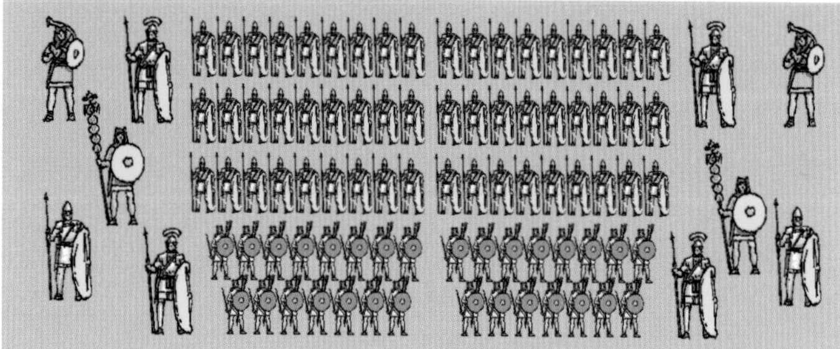

Above: A maniple of *triarii* always consisted of 60 veterans bearing spears with a number of velites. The maniple of *triarii* was also organized into two centuries and commanded as the *hastati/principes.*

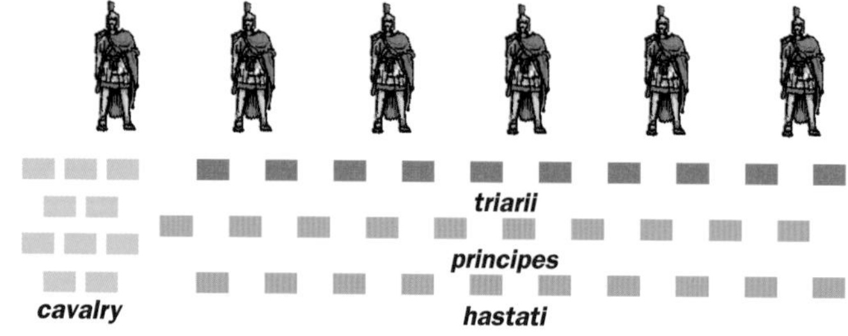
triarii
principes
cavalry
hastati

Above: A legion was composed of 30 maniples: 10 of hastati in the front rank, 10 of principes in the middle rank, and 10 of triarii in the rear rank. 300 cavalry were organized as 10 *turmae.* Each *turma* consisted of 30 horsemen divided into three squadrons of 10 men, including a *decurion* and his *optio.* The whole legion was commanded by six tribunes, usually young aristocrats pursuing political careers.

the front line and the *principes* in the second. In full armor, they each carried a sword and two long *pila* (javelins). *Triarii* were veterans who were similarly armored, but carried one long spear. Standing in the rear rank, they were seldom used in battle and the expression "the battle came to the *triarii*" described a desperate situation. The fourth type of legionary were the *velites*. Armed with only a helmet and shield and carrying a sword and short pila, *velites* were used for skirmishing.

The centurions then chose their *optio* (second-in-command), *signifer* (standard bearer), *cornicen* (bugler), and *tessarius* (guard commander), who received the day's password written on a *tessera* (tablet). The centurion who had been elected was the senior of the two and commanded the right-hand century. The first centurion to be elected by the men became the *primus pilus* or highest ranking centurion of the legion.

At the middle of the command structure were six tribunes per legion reporting to the general's *legatus* (legate). A *legatus* had to be a man of senatorial status, and was often of consular rank. By the time of the Punic Wars, a general usually had several legates working for him, especially if the campaign looked an interesting one, since these elder statesmen often enjoyed an active period away from the political rigors of Rome and willingly volunteered their services.

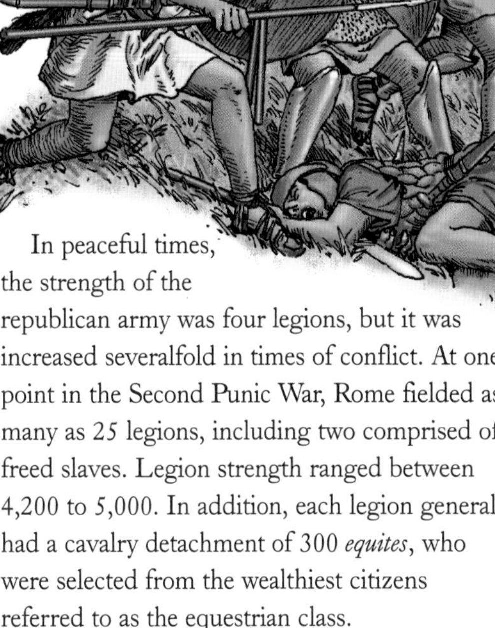

Below: The *velites*—one *veles* on the left and one on the right, with green shields—skirmish with the enemy, while the *hastati* and *principes* in the center engage with javelins. The *triari* stand in reserve in the rear. A *turma* of *equites* supports the forward push.

In peaceful times, the strength of the republican army was four legions, but it was increased severalfold in times of conflict. At one point in the Second Punic War, Rome fielded as many as 25 legions, including two comprised of freed slaves. Legion strength ranged between 4,200 to 5,000. In addition, each legion generally had a cavalry detachment of 300 *equites*, who were selected from the wealthiest citizens referred to as the equestrian class.

Structure of the legions

Each legion was divided into 60 units called centuries, an echo of the original centuries created by Romulus. Centuries were organized in couples and the pair was called a maniple. The *hastati*, *principes*, and *triarii* were each divided into ten maniples, with the *velites* distributed among them.

Each legion elected 30 centurions to command the maniples, and each of these nominated a second centurion to make up the full strength.

Allied forces were organized along similar lines to the legions, but supplied up to three times the number of cavalry. Command of the allied force was in the hands of three *praefecti* (prefects) nominated by the consul. In this period, the army's general was invariably one of the two consuls, a situation that did not necessarily pertain after the reforms of Marius.

An important point about the army of the middle republican period is that the legions had no permanence. Legions were raised at one time when needed, and continued to exist until the citizen-soldiers raised in it were dismissed from duty. This would change with Marius's reforms.

CHAPTER 4

The Late Republic

For centuries, Romans were raised to believe that they waged only just wars, rather than conflicts inspired by greed. The confederacy of Italian states came about more as a civilizing drive than one of pure conquest for gain. Romans had little taste for enemy annihilation. But after the First and Second Punic Wars, the national character changed. Forays into foreign lands had reaped dividends and a new age dawned for the republic in which territorial acquisition became paramount.

At the end of the Punic Wars, Roman soldiers were posted in Spain, North Africa, Sicily, Sardinia, Corsica, Illyria, and Macedon, or Macedonia as Romans referred to it. This empire came together without too much evidence of imperialism. Rome, often acting defensively, had inadvertently gained massively extended territory.

Now the new possessions abroad obliged Rome to maintain friendly and protected routes to supply its legions in those lands. For Roman soldiers, the reward for a successful expedition was an enviable amount of booty, officially

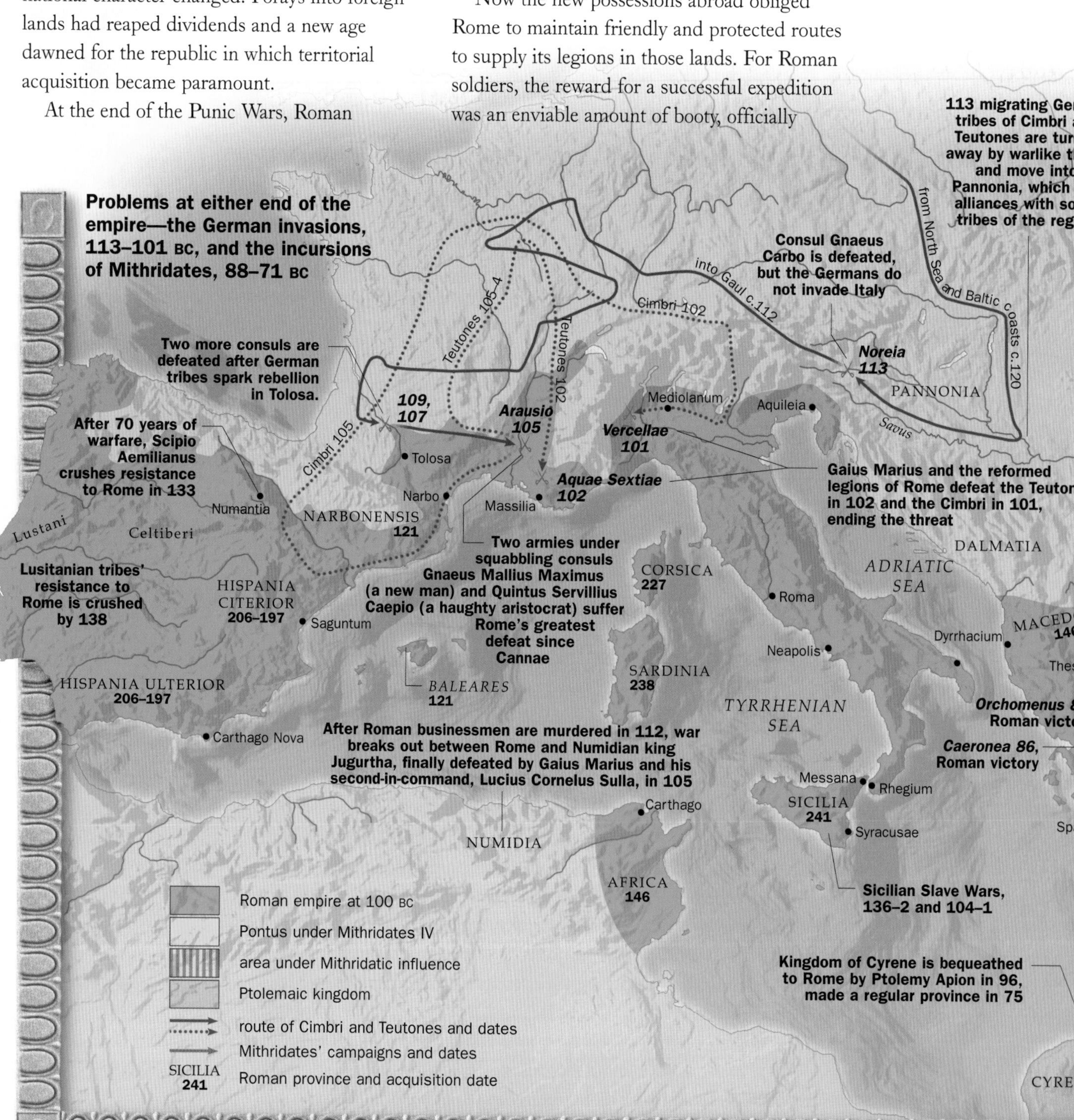

Problems at either end of the empire—the German invasions, 113–101 BC, and the incursions of Mithridates, 88–71 BC
Two more consuls are defeated after German tribes spark rebellion in Tolosa.
After 70 years of warfare, Scipio Aemilianus crushes resistance to Rome in 133
Lusitanian tribes' resistance to Rome is crushed by 138
Consul Gnaeus Carbo is defeated, but the Germans do not invade Italy
Gaius Marius and the reformed legions of Rome defeat the Teutone in 102 and the Cimbri in 101, ending the threat
Two armies under squabbling consuls Gnaeus Mallius Maximus (a new man) and Quintus Servillius Caepio (a haughty aristocrat) suffer Rome's greatest defeat since Cannae
After Roman businessmen are murdered in 112, war breaks out between Rome and Numidian king Jugurtha, finally defeated by Gaius Marius and his second-in-command, Lucius Cornelus Sulla, in 105
Sicilian Slave Wars, 136–2 and 104–1
Kingdom of Cyrene is bequeathed to Rome by Ptolemy Apion in 96, made a regular province in 75
Orchomenus 85 Roman victor
Caeronea 86, Roman victory
from North Sea and Baltic coasts c.120
into Gaul c.112
Cimbri 102
Cimbri 105
Teutones 105–4
Teutones 102
109, 107
Arausio 105
Vercellae 101
Aquae Sextiae 102
Noreia 113
PANNONIA
Savus
Mediolanum
Aquileia
Tolosa
Narbo
Massilia
Numantia
NARBONENSIS 121
Lustani
Celtiberi
HISPANIA CITERIOR 206–197
Saguntum
HISPANIA ULTERIOR 206–197
Carthago Nova
BALEARES 121
CORSICA 227
SARDINIA 238
Roma
Neapolis
TYRRHENIAN SEA
ADRIATIC SEA
DALMATIA
Dyrrhacium
MACEDO 146
Thess
Messana
Rhegium
SICILIA 241
Syracusae
Carthago
NUMIDIA
AFRICA 146
Spar
CYREN
Roman empire at 100 BC
Pontus under Mithridates IV
area under Mithridatic influence
Ptolemaic kingdom
route of Cimbri and Teutones and dates
Mithridates' campaigns and dates
SICILIA 241 Roman province and acquisition date

The Social War, 91–89 BC
Also known as the Marsic War or the War of the Allies, this conflict was sparked by Rome's consistent refusal to give her Italian allies the rights of citizenship. Since citizens paid no taxes, the full burden of raising finance to maintain Rome's growing number of legions fell primarily on the Italian allies, in addition to supplying most of the legionaries for the ranks. The attempts of Marcus Livius Drusus to champion their cause in 91 were vigorously resisted by the patricians and senate. When he was mysteriously murdered, revolt broke out in Asculum in Picenum and rapidly spread. The strength of resistance alarmed Rome, and in 90 BC, the consul Lucius Julius Caesar passed a law (lex Julia) granting citizenship to all loyal communities and any others that laid down their arms. The response was encouraging in central Italy, but it took rising star L. Cornelius Sulla to conclude the war in the south. The crisis was concluded just in time for Rome to reorganize and counter with the threat posed by Mithridates (see main map).
115
Mithridates (121–63 BC) seizes power and expands kingdom, aiming to "free" Greeks from Roman rule. Early successes in the First Mithridatic War are turned by Lucius Cornelius Sulla in 88, who wins victories in Greece and makes treaty in 85. Mithridates starts second war in 83, defeated in 82, only to return a third time, to be defeated again in 71. A fourth war is avoided by his death.
Italy during the Social War
Latin territory
allied territory
rebels' territory, 91 BC
allies who joined the rebels
Bruttii
tribal name
Pisae
Arnus
Picentes
Arretium
Sentinum
Etrusci
Cortona
Igvium
Perusia
Camerinum
Firmum Picenum
Clusium
Nuceria
Fulginum
Asculum
Spoletium
Interamina
Narnia
Pinna
Ostia Aterne
Reate
Amiternum
Paeligni
Marrucini
Teate
Tarquini
Nepet
Corfinum
Histonium
Caere
Tiberis
Tibur
Cluviae
Frentani
Roma
Praeneste
Terventum
Larinum
Anagnia
Aufidena
Samnites
Teanum Apulum
Velitrae
Cora
Signia
Arpinum
Aesernia
Sipontum
Venafrum
Bovianum
Luceria
Arpi
Casinum
Saepinum
Salapia
Tarracina
Allifae
Herdonia
Aequum Tuticum
Hirpini
Canusium
Formiae
Minturnae
Teanum
Cales
Suessa
Beneventum
Ausculum
Barium
Capua
Aquilonia
Suessula
Aeclanum
Venusia
Acerrae
Nola
Venusini
Cumae
Campani
Silvium
Neapolis
Pompeii
Herculaneum
Salernum
Potentia
Brundisium
Surrentum
Eburum
Tarentum
Paestum
Mesapii
Grumentum
Heraclea
Thurii
Bruttii
Rhegium
BOSPORUS
110 joins Pontus
COLCHIS
BLACK SEA
Chalcedon
74 Roman defeat
Sinope
Trapezus
74
74
Amasea
ARMENIA
Byzantium
BITHYNIA
PONTUS
73
Nicopolis 71, Mithridates defeated, flees to Armenia to regroup
GALATIA
88
ASIA
133
CAPPADOCIA
Pergamum
Edessa
Sardis
CILICIA
101
PARTHIAN EMPIRE
Ephesus
PISIDIA
Antiochia
LYCIA
SELEUCID EMPIRE
Rhodus
CYPRUS
MEDITERRANEAN SEA
HASMONEAN STATE
Alexandria

distributed by the consul, unofficially gathered *en route*, and the glory of a triumph, a lavish parade, and conspicuous public honor.

The more successful Rome became, the easier it was to beckon realms outside the empire into agreements that defended Roman interests. Ultimately, it regarded the whole Mediterranean basin as its backyard. But not everything went Rome's way. It is apparent that Rome won its war with Greece, but Greece won much of the peace. Greek culture came to permeate every area of Roman life. As the poet Horace put it, "Conquered Greece conquered in turn the uncultivated victor and introduced the arts in rustic Latium."

The Absorption of Greece

The events of the Second Punic War spilled over into a wider theater when Philip V of Macedon took advantage of Rome's perceived weakness after the defeat at Cannae. Eventually, Romans could not ignore the situation across the Adriatic—and it spelled the end for Greek independence.

Below: Spectacle in religious rites was a common factor of Roman life, but there is little to show that Romans enjoyed theater for its literary drama. But with the acquisition of Greek culture, Greek-style theaters began to appear in Italy and eventually all over the Roman empire, like this much restored one at Arausio (Orange), France.

When Carthage was defeated for a second time in 201 BC, the Greeks were generally pleased to see a time-honored enemy humbled. Rome had already won a degree of trust among the Italian Greek city-states and this was generally reflected in the Aegean mainland. The fact that Macedon supported the doomed Carthaginians gave Greeks further cause to rejoice; since Philip II and Alexander the Great's days, Macedon had been the oppressor of Aetolian and Achaean Greeks for more than 200 years.

For its part, Rome had no desire to make war with the Greeks. It already controlled a region along the eastern Adriatic coast, gained in small-scale campaigns (the First and Second Illyrian Wars of 229–8 and 221–19). These actions

aroused Philip's suspicions and resulted in his alliance with Carthage in 215. Rome responded in 211 by allying with the Aetolian Greeks, which had the advantage of containing Philip without their having to commit any large forces. This First Macedonian War left the Aetolians taking the brunt of the conflict, and in 206 they made peace with Philip.

With Carthage beaten, Rome turned to Greece in 200, and the Second Macedonian War began. Over two years, the struggle remained indecisive, although the Roman general Titus Quinctius Flaminius (*see picture page 57*) was successful on the diplomatic front, rallying the Greeks against Macedon with the enticing slogan "Greece for the Greeks." After Philip's forces were roundly beaten at Cynoscephalae in 197 BC, Flaminius pledged the withdrawal of all Roman troops from Greek territory, which was done by 194.

Their return six years later was to eject the Seleucid king Antiochus III, who had invaded. Having invaded Thrace in 196, Antiochus saw a request from Aetolians to rid them of Rome (they were disgruntled because Rome had refused to let them reoccupy some territories vacated by Philip) as a golden opportunity. The legions proved their worth when they routed the Seleucid force at Thermopylae, a site celebrated by Greeks for the heroic resistance shown by its *hoplites* during the Persian War of 480. The Romans then invaded Asia Minor under the command of Lucius Scipio (brother of Africanus, who accompanied the expedition), and defeated Antiochus in pitched battle at Magnesia in 190.

After a short campaign in Galatia in the following year, Rome withdrew from Asia Minor and again from Greece. Almost 20 years passed before intervention across the Adriatic in 171 became necessary. The cause was Macedon again, now in the hands of Philip's son Perseus, who had succeeded his father in 179. Perseus enjoyed early successes

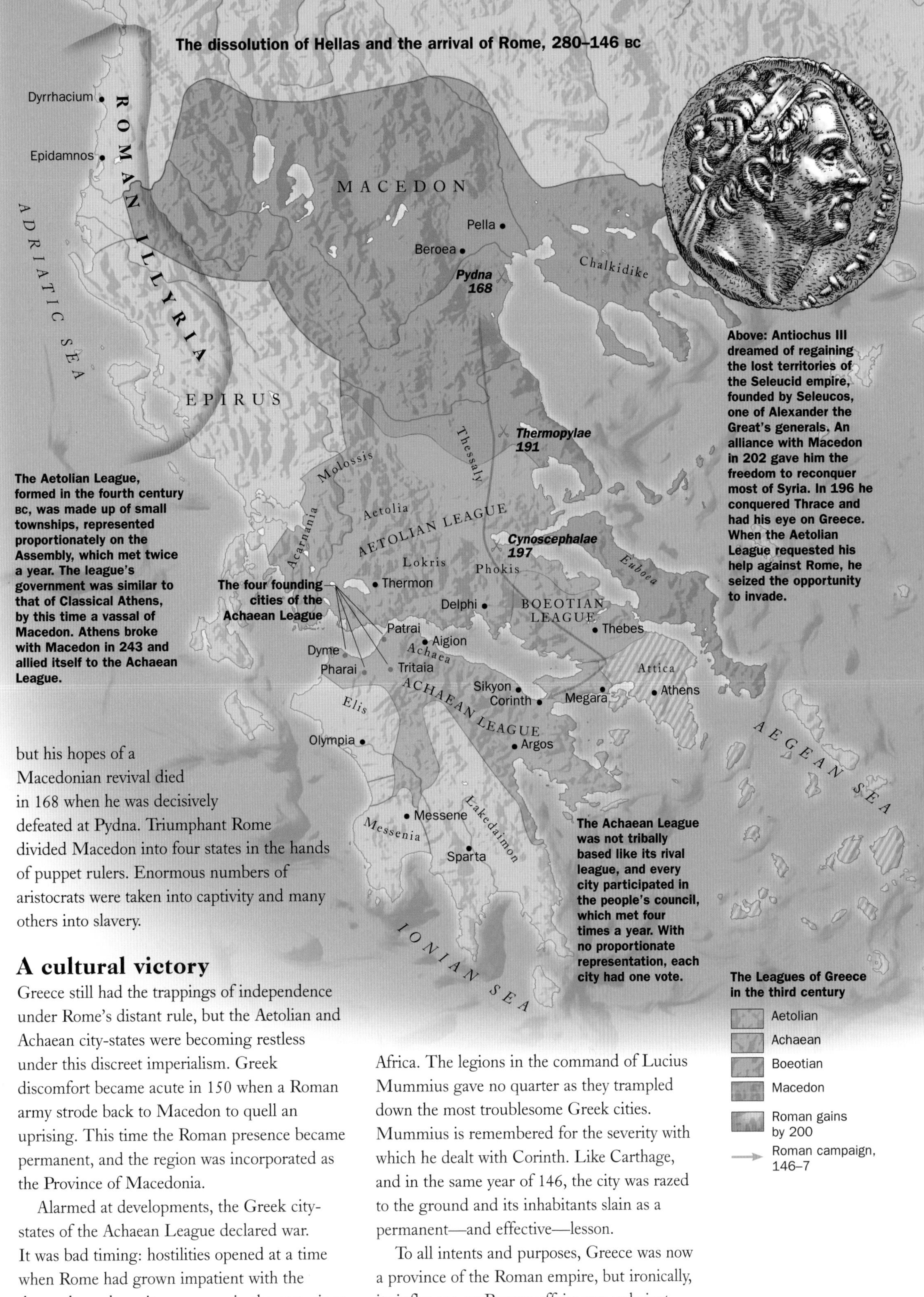
The dissolution of Hellas and the arrival of Rome, 280–146 BC
Dyrrhacium
Epidamnos
ROMAN ILLYRIA
ADRIATIC SEA
MACEDON
Pella
Beroea
Pydna 168
Chalkidike
EPIRUS
Thessaly
Thermopylae 191
Molossis
Acarnania
Aetolia
AETOLIAN LEAGUE
Cynoscephalae 197
Lokris
Phokis
Euboea
The four founding cities of the Achaean League
Thermon
Delphi
BOEOTIAN LEAGUE
Thebes
Patrai
Aigion
Achaea
Dyme
Pharai
Tritaia
Attica
Sikyon
Corinth
Megara
Athens
Elis
ACHAEAN LEAGUE
Olympia
Argos
AEGEAN SEA
Messene
Messenia
Lakedaimon
Sparta
IONIAN SEA
The Leagues of Greece in the third century
Aetolian
Achaean
Boeotian
Macedon
Roman gains by 200
Roman campaign, 146–7

Above: Antiochus III dreamed of regaining the lost territories of the Seleucid empire, founded by Seleucos, one of Alexander the Great's generals. An alliance with Macedon in 202 gave him the freedom to reconquer most of Syria. In 196 he conquered Thrace and had his eye on Greece. When the Aetolian League requested his help against Rome, he seized the opportunity to invade.

The Aetolian League, formed in the fourth century BC, was made up of small townships, represented proportionately on the Assembly, which met twice a year. The league's government was similar to that of Classical Athens, by this time a vassal of Macedon. Athens broke with Macedon in 243 and allied itself to the Achaean League.

The Achaean League was not tribally based like its rival league, and every city participated in the people's council, which met four times a year. With no proportionate representation, each city had one vote.

but his hopes of a Macedonian revival died in 168 when he was decisively defeated at Pydna. Triumphant Rome divided Macedon into four states in the hands of puppet rulers. Enormous numbers of aristocrats were taken into captivity and many others into slavery.

A cultural victory

Greece still had the trappings of independence under Rome's distant rule, but the Aetolian and Achaean city-states were becoming restless under this discreet imperialism. Greek discomfort became acute in 150 when a Roman army strode back to Macedon to quell an uprising. This time the Roman presence became permanent, and the region was incorporated as the Province of Macedonia.

Alarmed at developments, the Greek city-states of the Achaean League declared war. It was bad timing: hostilities opened at a time when Rome had grown impatient with the demands made on its resources in the east, since it was again fighting a war against Carthage in Africa. The legions in the command of Lucius Mummius gave no quarter as they trampled down the most troublesome Greek cities. Mummius is remembered for the severity with which he dealt with Corinth. Like Carthage, and in the same year of 146, the city was razed to the ground and its inhabitants slain as a permanent—and effective—lesson.

To all intents and purposes, Greece was now a province of the Roman empire, but ironically, its influence on Roman affairs was only just beginning.

HELLENISTIC INFLUENCE

The conquest of the Mediterranean brought about profound changes to Rome and Italy's social, political, and economic life, not least of which was a process of Hellenization that appeared to fly in the face of old Rome's homespun virtues.

Below: Remains of the Greek-inspired 3rd-century temple in the Largo Argentina complex, near Pompey's Theater.

Military necessity during the lengthy Second Punic War had prolonging the commands of successful generals beyond the statutory limit of one year. While a sensible innovation at the time, it set a dangerous political precedent by freeing ambitious men like Scipio

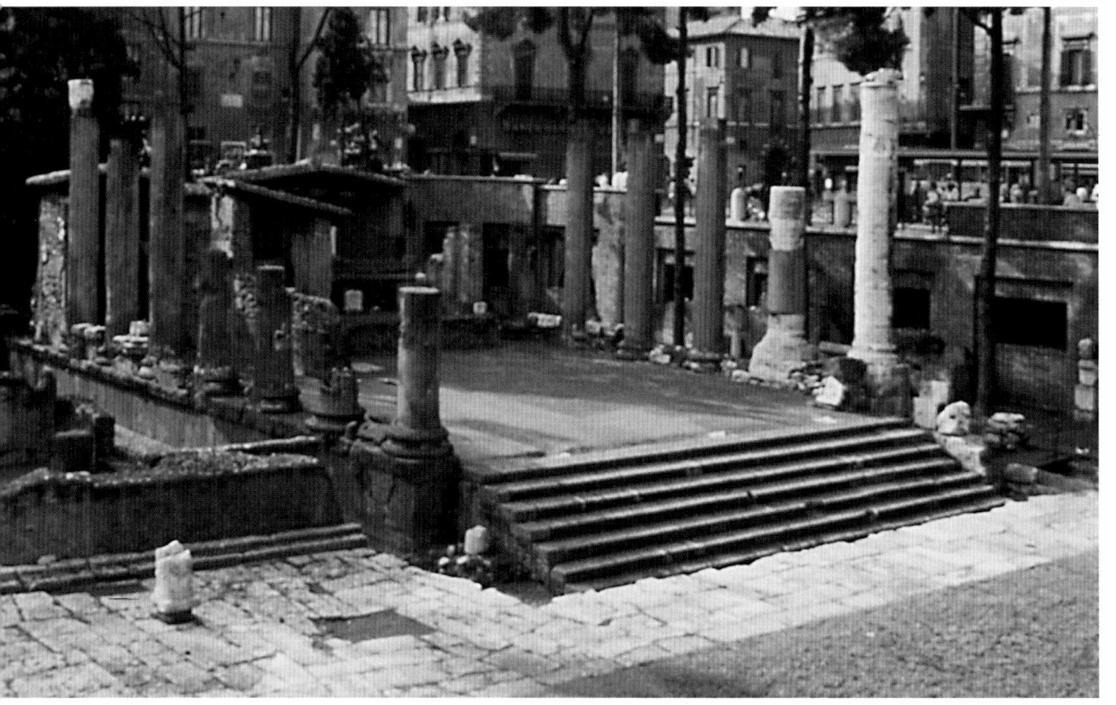

Facing: Commonly known as the temple of Fortuna Virilis, this late 1st-century BC building is more likely to be the temple of Portunus, the deity of the nearby harbor. It stands in the Forum Boarium.

Africanus from the constraints of annual elections and gave them the sense that they could do as they liked without consulting the senate. Magistrates enjoyed a large degree of independence, but there was an unwritten rule that it should always be consulted. Eventually, the concept was extended even to collegiate elections, and men like Marius would seek multiple re-elections as consuls—something that would have been unthinkable before.

These men, made wealthy through spoils of war, began to affect an ostentatious lifestyle characterized by their preference for the new Greek culture. Other nobles quickly followed suit, and the cult of Hellenism spread. Voices were raised against them, with the opposition to the trend being led by Cato the Censor (234–149 BC). Marcus Porcius Cato, also known as Cato the Elder, was strong on rhetoric and righteousness. He never spared a thought for human frailty as he expounded the old Italic ideals of frugal living and piety. It was inevitable that he should clash with the Hellenists.

Cato found the Greeks reprehensible, "a most wicked and retractable race" whom he suspected of trying to wipe out the Romans with poisonous Hellenism. Chief among his loathings was homosexuality, a long accepted part of Greek life. The Greeks were altogether too relaxed about life for the upright Cato.

However, he was not entirely opposed to Greek culture—and in fact spoke Greek—as long as it could be adapted to Roman needs. He also ordered the construction of Rome's first basilica, which was built entirely in the Greek style. Cato clearly approved of Greek writing, and was instrumental in adapting its style and construction to Latin needs. His real opposition was toward the corrupting influence of wealth, luxury, and the pursuit of power, which he associated with Hellenism.

Sticking to his views

His most abiding battle was with the pro-Greek Scipio. An ardent republican, Cato watched with horror as Scipio was hailed king by the troops

197 BC	195 BC	191 BC	190 BC	184 BC	168 BC	149 BC	147–46 BC
Romans defeat Philip of Macedon at Cynoscephalae, ending the Second Macedonian War	Hannibal flees Carthage after Rome demands he be surrendered	Rome defeats Greek Seleucids at Thermopylae, driving them out of Europe	The Seleucid empire is defeated in Asia Minor at the Battle of Magnesia	Conservative politician Cato becomes censor of Rome	Rome wins the Third Macedonian War at the Battle of Pydna	Carthage is drawn into Third Punic War by Rome's wily ally Massinissa	Roman empire defeats the Achaean League and destroys Corinth

serving him in Spain. Scipio swiftly introduced the title *imperator* for their use instead, which came to mean "successful general." The victory that won Scipio the cognomen Africanus added to his immense popularity and made him even more suspect in Cato's eyes, as did a claim to a special relationship with Jupiter. Cato detected the weakness of vanity in the overt Hellenist and was concerned it would endanger the republic. He undertook various machinations in an attempt to disgrace Scipio. The old warrior was finally worn down by Cato's persistence and retired from public life in 184, dying a year later.

Cato's second recurrent theme was a virulent hatred of Carthage. He was 32 when the Romans defeated Hannibal at the Battle of Zama. After, he watched in trepidation as Carthage enjoyed an economic revival. Ever-fearful that Carthage might rise phoenix-like from its military ashes, he maintained opposition to its very existence. He closed every speech he made to the senate with the words *Carthago est delenda*—Carthage must be destroyed. He lived to see war declared upon Carthage for a third time, but died before it and Corinth, the key Greek city, were destroyed by Roman forces.

In partnership with his patron, Lucius Valerius Flaccus, Cato held a number of public offices. His conduct was inevitably stern, his attitude unyielding. In 184 he was appointed censor, the man who would guard public morals against—in his view—a broad spectrum of external menaces. Unsurprisingly, he possessed little popular appeal. There were no fewer than 44 attempts to remove him from the senate.

A sympathetic trait was an assiduous devotion to his family. Cato was also a prolific writer, although few examples of his work have survived. He is the source of several popular maxims, however. Giving advice on public speaking he once said "*Rem tene, verba sequenter*," meaning: stick to the point, the words will follow.

Above: Marcus Porcius Cato represented the conservative values of old republican Rome in the face of the new Hellenization that he despised.

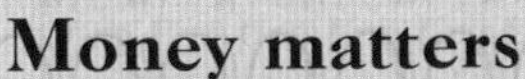

Money matters

Coinage first appeared in Asia Minor during the seventh century BC, but was put into wide circulation by the Greeks in the sixth century. The Romans came relatively late to the concept, in about the middle of the third century, adopting coinage from the Greek cities of Italy. They may have resisted it as a foreign invention. Certainly they began to use coins at the same time as they accepted other Greek cultural influences.

Early Roman coins did not carry portraits on the obverse (front). The first known to do so was struck in 197 BC in Macedonia to commemorate the victory of Titus Quinctius Flaminius at the Battle of Cynoscephalae, and it shows his profile. Portraits would not appear on coins of the mint of Rome until the time of Julius Caesar, some 150 years later.

Equating Roman monetary values with modern ones is not easy, since most modern currencies are no longer related to the gold standard. However, as a rough estimate, the gold *aureus*, the main gold coin of the early imperial period, is equivalent to about $75. The main silver coin of the late republic and early empire, the *denarius*, was worth about $3.

Greek gold coin with the earliest coin-portrait of a Roman, depicts general Flaminius.

146 BC	141 BC	123 BC	106 BC	102 BC	89 BC	87 BC	88–86 BC
Romans finally take Carthage, razing the city and adding it to the republic	Seleucids lose control of Mesopotamia and Persia to the Parthians	Southern Gaul is added to Rome's territories	Gaius Marius defeats King Jugurtha's Numidians (Algeria)	Marius defeats Germanic Cimbri and Teutons in Gaul	Rome quells an uprising of Italian states in the Social War	Gaius Marius is dictator of Rome	Lucius Cornelius Sulla wins the Roman civil war against Marius

NEW ROME

With mastery over the Mediterranean Sea and surrounding lands achieved, Rome was the epicenter of the known world. Now the city itself began to reflect due grandeur with ambitious building projects.

Carneades (c.214–129 BC) was a Greek philosopher, whose methodology was to propound equally convincing arguments for incompatible conclusions. While on a mission to Rome, he defended traditional views on justice one day, and the next day offered an equally eloquent attack on those same views. Unamused traditionalist Romans expelled Carneades from the city as a result, but were unable to stop the spread of stoicism.

After the Punic Wars, large numbers of peasants, many of whom saw their land destroyed in the conflict, descended on Rome. Slaves and freed men from Greece were close behind them, making Rome the most populous city in the world. Its population had probably risen to about 100,000 by 300 BC, and was nearing the million mark in the time of Caesar.

The influx meant there was abundant labor for building projects commensurate with a bustling metropolis. It needed aqueducts, roads, markets, temples, and other public buildings, and tenement blocks to house the workers. For the laborer, Greek-style bread replaced the staple of porridge and men chose to be clean-shaven rather than bearded.

With a steady stream of money generated by Rome's healthy overseas trade, financing these projects was not a problem. To give some idea of the scale of expense confronting the city, it cost an incredible 45 million denarii (about $135 million) to complete the high-level aqueduct Aqua Marcia in the 140s and 130s. This aqueduct brought pure water into Rome from the Anio valley, some 36 miles distant.

Until the third century BC the commonest building material was tufa, a soft volcanic ash. Later buildings were generally made of bricks and concrete derived from volcanic ash, lime, and tufa rubble. For aesthetic reasons, concrete façades were ultimately coated with thin layers of marble or travertine, a form of limestone—a process adopted from the Greeks.

Marble was more favored after the passing of the republic during the time of Augustus, although the round temple of Hercules in Rome's Forum Boarium (*see picture page 33*) was an exception. It remains the earliest surviving marble temple in Rome, probably the work of the Greek architect Hermodorus of Salamis, who is also credited with a further temple and a naval base between 146 and 102.

The first basilica, ordered by Cato, was constructed in Rome in 184. Basilicas were covered halls that provided a home to local law courts, public meetings, and markets. The concept of the basilica (even the word) was imported directly from Greece. Two more had been built by 170. At the same time, triumphal arches for generals became fashionable. Two appeared in 196 to mark victories in Spain and six years later Scipio Africanus added a third.

The power of wealth

A ripple action meant buildings of the style of Rome were built in provincial centers, like the Doric temple at Cora (Cori) and the Fortuna Primigenia at Praeneste. Meanwhile, Hellenization was continuing apace. Rome was quickly adorned with looted art treasures. Much arrived from the subdued Greek city-states, thus elevating Greek influence in Roman culture in general and architecture in particular. Doric, Corinthian, and Ionian pillars became the norm.

Intellectually, Greek ideas gained ground too. Although the Greek philosopher Carneades was expelled from Rome in 150 after questioning Roman imperialism, the city went on to embrace stoicism as expounded by Panaetius of Rhodes. The rich filled their houses with Greek slaves who carried out domestic duties but also became secretaries, clerks, and tutors, and so the march of Greek philosophy continued.

Private wealth increased. Among those best placed to gather riches were the consular generals who secured victories overseas and benefited from the booty that entailed. The amount of wealth encouraged bribery to flourish among those seeking political advancement. Polybius would have us believe otherwise, for he insisted that Romans believed "nothing is held more base than to be corrupted by gifts, or to covet an increase of wealth by means that are unjust." But he failed to appreciate that military commanders were exercising more power and influence than the senate and patriciate. More pragmatic than the nobility, generals were prepared to do whatever was necessary to achieve their ambitions.

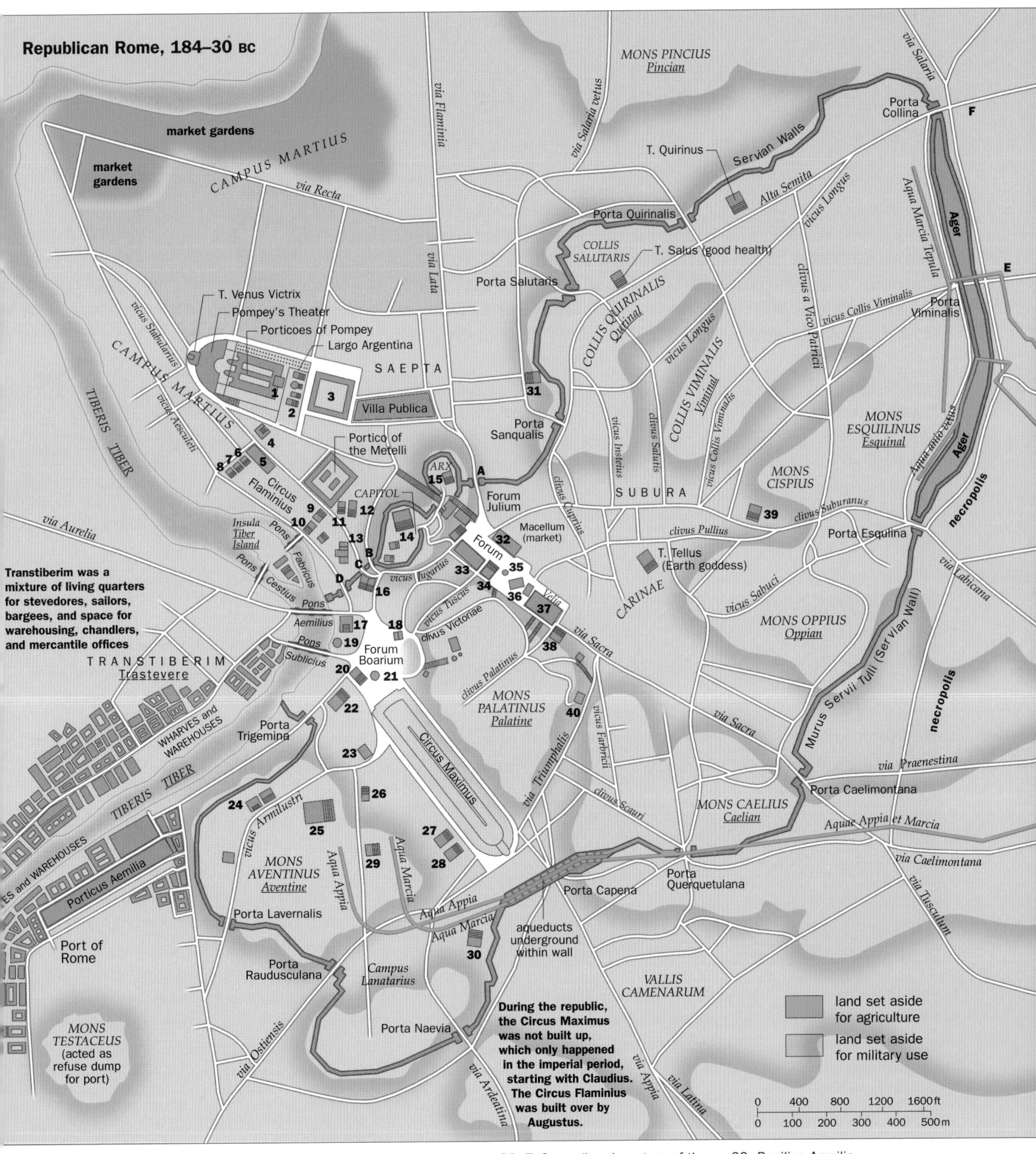
Republican Rome, 184–30 BC
market gardens
market gardens
CAMPUS MARTIUS
via Recta
via Flaminia
via Salaria vetus
MONS PINCIUS
Pincian
via Salaria
Porta Collina
F
T. Quirinus
Servian Walls
Alta Semita
vicus Longus
Aqua Marcia Tepula
Ager
Porta Quirinalis
COLLIS SALUTARIS
T. Salus (good health)
clivus a Vico Patricii
E
via Lata
Porta Salutaris
COLLIS QUIRINALIS
Quirinal
vicus Collis Viminalis
Porta Viminalis
T. Venus Victrix
Pompey's Theater
Porticoes of Pompey
Largo Argentina
vicus Stabularius
SAEPTA
vicus Longus
COLLIS VIMINALIS
Viminal
CAMPUS MARTIUS
vicus Aesculeti
TIBERIS TIBER
Villa Publica
31
Porta Sanqualis
vicus Insteius
clivus Salutis
vicus Collis Viminalis
MONS ESQUILINUS
Esquinal
Aqua anio vetus
Ager
Portico of the Metelli
ARX
A
Forum Julium
MONS CISPIUS
CAPITOL
Circus Flaminius
clivus Cuprius
SUBURA
39
clivus Suburanus
necropolis
via Aurelia
Insula Tiber Island
Pons Fabricius
Pons Cestius
Macellum (market)
Forum
clivus Pullius
Porta Esquilina
T. Tellus (Earth goddess)
Transtiberim was a mixture of living quarters for stevedores, sailors, bargees, and space for warehousing, chandlers, and mercantile offices
vicus Iugarius
Pons Aemilius
vicus Tuscus
clivus Victoriae
Velia
CARINAE
vicus Sabuci
via Labicana
Pons Sublicius
Forum Boarium
via Sacra
MONS OPPIUS
Oppian
Murus Servii Tulli (Servian Wall)
TRANSTIBERIM
Trastevere
clivus Palatinus
MONS PALATINUS
Palatine
vicus Fabricii
via Sacra
necropolis
WHARVES and WAREHOUSES
Porta Trigemina
Circus Maximus
via Triumphalis
via Praenestina
TIBERIS TIBER
vicus Armilustri
clivus Scauri
MONS CAELIUS
Caelian
Porta Caelimontana
Aquae Appia et Marcia
ES and WAREHOUSES
Porticus Aemilia
MONS AVENTINUS
Aventine
Aqua Appia
Aqua Marcia
via Caelimontana
Porta Querquetulana
Porta Capena
Aqua Appia
Aqua Marcia
via Tusculum
Porta Lavernalis
aqueducts underground within wall
Port of Rome
Porta Raudusculana
Campus Lanatarius
VALLIS CAMENARUM
MONS TESTACEUS (acted as refuse dump for port)
Porta Naevia
During the republic, the Circus Maximus was not built up, which only happened in the imperial period, starting with Claudius. The Circus Flaminius was built over by Augustus.
via Ostiensis
via Ardeatina
via Appia
via Latina
land set aside for agriculture
land set aside for military use
0 400 800 1200 1600 ft
0 100 200 300 400 500 m

A Porta Fontinalis
B Porta Triumphalis
C Porta Carmentalis
D Porta Flumentana
E via Tiburtina
F via Nomentana

1 Pompey's meeting house, site of Caesar's murder
2 four temples, part of Pompey's complex
3 possible site of Pompey's villa
4 T. Herculis Musarum
5 Porticus Minucia
6 T. Vulcan
7 T. Hercules Custos
8 T. Mars Invictus
9 T. Juno Regina
10 T. Jupiter Stator
11 T. Apollo Sosianus (healing)
12 T. Bellona (foreign war)
13 temples to Pietas, Janus, Spes (hope), Juno Sospita
14 T. Jupiter Optimus Maximus
15 T. Juno Moneta
16 T. Fortuna & T. Mater Matuta
17 T. Portunus (god of the harbor)
18 T. Janus
19 T. Hercules Olivarius (olives)
20 Ara Maxima Herculis (great altar of Hercules)
21 T. Hercules Invictus
22 T. Ceres (headquarters of the Plebeian Aediles)
23 T. Flora (vegetation)
24 two temples for the cult of Free Citizens
25 T. Diana (looks after slaves)
26 T. Luna (moon)
27 T. Mercury (headquarters of Guild of Merchants)
28 T. Venus Obaequens (protects prostitutes & adulterers)
29 T. Juventas (coming of age for boys)
30 T. Bona Dea (protects women)
31 T. Semo Sancus Dius Fidius (oaths and treaties)
32 Basilica Aemilia
33 Basilica Julia
34 T. Castor & Pollux
35 T. Vesta
36 Domus Publicus (home of the Vestal Virgins & Pontifex Maximus)
37 Porticus Margaritaria (jewelers, perfumiers, and luxury shops)
38 the hut of Romulus
39 T. Juno Lucina (registry of Roman citizen births)
40 Curiae Veteres (ancient meeting halls)

Agrarian Reform and the Gracchi

When two brothers identified troublesome weaknesses in the administration of the Roman Republic, they drew up legal measures to remedy the flaws. Instead of shoring up the power of the republic, they undermined its foundations and sparked a century of civil strife.

Right: Gaius and Tiberius Gracchus attempted reforms of Roman government that inevitably led to a destabilizing anarchy.

The Gracchis came from a distinguished family, their father being a former censor and consul and their mother the daughter of Scipio Africanus. Neither Tiberius (163–133 BC) nor Gaius (153–121) were at first sight candidates for political martyrdom. They were, however, keenly aware of shortcomings in existing Roman policy, most particularly of the pressing need for fair deals in land distribution.

Above: The land distributed to Roman colonists was marked out in rectangles made up from 100 2-*iguera* units called *centuriae* (123 acres). Evidence of centuriation can be seen all over Italy. As this photograph taken near Siena, Tuscany shows, modern farmers still tend to follow the ancient centuriation lines.

A series of wars had left the Roman army starved of men. By tradition the best recruitment grounds were among the *adsidui* (*see panel*) but these had diminished in number while the city of Rome was bursting at the seams. Most of those working on the land were slaves in the service of large land-owners. The folly of mass slave ownership was highlighted in 136 BC when an estimated 60,000 slaves in Sicily rose up against their masters and achieved considerable success for two years before being ruthlessly suppressed.

Tiberius, an elected tribune, came up with proposals to increase the number of small freeholders by distributing parcels of *ager publicus* (public land) seized by Rome from disloyal allies after the Second Punic War. In addition he made provision to reclaim land in the name of the state from wealthy land-owners who exceeded ancient limits, but who were largely ignoring the statutes. Non-Roman citizens were not part of the equation.

Popular support was assured, but his proposals aroused anger among the many wealthy land-owners. When an attempt was made to veto the bill, Tiberius had the offending tribute voted out of office. Anger turned to alarm when Tiberius cut out senate debate on the issue. The bill was passed into law, and a land commission of three men set up (himself, younger brother Gaius, and father-in-law Claudius Appius) to administer the parceling of plots. Undeterred by mounting hostility, Tiberius announced his intention to seek a second term as tribune, and hinted at even further reform. It was too much. On the day of the election he and hundreds of supporters were killed in a riot provoked by angry senators.

It is difficult to determine definitive motives for Tiberius Gracchus. At a glance he appears a just and wise social reformer, possibly acting in accordance with a Greek political theory of the day. Others believe him to be an ambitious self-seeker, yearning to be the tyrant of Rome and manipulating the mob to achieve this aim.

The senate's problems were doubled. Tiberius's law still stood, angering the aristocrats, and extreme violence—even bloodshed—had been introduced into the Roman political process for the first time, a state of affairs t would continue for decade

New corn laws

Gaius Gracchus took the of social reformer. A pow orator and persuasive pol he introduced an innovat that compelled the state corn surpluses and sell t people at below market It meant the populace v protected from boom-c market forces in basic foodstuffs, just as Gre been for years.

Conservatives wer unimpressed and we troubled by his move conscription banned age of 17, Carthage colony, and to exten Concerned senator to believe rumors t was plotting a cou pitched battle of t the death of Gaiu rest were hounde

The Gracchi v their efforts to re operating in hith up against those sentiment, the s which proved t Gaius was a tri of Rome, but i *populares* (Gra senatorial inco disasters between 113 and 105 at the hands of migrating German tribes (*see following spread*) and the failure to successfully prosecute the war against Jugurtha of Numidia, it left the way open for the *populares* to elect their champion Gaius Marius to the consulship in 108.

This was almost unthinkable—Marius was a "new man" from Arpinum, the antithesis of everything the patriciate thought it stood for. Marius was also appointed by plebiscite to take

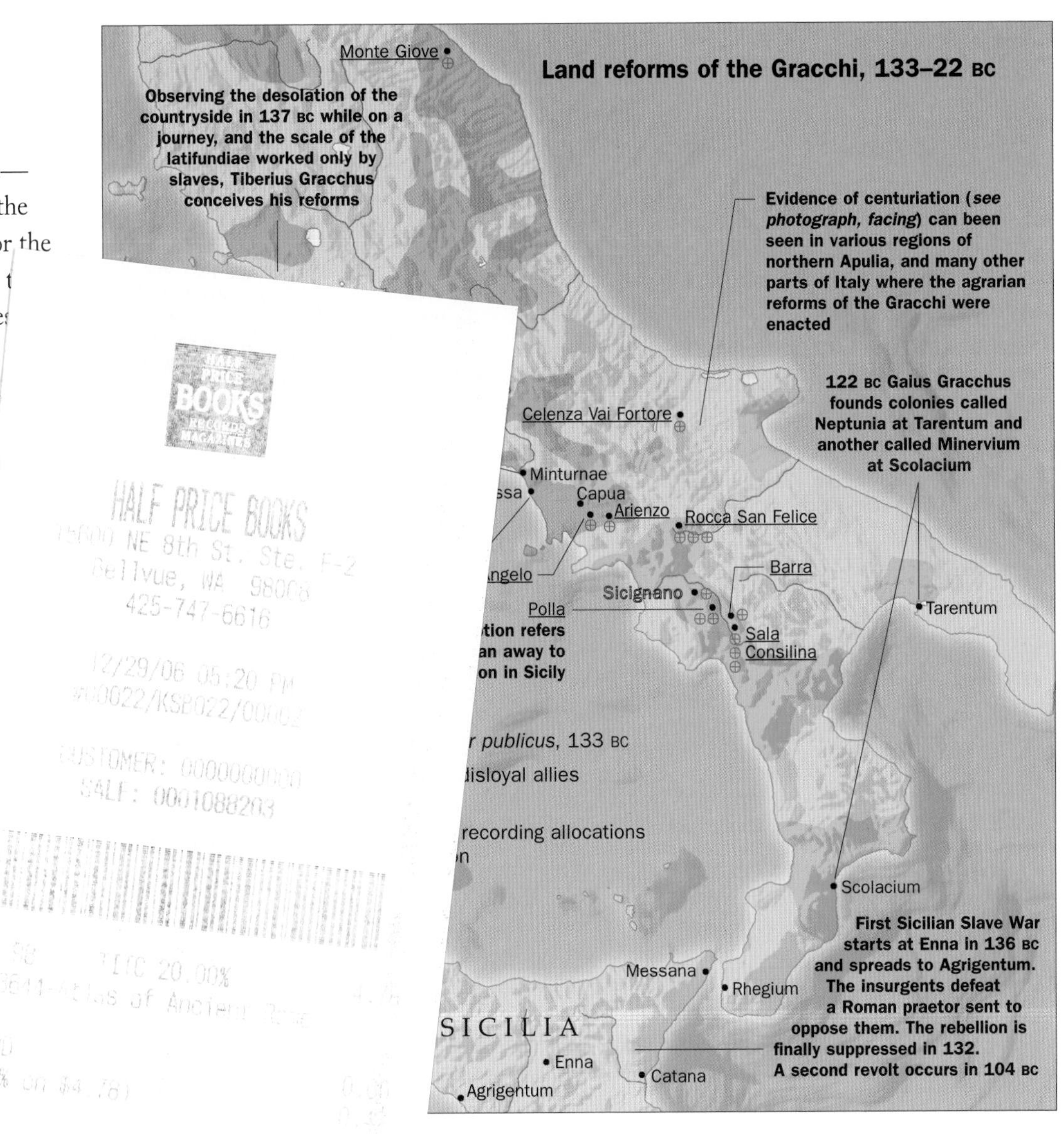

Land reforms of the Gracchi, 133–22 BC
Monte Giove
Observing the desolation of the countryside in 137 BC while on a journey, and the scale of the latifundiae worked only by slaves, Tiberius Gracchus conceives his reforms
Evidence of centuriation (see photograph, facing) can been seen in various regions of northern Apulia, and many other parts of Italy where the agrarian reforms of the Gracchi were enacted
122 BC Gaius Gracchus founds colonies called Neptunia at Tarentum and another called Minervium at Scolacium
Celenza Vai Fortore
Minturnae
Capua
Arienzo
Rocca San Felice
Barra
Sicignano
Polla
Sala
Consilina
Tarentum
Scolacium
r publicus, 133 BC
isloyal allies
recording allocations
First Sicilian Slave War starts at Enna in 136 BC and spreads to Agrigentum. The insurgents defeat a Roman praetor sent to oppose them. The rebellion is finally suppressed in 132. A second revolt occurs in 104 BC
Messana
Rhegium
SICILIA
Enna
Catana
Agrigentum

war against Jugurtha in place of nominee. Now he had the task of ns from among the depleted *adsidui*, ere not enough men to fill the ranks.

ne of the adsidui

an army was largely comprised of *adsidui*, men who owned the n amount of property to be classed as land-owners. The poor, e *infra classem* (beneath the class), were excluded from the army, e referred to as *proletarii*, since they only produced offspring, Dispossessed of his land, an *adsidui* became a proletarian. nibal's invasion had damaged the agricultural land that the relied on. Many farms had lost generations of their men. Unable debts, new factions of wealthy Romans seized the land and accumulated large estates (*latifundia*), which they worked with slaves made plentiful by the many conquests of the Punic and Macedonian wars, or dispossessed *adsidui*—who were little better off than the slaves. By 107, this situation had become so serious, despite attempts by the Gracchi to reverse it, that there were not enough land-owning *adsidui* from which to recruit the legions Gaius Marius needed to fight Jugurtha and the German invaders. This is why he turned to the *proletarii* (*see following page*).

Reform of the Legions

The republican army relied on its land-owning citizens for defense in times of war. But as the Roman state expanded, a need arose for a new style of army based around a core of professional soldiers.

Right: By making sweeping changes to the way Roman legions were raised, Gaius Marius helped create the modern army that would put its general's welfare before Rome's.

The structure of the early and middle republican army (*see pages 50–1*) had made it an effective force, but it suffered from two major drawbacks in the new era of growing empire. One was the tradition that required legionaries to be *adsidui*, and therefore men who wanted to return to their civic duties at the conclusion of a conflict, leading to the dissolution of their legion.

German invasions

Migrating Germanic tribes created a crisis situation for Rome when one tribe, the Cimbri, defeated the consul Gnaius Papirius Carbo in battle at Noreia, northern Illyria, in 113 BC. The Germans, however, left Italy alone, marching west into Gaul. They returned to again defeat Roman armies in 109, 107, and 105, the last at Arausio, where two Roman armies were massacred. Before Marius could turn his attention to the Germans, he first had to settle accounts with Jugurtha in Africa, which he did in 105. The Germans gave Marius a convenient lull, while he reformed the army, which met and defeated the Teutones at Aquae Sextiae in 102, and the Cimbri at Vercellae in 101.

The second was the division of the legions into rigid lines of various types of infantrymen. This weakness showed up particularly in 113–105 BC, when Rome was threatened by the Germanic Cimbri, Tutones, and Ambrones tribes, who danced around the inflexible legions, resulting in defeats in four major battles (*see panel*).

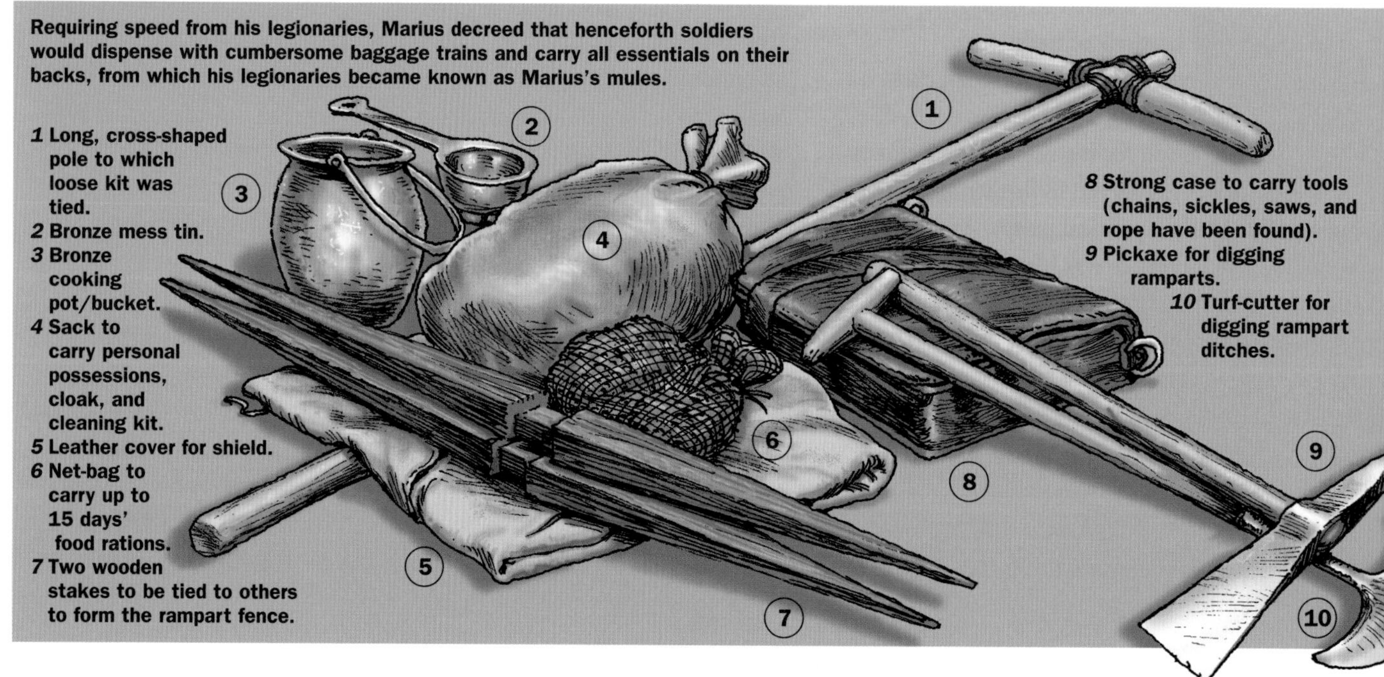
1
2
3
4
5
6
7
8
9
10

Requiring speed from his legionaries, Marius decreed that henceforth soldiers would dispense with cumbersome baggage trains and carry all essentials on their backs, from which his legionaries became known as Marius's mules.

1 Long, cross-shaped pole to which loose kit was tied.
2 Bronze mess tin.
3 Bronze cooking pot/bucket.
4 Sack to carry personal possessions, cloak, and cleaning kit.
5 Leather cover for shield.
6 Net-bag to carry up to 15 days' food rations.
7 Two wooden stakes to be tied to others to form the rampart fence.
8 Strong case to carry tools (chains, sickles, saws, and rope have been found).
9 Pickaxe for digging ramparts.
10 Turf-cutter for digging rampart ditches.

The necessary reforms of the army are credited to Gaius Marius, but there is no direct evidence to support this. It seems that many tactical changes were already ocurring during the first two Punic Wars. Marius, however, certainly codified the tactical reforms and made the major change—scrapping the property-owning requirement for military service.

By the time of Marius, *velites* had ceased as an independent category in favor of increased use of allied troops, such as slingers and bowmen from Thracian tribes. The rigid division of the lines by age and experience had also stopped and troops were distributed randomly through the legion. The concept of the maniple itself had also fallen into disuse. Instead, the fixed three lines were given up in favor of a freer organization based on a new unit, the cohort.

Whereas the maniples of each of the old fixed battle lines—*hastati*, *principes*, *triarii*—were under separate commands, the legion contained ten cohorts, each with its own *hastati*, *principes*, and *triarii*. This arrangement allowed far greater flexibility in maneuvering separate elements. For instance, if the general wanted some troops to turn 90 degrees, advance laterally, and then fall on the enemy's flank, he had a unit of sufficient strength at the end of his battle line that contained all three maniples. This arrangement proved to be so useful that the joining of maniples into cohorts, each of about 600 men, was made permanent.

Raising the eagles

The legions continued to have six military tribunes as officers, but their prestige had declined. Usually young aristocrats furthering political careers, their lack of experience was often an embarassment. Real command lay with the centurions and with the older, more experienced lagates. Originally envoys of the senate, lagates came increasingly to be used as subordinate commanders by generals, who asked the senate to appoint their choices. Legates often led small independent commands or commanded parts of the battle line during combat.

When he was elected consul in 108 BC, Marius faced a campaign in Numidia against King Jugurtha, who had been fighting Rome since 112. Because there had been a severe decline in land-owning citizens (*see page 60*), Marius abandoned the traditional practice of raising troops from among them, and simply enlisted volunteers from the proletariat. It followed that these poorer soldiers had to receive increased pay to afford their arms and armor. This in turn resulted in a dramatic increase in cheaply mass-produced equipment.

Perhaps most lastingly, Marius's decision to enroll paid professional soldiers was that they expected to be kept in service to the end of their useful lives, and then settled on a smallholding for their old age. In effect, the legion had become a permanent organization into which new recruits could be added.

To mark this change, Marius gave each legion a standard to represent it in the form of an eagle. The legion's eagle became a religious object, kept in a shrine and had a man assigned to carry it into battle. Loss of the eagle was now considered a major disgrace.

Above: A coin of King Jugurtha. On the death of Micipsa, son of Rome's ally Massinissa, the kingdom was split between Micipsa's two sons, Hiempsal and Adherbal, and his nephew Jugurtha. After murdering Hiempsal, Jugurtha declared war on Adherbal. Rome may have been left alone except that Italian merchants living in Adherbal's capital of Cirta were killed when Jugurtha sacked the city. War was declared in 112. Against unprepared Roman troops, Jugurtha won several victories, but was brought to heel by Marius in 105 BC when he became the first to face the new-style legions of Rome.

Left: A centurion exhorts his men in battle. At this period he wore the same clothes and armor as the common legionary, except for more elaborate helmet plumes and protective greaves.

CHAPTER 5

FALL OF THE REPUBLIC

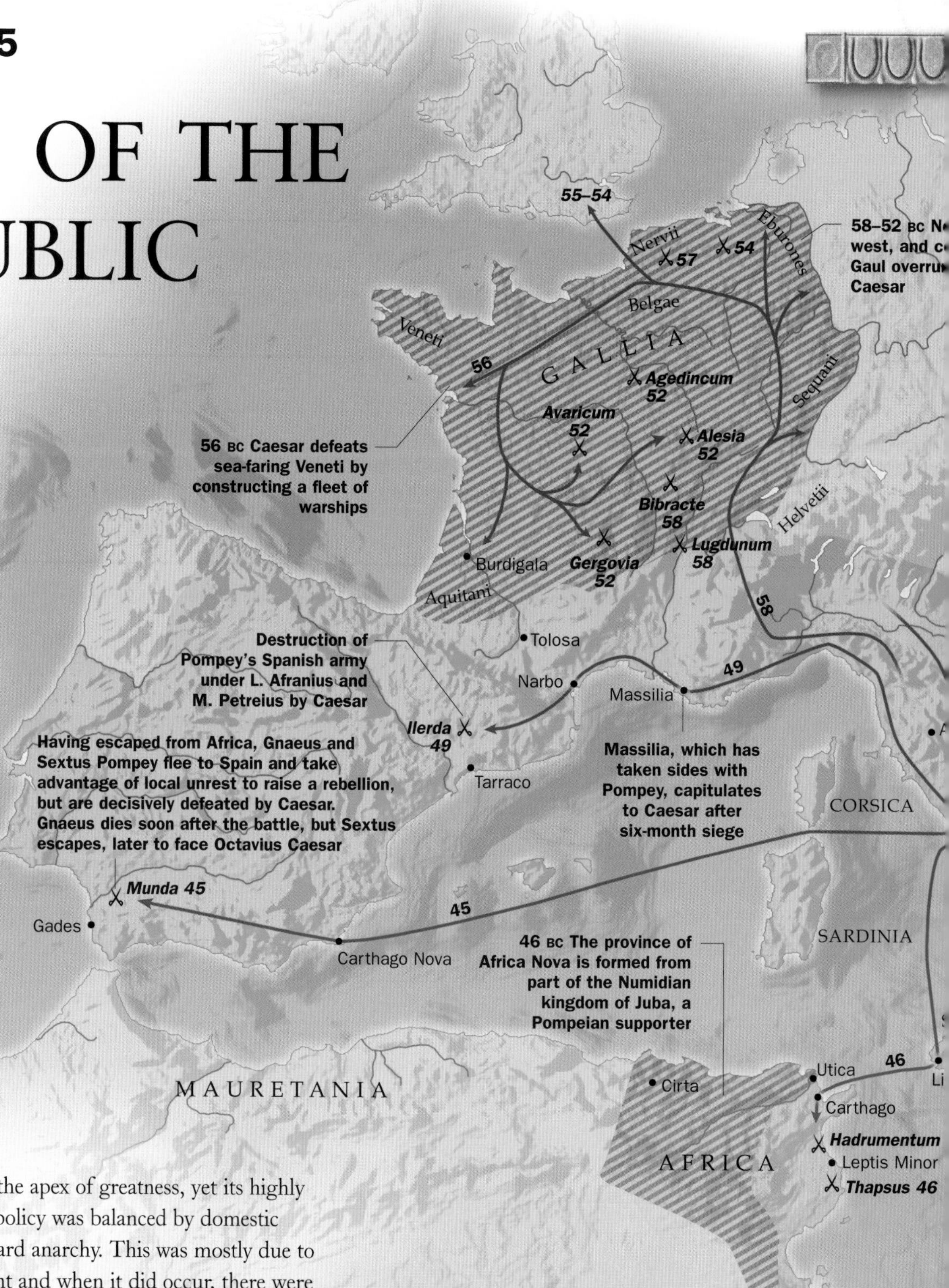

55–54
58–52 BC N
west, and c
Gaul overru
Caesar
Nervii
57
54
Eburones
Belgae
Veneti
GALLIA
56
Agedincum
52
Avaricum
52
Alesia
52
Sequani
56 BC Caesar defeats sea-faring Veneti by constructing a fleet of warships
Bibracte
58
Helvetii
Lugdunum
58
Burdigala
Gergovia
52
Aquitani
58
Destruction of Pompey's Spanish army under L. Afranius and M. Petreius by Caesar
Tolosa
Narbo
Massilia
49
Ilerda
49
Having escaped from Africa, Gnaeus and Sextus Pompey flee to Spain and take advantage of local unrest to raise a rebellion, but are decisively defeated by Caesar. Gnaeus dies soon after the battle, but Sextus escapes, later to face Octavius Caesar
Tarraco
Massilia, which has taken sides with Pompey, capitulates to Caesar after six-month siege
CORSICA
Munda 45
45
Gades
Carthago Nova
46 BC The province of Africa Nova is formed from part of the Numidian kingdom of Juba, a Pompeian supporter
SARDINIA
MAURETANIA
Cirta
Utica
46
Carthago
Hadrumentum
Leptis Minor
Thapsus 46
AFRICA
Leptis Mag

Rome was poised at the apex of greatness, yet its highly successful foreign policy was balanced by domestic disorder that veered toward anarchy. This was mostly due to a lack of firm government and when it did occur, there were always strings attached. For some, the reason for Rome's decline into chaos stemmed from the victory over Carthage. It was as though without an eminent rival, the republic suffered from a lack of self-discipline. Greed was permitted to gain the upper hand. Bad management had led to insurrection on the Italian peninsula as erstwhile allies reared up against Rome. The Social War of 91–89 BC was quickly suppressed but was occasioned because of Roman high-handedness in the first place.

The mob became a feature of Roman street life. Cunning rulers often rallied the loud, leaderless rabble to serve their own ends. But the loyalties of the mob blew in the wind and was likely to switch chariots mid-race.

Another problem can be seen in the growing strength of the army and its generals. One of these was Julius Caesar, whose name is synonymous with the highs and lows of Rome at the time. Eventually it was Caesar and his assassins that determined the future of Rome, discarding the Roman Republic in favor of totalitarianism. Perhaps Rome had simply become too big for an ostensibly democratic government to rule.

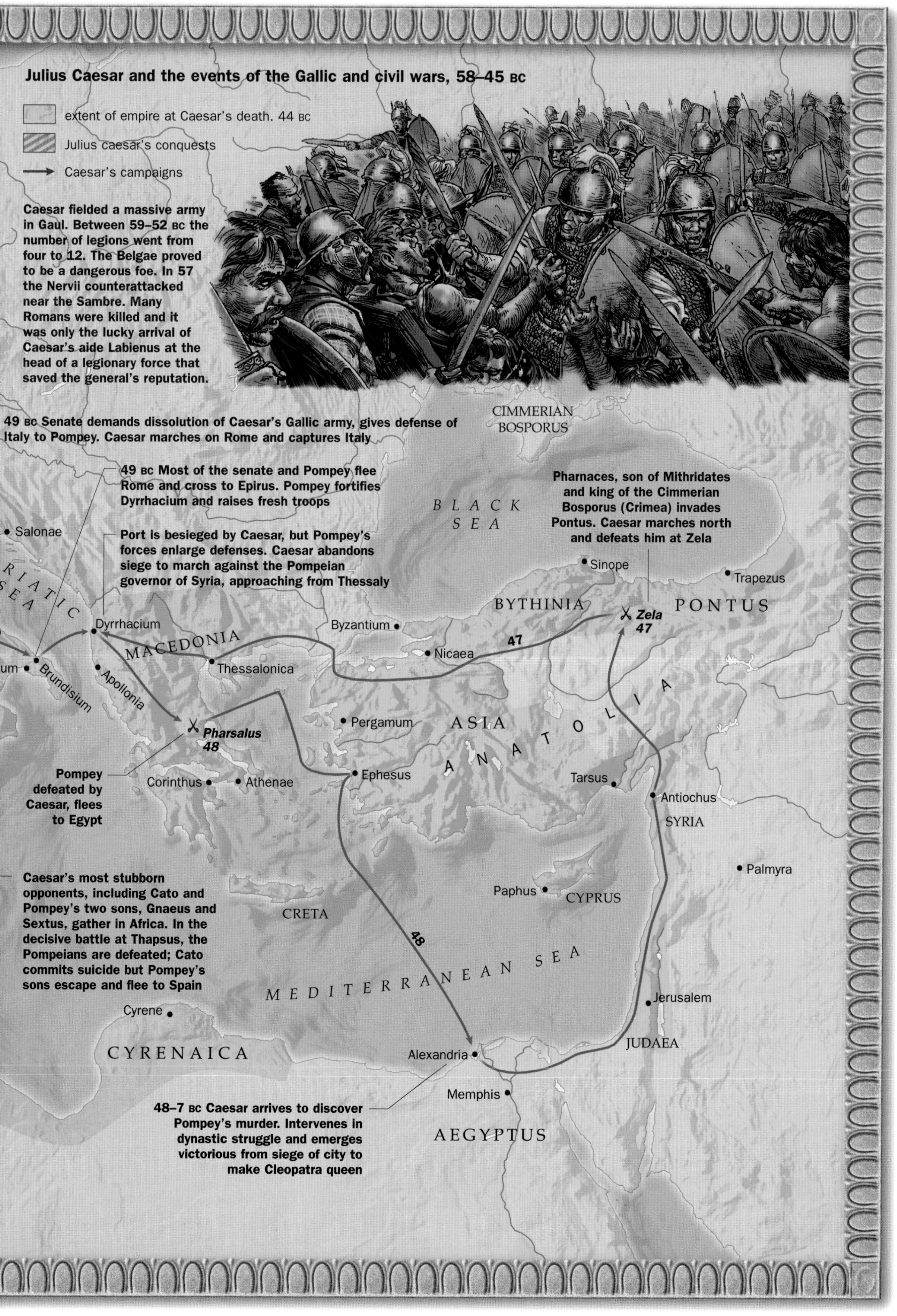
Julius Caesar and the events of the Gallic and civil wars, 58–45 BC
extent of empire at Caesar's death. 44 BC
Julius caesar's conquests
Caesar's campaigns
Caesar fielded a massive army in Gaul. Between 59–52 BC the number of legions went from four to 12. The Belgae proved to be a dangerous foe. In 57 the Nervii counterattacked near the Sambre. Many Romans were killed and it was only the lucky arrival of Caesar's aide Labienus at the head of a legionary force that saved the general's reputation.
49 BC Senate demands dissolution of Caesar's Gallic army, gives defense of Italy to Pompey. Caesar marches on Rome and captures Italy
49 BC Most of the senate and Pompey flee Rome and cross to Epirus. Pompey fortifies Dyrrhacium and raises fresh troops
Port is besieged by Caesar, but Pompey's forces enlarge defenses. Caesar abandons siege to march against the Pompeian governor of Syria, approaching from Thessaly
Pharnaces, son of Mithridates and king of the Cimmerian Bosporus (Crimea) invades Pontus. Caesar marches north and defeats him at Zela
CIMMERIAN BOSPORUS
BLACK SEA
Salonae
RIATIC SEA
Dyrrhacium
MACEDONIA
Thessalonica
Brundisium
Apollonia
Byzantium
Nicaea
47
BYTHINIA
Sinope
Trapezus
PONTUS
Zela 47
Pharsalus 48
Pergamum
ASIA
ANATOLIA
Ephesus
Corinthus
Athenae
Tarsus
Antiochus
SYRIA
Palmyra
Pompey defeated by Caesar, flees to Egypt
Caesar's most stubborn opponents, including Cato and Pompey's two sons, Gnaeus and Sextus, gather in Africa. In the decisive battle at Thapsus, the Pompeians are defeated; Cato commits suicide but Pompey's sons escape and flee to Spain
Paphus
CYPRUS
CRETA
48
MEDITERRANEAN SEA
Jerusalem
Cyrene
CYRENAICA
Alexandria
JUDAEA
Memphis
48–7 BC Caesar arrives to discover Pompey's murder. Intervenes in dynastic struggle and emerges victorious from siege of city to make Cleopatra queen
AEGYPTUS

MARIUS AND SULLA, DICTATOR

As factions and eminent families vied for power, deepening rifts in Rome undermined the republic. Weak leadership promoted street violence—the state's future hung in the balance. Strong men were needed.

Right: Lucius Cornelius Sulla (c.138–78 BC) adopted the cognomen Felix (fortunate), and in this he eventually was. His enemies were less so after he was made dictator in 82 BC—their properties were confiscated and their lives forfeit in the worst reign of terror Rome had witnessed. Notwithstanding his bloodthirsty actions, Sulla's reforms led to the restoration of constitutional government.

The precedent set during the Second Punic War of prolonging consular commands beyond the statutory limit of one year (*see page 56*) was eagerly seized upon by ambitious men. First of these was the "new man" Gaius Marius. Elected consul on a wave of popular support in 108 BC, he was elected again in 104 and then every year—first warring against Jugurtha, and then against the invading Germans—until his sixth consulship in 100. This was contrary to all law and precedent.

However, Marius, having achieved his aims of passing laws that settled his veterans on parcels of the *ager publicus* (thus making his proletariat army property-owning citizens), retired in 99 BC. His return to public life as a legate during the Social War brought him back in contact with his erstwhile lieutenant, Lucius Cornelius Sulla (138–78 BC). If Marius—a jumped-up man from the country—had been ambitious, the aristocratic but impoverished Sulla was about to redefine the word.

Sulla's record during the Social War elevated his stature with the Roman nobility, and he was elected consul in 88 to deal with Mithridates, who by this year had overrun all the Aegean and Greece. Marius, who felt he should have been elected, was furious and the distrust between the two that had developed after a squabble in Africa over Sulla's handling of a campaign increased. Marius used the tribune Publius Sulpicius to enact a law giving him command of the legions, which was passed amid much mob violence. Sulla's strength lay in the loyalty of the soldiers who served alongside him. He promptly left for Nola, where thay were still encamped after the Social War, and persuaded them to march with him on Rome.

Taken by surprise, Marius fled to Africa. Sulpicius was killed, and his law canceled amid a reign of terror. Sulla then left for the east, where he was unable to secure a lasting victory against Mithridates. However, he did rampage through Greece and was merciless in the face of insurrection, setting a trend for subsequent rulers of the republic.

This was a poor century for Greece. It became a battlefield, its past glories reduced to rubble. Centuries later, Greek historian Sir William Tarn wrote, "Whole districts were half depopulated; Thebes became a village, Megalopolis a desert, Megara, Aegina, Piraeus heaps of stones; Aetolia, like Epirus, was ruined forever."

While Sulla was thus occupied, Marius returned to Italy, raised fresh troops, and also marched on Rome. There was another reign of terror, as Sulla's supporters were massacred, before Marius was elected to his seventh consulship. However, he died a few days later in 86 BC. Despite his death, the Marian powerbase remained effective under the consulship of his supporter Lucius Cornelius Cinna. When Cinna was killed in a mutiny in 84, the majority of senators still avoided supporting Sulla.

Creating a vacuum

So when Sulla returned to Rome in 83, he was not assured of a warm welcome. He sought friends among the young opportunists of the aristocracy, including Marcus Crassus and the young Pompey, who had raised three legions on his own initiative to support Sulla. There now followed what was effectively a civil war, but the poorly organized resistance of the Marian faction gave Sulla victory by 82. Further resistance in Sicily and Africa was ruthlessly put down by Pompey, who was awarded a triumph by Sulla and given the title "Magnus"—Pompey the Great. He allied himself further by marrying Sulla's stepdaughter.

In 81 BC, Sulla declared himself dictator and embarked on a purge of his opponents, who were hunted down and put to death without trial, their property confiscated and given to Sulla's supporters. Many became instantly wealthy (most notably Marcus Crassus), including Sulla himself. He now ruled Rome without limitation to the term of his office.

The executions and confiscations—thousands died, including senators and men of the equestrian class—also benefitted his legionaries to whom he was obligated to find land. There were reforms of government, too. He empowered the senate above all other *comitia*, significantly enlarging its membership. Senators were not especially wise but elevating them to a single focus for legislation helped to make the cracks in the republic less conspicuous.

Sulla laid down the dictatorship in 81, was elected consul in 80, and retired into private life in 79. He died in 78. His retirement left Rome in a political vacuum. An array of incompetent nobles stepped into the breach but none had the charisma to pull the Roman mob into line. Pompey was one of several contenders. As Sulla's henchman, he had earned the nickname "teenage butcher," but his path to power was littered with opponents.

Above: The young Gnaeus Pompeius (106–48 BC) was one of Sulla's most devoted officers. He never held any high offices but his military reputation was sufficient to make him a power in later years. Plutarch wrote of him: "Pompey had a very engaging countenance, which spoke for him before he opened his lips."

Left: Mithridates remained a thorn in Rome's side for years. He was opposed by both Sulla (87) and Pompey (66), victories that were concluded by treaty rather than outright defeat. This relief sculpture depicts Mithridates standing with Hercules.

Cicero, Voice of Reason

Orator, writer, barrister, poet, political animal... Cicero was all of these and more. He presided—in words at least—over the tumultuous events of the republic's final days. In its last years he was its inspirational, intellectual beacon, giving it (false) hope for the future.

Facing: Cicero—his cognomen means "chickpea"—was another *novus homo* (new man), like Marius, from rural Italy. Opposed to Julius Caesar, he supported Pompey in the civil war. Caesar forgave him, but after his series of speeches to the senate (the Philippics) against Mark Antony, Antony did not, and had him executed.

Marcus Tullius Cicero (106–43 BC) was high born to a family of equestrian status in Arpinum (home town of Marius), some 70 miles east of Rome. His mother Helvia was, by all accounts, a frugal disciplinarian, while his father was bookish. In his teens he was sent with his younger brother Quintus to Rome for a formal education. This extended to trips to Greece and Asia Minor.

Cicero fathered a daughter, Tullia, and a son called Marcus by his first wife Terentia. It was the premature death of his daughter that shadowed Cicero's last years. She had married three times but the infants she bore all died. In grief Cicero divorced Terentia, although he alluded to her dishonesty. He married again and quickly divorced.

Cicero became a consul in 63 BC, the first in his family to do so. Afterward he became the center of political machinations in a tumultuous age, siding with one contender against another, striving to achieve a workable balance of power. As a lawyer his abiding concern was the constitution's well being and his commonly heard cry was "Lest the constitution of the republic be changed."

He was a great supporter of Pompey the Great, although he profoundly disliked Pompey's political associates Marcus Crassus, whose fabulous wealth stemmed initially from his gains under Sulla's proscriptions, and Julius Caesar, whose naked ambition he viewed as a danger to the republic. Politically he is remembered for securing the summary execution of the Catiline conspirators, supporters of a politician-turned-rabble rouser who tried to co-ordinate a march on Rome. Cicero, ably supported by Cato the Younger, great grandson of Cato the Censor, argued in the senate for capital punishment without trial as an example to other potential renegades.

The legality of the action was highly questionable, and Julius Caesar rose in opposition, urging the use of the hitherto underused sentence of life imprisonment.

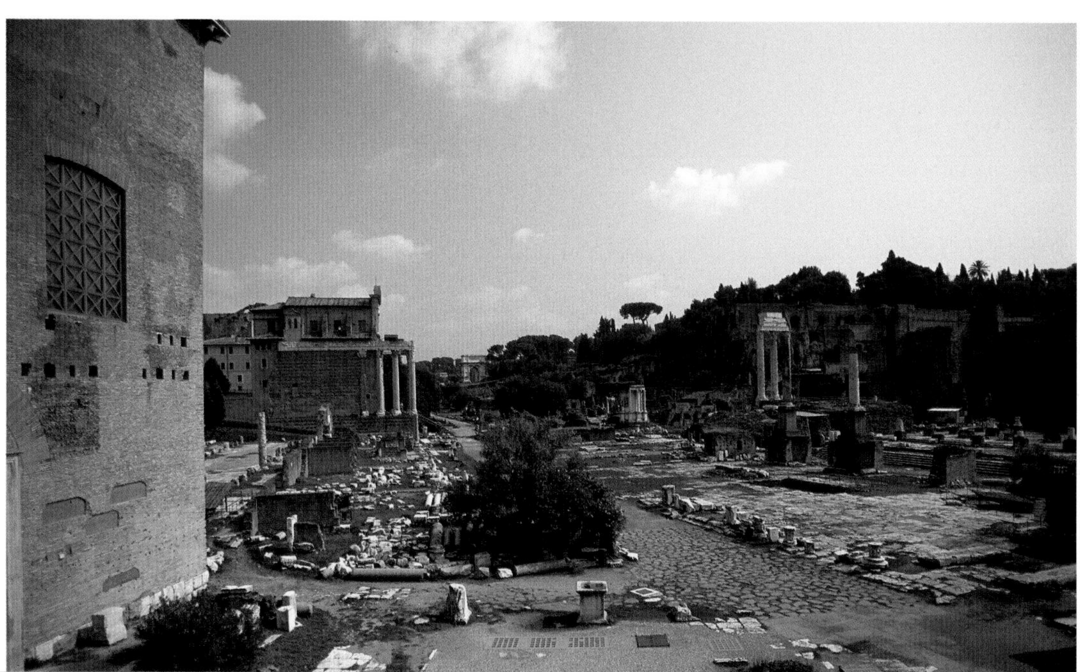

Right: View of the Forum Romanum, looking east, with the Palatine hill on the right. The Forum was the center of the republic's politics and government. Orators like Cicero addressed their colleagues and the people from many places within the Forum, not only in the *Curia Hostilia* (senate house) seen at the left foreground.

88–86 BC	85 BC	82 BC	79 BC	73–71 BC	70 BC	67 BC	64 BC
Romans fight Mithridates of Pontus in Asia Minor	Sulla agrees peace with Mithridates	Sulla drives out opposition and becomes dictator of Rome	A political void is left on Sulla's retirement	A slave rebellion led by Spartacus is quelled by Marcus Crassus	Pompey the Great and Marcus Crassus are elected co-consuls	An anti-pirate campaign by Pompey the Great eliminates Cicilian sea raiders	Julius Caesar becomes *pontifex maximus*

The accused were duly executed, although Cicero ultimately served some months in exile, having lost significant support during the episode. Beyond the Catiline affair, he failed to secure any constitutional reform during his tenure.

Bitter-sweet words

More positively, he transposed Greek philosophy into Latin, created philosophical texts for Rome, and put the republic on an intellectual par with Greece. Thanks to Cicero, we have bountiful evidence of life in Rome more than 2,000 years ago, although it is presented with bias.

Cicero was a prolifically versatile writer and astonishing numbers of his letters and essays have been preserved. This was mostly due to the efforts of Tiro, a slave freed by Cicero in 53 BC who thereafter became his devoted secretary. Tiro spent the last 35 years of his life collecting and publishing his former master's writings and collating a biography.

Cicero's eloquence continues to strike a chord and it is easy to see why he had both fervent supporters and bitter enemies. He said of Mark Antony: "At first you were just a public prostitute, with a fixed price: quite a high one too. But very soon Curio intervened and took you off the streets, promoting you, one might say, to wifely status, and making a sound, steady married woman out of you." (Antony responded by having Cicero killed in the proscriptions following Julius Caesar's death.)

Like the Catos, he elaborated the virtues of living off the land, saying "of all things from which one may acquire wealth, none is better than agriculture, none more fruitful, none sweeter, none more fitting for a free man."

Cicero was aware of the importance of religion in Roman society. It was, he felt, important for men to believe that their every word and deed was being observed by a higher power. "Minds that are imbued with [devout religion] will scarcely shrink from useful or correct opinions." He was the first Roman awarded the title *pater patriae* in 63, indicating his role as "father of the nation." Ironically, the title thereafter went to his sworn enemy Julius Caesar.

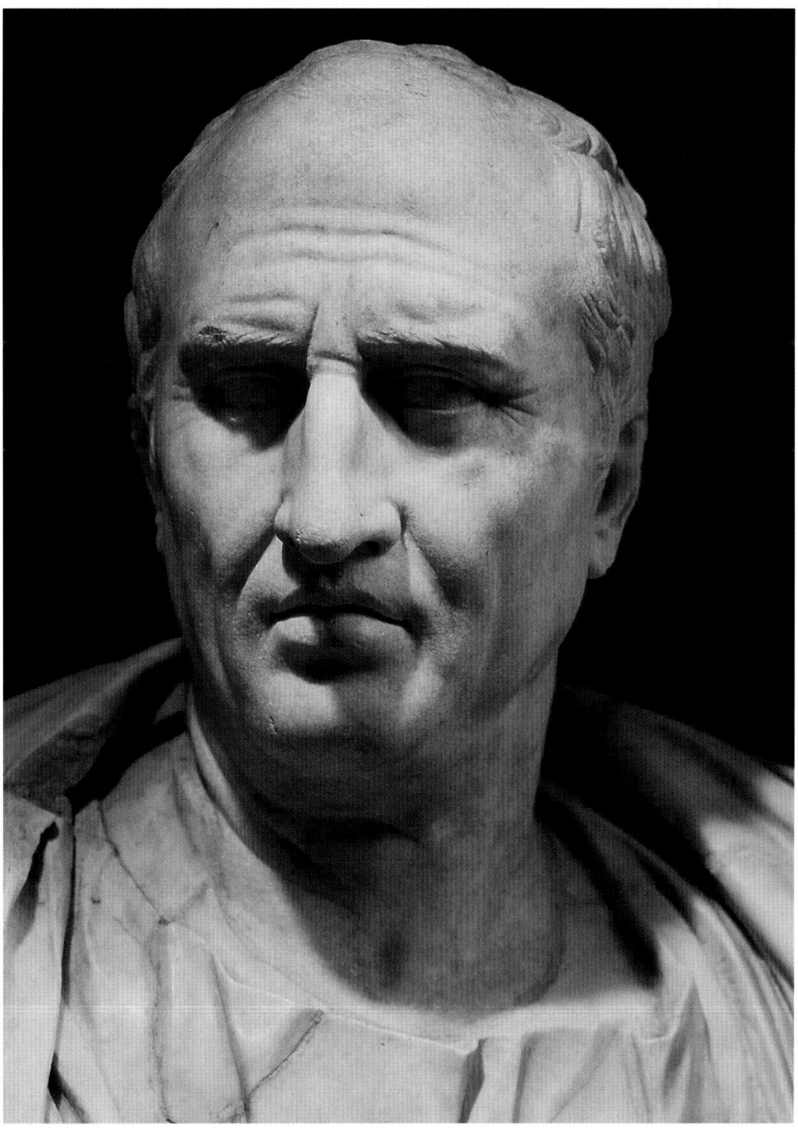

The Roman naming convention

Any Roman history is complicated by the participants' names, so many appear to be constantly repeated. The Roman name was usually comprised of three parts: *praenomen* (given name); *nomen*, or *gens* (family name); *cognomen* (nickname). During the republic, there were probably only 20 *praenomina* in common use, and each family seemed to favor certain ones. Among the Julii, for instance, the only *praenomia* in use were Gaius, Sextus, and Lucius, which meant that the naming of male children was extremely limited (*see also page 186*).

The *cognomina* were derived either from an honor given, such as "Africanus," or from a distinguishing feature (Cicero means "chick-pea," and Caesar a "fine head of hair," although Julius Caesar had thinning hair). There were exceptions; the Antonii never had a *cognomen* (Marcus Antonius) and the Caecilii Metelli routinely had four or more, which makes them easier to identify as individuals. By Caesar's day, the *cognomen* was applied to his whole branch of the *gens* Julia, and would be handed down increasingly as a regal title rather than an affectionate nickname.

63 BC Consul and writer Cicero becomes the first Roman *pater patriae*

60 BC Caesar, Pompey, and Crassus form the First Triumvirate

58–52 BC Roman forces led by Caesar conquer Gaul

55–54 BC Julius Caesar invades Britain

53 BC Crassus is killed at the Battle of Carrhae, Mesopotamia

c.50 BC Romans trade with China and India

c.50 BC Peoples of client kingdoms are offered Roman citizenship

47 BC Caesar and Pompey's civil war; Caesar becomes dictator after Pompey's death

Gaius Julius Caesar

Caesar's name has rung down the centuries in regal titles such as kaiser and czar. He proved pivotal in Rome's history, doing much to dismantle the republic and pave the way for the emperors who would give Romans tyranny and stability in equal measure.

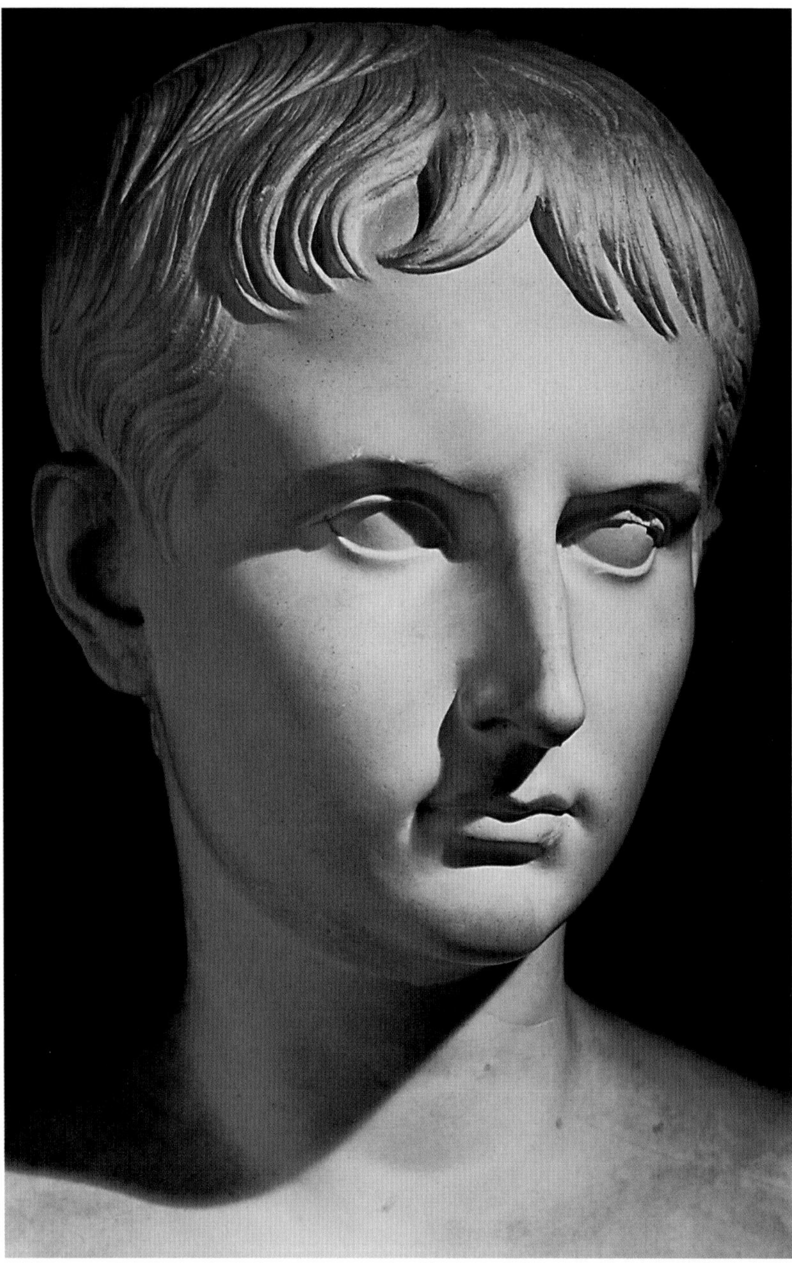

Above: Bust of the young Julius Caesar. Aristocrat but impoverished, Caesar remained frugal throughout his life but greedy for power.

Genius military commander, gifted orator, prolific writer, and law-maker, Gaius Julius Caesar (100–44 BC) was a man of many parts. Famous for clemency, pointedly sparing the lives of political enemies, he was cruel in his treatment of the Celts in Gaul. He spoke the language of the common legionary, but moved among Rome's elite on equal terms. His championing of the proletariat while accruing all honors he felt were owed to him made many of his aristocratic colleagues suspicous of his motives. Julius Caesar had no time for the nostalgic sentiment that was symptomatic of republican Rome.

From the ancient Julian line, the very young Julius was raised in luxury, but it was not to last. He was instilled with pride in Roman history, which must have been shaken when his father became a victim of political scheming and fell from grace, losing the family wealth along the way. Julius Caesar was raised in Rome's poor Subura quarter, and until his middle adult years he remained imured in poverty. This may have contributed to his famous frugality. As the Roman historian Suetonius (c.AD 69–122) wrote: "That he drank very little wine not even his enemies denied. There is a saying of Marcus Cato that Caesar was the only man who undertook to overthrow the state when sober. Even in the matter of food Gaius Oppius tells us that he was so indifferent…."

At 15, on the death of his father, Caesar joined the army. Four years spent on hectic military campaigns earned him a reputation for valor and physical strength that belied the epilepsy from which he occasionally suffered. Aged 20 he won the *corona civica* or civic cross for saving a fellow soldier's life in a campaign on the Black Sea.

Indisposed to agree with Sulla, there is no evidence that he was involved in any attempts to overthrow Sulla's constitution. However, Caesar deemed it prudent to be away from Rome during the proscriptions, and left for scholarly study in Rhodes.

The triumvirate gathers

He first came to notice as a prominent political figure as a client of Marcus Licinius Crassus—thus apparently hitching himself to the Sullan *optimates* party. But his marriage to Cornelia, daughter of eminent Marian supporter Cinna, and the fact that Gaius Marius was his uncle, tied him to the democratic cause. To this he remained constant, and all his life was an opponent of the senate. Marius, who used his position to appoint Caesar to the ancient priesthood, rated him as a fellow radical—in this he was only partly correct, although Caesar was to use radical tactics.

First he was sent to administer the colony of Spain—recently subdued by Pompey (*see panel*)—then he was given responsibility for Rome's entertainment. He staged elaborate shows with exotic animals from Africa and gladiatorial combat. He is even said to have flooded arenas to stage naval battles. At the same time he courted the city-dwellers, visiting slums where he still felt entirely at home and where few aristocrats dared venture.

All this without an aristocrat's money; his personal debts mounted, alleviated to some extent by generous handouts from Crassus in return for Caesar's gift of public oratory. His problems were eased when, at 36, he was elected *pontifex maximus*, supreme priest of Rome. This unexpected appointment gave him funds, an official residence, and enhanced prestige.

The rival statesman to Crassus was Pompey. They both stood for consulship in 70 BC, even though Pompey had never held a magistracy of any kind and at 36 was too young to hold the office according to Sulla's new laws. Between them, they reversed much of Sulla's constitution, which effectively took away the powers he had granted to the senate, and handed them back to the tribunate. It was inevitable that Caesar, ambitious for military glory and political position, would throw in his lot with these powerful men. His next move was to marry his daughter Julia to Pompey, who by all accounts was head over heels in love with her.

It is doubtful that Caesar would have won his first consulship in 59 with the backing of only Crassus, but with Pompey behind him as well, it became a foregone conlcusion. The three men decided on a mutually beneficial policy of control by inclusion and so came about the First Triumvirate, with Caesar apparently the junior partner, a situation he did not tolerate for long.

Below: A frieze along one side of the monument (70 BC) known as Altar of Domitius Ahenobarbus shows scenes from a Roman census. On the left a citizen is registered. In the center the *pontifex maximus* (high priest, the office held by Caesar) presides over the sacrifice of a bull and a sheep.

Rebellion in Spain

Under Sulla, the Roman empire acknowledged the supremacy of the senate, with the exception of Spain. There, the governor, a democrat called Quintus Sertorius (*pictured here*), remained opposed. Sulla sent a new governor, and Sertorius took to the hills with some 8,000 men, eventually accepting the offer of the Lusitanian tribes to become their leader in 80 BC.

After successfully holding at bay the legions of Metellus Pius sent to destroy him, Sertorius was faced by the addition of Pompey and reinforcements in 76. Over another three years, the two Roman generals wore down Sertorius and his army of Roman refugees and Spanish guerrillas. The rebellion collapsed when Sertorius was assassinated in 72, and Pompey was given the credit and the hero worship of the nation.

GOVERNMENT BY TRIUMVIRATE

No man was sufficiently strong to grasp the reigns of power in Rome on Sulla's demise, so rule reverted to republican government. Three of the most able men of the age combined in opposition to the senate to form the First Triumvirate.

After Sulla's resignation as dictator, the first to compete for outright power were Marcus Aemilius Lepidus and Pompey the Great. Lepidus and Quintus Lutatius Catulus were elected consuls for 78 BC, Lepidus in spite of Sulla's dark warnings. After Sulla's death, Lepidus wasted no time in rousing large areas of Italy against Sulla's constitution, and soon found himself at the head of a large army, prepared to march on Rome and divest the senate of its enlarged powers.

Pompey had supported Lepidus in the elections, but found the opportunity to raise arms against him on behalf of the senate irresistable. The rebellion was short-lived. Pompey cornered Lepidus and defeated him in battle near Cosa. Lepidus withdrew his forces to Sardinia, where he died soon after. His men went on to join Sertorius in Spain (*see previous page*) and eventually suffered defeat at Pompey's hands in 72 BC.

Above: Marcus Licinius Crassus (115–53 BC) was one of Sulla's officers in 83, and subsequently held several consulships. His fabulous wealth started with the confiscation of property during Sulla's proscriptions, but Crassus enlarged it through buying fire-damaged houses cheaply and rebuilding them for profit.

While Pompey was busy in Spain, and Roman legions under Licinus Lucullus were winning glory in again fighting Mithridates in Asia, Marcus Crassus was given an opportunity to show his mettle. When Rome was paralyzed by another slave rebellion in 73 BC, it was Crassus who finally brought the insurgents and their remarkably successful leader, Spartacus, to heel after a two-year campaign. To mark his victory he lined the via Appia with 6,000 crucified slaves, to the very gates of Rome.

Pompey and Crassus were now titans on the Roman political stage. Each stood at the head of legions of men and sat on substantial wealth. A clash between the two—who made little secrecy of their mutual dislike—would have resulted in wholesale death and destruction. Accordingly, each skirted around the other, coaxing and courting to such a great degree that in 70 they were elected co-consuls. It was an uneasy partnership. When it came to an end, Pompey was largely absent from Rome.

First, in 67, he undertook a campaign to wipe out the ever-expanding numbers of pirates along the Cilician coast. Then, because he was on the spot, he took over from Lucullus to conclude the war against Mithridates. Although Lucullus had done all the work, Pompey received the glory, and was even said to be the greatest general since Alexander.

Crassus and Julius Caesar were apprehensive about his return in 62, for Pompey alone had sufficient wealth and standing to topple them from grace. However, senators subsumed in their own self-importance unwittingly intervened to unite the unlikely trio. Despite the glory he had won for Rome, the senate, fearful of a coup, denied Pompey land with which to reward his soldiers. Reeling from the insult, he threw in his lot with Crassus and Caesar, forming the First Triumvirate in 60 BC, a bulwark against the intransigent senate.

The three leaders

Crassus had the money. Caesar brought a common touch—he was at home with ordinary folk, and overpopulated Rome had plenty of these. But Pompey had little to offer the triumvirate except his immense popularity among the legions. Even Cicero, one of his most adamant supporters, said Pompey was "nothing great, nothing outstanding, nothing that is not low and popular."

There was nothing official about the triumvirate. It was a private agreement assuring its members of co-operation. Each acted ostensibly in the interests of the others, while in reality they worked to secure increased power and wealth for themselves. The busiest was Caesar, who, after his first election as consulship in 59, acted on behalf of the triumvirate from a position of strength.

Through collaboration and with the use of their clients and supporters, the triumvirs exerted influence on the government apparatus, despite senate attempts to thwart them at every turn. They pursued policies that would win the support of the *plebs*, including the presentation of free public games and extra grain rations. Pompey's soldiers received the land they were promised. All this was costly, so in response the triumvirate secured overseas posts that would replenish their fortunes. Pompey went to Spain, Crassus pitched himself and his forces into Syria, while Caesar sought new acquisitions in Gaul.

The strain of this unnatural bonding soon became intolerable. Emergency talks dubbed the Luca Conference took place in 56 to avoid a falling out. The triumvirate was endorsed in 55 when Pompey and Crassus were once again consuls. But in 54, the link that kept Caesar and Pompey allied was severed when Julia died. By all accounts, Julia was the wife that Pompey loved best. A year later, Crassus was killed in the Battle of Carrhae (modern Harran) in Mesopotamia. Pompey and Caesar were left tentatively circling one another, waiting and watching.

Above: Crassus and Pompey were not the only very wealthy men in the late republic. This fresco from Pompeii shows a seaside villa (*villa marittima*), a luxury dwelling that became common for fashionable Romans to spend time relaxing away from the city. The majority were built around the Bay of Naples and boasted every luxury of the period.

Caesar's Gallic War

In Gaul, Caesar's brilliance as a strategist, tactician, and diplomat came to the fore. In a seven-year campaign against the Celts and Germans, he schemed, allied, and fought his way to victory time and again.

Above: Vercingetorix, a prince of the Averni, roused the common people with his eloquence and soon won the support of the tribes of central and western Gaul. After many successes against the Roman legions, Caesar finally cornered him at the hill fort of Alesia, seen below today.

Opportunity beckoned in 58 BC, when the Helvetii, threatened by the Germanic Suevi tribe from the north and allied Dacian tribes from the east, asked Rome if they could migrate across a portion of Transalpine Gaul (a province since 120 BC)—through lands of the neighboring Allobroges—into Gaul itself. Since the situation in Gaul was highly unstable, which affected Rome's interests, Caesar refused them permission. The Helvetii ignored his edict and marched west, entering Gallic Sequani lands. Caesar painted a picture of extreme danger to the senate, and took four legions to the Rhône, reinforced by a further three that were wintering in Cisalpine Gaul.

At the Battle of Bibracte in the same year, the Romans defeated a far larger number of Helvetii and their allies, and pushed them back into the Swiss Alps. In gratitude, a number of pro-Roman Celtic chiefs helped Caesar force the senate into appointing him Protector of the Gauls—they wanted protection against the ambitious Aviovistus of the German Suevi. Caesar obliged, marching north with his seven legions to Alsace. In another decisive battle in the Vosges in 58, Caesar drove the Germans back over the Rhine and saved Gaul from barbarian invasion.

The Roman army went into winter quarters, but emerged in the spring of 57 to defend the Gallic Remi tribe against threatening Belgae. Caesar attacked each of the 11 Belgae tribes in turn before they could join forces. Two—the Nervii and Aduactui—almost checked him when they launched a surprise attack on the Roman camp. It nearly ended in disaster, but the indefatigable general rallied his troops, led a counterattack, and ultimately claimed victory in the Battle of the Sambre. Caesar followed up his victory by conquering the Veneti in northwestern France.

Between campaigns, Caesar returned to Cisalpine Gaul to meet with his fellow triumvirs and conduct mutual business. One essential was to ensure his command was extended for a five-year period, which as co-consuls again Crassus and Pompey were able to do.

Crossing the Rubicon

In 55, Caesar repelled another Germanic invasion before leading a cross-channel reconnaissance into Britain to attack the Belgae tribes living there. His invasion was cut short, however, by an uprising in central Gaul led by Vercingetorix, a prince of the Averni. A shrewd realist, Vercingetorix adopted guerrilla tactics to harrass the Romans, but made the mistake of entering into a full-scale engagement when he thought the legions were retreating to Transalpine Gaul. Caesar turned, and pushed the Celts into their hilltop fortress of Alesia.

In what would become the best known siege in ancient history, Caesar encircled the city then defeated a Gallic relief army from behind an outer circumvallation. In 52 BC Vercingetorix was forced to surrender and taken captive, ready for Caesar's eventual triumph in Rome. Although it took another year to fully pacify Gaul, the region had become a Roman province.

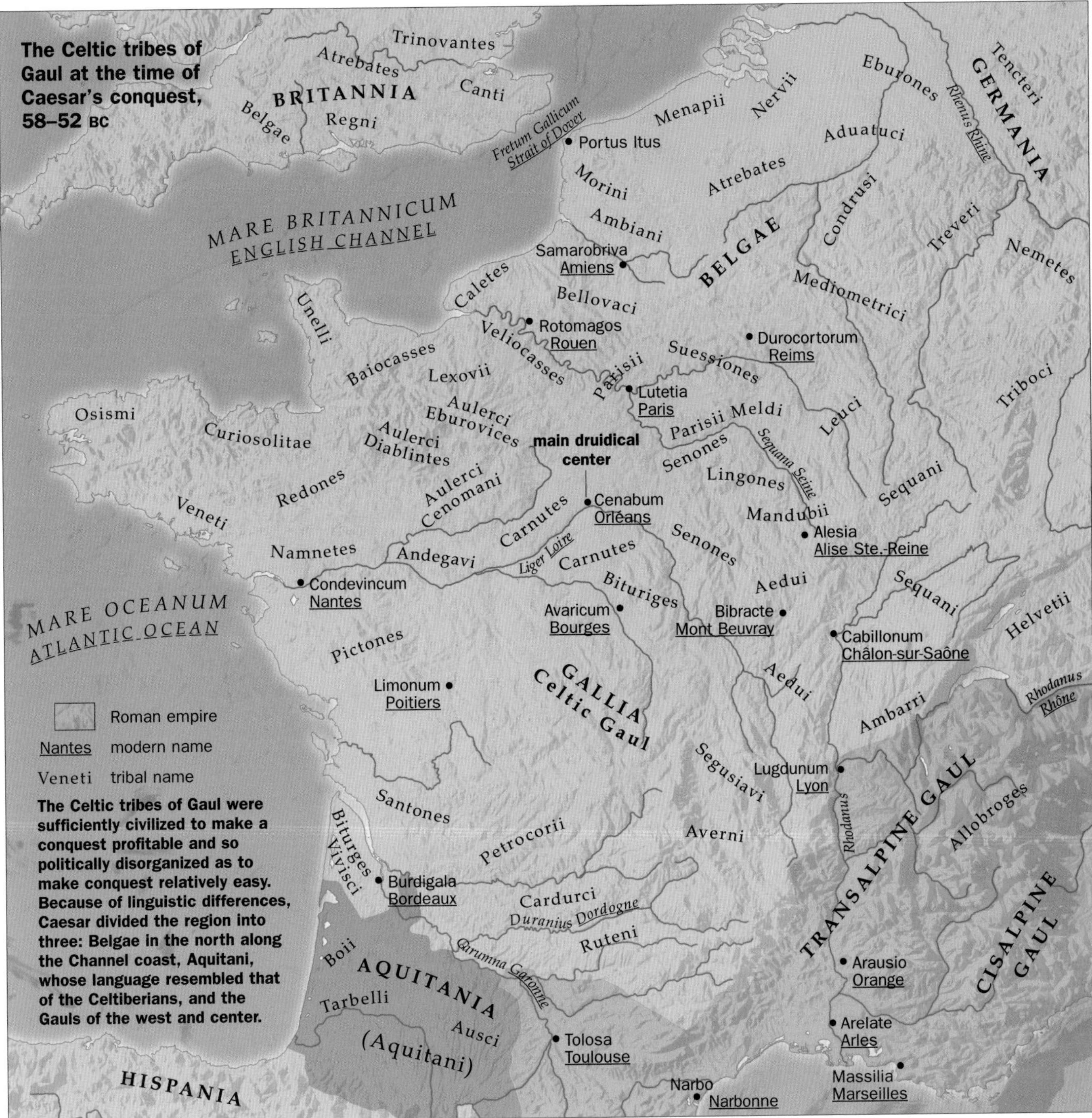
Trinovantes
Atrebates
BRITANNIA
Canti
Belgae
Regni
Fretum Gallicum
Strait of Dover
Portus Itus
Menapii
Nervii
Eburones
Tencteri
GERMANIA
Rhenus Rhine
Aduatuci
Morini
Atrebates
MARE BRITANNICUM
ENGLISH CHANNEL
Ambiani
Condrusi
Treveri
Nemetes
Samarobriva
Amiens
BELGAE
Mediomatrici
Caletes
Bellovaci
Unelli
Rotomagos
Rouen
Veliocasses
Durocortorum
Reims
Suessiones
Baiocasses
Lexovii
Parisii
Lutetia
Paris
Triboci
Osismi
Curiosolitae
Aulerci Eburovices
Aulerci Diablintes
main druidical center
Parisii
Meldi
Leuci
Senones
Sequana Seine
Lingones
Redones
Aulerci Cenomani
Carnutes
Cenabum
Orléans
Mandubii
Sequani
Veneti
Alesia
Alise Ste.-Reine
Namnetes
Andegavi
Liger Loire
Carnutes
Senones
Condevincum
Nantes
Bituriges
Aedui
Sequani
MARE OCEANUM
ATLANTIC OCEAN
Avaricum
Bourges
Bibracte
Mont Beuvray
Cabillonum
Châlon-sur-Saône
Helvetii
Pictones
GALLIA
Celtic Gaul
Aedui
Limonum
Poitiers
Rhodanus
Rhône
Ambarri
Roman empire
Nantes modern name
Veneti tribal name
Segusiavi
Lugdunum
Lyon
TRANSALPINE GAUL
Santones
Rhodanus
Allobroges
Bituriges Vivisci
Petrocorii
Averni
Burdigala
Bordeaux
Cardurci
Duranius Dordogne
Ruteni
CISALPINE GAUL
Boii
AQUITANIA
(Aquitani)
Garumna Garonne
Arausio
Orange
Tarbelli
Ausci
Arelate
Arles
Tolosa
Toulouse
HISPANIA
Narbo
Narbonne
Massilia
Marseilles

The Celtic tribes of Gaul at the time of Caesar's conquest, 58–52 BC

The Celtic tribes of Gaul were sufficiently civilized to make a conquest profitable and so politically disorganized as to make conquest relatively easy. Because of linguistic differences, Caesar divided the region into three: Belgae in the north along the Channel coast, Aquitani, whose language resembled that of the Celtiberians, and the Gauls of the west and center.

Caesar now turned his attention to the political crisis at home. In 52, an unwilling senate had given Pompey a third consulship with the purpose of his quelling the political street fighting, which had gotten out of hand—but without a colleague to hinder him. This virtual dictatorship was more than the Luca Conference had allowed for between the triumvirs. Caesar needed to be elected consul while still governor of Gaul, thus continuing his *imperium* and immunity to legal prosecution for any illegal acts he may have carried out as a governor—of which there were plenty. The senate insisted on the statutes, that he enter Rome as a private citizen to canvas for the election.

Although Pompey agreed to use his position to waive the regulations, Caesar no longer trusted him, or he may have not believed that Pompey could carry the senate with him. In any event, Caesar invaded Italy at the beginning of 49, crossing the Rubicon river, which marked the boundary between Cisalpine Gaul and Italy at the head of his devoted legions, occupying Ariminum. Caesar seems to have striven for a peaceful situation, if one was possible on his own terms. One source tells how Caesar had pondered his alternatives. "To refrain from crossing will bring me misfortune; but to cross will bring misfortune to all men." But he would not lose the initiatve through caution, and it was clear he had taken Pompey completely by surprise. Pompey chose not to face him, and instead withdrew across the Adriatic to begin marshaling his forces in the Balkans.

END OF THE REPUBLIC

In less than five years, Julius Caesar changed the destiny of Rome through decisive battles, a mass of innovative legislation, and by becoming to some the most dangerous man in the known world.

Rome and all Italy fell to Caesar with scarcely any fighting, but the city had emptied of most of the magistrates. His first task, therefore, was to provide some sort of government. However, he did this without entering the city, still adhering to constitutional forms. He even attempted to persuade Cicero to return, but the orator refused, and eventually slipped across the Adriatic after Pompey.

The first act of the civil war took place in Spain, where Pompey still had a powerful army. Hoping to deal with them before Pompey had time to organize another army in Illyria, Caesar dashed overland to Spain. In his brief absence, Marcus Antonius (Mark Antony), a young tribune who had won his favor in Gaul, was in charge of Italy. Pompey's cause fell rapidly in the hands of his poorly chosen generals, Lucius Afranius and Marcus Petreius. They surrendered in return for a pardon and the disbandment of Pompey's legions. Caesar hurried back to Itay, where he was elected consul again, to begin a round of diplomatic missions to help restore proper government. And then, at the end of a very hectic 49 BC, he set off for the east.

After failing to dislodge Pompey's well-entrenched forces at Dyrrhacium, Caesar marched into Thessaly to intercept Metellus Scipio, the governor of Syria, who was coming overland to join the Pompeian army. Pompey followed him, and the three forces finally clashed in the summer of 48 at Pharsalus, in northern Greece. Despite being outnumbered two to one, Caesar's infantry broke Pompey's massed cavalry and then pressed the Pompeian army to the point of routing it completely.

Pompey fled to the coast and took a ship to Egypt in the hope that the children of King Ptolemy Auletes, Cleopatra and Ptolemy XII, would remember that when he was alive their father owed his throne to Pompey's generosity. They did not—perhaps they feared Caesar more. When he landed, Pompey was treacherously murdered on the beach, and his head handed to a horrified Caesar on his arrival in Alexandria early in 47.

When news of his victory at Pharsalus reached Rome, Caesar was appointed dictator for an indefinite period. Now undisputed ruler of the Roman world, he mediated between the squabbling factions at the Alexandrian court, eventually siding with Cleopatra. He then returned to Rome by way of Asia Minor, where he put down a revolt led by the son of Mithridates. The sojourn was brief; in 46, he went to Africa and defeated Pompey's remaining republicans at Thapsus.

Death of a tyrant

Having labored long and hard for this cherished position of power, Caesar set about enjoying the rewards. In 46 he was made dictator for ten years, and in 44 the office was given to him for life. Honors were heaped on him by obsequious senators trying to outdo one another. His birthday became a public holiday. The month of his birth was renamed "Julius" (July) after him. There seemed no end to his exaltation.

Although he refused the title *rex*, and rejected the crown Antony offered him in 44 at the festival of Lupercalia, Caesar adopted many kingly trappings. He took to wearing a purple toga, the regal color. He was awarded the right to sit on a golden chair during senate meetings, wearing a golden wreath. That Queen Cleopatra of Egypt came to reside outside Rome's walls as his mistress, with her son by Caesar, Caesarion, only added to patrician disquiet. Rome still did not take kindly to monarchs. It became too much for some.

According to Cicero, the conspiracy was contrived by people with "the courage of men but the understanding of boys"—in other words, they were naïve if they believed the death of Caesar would restore the republic. On the agreed day, the Ides (15th) of March, 44, Caesar went to the senate at its appointed place, the meeting hall in the Portico of Pompey. There, at the foot of Pompey's oversize statue, the large group of conspirators murdered him. Perhaps Caesar knew it was coming, for he made little attempt to defend himself—he had even dismissed his lictors earlier. He succumbed to 23 stab wounds.

After his death, Cleopatra returned with Caesar's son to Egypt, vituperatively declaiming that the conspirators were traitors. Although there were certainly lofty as well as less noble motives for the murder, this cruel and senseless act unleashed a civil war worse than any in Rome's history and ensured the end of the republic forever.

Clash of the Titans: when the two most powerful men in the empire came to blows, it spelled the end of the republic. Pompey (left) gambled on his miltary prowess, Caesar (right) on his strategic genius.

LEX JULIA MUNICIPALIS

Although Caesar spent comparatively few months in Rome between 49 and 44 BC, he accomplished a great deal, launching a vast program of reforms, politically, socially, and administratively. What he might have accomplished had he lived longer is a matter of conjecture, beyond those projects he was known to be considering at the time of his murder.

The most pressing matter was alleviating poverty and debt. Everything in Rome and Italy was in disorder after the long political struggle. In times of conflict, interest rates went sky high, and few could afford their repayments. As early as 49, Caesar reduced debts by a quarter, but assured those holding notes that he would not cancel all debts, as had been done by populist dictators in the past. He decreed that for purposes of repayment property should be valued at prewar levels, and a remission of rents was given in 48. In Rome the mob had become used to free corn, which had encouraged a mass exodus of the land for the city. By 48 as many as 320,000 received the corn-dole. Caesar reviewed the civic lists, and reduced the number of dependents by half.

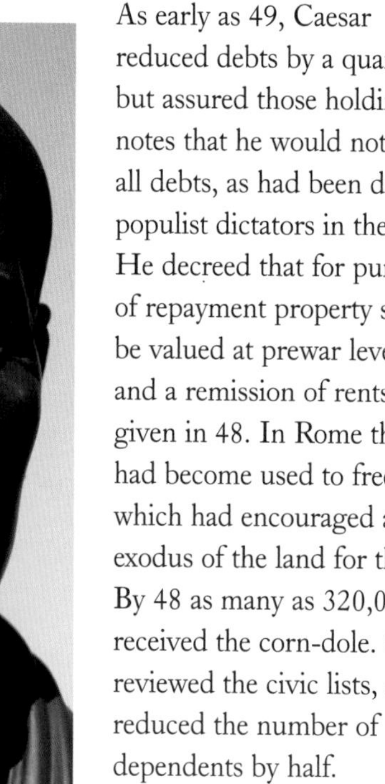

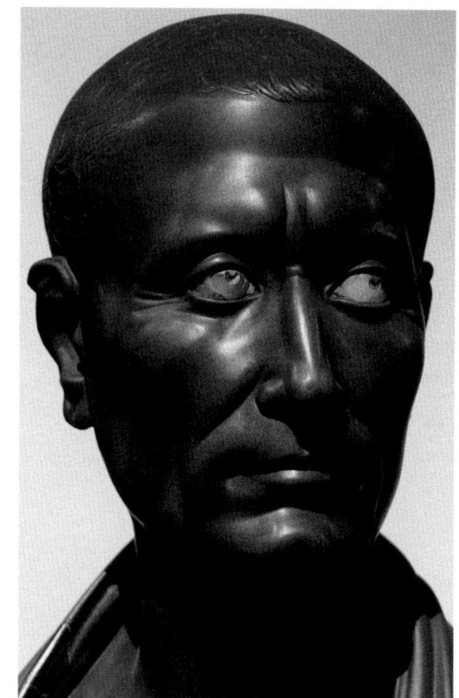

Above: Law-maker and architect, Caesar's reforms of the constitution went in hand with a massive building program, especially in the Forum, centered around his great new temple of Venus Genetrix. These three columns (**facing**) are all that remain standing today.

Large numbers of poor citizens and discharged soldiers were settled in colonies in Italy and especially in the provinces (*see map page 96*). About 80,000 families were offered a new life in more than 20 newly founded colonies, among them the rebuilt Carthage and Corinth. Caesar's soldiers each received 5,000 *denarii* at his triumph in 46, and veterans were allotted farms and a bonus.

His generosity in granting citizenship to many in the provinces was part of a comprehensive Romanization policy, particularly in Gaul, Spain, and Africa. For the administration of this vast undertaking he drew up laws for the governing of these new towns. The *Lex Julia municipalis* would become the cornerstone and foundation not only for municipal but also provincial administration and would last until the fall of the western empire.

A new calendar

Caesar's wide travels had convinced him that Rome could no longer be a city-state. He foresaw a time when citizenship would be extended to all peoples, not just the citizens of Rome, and that they would be bound to Rome the empire, not Rome the city. An empire would need an expanded, workable government. To this end he enlarged the senate from 600 to 900, including many new citizens from the provinces. However, since most of the new senators were his clients, this also strengthened his control of the senate.

Other measures included new traffic congestion controls for the city, which banned wheeled vehicles from the streets during daylight hours. He reformed the laws of bribery, extortion, and treason, and ended the system of "tax-farming" in the provinces, which had made many *equites* very rich at the expense of the people. The provinces were to be governed by legates appointed by Caesar himself, but their tenure would be strictly controlled by law.

In Rome, a series of grandiose building projects was begun, which created work for many of the rabble. The most impressive was an entirely new Forum, including a refurbished senate house, new law courts, a state library, and temples in the Hellenistic style. Work on this began in 54 and was completed by 46.

He also overhauled the Roman calendar, which had fallen out of harmony with the seasons due to the way priests randomly added the necessary leap-days. To correct this, Caesar—with the help of an Alexandrian astronomer—made the year 46 BC 445 days long to regain harmony, and on January 1, 45 a year of $365\frac{1}{4}$ days was introduced, with every fourth being a leap year. This reform lasted until 1582, when Pope Gregory XIII made a slight adjustment to the calendar to its current form.

Caesar had plans for massive civil engineering projects that included draining the

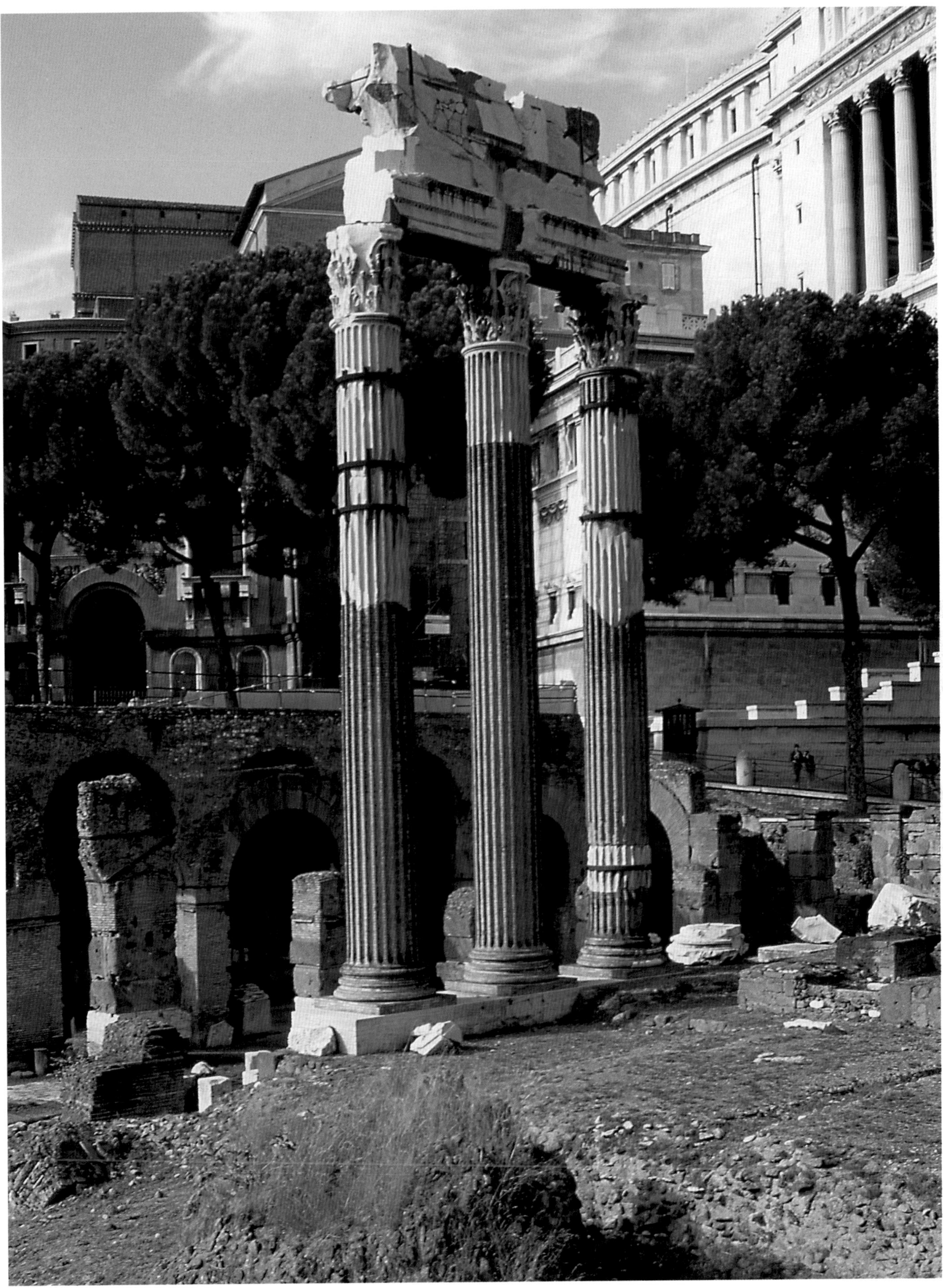

Fucine Lake and the Pomptine marshes, building a road through the Appenines, and constructing a canal across the Isthmus of Corinth.

Although all these reforms were handled within the constitutional traditions of the republic, and despite his clemency to former enemies, his moderation did little to dispell growing fears that Caesar had become a tyrant in the despised oriental manner.

CHAPTER 6

THE NEW CAESARS

The Roman Republic had endured for more than 400 years. It was not always in the best of health, but its survival was testament to the strength of the political system. Tacitus sums up the history of Rome to date: "In the beginning, kings ruled the city of Rome; Lucius Brutus brought freedom and instituted consuls. On occasion there were dictatorships; the Decemvirate lasted no more than two years, and the military tribunes with consular power not long. Neither Cinna nor Sulla exercised mastery for more than a brief space; the power of Pompey and Crassus swiftly passed to Caesar, the armed strength of Lepidus and Antony to Augustus: and he, now that the whole state was exhausted by civil war, assumed the name of *princeps*, and took it under his control."

But before he would become Augustus, Caesar's grand-nephew and adopted son Gaius Octavius had much to do. Rome's move into true empire was not completed overnight. The senate's greed, Sulla's dictatorship, and Caesar's power mania all contributed to the downfall of the republic before Octavius had come of age.

Yet it was down to Octavius as Augustus, supreme ruler of Rome, to define his role and that of his successors. He chose not to make sweeping changes and maintained the senate and other government offices, so that the accusation of tyranny that damaged Caesar could not be wielded against him. His acquisition of power was slow but sure, undertaken in the knowledge that Romans were wary of sudden change. His considered approach put the Roman empire on a steady footing and ensured it would continue for centuries rather than decades, its contribution to the modern world still discernible today.

The *Forum Romanum* was the hub of the empire—seen here in its final 3rd-century AD architectural glory—the result of continued enhancement projects begun by Augustus.

OLIVER FREY

Octavius Caesar

Gaius Octavius bore no obvious hallmarks of greatness, yet he made Rome illustrious. He built on the past glories and laid firm foundations for Rome's future. He also proved to be as politically astute as his adoptive, and now murdered father, Julius Caesar.

Below: Marcus Antonius (83–40 BC) thought he was Caesar's heir, but was forced to accept that his rival Octavius was the chosen one.

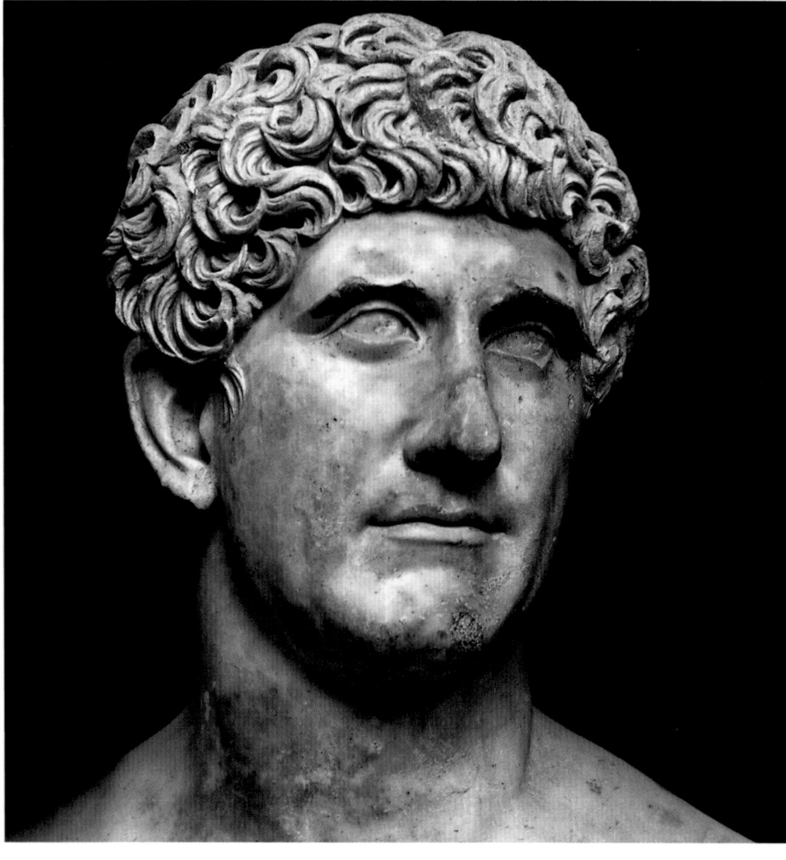

As Caesar's great nephew and adopted son, Gaius Octavius had his first taste of public speaking aged 12 at the funeral of his grandmother, Julia, Caesar's daughter. Although his natural father was a senator, it was Caesar who was the greater influence in the young man's life. He had already served as one of Caesar's tribunes in Spain and was in Epirus preparing for an expedition with him against the Parthians when Caesar was assassinated. Since—to almost everyone's surprise—he was named as Caesar's heir in the will, he ignored his mother's pleas to stay away from politically dangerous Rome.

Caesar's wealth (much of it also the state's) and the loyalty of his legions were in the hands of Mark Antony, Caesar's trusted lieutenant, and the surviving consul, supported by Marcus Aemilius Lepidus, master of the horse. Antony had assumed he was Caesar's heir, and was displaying all the signs of becoming the next dictator. The eventual reading of the will was an upset and he was cool in his reception of Octavius, who he called "the boy." Meanwhile, thanks to Antony, Marcus Junius Brutus and Gaius Cassius Longinus, the most reputable among Caesar's assassins, had been allowed to leave Rome as free men.

Antony's actions drove Octavius into the hands of the senatorial party, who felt they could use his name against Antony's naked ambition. Cicero—so opposed to the Caesarian faction—summed up their feelings when he said "praise [Octavius], honor him then get rid of him." In 43 BC Antony, feeling a cold wind blowing, went to his provincial command in Gaul. Cicero then persuaded the senate with a series of impassioned speeches (the Philippics) to send an army after him under the two consuls of the year, together with Octavius.

Antony moved back into Italy and the two armies met at Mutina (Modena), where Antony was defeated. However, the two consuls were killed in the action. Octavius seized control and demanded the consulship. The soldiers of the legions would follow any with the name Caesar—even though it was not yet legally his—so when the senate refused, Octavius marched on Rome and secured the consulship by force. He now officially became Gaius Julius Caesar Octavianus (Octavian), and basked in his unparalleled popularity among the armies in Italy and the *plebs* as Caesar's heir.

It seems apparent, however, that Octavian did not feel ready to tackle Antony and

44 BC	43 BC	42 BC	41 BC	40 BC	37 BC	36 BC	31 BC
Conspirators assassinate Gaius Julius Caesar	Octavian, Mark Antony, and Marcus Aemilius Lepidus form the Second Triumvirate	The conspirators against Caesar commit suicide on their defeat at Philippi, Macedonia	Mark Antony meets Cleopatra at Tarsus	Perusine War between Octavian and Lucius, brother of Mark Antony	Agrippa defeats Sextus, son of Pompey, on behalf of Octavian	Lepidus is stripped of power, leaving Octavian and Antony as co-rulers	Octavian is sole ruler after defeating Antony in a sea battle at Actium

Lepidus, who still commanded greater forces. Instead, the two sides settled their differences and met at Bononia (Bologna) in 43. The result, intended to present a united front against the senate and the assassins, was the *Triumviri reipublicae constituendae* (Triumvirs for the Regulation of the Republic). Unlike the First Triumvirate, the second was set up by law, and was effectively a joint dictatorship.

Virtually at sword point, the senate granted the triumvirs draconian powers to hunt down Caesar's killers. In the ensuing purge, more than 2,000 senators and knights were proscribed and executed, including Cicero. However, the real enemy was massing across the Adriatic under the banners of Brutus and Cassius.

Betrothals and betrayals

The triumvirs crossed the Adriatic in 42 and were victorious against Brutus and Cassius with 17 rebel legions at Philippi in Macedonia. Rather than risk capture, the assassins committed suicide. In the same year, Julius Caesar was deified and Octavian basked in reflected glory—the son of a god. Antony and Octavian now redistributed the empire between them. Octavian received Italy and the western provinces, which included the command against Sextus Pompey (son of Pompey the Great), who had seized Sicily. Antony took the east, and Lepidus was edged out by being given Africa.

Back in Rome, Octavian faced a new conflict. Known as the Perusine War, it was sparked when he attempted to settle the Philippi veterans on confiscated land. One of the consuls, Antony's brother Lucius backed by Antony's wife Fulvia, took up arms on behalf of the dispossessed Italians. After months of fighting, Lucius surrendered at Perusia (Perugia). Fulvia died shortly after. The conflict might have spiraled into full-scale civil war when Antony landed at Brundisium in 40, but both armies—all from Caesar's legions—forced the two men to make peace. The triumvirate was re-established and the division between east and west confirmed. To secure the partnership, Octavian married his sister Octavia to Antony.

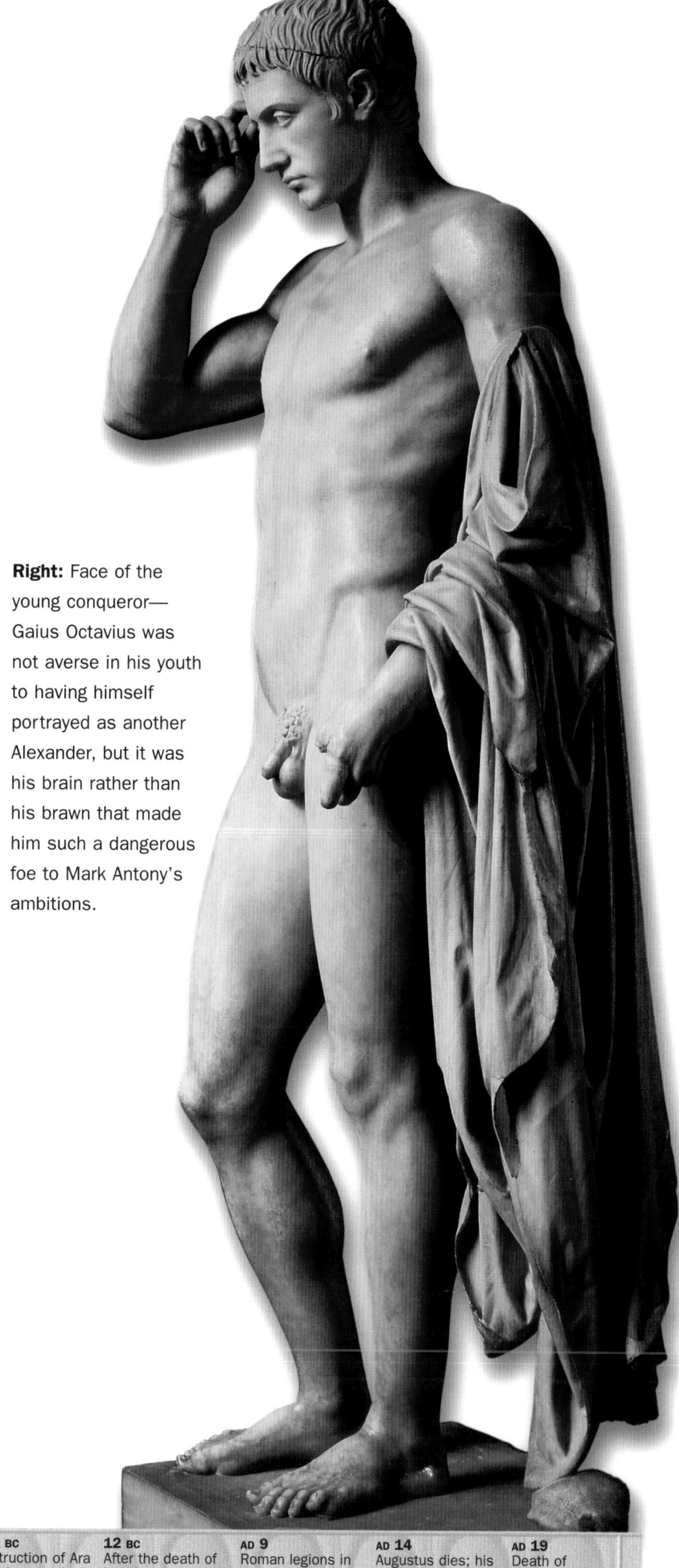

Right: Face of the young conqueror—Gaius Octavius was not averse in his youth to having himself portrayed as another Alexander, but it was his brain rather than his brawn that made him such a dangerous foe to Mark Antony's ambitions.

30 BC Suicide of Antony and Cleopatra; Egypt becomes a Roman province

27 BC Octavian changes his name to Augustus; end of the republic, start of the empire

26–25 BC Augustus reasserts Roman control of Spain and Gaul

13–9 BC Construction of Ara Pacis (peace altar), symbolic of the peace of Augustus's reign

12 BC After the death of Lepidus, Augustus becomes *pontifex maximus*

AD 9 Roman legions in Germany are decimated by tribes at Teutoberg Forest

AD 14 Augustus dies; his will names Tiberius as successor

AD 19 Death of Germanicus, co-consul, general, and heir to Tiberius

MASTER OF ROME

Antony and Octavian were united, but the divisions between them were evident. While Antony consorted with Cleopatra in Egypt, Octavian laid the groundwork to defeat his rival in battle.

Right: Marcus Vipsanius Agrippa (64–12 BC), lifelong supporter of Augustus and inspired general, was also a fine naval admiral.

Facing: The face of the conqueror—a statue of Augustus stands at Prima Porta, near Rome. The central scene on the breastplate depicts the recovery of an eagle from a defeated barbarian, although the meaning of the other figures is not clearly understood.

Sextus Pompey's occupation of Sicily had dried up Rome's grain supply and famine threatened. When complex peace overtures between Sextus, Antony, and Octavian failed, Antony left the matter in Octavian's hands and left for the east in 37 BC. Well served by his friend and fellow tribune of Caesar's, Marcus Vipsanius Agrippa, Octavian invaded Sicily. Agrippa's massive fleet swung the balance when it annihilated Pompey's at Naulochus in September 36. Sextus fled to join Antony in the east, while Octavian confronted Lepidus. He had brought his army from Africa for the campaign but now looked intent on taking Sicily for himself. The situation was critical, but Octavian gambled that the legions had little love for Lepidus. He persuaded the soldiers to desert and deposed Lepidus from the triumvirate.

In the east, Antony's campaign against the Parthians ended in failure in 36, and he returned to Alexandria... and his mistress Queen Cleopatra. This affair had started in 41 BC, when Antony summoned her to Tarsus to explain her actions since Caesar's death. Plutarch wrote of her exotic arrival: "She came sailing up on a galley whose stern was golden; the sails were purple, and the oars silver. The queen, in a dress and character of Aphrodite, lay on a couch of gold brocade, as though in a picture, while about her were pretty boys like cupids who fanned her."

Her effect on Antony may have been erotic, but a more plausible explanation lies in politics. At some point after 37 BC he married Cleopatra. This foreign wedding was not recognized in Rome—beyond contributing to a further deterioration in relations with Octavian—but to Egyptians, Antony had become their king. For Cleopatra, first Julius Caesar, now Antony, represented the power of Rome. But Rome was a force that had undercut the traditional means of maintaining Ptolemaic power in Egypt, which relied on an army of Greek mercenaries to keep the Egyptians in subjection. These were raised in the Greek lands, over which Rome was now master. Since the conquest, Egypt's military strength had declined. Using her charms on Caesar and Antony can be seen as a natural way of influencing Rome to give back some of Egypt's old recruiting grounds.

Ptolemaic Egypt

The Egypt of 30 BC was no longer in the hands of the ancient pharaohs. Already a part of the Persian empire, Alexander the Great conquered Egypt in 332 BC. Following Alexander's death in 323, his generals divided his empire, each setting up their own kingdoms.

In charge of Egypt, Ptolemy took the country as his share and ruled as Ptolemy I Soter. For the next three centuries, the Ptolemaic dynasty of the Greeks ruled Egypt, mingling Hellenistic tradition with the legacy of the pharaohs. Under them Alexandria grew prosperous, the center of a commercial empire that extended around the coast of Syria to the Aegean Sea.

However, it was rarely a peaceful city. The Ptolemies suffered endless family feuds while contending with the restless Egyptian population, held in subjection by hated armies of Greek mercenaries. Later successors failed to live up to the standards set by their forebears, and failed foreign policies brought Egypt increasingly under the influence of Rome.

Brash and overconfident

For Antony, he had a choice: stay in the east and create a new oriental Roman empire with Cleopatra, or invade the west and deal with Octavian. Being Antony, he wanted to combine both, on the grounds that if he failed in the west, he could always fall back on the east and hold it against Octavian.

Antony had goaded the Roman establishment in several ways: by (illegally) marrying a reigning monarch; by holding a sacred Roman triumph in Alexandria; by declaring Caesar's son Caesarion to be true ruler of the west; by humiliating his virtuous wife, Octavia. He had fathered twins with Cleopatra even before Octavia's second pregnancy and abandoned her in Italy to raise his two daughters. When he divorced Octavia, it was merely a formal end to an already dead marriage. Romans were outraged.

In Rome, Octavian had cleared the senate of the Antonian party, so he found little difficulty in rousing war talk. Antony's actions left himself vulnerable to his rival, who ably portrayed his former triumvir as either blind to reason or plain mad. Octavian determined to redeem Rome's honor and forced Italian citizens to swear allegiance to his cause (the *coiuratio Italiae*). Antony tried to enlist the support of Roman allies and client states. But he could not overcome the difficulty of being so far from the recruiting grounds in and around Rome, where the best soldiers were to be found.

War was declared in 32 and the following year the rivals' fleets clashed at Actium in the Ionian Sea. Under Agrippa's masterly command, Octavian's fleet was swiftly triumphant. Immediately, Octavian established his control over Antonine Greece and Asia Minor. He then invaded Egypt. Cornered in 30, Antony and Cleopatra committed suicide. Octavian ordered the death of Caesarion, thereby removing a legitimate contender for Roman rule. Egypt became imperial property, and Octavian was master of Rome's empire.

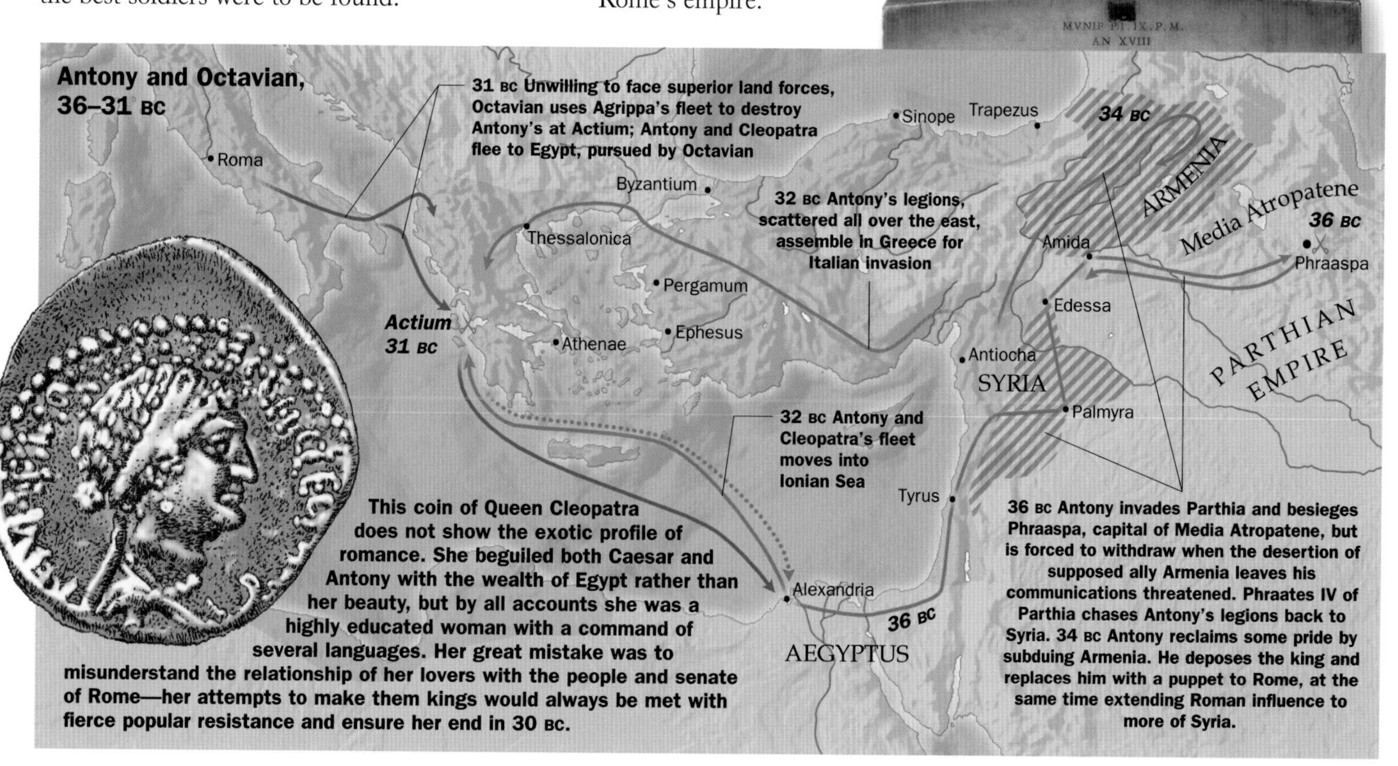
Antony and Octavian, 36–31 BC
31 BC Unwilling to face superior land forces, Octavian uses Agrippa's fleet to destroy Antony's at Actium; Antony and Cleopatra flee to Egypt, pursued by Octavian
32 BC Antony's legions, scattered all over the east, assemble in Greece for Italian invasion
32 BC Antony and Cleopatra's fleet moves into Ionian Sea
36 BC Antony invades Parthia and besieges Phraaspa, capital of Media Atropatene, but is forced to withdraw when the desertion of supposed ally Armenia leaves his communications threatened. Phraates IV of Parthia chases Antony's legions back to Syria. 34 BC Antony reclaims some pride by subduing Armenia. He deposes the king and replaces him with a puppet to Rome, at the same time extending Roman influence to more of Syria.
Roma
Byzantium
Thessalonica
Pergamum
Actium
31 BC
Athenae
Ephesus
Sinope
Trapezus
34 BC
ARMENIA
Media Atropatene
36 BC
Phraaspa
Amida
Edessa
Antiocha
SYRIA
PARTHIAN EMPIRE
Palmyra
Tyrus
Alexandria
36 BC
AEGYPTUS

This coin of Queen Cleopatra does not show the exotic profile of romance. She beguiled both Caesar and Antony with the wealth of Egypt rather than her beauty, but by all accounts she was a highly educated woman with a command of several languages. Her great mistake was to misunderstand the relationship of her lovers with the people and senate of Rome—her attempts to make them kings would always be met with fierce popular resistance and ensure her end in 30 BC.

The Imperial Throne

Although he aspired to absolute power, Octavian had learned from the mistakes of his adoptive father Caesar and opted for a subtle approach to politics. He gradually acquired titles, respect, and absolute power.

Facing: Face of the priest—in his role of *pontifex maximus,* Augustus symbolized republican religious traditions. He was responsible for the revival of many ancient festivals and the restoration of numerous temples. Among his new projects, the Temple of Apollo, **below**, was later incorporated into Domitian's palace.

Drawing a halt to his momentum after Actium, Octavian graciously offered the power that lay in his grasp to the senate, and in doing so appeared benign and bountiful. He avoided the overt dictatorship of Caesar and instead ruled in the guise of a constitutional *princeps* (first citizen, the literal meaning of the word "prince"). The senate responded just as he had hoped, by offering him more authority than ever before. Crucially, Octavian held these new powers for an unlimited time.

His own position was arbitrary, although backed by the power of the legions. In return for handing the state back to the senate, he was awarded an *imperium* that included Gaul, Spain, Syria, and Cilicia, which he would govern through his legates. This legalized his position in a manner that had clear republican precedents. In a continuing modest manner, he courted senate, reiterating all the while that its main function was to advise rather than rule. Had he stepped outside the law, he might have lost the core support of the *plebs*, the non-political aristocrats of Rome, and the army. But he stayed within acceptable boundaries, seeming to personify parsimony and moderation.

On January 16, 27 BC Octavian changed his name to Augustus (noble one). It was the first of a string of honors conferred by a respectful senate. Augustus became senate speaker, dictator for life, life consul, life tribune, *pater patriae*, and, from March 6, 12 BC, *pontifex maximus*. He now held all the significant posts of government and the population developed a psychological dependency on him, similar to that once fostered for the republic. Most importantly, he was commander-in-chief of the army and strictly controlled the careers of its generals. There may

have been politicians at least as able as Augustus, but none was permitted to shine as brightly, and so none presented himself.

Gradually, Augustus absorbed more of the mechanics of government by employing men of the *equites* as semi-professional administrators. At first they were his personal *procuratores* (agents), but increasingly they became financial adminstrators and provincial governors, posts once the gift of the senate to patricians.

That a people drilled in the rewards of republicanism should permit a takeover, even one carried out by stealth, is not such a mystery. Consider the plight of ordinary Romans, who had seen a century of unprecedented domestic violence. As more men were recruited into the army, vast tracts of land lay untended, causing economic hardship and shortages. The republic had offered no comfort in difficult times, while the reign of Augustus heralded peace and stability. Under his auspices there was a new era of enhanced personal safety and recourse to law.

Encouraging marriage

In 29 the doors of the Janus temple in Rome remained closed, official recognition that a state of peace existed. As if to underscore the new era, work on Rome's Ara Pacis, the peace altar, began in 13, taking four years to complete. For the 4,063,000 Roman citizens throughout the empire who had been buffeted by civil and foreign wars, this was good news indeed.

Among other reforms, Augustus revived religious festivals that had fallen into disuse, filled the gaping vacancies in the priesthoods, and repaired Rome's sacred buildings (*see page 90*). He introduced laws designed to curb divorce and make adultery a criminal offense. In 18 and 17 BC he imposed penalties on the *plebs* and especially the *equites* for remaining unmarried. There were rewards for those couple who produced children. These marriage laws may have been designed to counter a worrying drop in the birth rate of Roman citizens, but it is more probable that they were intended to regulate the lifestyle of the aristocrats, whose decadent lifestyle in the late republic had become notorious.

After a plot against his life was uncovered in 23, Augustus took practical steps to ensure his survival. He made the Praetorian Guards his personal bodyguards (*see following page*), while keeping the senate unarmed. But there appears to have been no significant threat to his regime, at least none that gathered any measure of popular support.

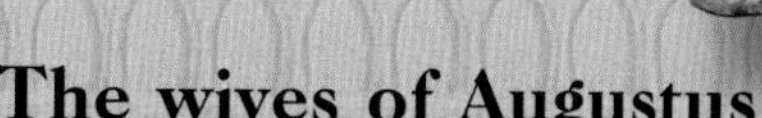

The wives of Augustus

During the peace overtures with Sextus Pompey in 39, Octavian had agreed to marry Scribonia, a relative of Pompey's. This political expedient was doomed to failure, since the two were ill-matched and war shortly seemed inevitable. He divorced Scribonia in 38, when she was pregnant with his daughter (Julia), and married Livia Drusilla (58 BC–AD 29). Livia (a bust of her pictured left) was a member of the powerful and ancient Claudian family, daughter of Marcus Livia Drusus Claudius. She married her cousin, Tiberius Claudius Nero, when she was 16. She bore one son, Tiberius, and was pregnant with a second (Drusus) when she divorced Tiberius and married Octavian. Whether the divorce and remarriage was a political or a love match is not known. But the abruptness of the marriage caused a scandal that Octavian had to live down. Livia had no children by Augustus, which partly explains the succession problems that followed, but the marriage lasted, spanning 52 turbulent years until Augustus's death in AD 14.

THE PRAETORIAN GUARD

Starting out as the personal guard of a Roman consul on campaign, the Praetorian Guard became an elite force under Augustus. In time, under successive imperial dynasties, the Praetorians grew into a military power that shaped imperial policy, including the making and deposing of emperors.

The first mention of the Praetorians is in 133 BC. Scipio Aemilianus—the man who finally destroyed Carthage in the Third Punic War—was engaged in a siege of the Celtiberian stronghold of Numantia, in Spain. He formed a personal bodyguard that became known as the *cohors praetoria*, after the *praetorium*, the area of a Roman camp in which the consul-general's tent was pitched. By the fall of the republic it was customary for all generals to have a cohort of Praetorian Guards, usually raised specifically for the campaign in hand and dismissed at its conclusion. Most were from the infantry, although the more experienced could apply to become knights or *equites*.

It was Augustus who elevated the Praetorians to a pivotal position within the military hierarchy. He combined the Guard of his defeated opponent Antony with his own to form a total of nine cohorts consisting of 4,500, with a small mounted contingent. These were stationed in and around Rome to be deployed immediately in the event of civil unrest. To encourage their loyalty, he reduced the length of service by a quarter (12 years, as opposed to 16 in the legions), and by AD 14 was paying them treble the standard annual wage of 225 denarii. It is little surprise that the Praetorians began to see themselves in a strong bargaining position.

Loyalty to Augustus was strengthened through daily contact. At first there was no overall command other than that of Augustus. In 2 BC Augustus appointed two equestrian *praefecti praetorio* (praetorian prefects) to take joint control. Every afternoon one *praefectus* received the day's watchword from the emperor in person at his palace on the Palatine. When he had business in the city, units of the Guard escorted him and his family, mingling with the crowds, ready to quash trouble. They rarely appeared in armor—a sop to old republican sentiments—but were easily identifiable from the formal cut of their togas.

At some point during the reign of Tiberius, the joint praefecti split into a hierarchy, with one becoming the senior—a situation that among the legions was natural became a cause for ambitious powermongering in the Praetorians. Because of

Left: The Ara Pacis illustrates scenes from the new Augustan age of peace and prosperity, much of which was maintained by the presence of the Praetorian Guard.

Facing: A Praetorian Guard from the Arch of Trajan showing that—in Rome at least—Praetorians wore tunic and *pallium*, rather than full body armor. In later imperial times, the Praetorians were responsible for the murder of several emperors, including the insane Commodus, seen **below** as a youth, whose death resulted in a period of chaos for Rome.

their access to the imperial court, the character of a Praetorian had to be beyond question. Applicants were expected to produce excellent references and prove they came from the "right" family. Given the Guard's later history, the merit of this vetting has to be questioned.

Buying into office

Praetorian Guard officers were directly responsible for the murders of the emperors Commodus, Pertinax, Elagabus, Balbinus, and Maximus, and in the later empire the *praefectus* could virtually make or break an emperor at whim. One of the most famous episodes was orchestrated by *praefectus* Laetus, who had the paranoiacally insane Commodus strangled on New Year's Eve 192 (*see page 138*). Laetus then put Pertinax in power, only to have him murdered three months later.

As the Roman historian Cassius Dio put it, "Thus ensued a most disgraceful business and one unworthy of Rome. For, just as if it had been in some market or auction room, both the city and its entire empire were auctioned off." The soldiers conducted bidding in their Praetorian Camp, on the Viminal, egging on the two main rivals to come up with bigger cash bribes. In the end, city prefect Titus Flavius Sulpicianus lost out to the wealthy senator Didius Severus Julianus, who agreed to pay each man some 25,000 sestertii each (the entire career income of a legionary private)—a total equivalent value of ten tons of gold.

Unfortunately for Julianus, the Danube legions had already elected their Pannonian governor, Lucius Septimius Severus, as the new emperor. Severus marched on Rome, where he tricked the Praetorians into leaving the *castra praetoria*, their fortified camp on the northeast side of Rome, unarmed. They were promptly replaced with his own Germanic troops.

Roman documents of the third century AD say comparatively little about Praetorian activities. Senior officers continued to meddle in imperial succession and were not beyond murdering prospective emperors. However, when Constantine fought his way to the throne in 312, one of his first acts was to abolish it.

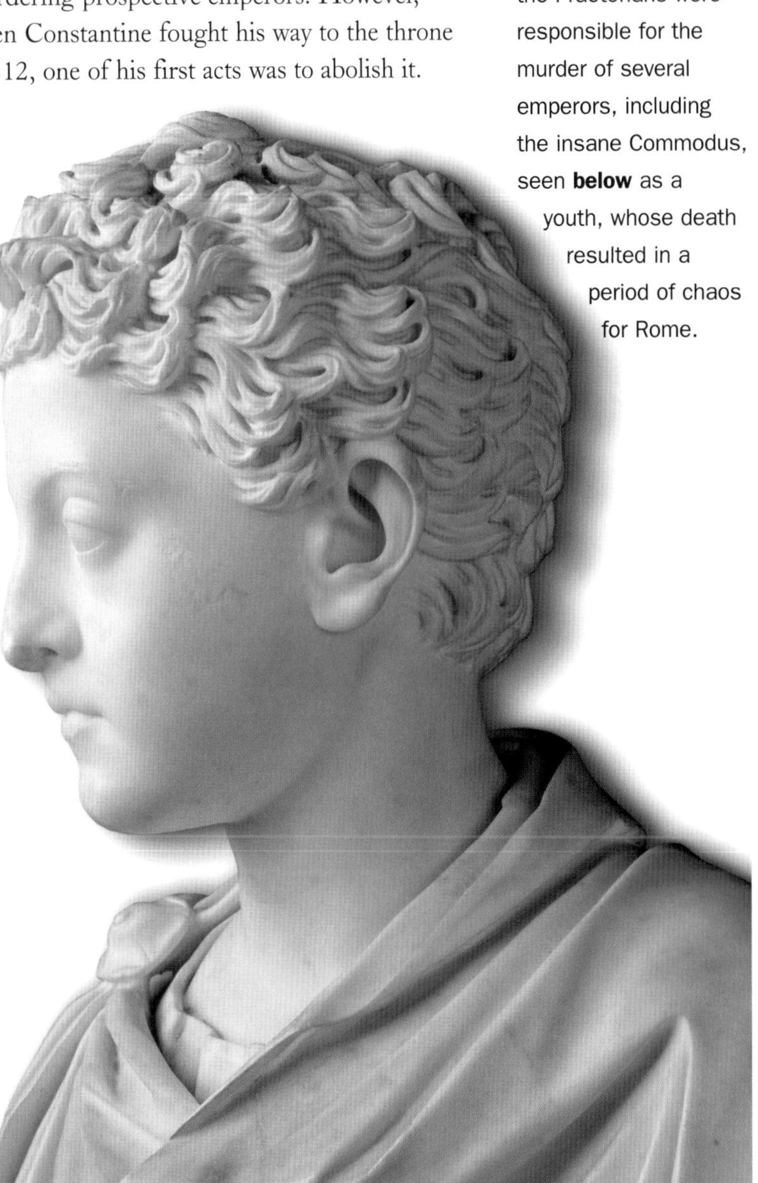

A New Empire

Julius Caesar had drawn up reconstruction plans for Rome, some of which were already underway at the time of his death. Augustus now continued the program, adding his own projects to revitalize Roman morale by restoring the city's fabric.

Below: The Theater of Marcellus stands at the edge of the Campus Martius, close to the Tiber at the foot of the Capitoline. Construction was started under Caesar and completed by Augustus, who dedicated it to the memory of his nephew Marcellus. Only the two lower tiers of the rear semi-circle survive today.

Under Augustan guidance, the architectural overhaul that was transforming Rome continued until it befitted an imperial age. Augustus claimed to have repaired no less than 82 temples during 28 BC. On the Campus Martius (Field of Mars), he repaired Pompey's Theater and two new ones were built, the Theater of Marcellus and the Theater of Balbus. In the same district, Agrippa built the Pantheon (later completely rebuilt by Hadrian) and the first of Rome's great public baths (*see also pages 140–1*). Agrippa also repaired the old aqueducts and built a new one, the Aqua Virgo.

Augustus also built an aqueduct, the Aqua Alsietina, constructed to supply an artificial lake for naval displays. The Temple of Apollo on the Palatine, Forum of Augustus, and Temple of Mars Ultor were only the most obvious of his prestige buildings. Augustus divided the city into 14 districts, each with its own administrative and technical services, and access to a fire brigade (*vigiles*). He found the funding for this mammoth program from the taxes channeled back to Rome from well-governed provinces. Augustus was said to have boasted that he found the city in brick and left it in marble.

Enriched culture helped to smooth the way for the Augustan age. Remarkable writers including Horace, Virgil, and Livy came to prominence under the patronage of Maecenas, a loyal aristocrat who operated a literary stable on behalf of the emperor. Critics have been quick to point out the propaganda value of Virgil's *Aeneid*, which celebrated Roman heroes and implied a divine progress for the empire, rather than one wrought by humans (*for more on Roman literature, see pages 130–3*).

Within his family, however, there were problems. The worst, to the man who proposed

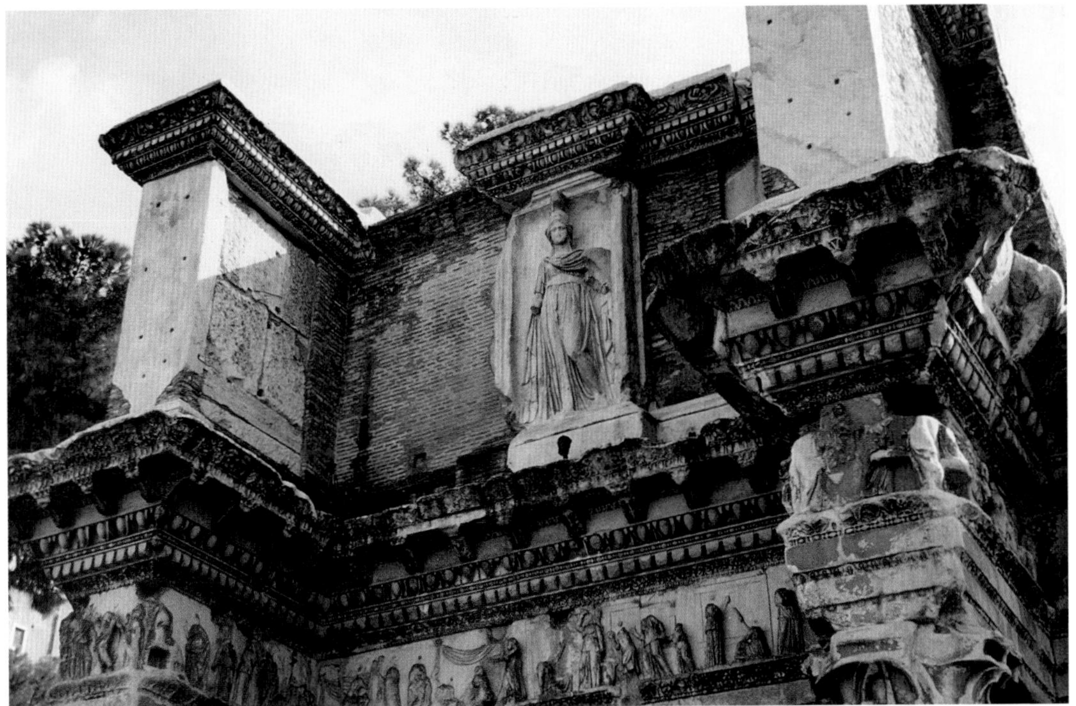

Left: A detail from the wall of the Forum of Augustus, seen from the Imperial Way, which now bisects the forae of Nerva, Augustus, and Trajan, and almost covers that of Julius Caesar. Augustus was the first to use a new source of white marble in northern Italy at Luna (Carrara). He also imported colored marbles from all over the provinces, which added new luster to Roman public building.

marriage and chastity laws, was that of his only daughter, Julia. Her sexual conduct became so scandalous that in 2 BC she was banished to a small island. In his will Augustus decreed that neither Julia nor her daughter of the same name should share his mausoleum in the Campus Martius.

Finding the limits

There was success abroad as well. Augustus mopped up the last vestiges of opposition in Gaul. He personally oversaw a campaign in Spain (26–5 BC). Ongoing difficulties presented by Parthia were exacerbated by the presence of a pro-Parthian king in Armenia, a state separating the warring empires.

Before taking sole command in Rome, Augustus had seen several attempts at conquering Parthia fail. He decided against mounting an attack and contented himself by installing a pro-Roman king in Armenia, while keeping the frontiers peaceful. Augustus also sponsored an expedition to Ethiopia, with exploitation of its resources in mind. Clearly the rewards of the venture were limited, since he withdrew from that corner of Africa, never to return.

Toward the end of his long life Augustus suffered a military reverse that left him reeling. Three Roman legions pushing across the Rhine in AD 9 under Varus, governor of Germany, were slaughtered almost to a man in battle by Arminius's Germanic tribes at Teutoberg Forest. Augustus was grief-stricken at the loss of the eagles and the ignominious label of failure. Insecurity swept the capital, inspiring a program of emergency army conscription. Augustus abandoned the policy of expansion and ordered his stepson Tiberius to do the same. For now, the limits of empire had been found.

Augustus died in Nola, to the east of Naples, in AD 14. According to accepted legend, he asked for a mirror, adjusted himself, and then asked assembled relations and advisors if they believed he had performed his part in the comedy of life well. He then quoted a familiar Greek poem, finishing with the line, "The play has ended, applaud!"

Augustus is remembered for many military triumphs, architectural legacies, and the internal harmony that was now the hallmark of the Roman empire. He had insufficient talent or color to be drawn as a heroic figure, yet he made the most of all he possessed, namely patience, determination, and steadfastness. He benefited enormously from good fortune. A personal achievement was that Augustus died in his bed, one of few Roman rulers to do so.

Below: The Mausoleum of Augustus is today a sad jumble of circular walls tightly shut into a small urban square. Although later enclosed by the Aurelian Wall, at the time it stood on the Campus Martius, outside the old Servian Wall and so outside Rome's sacred *pomerium*, inside of which no burials were allowed.

TIBERIUS

Having established an empire, Augustus was faced with the succession of his dynasty. As it happened, Augustus outlived most of his adopted descendants. On his death, his stepson Tiberius was the only Augustan candidate left alive.

Right: Augustus had never liked or approved of Tiberius, but in the end he was forced to accept him as his heir.

Below: A fragment of a cameo brooch depicts Livia and Tiberius. The relative sizes of the two figures was probably designed to show motherly love for her son, but effectively symbolizes the dominance Livia had over Tiberius for most of his life. Her ambition to make Tiberius the next emperor drove her to many lengths, including—according to Suetonius—the murder of any who stood in her way.

Born in 42 BC, Tiberius Claudius Nero Caesar (r.AD 14–37) was a compromise candidate—and he knew it. Augustus favored the sons of Julia, his daughter from his marriage to Scribonia. In 25 BC Julia married Marcellus, Augustus's nephew by his sister Octavia, but was quickly widowed. For her second husband Augustus chose his loyal friend Marcus Agrippa. Julia bore him three sons and two daughters, and the two eldest boys, Gaius and Lucius, were lauded as the heirs apparent.

Augustus's marriage to Livia Drusilla brought him two stepsons, Tiberius and Drusus. Both were successful generals in campaigns in Germany and the Balkans and were apparently content to remain in the political backwoods, to Livia's disgust. However, on Agrippa's death in 12 BC, Augustus cultivated one or both as regent, in case he should die before Gaius and Lucius came of age.

Augustus believed Tiberius arrogant and disagreeable, but convinced himself and those around him that this was merely an unfortunate manner. He forced Tiberius to divorce his wife Vipsania in favor of the widowed Julia. The ending of this love match distressed Tiberius but nevertheless his second wedding went ahead in 11 BC. It was an unhappy marriage and Tiberius had little affection for his precocious stepsons. Their brother, Agrippa Postumus, was so unlikeable that he was soon exiled. Tiberius withdrew into self-imposed exile on the island of Rhodes. And there he might have remained, but for the untimely deaths of Gaius and Lucius in the opening years of the first century. With his brother Drusus already dead, Tiberius alone was in line for the emperor's throne.

Augustus adopted Tiberius on June 26, AD 4, and instructed him to adopt Nero Claudius Germanicus. Germanicus was the son of his brother Drusus and a direct descendant of Julius Caesar on his mother's side. According to Suetonius, Germanicus was handsome, brave, intelligent, inspirational, and a perfect candidate for emperor.

An inauspicious successor

There was speculation—fueled by Suetonius—that Livia had a hand in the deaths of all those supposed to accede to the throne, in order to protect the position of her son, Tiberius. It is even mooted that she killed Augustus, by offering him poisoned figs. This protracted campaign—beginning with Marcellus in 23 BC and ending with Augustus in AD 14—may have taken place but it seems more likely those involved fell victim to disease.

Tiberius became emperor at the age of 54, inheriting power without precedent. According to Suetonius, "He was large and strong of frame, and of a stature above the average.... He strode along with his neck stiff and bent forward, usually with a stern countenance and for the most part in silence, never or very rarely conversing with his companions." His most pressing task was to dispose of the exiled Agrippa Postumus, the remaining adopted son of Augustus, who was speedily put to death.

Although Tiberius began his time as emperor with a disinterested approach to the senate, antagonism brewed between them. His reign began with unrest among the armed forces who spotted a fine opportunity to press for increased pay. Augustus's fears that his successor was plodding and unimaginative appear well grounded; the 23 years of Tiberius's reign were marked by a lack of creation and innovation. By any standards, he was ill-suited to the role of emperor, and even from its earliest years there was little to recommend his rule. He had no taste for public life and actively disliked spectacles and games, on which the crowds thrived. If this did not earn the enmity of the people, a massive rise in taxes did. He was, of course, already enormously wealthy, having inherited the extensive Augustan fortune.

Food and drink in the empire

The popular Hollywood image of vast feasts consisting of endless fanciful dishes accompanied by flowing wine is misleading. While the author and wit Petronius described such culinary orgies at the time of Nero, the general diet of Romans was frugal in the extreme; certainly Augustus and Tiberius were both simple eaters.

Romans usually ate one main meal a day, with breakfast (*ientaculum*) little more than a piece of bread and lunch (*prandium*) very light. The main meal (*cena*) was eaten at about sunset. For the well off, *cena* consisted of three courses: an appetizer (*gustatio*) of raw vegetables, eggs, and possibly fish or shellfish; a main course (*prima mensa*) of cooked vegetables and meats; and a dessert (*secunda mensa*) of sweet pastries and cakes, or fruit. Most meals of the poor consisted of cereals in the form of porridge, with a limited amount of vegetables when available and affordable, and meat only rarely (*see also legionary diets, page 109*).

Wine was the common Roman drink, always diluted with water (drinking undiluted wine was considered barbaric), with the poor drinking *posca*, made by watering down a low-quality vinegary wine called *acetum*. Milk was not drunk, and used only for making cheese. Another common liquid was *garum*, made by fermenting fish intestines. This strong sauce was used in all forms of cooking, including desserts.

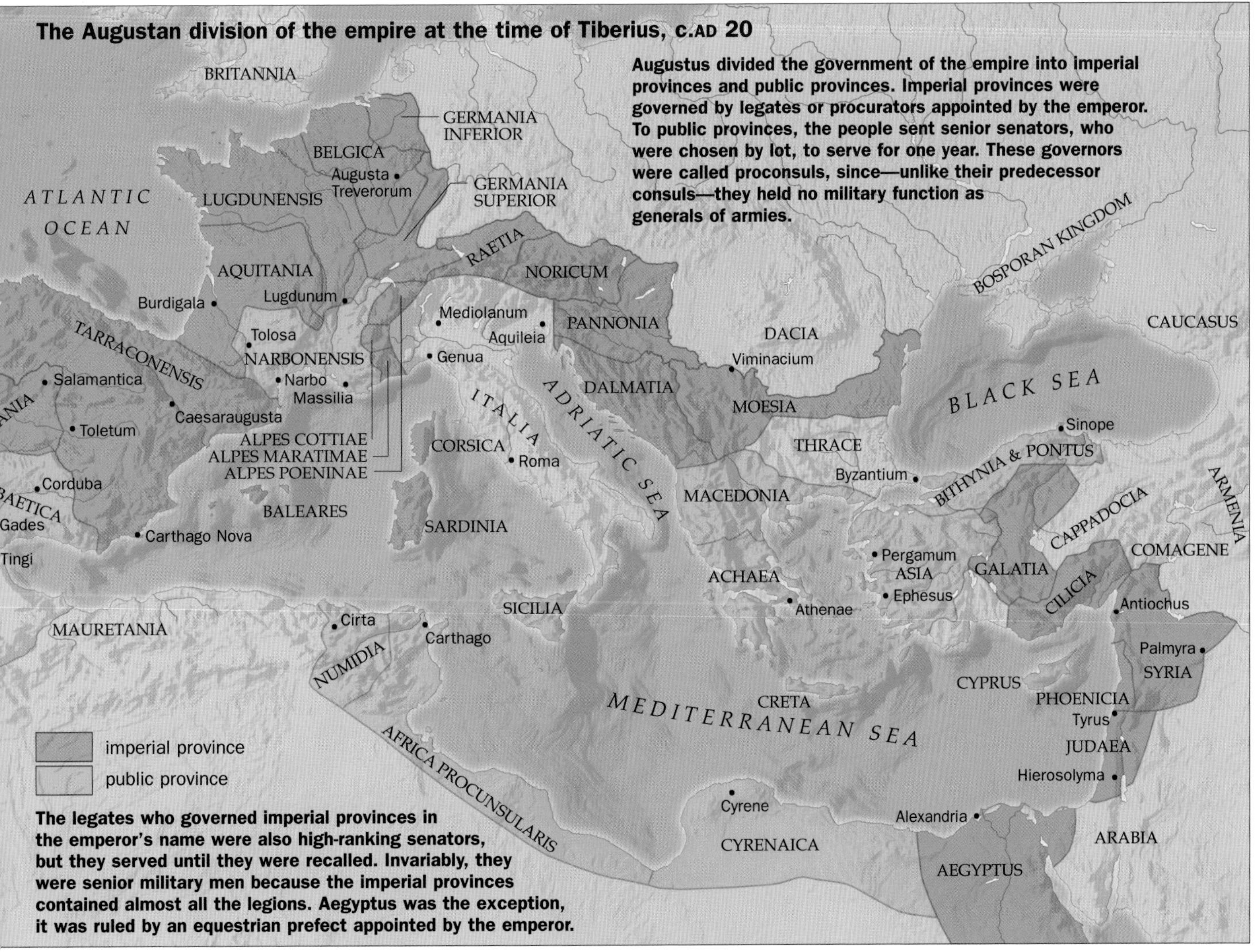
BRITANNIA
GERMANIA INFERIOR
BELGICA
Augusta Treverorum
GERMANIA SUPERIOR
ATLANTIC OCEAN
LUGDUNENSIS
RAETIA
NORICUM
AQUITANIA
Burdigala
Lugdunum
Mediolanum
PANNONIA
Aquileia
TARRACONENSIS
Tolosa
NARBONENSIS
Genua
Salamantica
Narbo
Massilia
Caesaraugusta
Toletum
ALPES COTTIAE
ALPES MARATIMAE
ALPES POENINAE
CORSICA
ITALIA
Roma
ADRIATIC SEA
DALMATIA
DACIA
Viminacium
MOESIA
BOSPORAN KINGDOM
CAUCASUS
BLACK SEA
Sinope
THRACE
Byzantium
BITHYNIA & PONTUS
ARMENIA
Corduba
BAETICA
Gades
BALEARES
Carthago Nova
SARDINIA
MACEDONIA
CAPPADOCIA
Tingi
Pergamum
ASIA
Ephesus
GALATIA
COMAGENE
ACHAEA
Athenae
CILICIA
Antiochus
SICILIA
MAURETANIA
Cirta
Carthago
NUMIDIA
Palmyra
SYRIA
CYPRUS
CRETA
MEDITERRANEAN SEA
PHOENICIA
Tyrus
JUDAEA
Hierosolyma
AFRICA PROCUNSULARIS
Cyrene
CYRENAICA
Alexandria
AEGYPTUS
ARABIA
imperial province
public province

The Augustan division of the empire at the time of Tiberius, c.AD 20

Augustus divided the government of the empire into imperial provinces and public provinces. Imperial provinces were governed by legates or procurators appointed by the emperor. To public provinces, the people sent senior senators, who were chosen by lot, to serve for one year. These governors were called proconsuls, since—unlike their predecessor consuls—they held no military function as generals of armies.

The legates who governed imperial provinces in the emperor's name were also high-ranking senators, but they served until they were recalled. Invariably, they were senior military men because the imperial provinces contained almost all the legions. Aegyptus was the exception, it was ruled by an equestrian prefect appointed by the emperor.

Imperial Intrigue

Tiberius did not relish his exalted position; in fact, there's every indication he resented oppressive power. His task was made more difficult by his rampantly suspicious mind, which sent many unwitting rivals to their unnecessary deaths.

Livia had been made Augusta by the terms of her husband's will, but Tiberius had no intention of permitting her undue power. He ignored her claims and effectively sidelined her. Relations deteriorated so badly that at her death in AD 29 aged 86 he refused to attend the funeral, nor would he abide by her final wishes.

Meanwhile, Germanicus was leading the successful campaign in Germany that gave him his cognomen. Redeeming Roman pride after the Teutoberg disaster of AD 9 and shouldered by the support of the army, he appeared poised for ultimate power. However, he showed every sign of remaining loyal to Tiberius. However, Germanicus fell ill and died in 19 on a trip to the East, allegedly poisoned by the Syrian leaders who some believed to have been in the pay of Tiberius.

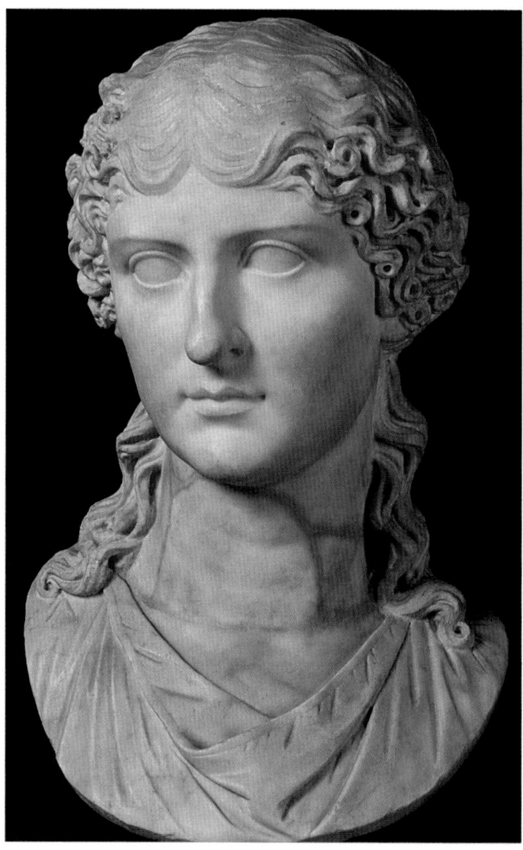

Right: Agrippina (the Elder, c.14 BC–AD 33) was the daughter of Marcus Agrippa. She had nine children, including Agrippina the Younger, who was later the mother of Nero, and Gaius Caligula. Her vendetta against Tiberius in the belief that he had her husband Germanicus killed led to her exile on the island of Pandateria, where she starved herself to death.

Right: Nero Claudius Germanicus, later Germanicus Julius Caesar (15 BC–AD 19), undertook two campaigns against the Germans (AD 14–16, 17) and was Rome's finest general of the period. It was in Germany that his legionaries took to calling his baby son Gaius "Caligula" because of the tiny soldier's boots (*caligae*) he customarily wore. Germanicus died in suspicious circumstances in Antioch.

Although his mother Agrippina had no proof, she began a life-long vendetta against Tiberius. He endured her damaging whispering campaign for a decade before having the senate banish her and two of her sons from Rome. Consequently they were either murdered or driven to suicide. The third son Gaius called Caligula (little boots), too young to be a threat, was kept in seclusion alongside the emperor.

At the age of 67, Tiberius withdrew from public life to the island of Capri. Lucius Aelius Sejanus, commander of the Praetorian Guard, seized the opportunity to become chief powerbroker. He persuaded Tiberius to stay away from Rome while he built his empire within an empire, filling top jobs with appointees loyal to him. He was involved together with his lover Livilla, widow of Germanicus, in the death by poison of Tiberius's son Drusus.

The emperor no longer had access to old constitutional methods to control Sejanus, so he artfully employed another ambitious Praetorian officer, Naevius Sutorius Macro, to fell Sejanus. Macro replaced the Praetorian Guard with ordinary soldiers before arresting Sejanus, who was hauled away to his death. From this act, the reign never shook off its oppressive atmosphere engendered by accusation and denunciation. When Tiberius died on March 16, 37 there were celebrations in the streets and calls for his body to be tossed into the Tiber as if he were a common criminal. However, it has to be said that, thanks in part to his own miserly instincts, Tiberius left imperial finances in even better shape than had Augustus.

Above: Gaius Julius Caesar Germanicus Caligula (AD 12–41) was the first Roman emperor to display the alarming effects of absolute power, but far from the last. The reasons for his assassination are legion, but his habit of giving the manly Praetorian Guards watchwords like "kiss me quick" did not help his cause.

Caligula's reign of terror

From the age of 18, Caligula (r.AD 37–41) had lived on Capri with Tiberius, who harbored few illusions about his young nephew, acidly remarking that he was "rearing a viper for the Roman people." His young, sickly cousin Tiberius Gemellus had the better right to the throne, but Macro saw more opportunity for himself in courting Caligula. Besides, the son of the heroic Germanicus and a descendant of Antony and Octavia had the pedigree to attract Romans eager for a new rule, and he was confirmed as emperor.

At first Caligula seemed like sunshine after the rain. He abolished the unpopular sales tax, staged public shows, and emphatically ended the hostility and suspicion that had prevailed in government. Alas, this enlightenment lasted but a few months. Caligula fell ill—the details of the affliction remain hazy—but, when he recovered, he was a changed man. Suetonius referred to him as "Caligula, the monster." He began to live in lavish splendor and soon squandered the colossal wealth left him by Tiberius. When new levels of taxation proved insufficient, Caligula persecuted aristocrats in order to seize their land and money.

His capriciousness knew no bounds. He rode roughshod over the senate, and outraged everyone by making his favorite horse Incitatus a consul. He organized an invasion of Britain, but on the coast of Gaul ordered the legionaries to collect seashells, then proclaimed a triumph in Rome for his victory over Neptune. He dressed in exotic garb, including women's clothing, and frequently presented himself as a god. He had Macro executed to be replaced by a more malleable Praetorian. On her death in 38, he made his favorite sister Drusilla (with whom he was rumored to have incestuous relations) into a goddess.

After just four years as emperor, knife-wielding assassins killed Caligula during the last day of the Palatine Games. His body was hastily disposed of and the name Caligula swiftly erased from the records. His cherished last wife Milonia Caesonia and their daughter Julia Drusilla were both slain immediately after him. Once again, there was a vacuum, and the Praetorian Guard filled it.

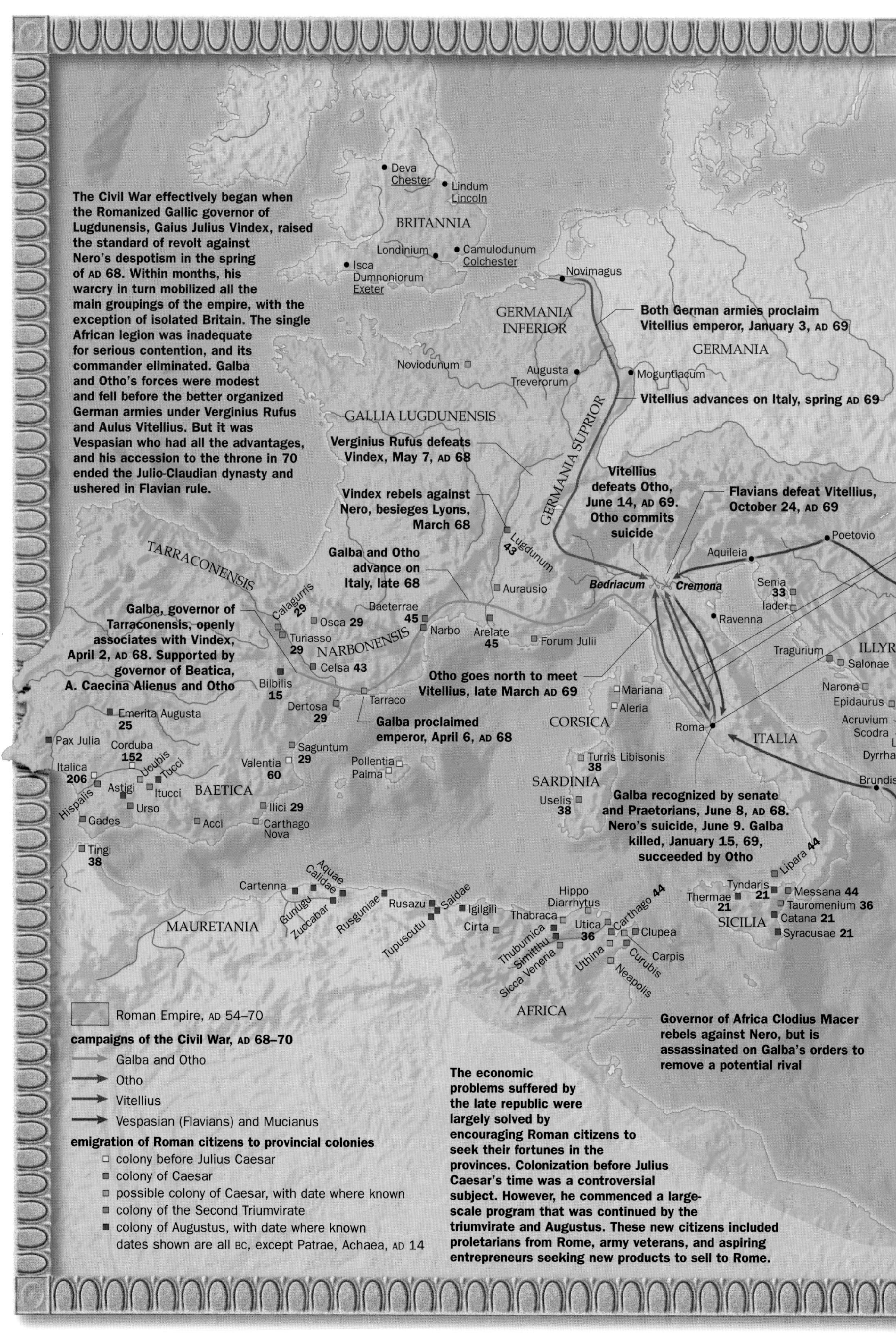
The Civil War effectively began when the Romanized Gallic governor of Lugdunensis, Gaius Julius Vindex, raised the standard of revolt against Nero's despotism in the spring of AD 68. Within months, his warcry in turn mobilized all the main groupings of the empire, with the exception of isolated Britain. The single African legion was inadequate for serious contention, and its commander eliminated. Galba and Otho's forces were modest and fell before the better organized German armies under Verginius Rufus and Aulus Vitellius. But it was Vespasian who had all the advantages, and his accession to the throne in 70 ended the Julio-Claudian dynasty and ushered in Flavian rule.
Deva
Chester
Lindum
Lincoln
BRITANNIA
Londinium
Camulodunum
Colchester
Isca Dumnoniorum
Exeter
Novimagus
Both German armies proclaim Vitellius emperor, January 3, AD 69
GERMANIA INFERIOR
GERMANIA
Noviodunum
Augusta Treverorum
Moguntiacum
Vitellius advances on Italy, spring AD 69
GALLIA LUGDUNENSIS
GERMANIA SUPRIOR
Verginius Rufus defeats Vindex, May 7, AD 68
Vindex rebels against Nero, besieges Lyons, March 68
Vitellius defeats Otho, June 14, AD 69. Otho commits suicide
Flavians defeat Vitellius, October 24, AD 69
Poetovio
TARRACONENSIS
Galba and Otho advance on Italy, late 68
Lugdunum 43
Aquileia
Bedriacum
Cremona
Auraúsio
Senia 33
Iader
Ravenna
Galba, governor of Tarraconensis, openly associates with Vindex, April 2, AD 68. Supported by governor of Beatica, A. Caecina Alienus and Otho
Calagurris 29
Osca 29
Baeterrae 45
Turiasso 29
NARBONENSIS
Narbo
Arelate 45
Forum Julii
Celsa 43
Tragurium
Salonae
ILLYRI
Bilbilis 15
Otho goes north to meet Vitellius, late March AD 69
Narona
Epidaurus
Dertosa 29
Tarraco
Mariana
Aleria
Emerita Augusta 25
Galba proclaimed emperor, April 6, AD 68
CORSICA
Roma
Acruvium
Scodra
Pax Julia
Corduba 152
Ucubis
Tucci
Saguntum 29
ITALIA
Dyrrhac
Italica 206
Valentia 60
Pollentia
Palma
Turris Libisonis 38
Brundis
Hispalis
Astigi
Itucci
BAETICA
SARDINIA
Urso
Ilici 29
Uselis 38
Galba recognized by senate and Praetorians, June 8, AD 68. Nero's suicide, June 9. Galba killed, January 15, 69, succeeded by Otho
Gades
Acci
Carthago Nova
Tingi 38
Lipara 44
Aquae Calidae
Cartenna
Hippo Diarrhytus
Tyndaris 21
Thermae 21
Messana 44
Rusazu
Saldae
Igilgili
Carthago 44
Tauromenium 36
Gunugu
Zuccabar
Rusguniae
Thabraca
SICILIA
Catana 21
MAURETANIA
Tupusuctu
Cirta
Utica 36
Clupea
Syracusae 21
Thuburnica
Simitthu
Sicca Veneria
Uthina
Curubis
Carpis
Neapolis
AFRICA
Governor of Africa Clodius Macer rebels against Nero, but is assassinated on Galba's orders to remove a potential rival
Roman Empire, AD 54–70
campaigns of the Civil War, AD 68–70
Galba and Otho
Otho
Vitellius
Vespasian (Flavians) and Mucianus
emigration of Roman citizens to provincial colonies
colony before Julius Caesar
colony of Caesar
possible colony of Caesar, with date where known
colony of the Second Triumvirate
colony of Augustus, with date where known
dates shown are all BC, except Patrae, Achaea, AD 14
The economic problems suffered by the late republic were largely solved by encouraging Roman citizens to seek their fortunes in the provinces. Colonization before Julius Caesar's time was a controversial subject. However, he commenced a large-scale program that was continued by the triumvirate and Augustus. These new citizens included proletarians from Rome, army veterans, and aspiring entrepreneurs seeking new products to sell to Rome.

CHAPTER 7

IMPERIAL DREAMS AND CIVIL WAR

After Augustus, the empire moved into an era dominated by unstable personalities prone to paranoia and persecution. Some were more able than others, but none conducted a reign unblemished by intrigue and the murder of opponents. Caligula summed up the attitude of that breed of emperors when he said of the people of Rome, "I wish they had one neck, so I could cut it off… let them hate me, so long as they fear me."

But Augustus had constructed a robust administration that could withstand the blows dealt by his successors. The Roman empire survived in spite of its inadequate leaders, not because of them.

Although leadership was uninspired, life for the everyday Roman was better than it had ever been. Internal peace was not unduly threatened by those idiosyncratic rulers and the empire was still expanding. This meant there was ample opportunity to trade using the excellent network of roads extending from Rome to the frontiers. Soldiers were also benefiting from the increased wealth and technology available to the empire. They were well paid and better protected than ever before.

Inevitably the succession of woeful leaders undermined the emperor's position. When ambitious soldiers stepped in to have their say, the future of imperial rule looked bleak.

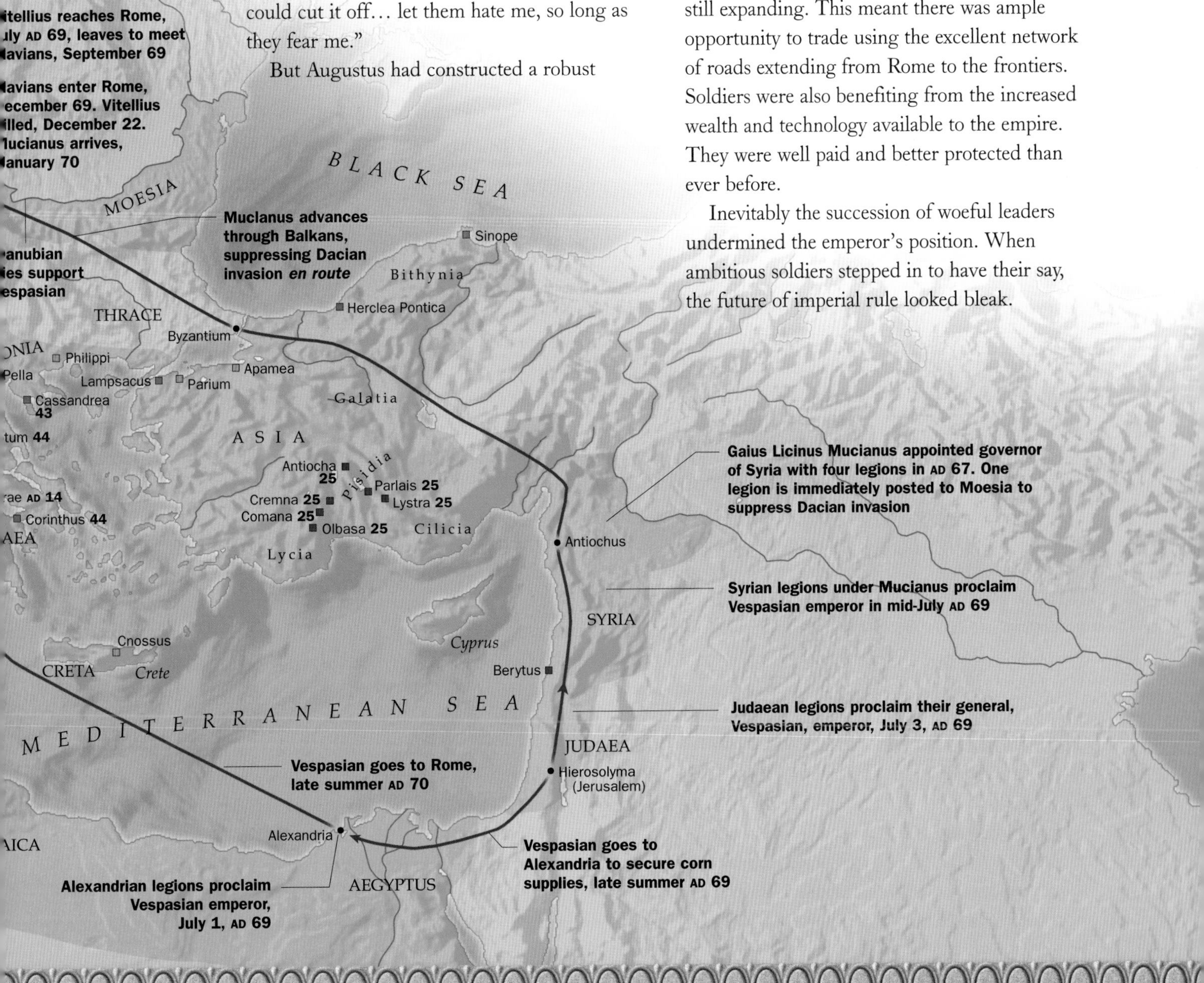

BLACK SEA
MOESIA
Muclanus advances through Balkans, suppressing Dacian invasion *en route*
Sinope
Bithynia
Herclea Pontica
THRACE
Byzantium
Philippi
Pella
Lampsacus
Parium
Apamea
Cassandrea 43
Galatia
ASIA
Antiocha 25
Pisidia
Parlais 25
Lystra 25
Cremna 25
Comana 25
Olbasa 25
Cilicia
Corinthus 44
Lycia
Gaius Licinus Mucianus appointed governor of Syria with four legions in AD 67. One legion is immediately posted to Moesia to suppress Dacian invasion
Antiochus
Syrian legions under Mucianus proclaim Vespasian emperor in mid-July AD 69
SYRIA
Cnossus
CRETA
Crete
Cyprus
Berytus
MEDITERRANEAN SEA
Judaean legions proclaim their general, Vespasian, emperor, July 3, AD 69
JUDAEA
Hierosolyma (Jerusalem)
Vespasian goes to Rome, late summer AD 70
Alexandria
Vespasian goes to Alexandria to secure corn supplies, late summer AD 69
Alexandrian legions proclaim Vespasian emperor, July 1, AD 69
AEGYPTUS

CLAUDIUS, CIVIL SERVANT

Suetonius drew a portrait of a drooling idiot. However, Claudius was mentally agile and well equipped to keep the wheels of empire in motion. His reign was largely one of prosperity for Rome, one also of expansion abroad and growth of the new bureaucracy.

Right: Any likeness of Claudius should be viewed with suspicion. Although Roman imperial sculpture is remarkably warts-and-all in its approach, Claudius was said to be grotesque in his appearance, due to a childhood illness which left him partially paralyzed. His brain, however, was unaffected—he was the most learned man on the throne since Julius Caesar.

Facing: Claudius was responsible for the redevelopment of Ostia, building a new harbor two miles to the north at Portus. The area in between rapidly became urbanized, boasting fine houses with ostentatious decoration (above) and tenements. The Aqua Claudia (below), completed in AD 52, was one of the two greatest aqueducts in terms of volume.

The tale of Tiberius Claudius Drusus (r.AD 41–54) quivering behind a curtain following the death of Caligula is told by Suetonius. When a Praetorian stalking the palace corridors discovered him, the son of Drusus, nephew of Tiberius, and grandson of both Mark Antony and Livia Drusilla fell at his feet pleading for his life. Not the best start for an imperial ruler, but Claudius had good reason to be fearful after the murder of his nephew Caligula resulted in a wave of reprisal killings carried out by loyal Praetorians.

As luck would have it, Claudius had been discovered by one of the those Guards opposed to the ambitions of the senate to redeem the republic. This nameless soldier took charge of the reluctant noble and propelled him toward his fellow Guardsmen. Regardless of his dismal reputation, they raised Claudius up and proclaimed him emperor on January 25, within a day of Caligula's death.

The senate was powerless to prevent the accession, and besides, those few who knew of his hidden accomplishments as a historian of the republic expected his rule to be favorable to their cause. Although he had some Julian blood from his grandmother Octavia's side, he had never been adopted into the Julian house, and remained a Claudian, also better favored by the senate. However, this did not prevent him adopting the populist name of Caesar.

On the face of it, Claudius did not seem an ideal candidate to rule the civilized world. Born at Lyon in 10 BC, an attack of paralysis in childhood had left him with an unattractive appearance. He is said to have foamed at the mouth, had a runny nose, stammered, and habitually trembled. As a result, his embarassed parents kept him out of the public eye, which gave him ample opportunity to study. He became an accomplished historian, producing books on Etruscan, Augustan, and Carthaginian history. None has survived.

A flawed character

Despite his apparent disabilities, Claudius was a surprisingly effective emperor, with a steady hand on the administrative, fiscal, and legal tiller. The tenor of his rule was one of steady, unalarming growth—apart from his invasion of Britain (*see following page*). Claudius continued the programs of civil reform of Caesar and Augustus. Tasks once performed by elected magistrates were now undertaken by a growing group of civil servants. These were generally recruited from among the ranks of his own freedmen and slaves, and eventually became the Imperial Civil Service. His secretaries Pallas, Narcissus, Calistus, and Polybius even sat in for him at senatorial sessions on occasions.

This increasing centralization of bureaucracy

was only hastened by several famines due to wheat shortage, which were largely the result of peculation among responsible *equites*. Claudius overhauled the food-providing institutions and went to lengths to improve agricultural productivity. He completed two aqueducts, begun in the time of his predecessor, and constructed a deep-water harbor at Portus, near Ostia. He also had the bed of Lake Fucinus (Fucine) drained to provide farming land. For 11 years, 30,000 men were employed on the project (which ultimately proved futile).

Claudius's domestic life was a disaster. One bride-to-be died on her wedding day. Claudius then divorced his first two wives, Plautia Urgulanilla and Aelia Paetina, had the third, Valeria Messallina, executed after she cuckolded him, and was poisoned by the fourth, Agrippina (the Younger). Socially, Claudius was clumsy and coarse, and had an unhealthy fascination with the death throes of gladiators at the many games he sponsored. His attitude to religion was reactionary, yet his foreign policy was forward-thinking and successful. The contradictions in his nature are summed up in his attitude toward Jews. While guilty of banishing them from Rome, possibly in response to unrest stirred up by Christians, he confirmed their rights in other locations. He also appealed for Jews and non-Jews in Egypt to stop the "destructive enmity" that existed between them.

THE CONQUEST OF BRITAIN

Julius Caesar's raids into Britain in 55 and 54 BC were militarily geared to find compliant kingdoms, obtain tribute, and prevent alliances with the Gauls. It would be another 96 years before the Roman army returned in force, with a different agenda.

Soon after being placed on the throne by the Praetorian Guard, Claudius needed a foreign policy event to popularize his reign in the eyes of the army and the people. A full-scale invasion of Britain offered the perfect opportunity. It was presented as the completion of Caesar's unfinished business, giving Rome unfettered access to important slave, hides, and metal markets. In fact, the entire venture was economically misguided.

Strabo neatly sums up the position in his *Geographical Sketches*, written a generation earlier: "Though Rome could have taken Britain she declined to do so. In the first place the Britons are no threat, having insufficient strength to cross over and attack us. In the second, there would be little to gain. It seems that we presently get more out of them in duty on their exports than we would by direct taxation, especially if the costs of an occupation army and of tax collecting be discounted."

Below: Detail from a bas-relief sculpture on the side of a Roman tomb at Colchester, England, dating from the 1st century AD, features a horse trampling a monkey.

Glossing over this, Claudius found his excuse for action in AD 42. The Roman client king Verica was defeated by Caratacus and Togodumnus, sons of the British ruler Cynobelinus, and fled to Rome from his kingdom in West Sussex. This left the whole of southeast Britain under Cynobelinus's control, a theoretical challenge to the empire. Managing the northwestern colonies required a divide-and-rule strategy in which incessantly quarreling barbarian tribes rarely became strong enough to engage imperial forces. If Cynobelinus allied with the Gauls, argued Claudius's advisers, it would be a recipe for rebellion.

Claudius's general, Aulus Plautius Silvanus, sailed his task force of four legions from Boulogne in the spring of 43, landing most of the troops at Richborough, Kent. From there they fought north, halting at the Thames to await the carefully stage-managed arrival of the emperor. It was eight weeks before the imperial bandwagon, complete with war elephants, caught up with them, by which time all immediate resistance had been crushed. Claudius continued unchallenged to Colchester, Cynobelinus's capital, where he held a victory parade. Sixteen days later he left the new province in the hands of Plautius and returned to Rome to prepare his triumph.

Romans sweep Britain

When the conquest resumed the following spring, it was a young commander (and future emperor) Titus Flavius Vespasianus (Vespasian) who claimed the glory. The Roman historian Suetonius said of him: "He went to Britain, where he fought 30 battles, subjugated two tribes and took more than 20 *oppida* [hill forts], Vectis [Isle of Wight] besides."

This hardly does Vespasian justice. His mastery of artillery pieces such as the *scorpio* and *ballista* allowed him to annihilate supposedly impregnable fortresses in Wessex and devastate native morale. With one quarter of the invasion force, his Legion II conquered three-quarters of the Romans' target territory, including a vast swathe across the south and southwest as far as Exeter. Legion IX pushed north as far as Lincoln, while Legion XIV and XX advanced to Leicester. The line connecting them was the 200-mile Fosse Way, the ancient limestone ridge between Devon and Lincolnshire that became the limit of the initial Claudian occupation.

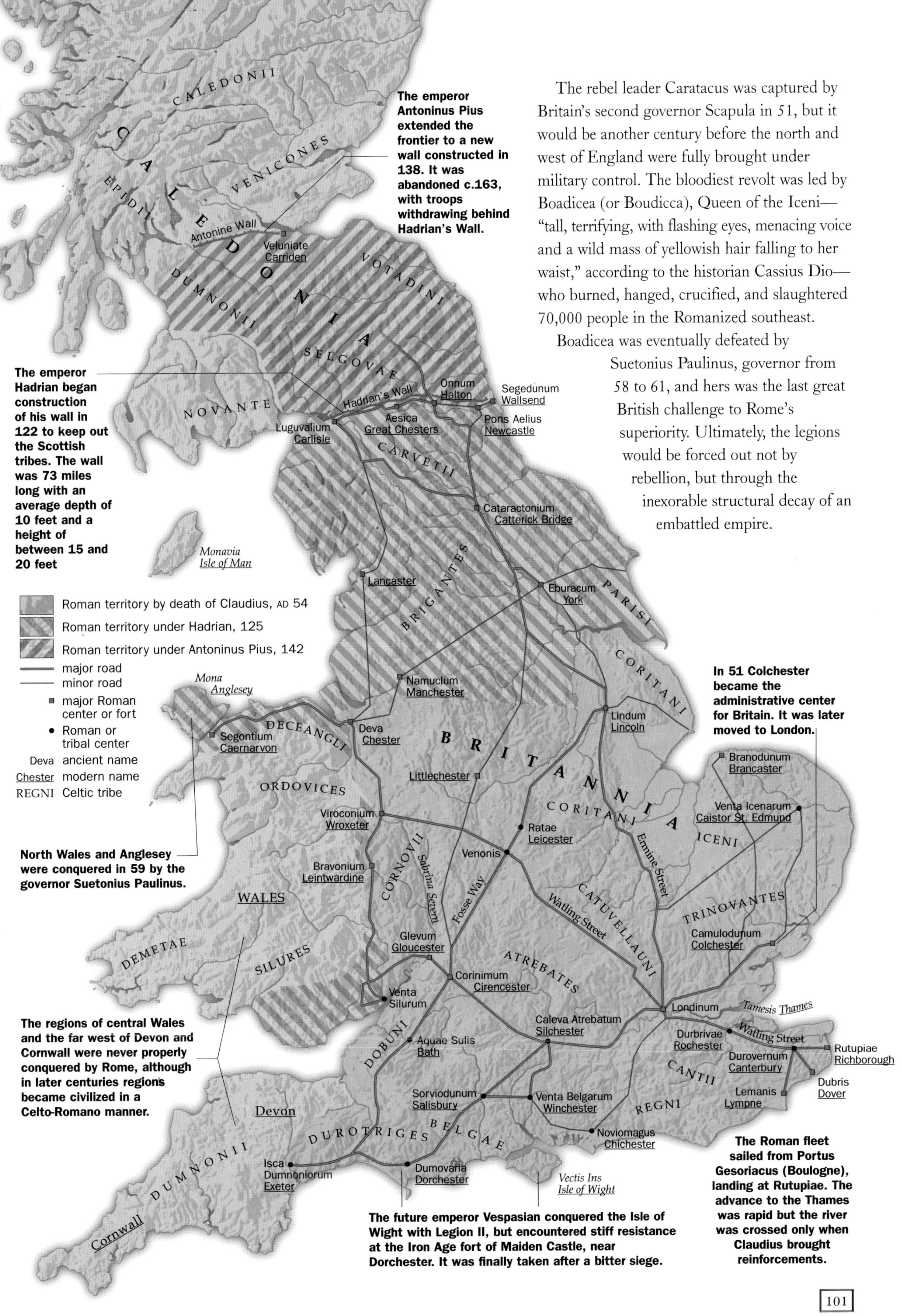
CALEDONII
CALEDONIA
VENICONES
EPIDII
Antonine Wall
Veluniate
Carriden
VOTADINI
DUMNONII
SELGOVAE
The emperor Antoninus Pius extended the frontier to a new wall constructed in 138. It was abandoned c.163, with troops withdrawing behind Hadrian's Wall.
The emperor Hadrian began construction of his wall in 122 to keep out the Scottish tribes. The wall was 73 miles long with an average depth of 10 feet and a height of between 15 and 20 feet
NOVANTE
Hadrian's Wall
Onnum
Halton
Segedunum
Wallsend
Aesica
Great Chesters
Pons Aelius
Newcastle
Luguvalium
Carlisle
CARVETII
Cataractonium
Catterick Bridge
Monavia
Isle of Man
BRIGANTES
Lancaster
Eburacum
York
PARISI
Roman territory by death of Claudius, AD 54
Roman territory under Hadrian, 125
Roman territory under Antonius Pius, 142
major road
minor road
major Roman center or fort
Roman or tribal center
Deva ancient name
Chester modern name
REGNI Celtic tribe
Mona
Anglesey
Namuclum
Manchester
CORITANI
In 51 Colchester became the administrative center for Britain. It was later moved to London.
DECEANGLI
Segontium
Caernarvon
Deva
Chester
BRITANNIA
Lindum
Lincoln
Branodunum
Brancaster
Littlechester
ORDOVICES
CORITANI
Venta Icenarum
Caistor St. Edmund
Viroconium
Wroxeter
Ratae
Leicester
ICENI
North Wales and Anglesey were conquered in 59 by the governor Suetonius Paulinus.
Bravonium
Leintwardine
CORNOVII
Sabrina Severn
Venonis
Fosse Way
Ermine Street
WALES
Watling Street
CATUVELLAUNI
TRINOVANTES
DEMETAE
SILURES
Glevum
Gloucester
Camulodunum
Colchester
ATREBATES
Corinimum
Cirencester
Venta
Silurum
Londinum
Tamesis Thames
The regions of central Wales and the far west of Devon and Cornwall were never properly conquered by Rome, although in later centuries regions became civilized in a Celto-Romano manner.
DOBUNI
Aquae Sulis
Bath
Caleva Atrebatum
Silchester
Durbrivae
Rochester
Watling Street
Rutupiae
Richborough
Durovernum
Canterbury
CANTII
Dubris
Dover
Lemanis
Lympne
Sorviodunum
Salisbury
Venta Belgarum
Winchester
REGNI
Devon
BELGAE
DUROTRIGES
Noviomagus
Chichester
DUMNONII
Isca
Dumnoniorum
Exeter
Dumovaria
Dorchester
Vectis Ins
Isle of Wight
Cornwall
The Roman fleet sailed from Portus Gesoriacus (Boulogne), landing at Rutupiae. The advance to the Thames was rapid but the river was crossed only when Claudius brought reinforcements.
The future emperor Vespasian conquered the Isle of Wight with Legion II, but encountered stiff resistance at the Iron Age fort of Maiden Castle, near Dorchester. It was finally taken after a bitter siege.

The rebel leader Caratacus was captured by Britain's second governor Scapula in 51, but it would be another century before the north and west of England were fully brought under military control. The bloodiest revolt was led by Boadicea (or Boudicca), Queen of the Iceni—"tall, terrifying, with flashing eyes, menacing voice and a wild mass of yellowish hair falling to her waist," according to the historian Cassius Dio—who burned, hanged, crucified, and slaughtered 70,000 people in the Romanized southeast.

Boadicea was eventually defeated by Suetonius Paulinus, governor from 58 to 61, and hers was the last great British challenge to Rome's superiority. Ultimately, the legions would be forced out not by rebellion, but through the inexorable structural decay of an embattled empire.

NERO, GILDING ROME

Nero was a curious blend of high culture and extreme cruelty. After a promising start, he emerged as the most unpalatable dictator Rome had ever known, eliminating series of rivals and even arranging the murders of his wife and mother.

Lucius Domitius Ahenobarbus was brought up at court with eminent tutors, under whose watchful eyes he developed an abiding interest in the arts. Caligula had exiled his mother Agrippina, but Claudius revived the family fortunes by not only recalling her to Rome, but also marrying her. She went on to contrive a marriage between her son and Octavia, Claudius's daughter, after which Claudius adopted him as Nero Claudius Caesar Drusus Germanicus. On the sudden death of Claudius, 18-year-old Nero (r.AD 54–68) was declared emperor.

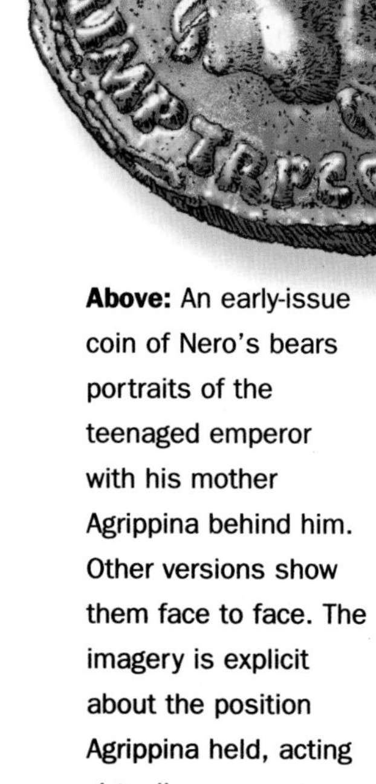

Above: An early-issue coin of Nero's bears portraits of the teenaged emperor with his mother Agrippina behind him. Other versions show them face to face. The imagery is explicit about the position Agrippina held, acting virtually as regent. This overt posturing led to her downfall, and Nero grew to loathe her so much that he eventually had her murdered.

Delighted, Agrippina styled herself as co-ruler alongside her son. The first coins minted during the era show their heads side by side. Her first actions were the elimination of the Claudian secretaries, and the few remaining Augustan descendants who may have posed a threat. However, Nero's tutors Seneca and Burrus were opposed to the idea of a woman ruling Rome, and persuaded him against his mother. Rebutted, Agrippina turned her affections toward Britannicus, son of the late Claudius and candidate for the throne.

Seneca urged wisdom and caution above impulsive response, but as the reality of absolute power dawned on Nero, he began to disregard Seneca and followed his instincts, most of which were base. Britannicus was the first victim. When he collapsed and died during a feast, Nero claimed an epileptic fit was to blame. Nero then exiled his mother on a ship which, unknown to her, was designed to fragment on the water. After Agrippina swam to safety, he ordered her murder. In matters of government, he was content to leave everything in Burrus and Seneca's hands. If historians see a happy period of five years during Nero's reign, it is down to these two, who managed things well.

A thuggish thrill-seeker, Nero is alleged to have prowled the streets of Rome in darkness with friends—including Otho, the future emperor—beating up revelers. When the joys of this pastime dried up, he turned his attentions to racing, scandalizing Roman aristocrats by becoming a chariot racer. Charioteers were generally trained slaves and Nero was the only noble-born among them. His passion for Helenistic sports resulted in the Neronian Games of AD 60, inspired by the Olympian Games in Greece.

A determined performance

His unseemly predilection for sport—contrary to popular belief, he was not interested in Roman gladiatorial contests—was accompanied by a growing zeal for the performing arts. Actors of the age were considered lowly, vulgar types, but Nero seized any opportunity to perform in the theater, prohibiting anyone to leave while he was on stage.

His reputation was further blackened when

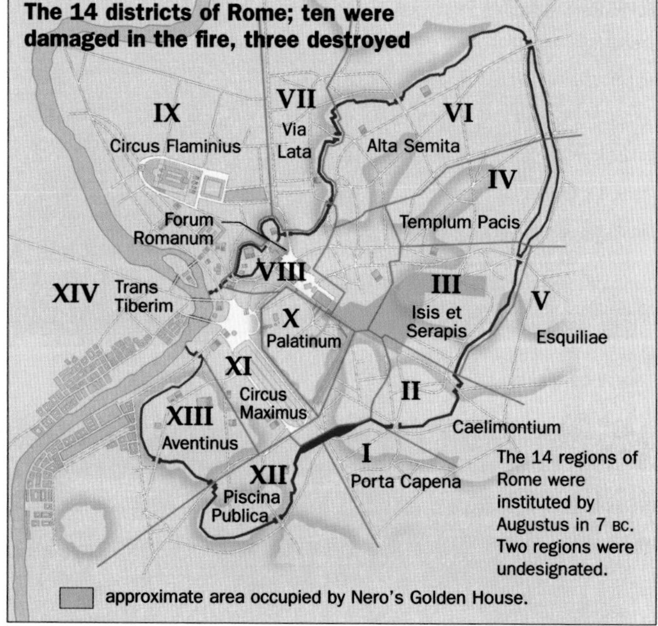
The 14 districts of Rome; ten were damaged in the fire, three destroyed
IX
Circus Flaminius
VII
Via Lata
VI
Alta Semita
IV
Templum Pacis
Forum Romanum
VIII
XIV
Trans Tiberim
III
Isis et Serapis
X
Palatinum
V
Esquiliae
XI
Circus Maximus
XIII
Aventinus
II
Caelimontium
I
Porta Capena
XII
Piscina Publica
The 14 regions of Rome were instituted by Augustus in 7 BC. Two regions were undesignated.
approximate area occupied by Nero's Golden House.

Left: Nero took much of central Rome for the construction of his Domus Aurea (Golden House). The anger it engendered contributed to his downfall. The enormous sums spent on the palace were such a drain on the treasury that Nero reduced the weight of gold and silver in his coins and introduced ones of cheaper bronze. In this he began the process of making coinage a symbol of currency instead of a real value based on the weight of precious metal.

he had his popular wife Octavia (always suspect as the sister of Britannicus) banished and murdered. He replaced her with the vain Poppaea Sabina, wife of his friend Otho, who had been sent as governor to Lusitania. His readiness to eliminate opposition through murder created an atmosphere of paranoia. Unwisely, Nero chose to eliminate some popular figures, including his former tutor Seneca and the celebrated general, Domitius Corbulo.

This act turned the disaffection of an army almost completely ignored by Nero into outright hostility. And then in 64, mob outrage overspilled after the great fire. Nero was cast as the villain, after he unguardedly suggested that the fire—which wiped out three of Rome's 14 regions—was a godsend, since it provided space for his new palace, The Golden House.

In fact Nero, who was miles away at Antium when the fire started, took energetic measures to bring the fire under control and provide relief for the victims. He was responsible for a host of new building and fire regulations to help prevent what was a common hazard in Rome.

Nero sought a scapegoat and lit on the Christians, members of a burgeoning religious sect on the margins of society. Thousands died in punishment for a crime they had not committed. Nero's reponse to his unpopularity was to purge any opposition. His *praetorian praefectus* Tigellinus was a willing executioner. With the mob now set firmly against him and open mutiny among the legions, the senate declared Nero a public enemy and declared for Galba, the governor of Tarraconensis on June 8, 68. The shamed emperor fled to the suburbs where on the following day, lacking the courage to take his own life, he ordered a servant to stab him. The Julio-Claudian dynasty ended when Nero fell, uttering the words, "What an artist I die."

The continual fire hazard

Rome and the larger urban centers of the early imperial period were packed with *insulae* (apartment blocks or tenements). Built around a courtyard, they were multi-storied with shops fronting the street. There were usually three stories, although in Rome's Subura they reached to six or seven floors, housing several families in cramped conditions. Augustus limited the height of *insulae* to a maximum of five floors. By the end of the republic, the majority of Rome's population was housed in rented rooms owned by a handful of wealthy landlords, like Marcus Crassus. *Insulae* earned a bad reputation for being unsafe.

Fire from cooking was a continual hazard. *Insulae* were built from timber frames and perishable mud bricks, which meant that they burned easily, and their height made them prone to disastrous collapse, burying the hapless victims of lower floors under tons of burning debris. Rome's great fire ravaged these densely clustered buildings, clearing the space that Nero used for his Golden House. Later *insulae*, like the model of the one pictured here from Ostia, were more soundly built from concrete and fired bricks, but they remained as cramped inside and lacked the basic amenities others took for granted, such as lavatories and running water.

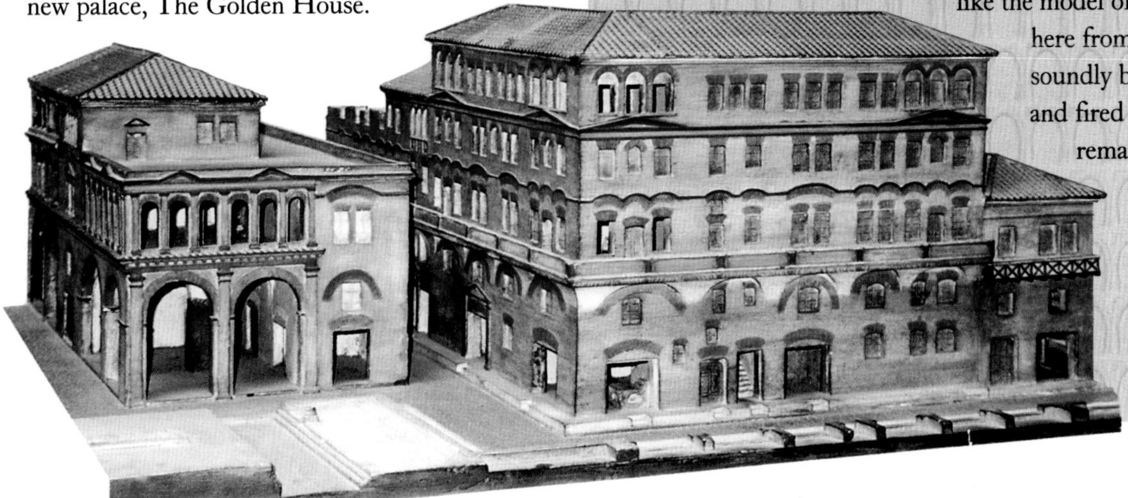

YEAR OF FOUR EMPERORS

The death of Nero again propelled Rome to the brink of civil war. Three prominent soldiers aspired to the Purple—Servius Sulpicius Galba, Marcus Salvius Otho, and Aulus Vitellius—but none could muster wholesale support and each met a sorry end.

Above: Galba (top) and Otho both claimed to be Julians and took the name Caesar to endear themselves to the troops. Vitellius, **above right**, refused the name but claimed to be Nero's chosen successor. None, however, had the strength of character of Vespasian, **right**.

Nero never visited his armies overseas. The Julio-Claudian emperors kept the military loyal through financial rewards, but Nero failed to do so. When the senate moved to depose him no soldiers supported Nero and, because the Praetorians could find no Julio-Claudian to elevate, the succession was finally decided outside Rome.

The first contender for power was the 70-year-old Servius Sulpicius Galba, governor of Hispania Tarraconensis for the past eight years. He had already aligned himself in rebellion against Nero by associating with the Gallic cause of Vindix (*see opening map of chapter*) and was now ready to seize the opportunity of Nero's death. In early June 68, having convinced the senate and mollified the Praetorians with a promised bonus, he was declared emperor and marched to Rome in company with his supporter Marcus Salvius Otho. As Tacitus put it: "the secret of empire was revealed: an Emperor could be made elsewhere than at Rome." Now anyone with a provincial army to back him could aspire to imperial position.

The treasury was in a deplorable state, and Galba, described by Tacitus as a "mediocre genius," tried to redeem cash from gifts given freely by Nero. He executed key members of the Neronian household, giving himself the hallmarks of a tyrant. His attempts to restore discipline in the army were also clumsy. When the legions of Upper and Lower Germany under the command of Aulus Vitellius rebelled, Galba adopted Piso Licinianus and gave the

younger noble command of the army to meet the threat. This was the position Otho had expected. Having nursed resentment against Nero for stealing his wife, this added act of ingratitude from Galba spurred him to action. With promises of bonuses, Otho won the support of the Praetorians, who seized the unfortunate Galba and killed him. Galba's head was paraded on a pole around the city.

Otho now had to deal with the Rhine armies. The legions had already declared Vitellius emperor on January 3, and the powerful force was marching south to invade Italy. With the legions of Judaea and Syria too far away to intervene, Otho only had an army of some 25,000 to counter Vitellius, but there was no alternative. He marched north on March 14.

Vespasian wins through

During the ensuing battle at Bedriacum, near Cremona, Otho's men were cut down in swathes. Nobly, Otho declined to pursue his cause and fell on his sword at dawn, ending a

AD 37 On Tiberius's death, Germanicus's son Caligula becomes emperor

40 Mauretania (Algeria and Morocco) is annexed by Caligula

41 Caligula is assassinated; Claudius is the new emperor

43–44 Claudius and Titus Flavius Vespasian conquer Britain

44 Agrippa, grandson of Herod, dies; Palestine becomes the Roman province of Judaea

c.50 Rome has a population of approximately one million

51 Britain's second governor Scapula captures rebel leader Caratacus

53–63 Rome clashes with Parthia (Iran) over Armenia

three-month rule. Vitellius proceeded to Rome at the head of troops, Roman and mercenary, plundering Italy on the way.

There was the by-now familiar round of revenge killings with which Vitellius hoped to secure his position. But no public display of strength could mask the fact that he lacked talent. He had been one of Tiberius's young men on Capri before emerging as a flattering courtier to Caligula, Claudius, and Nero. His highest achievements lay in gluttony and extravagance, in which he was said to be unmatched.

Provincial leaders, unhappy with Vitellius from the first, made overtures to Titus Flavius Vespasianus (Vespasian), the commander who had been so successful in Britain and was now general of Roman forces in Palestine. On July 1, 69, Vespasian's forces declared him emperor.

There was a two-front attack on Rome in which Vitellius's forces were trounced at Cremona. A bid by Vespasian's brother Flavius Sabinus to seize the city ended in his death when desperate Vitellians made a last stand. As a result, fire engulfed the Capitol and the Temple of Jupiter was destroyed. Despite attempts to disguise himself, Vitellius was discovered, tortured, and killed. His body was tossed into the Tiber. Vespasian proved to have greater staying power. When the dust settled on Rome, he gained control of the army, with help from loyal and able generals, and brought a year of civil strife to an end.

Disposition of the Legions in the provinces

Toward the end of the republic, the soldiers of the legions had become a vital factor in the succession of their generals first and then emperors. In the civil war after Caesar's murder, there was an explosion in the number of legions raised on all sides, but from the period of Augustus onward, the situation settled down and the numbers were reduced. Marius was responsible for introducing the numbering and nomenclature system of identifying the various legions, which became standardized during the reign of Augustus. Almost every legion of the imperial period had a title—essential when many legions shared the same number. Some titles were replaced—IX Hispaniensis (stationed in Spain) later became Hispana (Spanish)—or went out of use, and if a legion was lost, its number was never used again. The titles indicated either distinguished service or described particular qualities, such as Felix (lucky), Pia Fidelis (loyal and faithful), or Primigenia (firstborn), indicating a newly raised legion. The table below shows the known disposition of the legions at three times in the early imperial period.

Province	AD 24	AD 74	AD 150
Africa	II Augusta	III Augusta	III Augusta
Arabia			III Cyrenaica
Britannia		II Augusta II Adiutrix IX Hispana XX Valeria Victrix	II Augusta VI Victrix XX Valeria Victrix
Cappadocia		XII Fulminata XVI Flavia	XII Fulminata XV Apollinaris
Dalmatia	VII XI	IV Flavia Felix	XIII Gemima
Egypt	III Cyrenaica XXII Deiotariana	III Cyrenaica XXII Deiotariana	II Traiana Fortis
Germania Inferior	I Germana V Alaudae XX Valeria Victrix XXI Rapax	VI Victrix X Gemima XXI Rapax XXII Primigenia	I Minerva XXX Ulpia
Germania Superior	II Augusta XII Gemima XIV Gemima XVI Gallica	I Adiutrix VIII Augusta XI Claudia Pia Fidelis XIV Gemima	VIII Augusta XXII Primigenia
Hispania Tarraconensis	IV Macedonica VI Victrix X Gemima	VII Gemima	VII Gemima
Judaea		X Fretensis	VI Ferrata X Fretensis
Moesia	IV Scythica V Macedonica	I Italica V Alaudae V Macedonica VII Claudia Pia Fidelis	*Inferior*: I Italica V Macedonica XI Claudia Pia Fidelis
Moesia Superior			IV Flavia Felix VII Claudia Pia Fidelis
Pannonia	VIII Augusta IX Hispana XV Apollinaris	XIII Gemima XV Apollinaris	*Inferior*: XIV Gemima II Adiutrix
Pannonia Superior			I Adiutrix X Gemima
Syria	III Gallica VI Ferrata X Fretensis XII Fulminata	III Gallica IV Scythica	III Gallica IV Scythica XVI Flavia Firma

54 Nero becomes emperor on death of Claudius

61 Boadicea is pursued by Romans and dies after battle

64 Christians are blamed for the fire of Rome

67 Nero's Golden House is completed on a site cleared after the Great Fire

68 S. Sulpicius Galba becomes emperor, followed by M. Salvius Otho and Aulus Vitellius

69 Titus Flavius Vespasianus launches an attack on Rome and deposes Vitellius

70 Romans led by Titus sack Jerusalem and destroy the Temple

79 Vespasian is succeeded by his son, Titus

ROADS AND AQUEDUCTS

Roman roads spread like tentacles across conquered territories and, with roads, came communication and administration. Now Rome could efficiently maintain newly conquered territories, and enjoy the secondary function of easier trading during peace time.

Below: A section of the via Ostiensis looks peaceful today, but in ancient Roman times, this was the busy highway connecting Rome to its port at Ostia. It was continuousy thronged with carts bringing goods into the city.

One of the greatest gifts bequeathed by ancient Rome was the network of roads that ultimately linked the furthest outposts of the empire with its center. Before the fall of the empire, there were 29 military roads radiating out of Rome.

Construction of the first military road, the Appian Way, began in 312 BC, alongside the building of Rome's first aqueduct, the Aqua Appia, both named for the censor Appius Claudius Caecus. The initial section, stretching for 60 miles, was arrow-straight. Including curbs and sidelines, it measured 35 feet wide. Even before it connected with the port of Brindisi in 190 BC, it was known to ancient Romans as the *regina viarum*, or queen of roads. Ultimately, local populations became responsible for the roads within their neighborhood.

Roads were primarily built for soldiers to march down, but there were prolonged periods of peace under the early emperors, opening these arteries to trade and travelers. Road users took fresh ideas and innovations from one region of the empire to the next, speeding the development of trends and ideas. Christianity is one prime example of a movement that flourished thanks to the well-used road system.

Romans were not the instigators of road construction—as far as is known, that accolade goes to the residents of Ur, where the earliest road has been dated to c.4000 BC. However, the Romans were far more prolific than any previous civilization, building something in the order of 52,000 miles of roads in Europe, Asia, and North Africa. They drew on the expertise of those who had built roads before them, including the Etruscans, Carthaginians, and the Greeks.

Nothing emerged to rival the Roman manner

of road construction until the invention of Tarmacadam in the 19th century. The Romans refined construction techniques using cement, which became one of the great strengths of their highways. They were the first all-weather routes in operation.

The shortest distance

The most noticeable aspect of Roman roads was the directness of their routes. Surveyors quite simply built from one sighting point to the next, the builders countering obstacles as they went. Building work began with the digging of twin trenches 25–30 feet apart. The trenches provided drainage and material excavated from them helped raised the height of the road.

One feature of Roman roads above those from other civilizations was the milestone. While these small markers may not have included distances between points, they did give the name of the nearest towns and indicated their directions, as well as commemorating the emperor of the day.

With road building came the engineering necessity for bridge-building, cuttings, and fords. Minor bridges made of wood have fallen foul of the ravages of time, but some stone bridges still exist, including Tiberius's bridge over the Rubicon at Rimini.

Back down the roads toward Rome came goods as diverse as wild animals from Africa, silks and spices from China, glass from Sidon, and tin and wool from England. And with roads came revenue. Archaeologists have discovered Roman coins the length and breadth of the empire, and beyond, in India. New sea routes opened, backing up the land routes prone to attack and strengthening trade further.

Another monument to Roman engineering still in evidence today is the system of aqueducts. The Romans were not the first to channel water from one place to another, but no other civilization matched their building rate. Before the end of the third century they had constructed 11 aqueducts discharging some 298,000 gallons of water every day. Only 10% of the aqueducts ran above ground, with the rest routed at ground level or below. But as with the bridges it is the graceful examples that stand above ground that excite modern interest, especially where they are combined with roads or city walls.

Roman roads were constructed of four *strata* (layers, from which the word "street" is derived) to a depth of between three and six feet. Roads were cambered, or raised in the middle, for drainage and thus never became mired in mud. There was frequently sufficient space for one cart to pass by another, but no one knows if traffic was compelled to travel on the right- or left-hand side of the road.

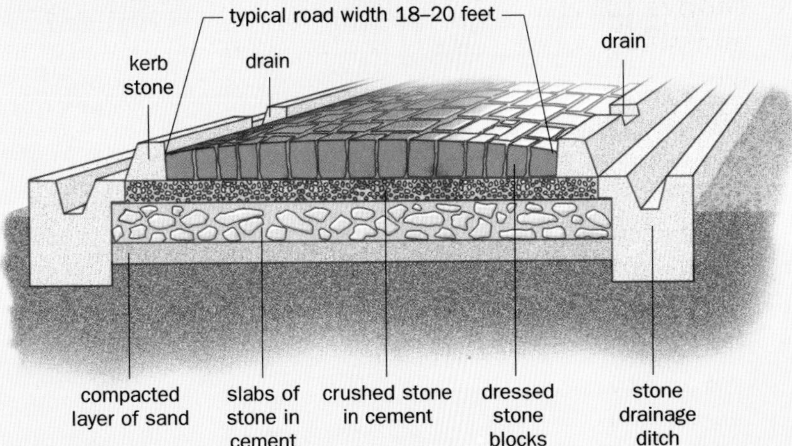

typical road width 18–20 feet
kerb stone
drain
drain
compacted layer of sand
slabs of stone in cement
crushed stone in cement
dressed stone blocks
stone drainage ditch

Left: The combined waters of the Anio Novus and Aqua Claudia are intersected by the Aqua Marcia. Running parallel to the Claudia, the via Latina stretches north toward Rome in the far distance. The line of trees at the top left of this reconstruction marks the route of the via Appia.

The Imperial Roman Army

Investment in the Roman army was increasing. Following the fall of the republic, emperors realized they could not rule without its goodwill. The best way to keep soldiers on their side was arm them adequately and line their pockets with money.

In the first century AD soldiers wore a sleeveless woolen undertunic belted at the waist so that its length fell to the mid-thigh. For wet weather there was the option of a hooded woolen cape called a *paenula*. Body armor was introduced during Tiberius's reign. Thanks to two complete outfits being excavated in 1964 along Hadrian's Wall we know it was made in segments and hinged for flexibility.

The advent of such body armor signaled the advent of a whole new industry of hammered ironwork. This was restricted to the legionaries, however, leaving auxiliaries dependent on mail or scale armor. Fine mail, favored by officers, was made of bronze rings, perhaps as small as an eighth of an inch in diameter, extremely costly to manufacture given the time it took.

Helmets, which had once been little more than skullcaps, became more effective, with detachable cheek protectors in addition to a substantial neck guard. Made of iron, they were sometimes intricately engraved. Surprisingly few helmets have survived into modern times. Military belts, known as *cingulum militare* or *balteus*, were an important part of the uniform. Each soldier wore two in a crossover style, one to hold his dagger, the other his sword. Officers wore their sword on the left, while lower ranks carried them on the right. Scabbards were attached to the belts with the aid of rings and straps.

Sword design and decoration would have varied depending on rank and individual preference. The bronze Sword of Tiberius found near the Rhine at Mainz dates from the early first century AD and is a good example of a typical personal weapon. It has a bone handle, with wooden pommel and hilt, and a sheath made of a leather-covered wooden lining. More valuable still is the sword found at Rheingonheim, Germany, which has a silver-encased wooden handle, surely the property of a nobleman or centurion.

Maintaining the standard

On their feet soldiers wore *caligae*, the upper made from strips of woven leather laced with leather thongs and the soles studded with hobnails. These are commonly depicted in Roman reliefs and some examples have been found at ancient battle sites.

In battle some soldiers, centurions, and cavalrymen in particular wore leather-lined metal shin guards or greaves covering the exposed area between ankle and knee.

Below: From the late republican period, Roman army engineers fought as part of combat units, putting their skills to the practice when required. One of the most important skills was bridge building. Many trestle bridges were erected to cross the Rhine and Danube, many of which were later rebuilt in stone.

A tripod is built on a log raft. One of the legs is a chute in which a heavy weight connected to a rope slides up and down. Engineers winch the weight to the top of the chute. On releasing it, the weight falls and, by repeating the process several times, drives a piling deep into the river bed at an angle. Pairs of pilings are cross-braced. A pair on the opposite side form a trestle to carry lengths of timber, across which are fastened the sawn timbers forming the bridge's surface.

Infantrymen were protected by their rectangular shields, made from three layers of plywood, covered in felt, with a round metal boss on the outside. Bearing all their equipment, it was usual for armies on the move to cover 20 miles a day. Earlier deficiencies in Roman cavalry had been remedied by the first century, and cavalry units staged equestrian games to hone their skills.

Artillery comprised of the *ballista*, a huge catapult, that could lob boulders or fireballs, and the smaller crossbow-style scorpion, that fired large arrows with great accuracy. Siege craft, including the construction of towers and ramps, was evolving all the time.

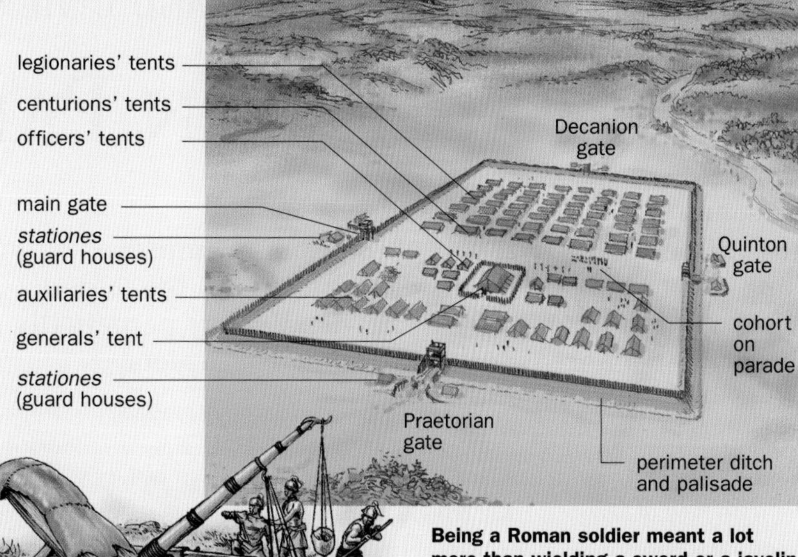
legionaries' tents
centurions' tents
officers' tents
main gate
stationes (guard houses)
auxiliaries' tents
generals' tent
stationes (guard houses)
Decanion gate
Quinton gate
cohort on parade
Praetorian gate
perimeter ditch and palisade

Being a Roman soldier meant a lot more than wielding a sword or a javelin. Every legionary also carried a spade and other digging implements. As soon as a camp site had been picked out, even for one night, the weary soldiers set about digging a 13-foot-wide ditch, which was palisaded by the stakes that they also carried as part of their packs. A camp of some 2,000 yards could house two legions. Larger and more permanent camps eventually grew into towns.

The lever-and-spring catapulta (top) was the Roman army's heavy artillery piece, capable of throwing stones weighing up to 220 lbs. The ballista (center) was the universal medium-range artillery of a besieging Roman army. Powered like the onager, or "wild ass," (right) and the catapulta by twisted skeins of sinew or hair, the ballista was more accurate in aim and rapid-fire in use. It hurled rounded stones of up 60 lbs for a range of up to 1,300 feet, and could also deliver large arrows or burning logs. It also came in a variety of sizes and power ranges. The onager was a giant sling-shot, and its fierce action gave rise to its nickname of the "scorpion."

The legionary's diet

Drawn from among the ranks of the poor, the imperial legionary was not used to a rich diet. And given the problems of transporting quantities of livestock, most soldiers dined regularly on bread and porridges made from cereals. When meat was available, it was usually bacon (which kept well on long marches) cooked with pulses such as lentils or chickpeas. On the rare occasions when feasting took place, we are told by contemporary historians that the legionaries were invariably sick for days from the effects of digesting cooked flesh.

Roman soldiers were superstitious and among their chief concerns was the fate of the legion's standard. At the time of the empire the standard, an *aquila* or eagle, was made entirely of gold (earlier versions were gold and silver) and stood proud on the end of a pole. It never left the camp unless the whole legion was on the move and was always closely guarded. When Varus led ill-fated legions to disaster in Germany during the reign of Augustus, three standards were lost, only two of which were recaptured by later missions. Augustus was said to have bemoaned the loss of his eagles for the rest of his life.

Legionaries served for 25 years, earning about three times as much as auxiliaries. Their pay was supplemented by bonuses paid by emperors when they pursued or gained power. At the time of Nero there were 28 Roman legions around the empire: three in England, one each in Spain, Gaul, Italy, and Northern Africa, two in Egypt, three each in Jerusalem and Syria, and no fewer than 13 along the Rhine and Danube rivers.

Right: Legionaries in segmented armor rush to the aid of their wounded centurion.

Insurrection in Palestine

Judaea became a vital part of the Roman empire, helping to shore up its eastern frontier. Yet the region seethed with rebellion, with Jewish Zealots perpetually advocating a holy war against Roman occupiers.

Below: Copy of a relief from the Arch of Titus shows legionaries carrying off the spoils of the Temple in AD 70. Surviving Jewish warriors retreated to the rock fortress of Masada, **facing**, where they held out for almost three years.

Palestine had a long, troubled history in the republican era, but peace was restored in 37 BC by Herod the Great, a king who ruled the region with Roman approval. On his death in AD 4 his realm was split among successors, some better than others. Those that faltered gave Rome the opportunity to install their chosen prefects into key locations, thus beginning the process of Romanization. Herod's grandson, Herod Agrippa I, briefly united the territory in 37 but, following his death in 44, the kingdom passed to Rome and became the province of Judaea.

While Rome was culturally tolerant and some emperors were actively pro-Jewish, there was a mutual contempt between Roman and Jew at grass roots level. At the heart of the Jewish faith was the Temple, built with Solomon's gold in Jerusalem. The first major clash occurred in 66, after Roman procurator Gessius Florus requisitioned a heavy tribute of gold from the Temple treasury. When Jews gathered to protest, soldiers set about them with swords, killing hundreds. In the revolt that followed, Jerusalem was taken over by Jews, who chased out the Roman rulers and slaughtered legionaries who remained.

Masada became another key Jewish stronghold and, elsewhere, Jews formed guerrilla bands, attacking Roman soldiers at will. Nero dispatched Vespasian to regain control. Among his initial victories were the taking of Jotapata, a small citadel in Galilee, where Jewish commander Josephus was the last alive, having failed to honor a suicide pact. At first a prisoner, Josephus became an informant, invaluable historian, and imperial confidante.

Ultimately, the ardor of the Jewish fighters proved no match for the ruthless organization that was the Roman army. Methodically, the Romans captured town after town until they arrived at the gates of the steeply walled Jerusalem. In 69 Vespasian departed in quest of the Purple in Rome (*see page 105*), leaving the task to his son, Titus. Finding the defenses impossible to assail, Titus resolved to starve the population of Jerusalem into submission.

Life or liberty

Josephus described the desperation of the Jews. "Need drove the starving to gnaw at anything. Refuse which even animals would reject was collected and turned into food. In the end they were eating belts and shoes and the leather stripped off their shields." Those caught smuggling

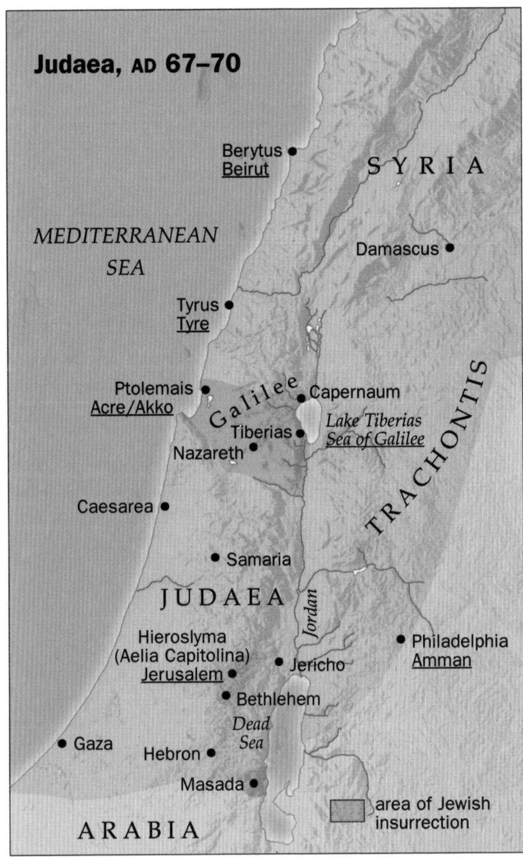
Judaea, AD 67–70
Berytus
Beirut
SYRIA
MEDITERRANEAN
SEA
Damascus
Tyrus
Tyre
Ptolemais
Acre/Akko
Galilee
Capernaum
Tiberias
Lake Tiberias
Sea of Galilee
TRACHONTIS
Nazareth
Caesarea
Samaria
JUDAEA
Jordan
Hieroslyma
(Aelia Capitolina)
Jerusalem
Jericho
Philadelphia
Amman
Bethlehem
Dead
Sea
Gaza
Hebron
Masada
ARABIA
area of Jewish
insurrection

supplies were crucified in view of the besieged Jews. In the face of a fresh onslaught, the Jews retreated to Herod's palace in 70, where they committed suicide rather than face Roman "justice." The victors torched the sacred temple and large sections of the city.

The last remaining Jewish stronghold was Masada, a mountaintop fortress overlooking the Dead Sea. The Romans encircled the fort with a wall so none could escape, then constructed a mighty earth ramp until it was level with the fortress walls. A battering ram finally gave entry to the Romans in May 73. Inside they found the corpses of almost a thousand occupants, dead by their own hands. The Jewish revolt was over, but bitter feelings against the Romans still ran high. Previously a part of the Roman province of Syria, Judaea ceased to exist as a name after 70 when it was renamed Syria-Palestina.

Yoked by severe repression, the Jews once again rallied to arms in 132 under the leadership of Simon Bar Kokhba, goaded by Hadrian's decision to transform the site of their temple into a place of pagan worship. Once again the Jews registered some initial success but were ground down by the size and strength of Roman forces pitched against them. Shrewdly, Bar Kokhba avoided open battles in favor of guerrilla tactics. But by 135 the flower of the Jewish forces were cornered at Bethar fortress, west of Jerusalem, to be cut down by the Romans.

Vengeance belonged to the emperor Hadrian, who killed or enslaved any Jews who had not fled the region in the great diaspora. Jerusalem was entirely Romanized and Judaism was banned. The Jews were without a homeland, and would remain so until 1948.

Above: Joseph ben Mattathias (Josephus) interpreted an ancient oracle that foretold the next emperor would arise from Judaea. When Vespasian became emperor, he rewarded Josephus and adopted him. Josephus wrote a history of the war that served to flatter his patron and to warn others against the folly of opposing Rome.

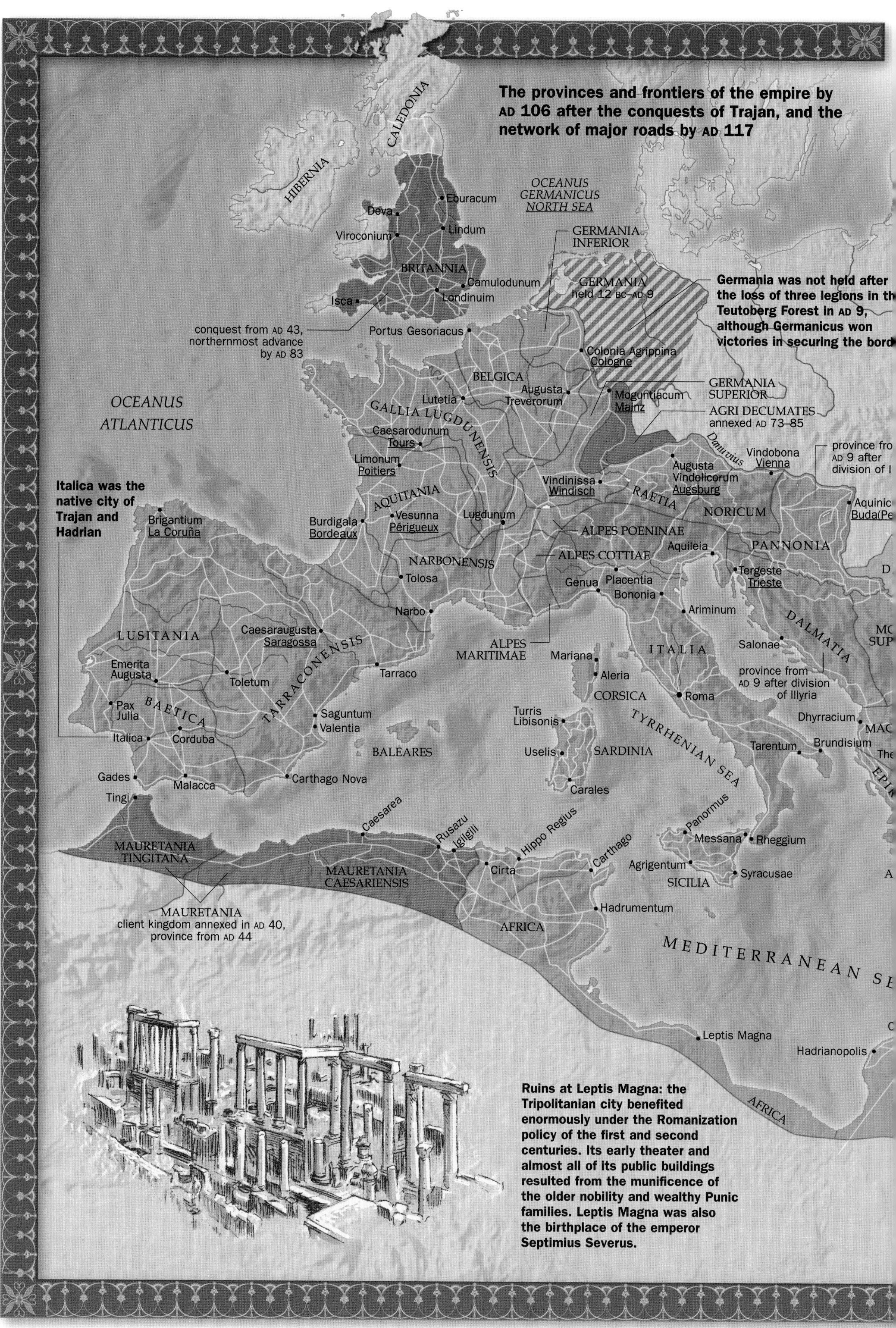
The provinces and frontiers of the empire by AD 106 after the conquests of Trajan, and the network of major roads by AD 117
CALEDONIA
HIBERNIA
OCEANUS GERMANICUS
NORTH SEA
Eburacum
Deva
Lindum
Viroconium
GERMANIA INFERIOR
BRITANNIA
Camulodunum
GERMANIA held 12 BC–AD 9
Isca
Londinium
Germania was not held after the loss of three legions in the Teutoberg Forest in AD 9, although Germanicus won victories in securing the bord
conquest from AD 43, northernmost advance by AD 83
Portus Gesoriacus
Colonia Agrippina
Cologne
BELGICA
GERMANIA SUPERIOR
Augusta Treverorum
Moguntiacum
Mainz
OCEANUS ATLANTICUS
Lutetia
GALLIA LUGDUNENSIS
AGRI DECUMATES annexed AD 73–85
Caesarodunum
Tours
Danuvius
Vindobona
Vienna
province fro
AD 9 after
division of I
Limonum
Poitiers
Augusta Vindelicorum
Augsburg
Italica was the native city of Trajan and Hadrian
Vindinissa
Windisch
RAETIA
AQUITANIA
Aquinic
Buda(Pe
Brigantium
La Coruña
Burdigala
Bordeaux
Vesunna
Périgueux
Lugdunum
NORICUM
ALPES POENINAE
Aquileia
PANNONIA
ALPES COTTIAE
NARBONENSIS
Tergeste
Trieste
Tolosa
Genua
Placentia
Bononia
Ariminum
Narbo
DALMATIA
LUSITANIA
Caesaraugusta
Saragossa
TARRACONENSIS
ALPES MARITIMAE
Mariana
ITALIA
Salonae
Emerita Augusta
Tarraco
Aleria
Toletum
CORSICA
province from AD 9 after division of Illyria
Roma
Pax Julia
BAETICA
Saguntum
Valentia
Turris Libisonis
TYRRHENIAN SEA
Dyrracium
Italica
Corduba
BALEARES
Uselis
SARDINIA
Tarentum
Brundisium
Gades
Malacca
Carthago Nova
Carales
Tingi
Caesarea
Rusazu
Igilgili
Hippo Regius
Panormus
Messana
Rheggium
MAURETANIA TINGITANA
Carthago
Cirta
Agrigentum
Syracusae
SICILIA
MAURETANIA CAESARIENSIS
Hadrumentum
MAURETANIA client kingdom annexed in AD 40, province from AD 44
AFRICA
MEDITERRANEAN SE
Leptis Magna
Hadrianopolis
AFRICA

Ruins at Leptis Magna: the Tripolitanian city benefited enormously under the Romanization policy of the first and second centuries. Its early theater and almost all of its public buildings resulted from the munificence of the older nobility and wealthy Punic families. Leptis Magna was also the birthplace of the emperor Septimius Severus.

CHAPTER 8

Pax Romana

With Vespasian's arrival in Italy, there began a period of peace (*Pax Romana*—it was not always peaceful for non-Roman citizens). Street fighting ceased once his accession was assured, the legions were satisfied that their man had won the day, so long-running rumblings of discontent in the ranks came to an end. In Palestine the Jewish revolt was entering its final stages. Border skirmishes continued—but they always had and always would.

This age, which began in the middle of the first century AD and closed after the first 20 years of the second—is regarded as the pinnacle of the empire. No other period compared in peace, prosperity, and internal harmony, marred only by further civil unrest in 193, from which emerged the Severan dynasty. It was a period of generally well-established imperial dynasties (Flavian, Nervo-Trajanic, and Antonine), the members of which ruled—with a few notable exceptions—with restraint. Some of its strength lay in the fact that succession did not necessarily fall between father and son. Emperors without an heir chose the best candidate from their immediate circle and this inevitably raised the caliber of the incumbents.

The longevity of emperors of this period also played its part. In 120 years there were only eight faces gracing the imperial coinage. The next eight emperors came and went in just 42 years and there were no fewer than 26 emperors in the following 62 years.

One disaster that even the most talented emperor could not fend off was the plague. It came from the east, carried by the rat-borne flea, showing no respect for rank, wealth, or imperial borders. It was centuries before the plague was sated. The death toll ran into countless thousands and one effect was a loss of labor and tax income.

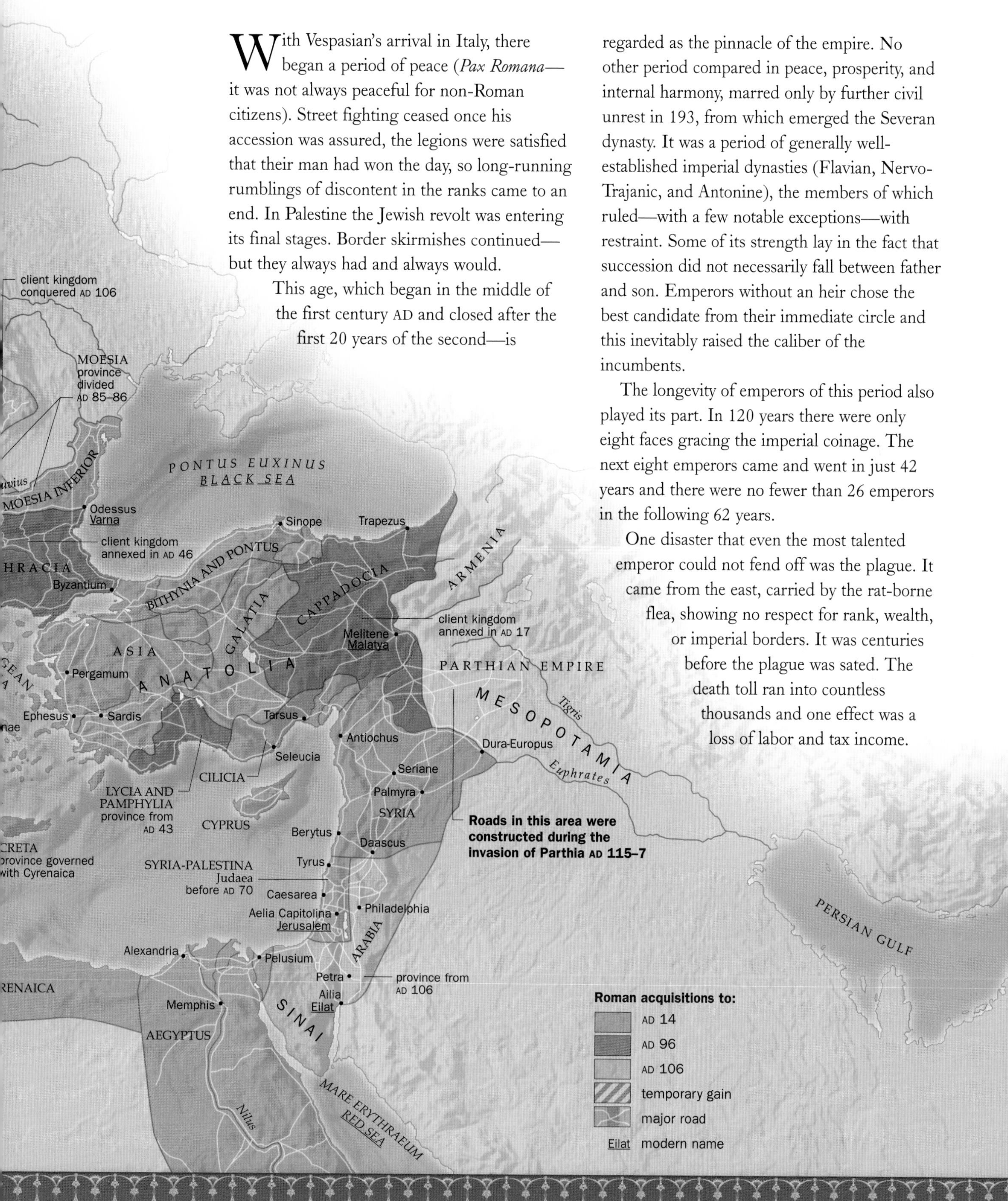

client kingdom conquered AD 106
MOESIA province divided AD 85–86
MOESIA INFERIOR
PONTUS EUXINUS
BLACK SEA
Odessus
Varna
client kingdom annexed in AD 46
HRACIA
Byzantium
Sinope
Trapezus
BITHYNIA AND PONTUS
GALATIA
CAPPADOCIA
ARMENIA
client kingdom annexed in AD 17
Melitene
Malatya
ASIA
ANATOLIA
Pergamum
Ephesus
Sardis
Tarsus
PARTHIAN EMPIRE
MESOPOTAMIA
Tigris
Euphrates
Antiochus
Dura-Europus
Seleucia
CILICIA
Seriane
LYCIA AND PAMPHYLIA province from AD 43
Palmyra
SYRIA
CYPRUS
Berytus
Daascus
Roads in this area were constructed during the invasion of Parthia AD 115–7
CRETA
province governed with Cyrenaica
SYRIA-PALESTINA
Tyrus
Judaea before AD 70
Caesarea
Aelia Capitolina
Jerusalem
Philadelphia
ARABIA
PERSIAN GULF
Alexandria
Pelusium
Petra
province from AD 106
RENAICA
Ailia
Eilat
Memphis
SINAI
AEGYPTUS
Nilus
MARE ERYTHRAEUM
RED SEA
Roman acquisitions to:
AD 14
AD 96
AD 106
temporary gain
major road
Eilat modern name

VESPASIAN'S FLAVIAN DYNASTY

It fell to the soldier Vespasian to restore order in Rome, a demanding task that he executed clinically and with flair. Lacking the paranoia of previous emperors, he brought a breath of fresh air to the capital.

Below: Vespasian brought to Rome a robust rustic wit and the native shrewdness of a countryman. In short order he had Rome back on course.

Vespasian (r.AD 69–79) was from the middle class *plebs*. He was born in AD 9 at Reate, in Sabine country, to a mother who had some aristocratic links, and a father who was was a mule breeder turned moneylender. Nevertheless, he enjoyed a good education, and the financial help of his mother propelled him into the legions as a tribune. Army service took Vespasian to Thrace, Crete, Cyrene, and Britain. Later he was made governor of Africa. He gained valuable experience overseas, not only in military matters but also learning the value of providing housing, sanitation, and an efficient tax-collecting system.

His future seemed assured when the well-placed Narcissus became his patron at Claudius's court. The death of Claudius and the accession of Nero, and specifically his mother Agrippina, cast Vespasian into the wilderness for some 15 years. This tactic was typically employed by emperors who perceived a threat to their own precarious security in the popularity of a successful general.

Vespasian continued to serve on the periphery of the empire until Nero, faced with the uprising in Palestine, called on him as a chief troubleshooter. Vespasian twice came close to death before becoming emperor, cornered during a battle during the Jewish revolt in Palestine and also falling asleep during a musical recital by Emperor Nero—a capital crime. He emerged as the capable pair of hands needed to steer the tottering empire back from the brink of destruction.

It was from Palestine that Vespasian surveyed the fast-moving events of AD 68 and 69. Initially, he had welcomed Galba as an alternative to Nero. But Galba had been dispatched before Vespasian's goodwill message could reach him. As further news of the deteriorating situation in Rome reached him, Vespasian determined to act.

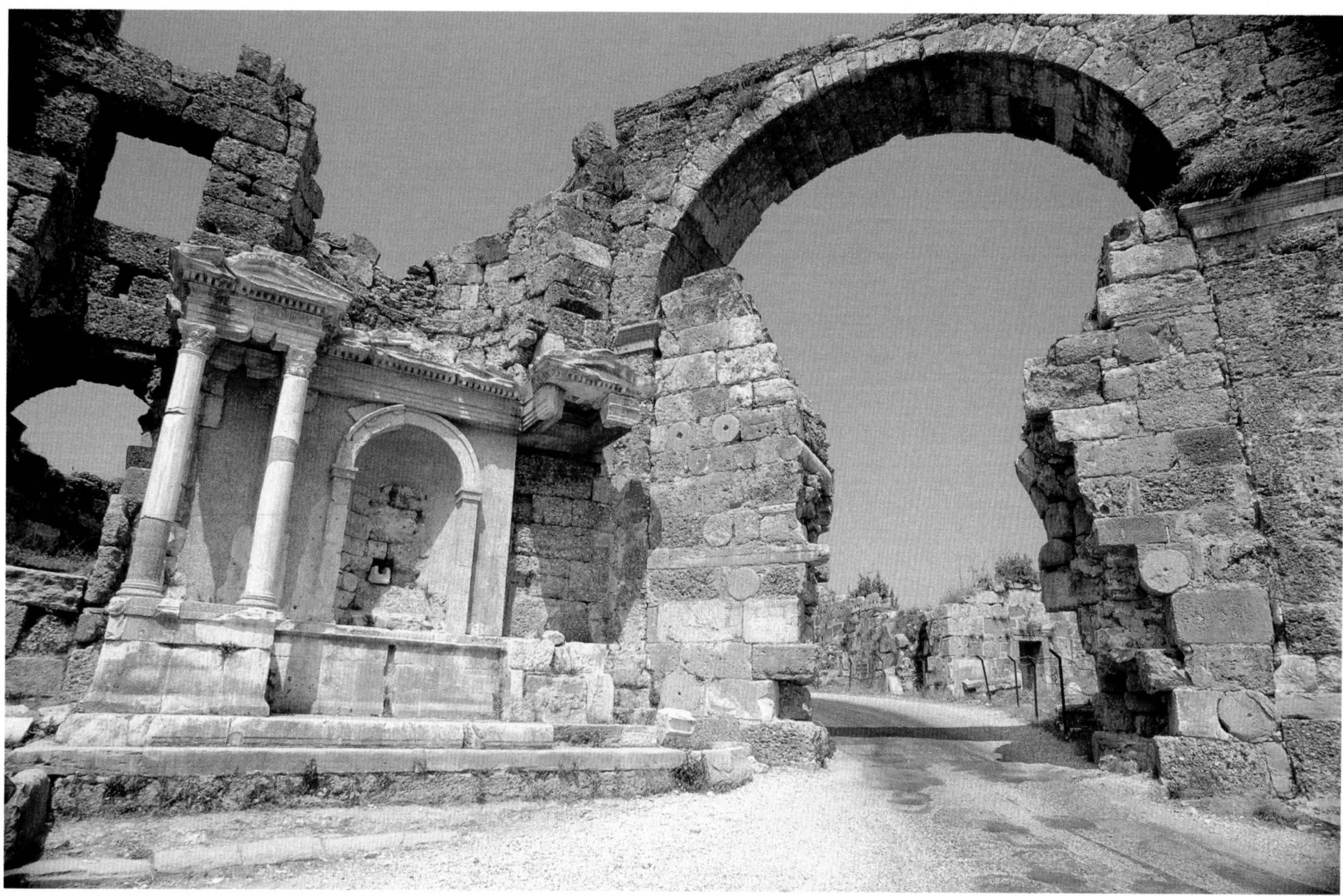

Above: The monumental gate of Sidon is graced by the Nymphaeum of Vespasian, on the left of the picture. Even missing the two columns on the right, it is easy to imagine how hot and dusty travelers would have wecomed its fountain and running water. Although he began construction of the mighty Colosseum, most of Vespasian's building projects were this kind of modest civic amenity, and they sprang up in provinces from one side of the empire to the other.

In this, as in everything he did, he showed the shrewdness of a Julius Caesar. Instead of marching directly on Rome, he first went to Alexandria to seize the corn supply. Egypt had now taken over from Sicily as Rome's chief granary, and this action effectively starved the Rome of Vitellius into submission. His delay also anticipated the fall of Jerusalem, which he needed since Jerusalem was wealthy and Rome's treasury stood empty. In the end he left Judaea in the capable hands of his son, Titus Flavius Vespasianus, and left for Rome before Jewish resistance crumbled.

Obscure but unashamed

In 73 he assumed the office of censor and used his position to fill the gaps in the senate with a new aristocracy drawn from the municipal towns of Italy. In this, he was quite open that, like Augustus, he intended to have a senate amenable to his actions—they should obey rather than just be co-operative. However, even those naturally opposed to him could not fear a return to the spendthrift years of Caligula or Nero; Vespasian was famous for his parsimony.

Among Vespasian's many achievements, a few stand out. He continued the programs of Caesar and Augustus in founding colonies in the provinces and conferring Latin rights on provincial towns. Between 74 and 84 no fewer than 350 Spanish towns received municipal charters. In Rome, he expanded the city's *pomerium* to outside the Servian Wall to help relieve crowding—an overt symbol of Rome's invulnerability to foreign attack that would remain until the later Aurelian Wall was built in less steady times. He also began construction of a massive amphitheater on the site of the lake of Nero's Golden House, known as the *amphitheatrum Flavaium*. We know it better today as the Colosseum (*see pages 118–9*).

Of the three Flavian emperors, Vespasian was undoubtedly the greatest. Suetonius, writing in *The Life of Vespasian*, described his rule like this: "The empire which for a long time had been unsettled and, as it were, drifting through the usurpation and violent death of three emperors, was at last taken in hand and given stability. This house was, it is true, obscure and without family portraits, yet it was one of which our country had no reason whatever to be ashamed...."

Unlike the majority of his predecessors, Vespasian died in his bed—perhaps fortunate that his two ambitious sons Titus and the younger Titus Flavius Domitianus (Domitian) were prepared to let nature take its course. His life finished on an ironic note when Vespasian, who never mustered faith in Roman religion or superstition, uttered, "Woe is me, I think I am turning into a god."

Titus and Domitian

The Flavian dynasty founded by Vespasian continued for a further 27 years as his sons, Titus and Domitian, took the empire's helm. In an almost fairytale manner, one was good and the other evil.

Facing: The Arch of Titus stands over the Sacred Way, looking across the Forum to the temples dedicated to Vespasian and Titus. The arch, finished by his brother Domitian (**far right**), is widely regarded as the finest example of Roman triumphal architecture.

Titus (r.AD 79–81) was 40 when he came to the imperial throne, and his path to the succession had been carefully groomed by Vespasian. There was little doubt to his abilities, having served well in Germany, Britain, and

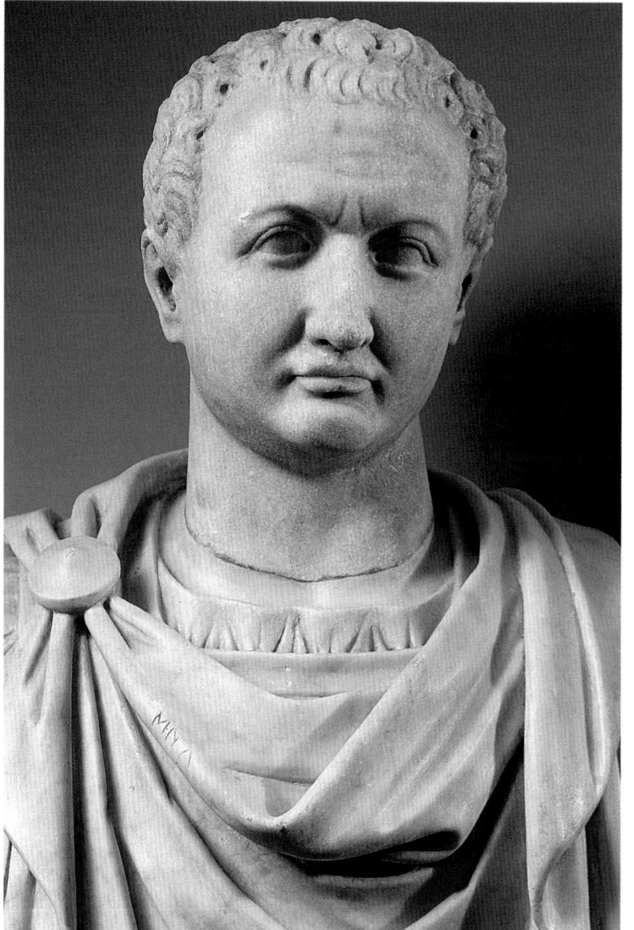

Right: Titus became Rome's most loved emperor, some cynical Romans said because the shortness of his reign allowed no time for him to develop into a monster.

Judaea. He was awarded a lavish triumph in 70 after the fall of Jerusalem, complete with an arch built into the eastern end of the Circus Maximus (now lost). But he had also earned a reputation for youthful extravagance and ruthlessness. Suetonius tells us that he was an adept forger who created evidence to win convictions against his family's enemies.

So it was that on Vespasian's death, few people relished the rule of Titus. It turned out differently, and Titus ended his short days as Rome's most loved emperor. He became a model of generosity, compassion, and wise leadership. Once, after an unaccustomed lapse in performing benevolent deeds, he declared *Amici, diem perdidi*—my friends, I have lost a day (in which to do good).

It seemed as though Rome had returned to the golden days, had it not been marked by two calamities. In 79, Vesuvius sensationally erupted, smothering the towns of Pompeii and Herculaneum (*see also pages 120–1*). Pliny the Younger experienced the terror and wrote: "You could hear the shrieks of women, the wailing of infants, and the shouting of men.... Many besought the aid of the gods, but still more imagined there were no gods left, and that the universe was plunged into eternal darkness for evermore." One of the victims was his uncle, the prolific writer Pliny the Elder.

Palatine palace

While Titus was visiting the disaster zone, a huge fire broke out in Rome, destroying the new Capitol (restored after its burning at the end of the Vitellian reign in December 69), Agrippa's Pantheon and Baths, and a sizeable residential area. Titus responded by pouring money and resources into stricken regions, alleviating some of the burden. He brightened people's lives in 80 with a hundred-day celebration to dedicate the Flavian Amphitheater, and gave gladiatorial shows to celebrate the opening of his luxurious new public baths.

His most visible reminder in Rome today is the triumphal arch that bears his name at the top of the Sacred Way into the Forum. Dedicated by Domitian in 81, it recalls his victories against Jewish insurgents in Palestine at the time when his father was assuming control in Rome. His death at Reate after reigning only two years, two months, and 20 days followed a short illness. Malaria was the probable cause, but because there was little love between Titus and his 30-year-old brother, the finger was pointed at Domitian.

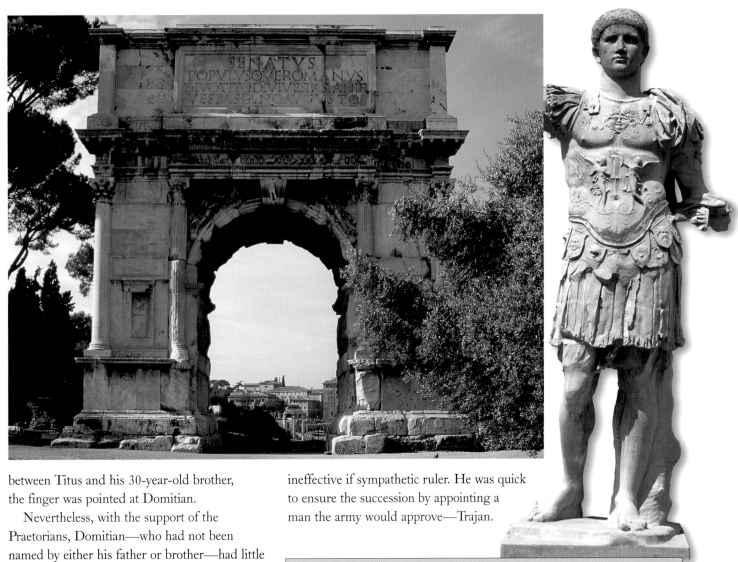

Nevertheless, with the support of the Praetorians, Domitian—who had not been named by either his father or brother—had little trouble in taking control. In contrast to Titus, history has few kinds words for Domitian (r.81–96). His reign appears to have begun well enough, with sound administrative and legal reforms. Expensive military campaigns in Germany during his tenure were conducted with varying degrees of success. Domitian continued to spend lavishly on buildings, including his own massive palace that eventually covered the whole central portion of the Palatine. The costs were compounded when Domitian awarded the legionaries a substantial pay rise, assuring him of their loyalty.

Eventually, competing emotions of paranoia and poor self-esteem apparently brought about a reign of terror. Hundreds of people were denounced and killed, from senators to Christians, as Domitian sought to rid himself of potential rivals. Ultimately, a disgruntled steward knifed Domitian and the Flavian dynasty came to an end. Hastily, the senate declared an emperor of its own, the 66-year-old Marcus Cocceius Nerva (r.96–8). Nerva avoided army mutinies and Praetorian dissent through the usual donatives and proved to be an ineffective if sympathetic ruler. He was quick to ensure the succession by appointing a man the army would approve—Trajan.

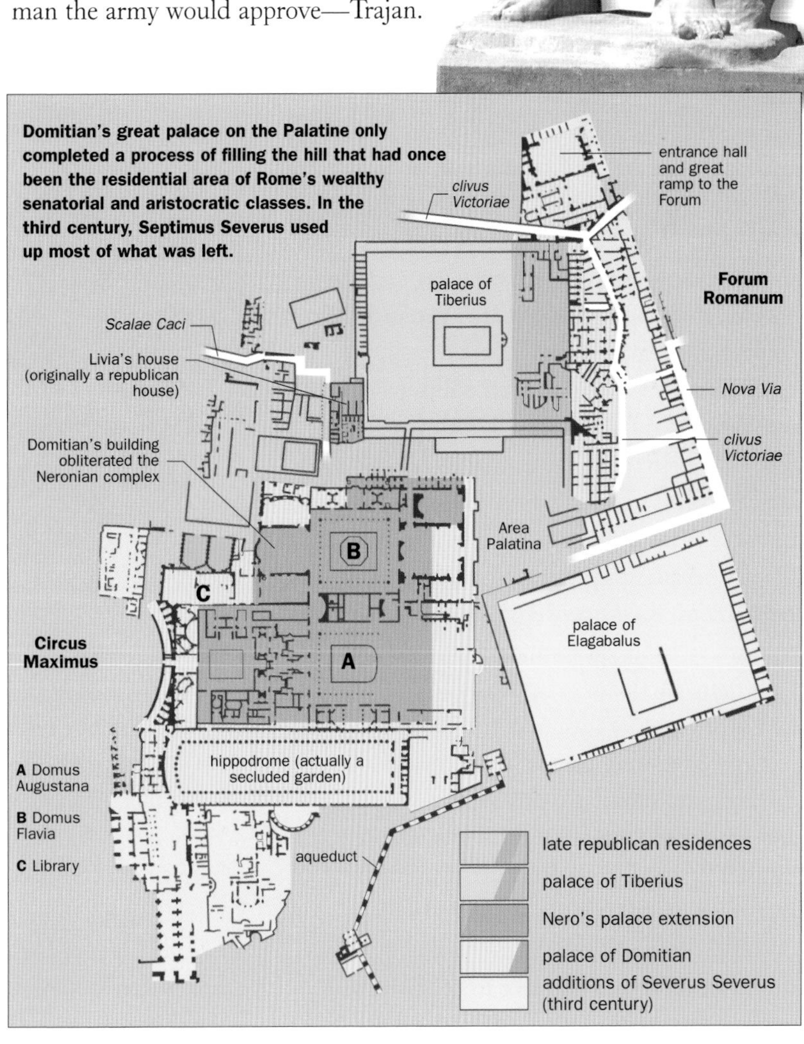
entrance hall and great ramp to the Forum
clivus Victoriae
palace of Tiberius
Forum Romanum
Scalae Caci
Livia's house (originally a republican house)
Nova Via
clivus Victoriae
Domitian's building obliterated the Neronian complex
Area Palatina
B
C
palace of Elagabalus
Circus Maximus
A
hippodrome (actually a secluded garden)
A Domus Augustana
B Domus Flavia
C Library
aqueduct
late republican residences
palace of Tiberius
Nero's palace extension
palace of Domitian
additions of Severus Severus (third century)

Domitian's great palace on the Palatine only completed a process of filling the hill that had once been the residential area of Rome's wealthy senatorial and aristocratic classes. In the third century, Septimus Severus used up most of what was left.

THE COLOSSEUM

From obscure beginnings as a religious rite, the gladiatorial games were the most dramatic aspect of the Roman taste for entertainment. Men fought for their lives before baying crowds, their blood raked over in the sand before the next combatants took to the arena.

The gladiatorial tradition began among the Etruscans or the Samnians as a funeral rite, its specific origins long forgotten. The first recorded gladiatorial combat took place in Rome in 264 BC, when three pairs of gladiators fought to the death in the Forum Boarium at the funeral of Marcus Junius Brutus. From this point, the scale and frequency of games

increased and they were exported around the empire, so many regional centers boasted their own amphitheater to host games.

Gladiator games illustrated military prowess and satisfied the need for religious sacrifice. They were also a mob anesthetic—consuls and later emperors cheerfully financed extravagant *ludi* (games) as insurance against urban insurrection. Games became an integral element of public celebrations. Rulers delivered additional spectacles to mark victories on competitively larger scales. One event in Trajan's reign lasted for 117 days and involved 4,941 pairs of gladiators.

Gladiators were generally drawn from among the lowborn: criminals, prisoners of war, slaves, and persecuted minorities. Caligula amused himself by making senators and knights fight, creating a scandal that contributed to his downfall. A few joined the profession by choice, desperate men with no place to go. Others enjoyed the prestige attached to the games.

Most gladiators had a short career, but the few that survived, such as Publius Ostorius, veteran of 51 clashes, emerged as national heroes.

Gladiators required training, and schools were established, particularly in Campania. The most famous was at Capua, and it was here in 73 BC that Spartacus led an uprising of gladiators. It grew into a nationwide slave rebellion that was finally put down by Crassus.

Gladiators were theatrically armored in the ring and bore a variety of armor and weapons. There were four main types: the Thracian was armed with a curved scimitar and small round shield, the Samnite had a short sword, oblong shield, and visored helmet, the *retiarus* was lightly armed with a net and trident or dagger, and the *murmillo* had

Left and below: The Colosseum today and reconstructed in a model of Rome. The Forum is immediately behind, Palatine left.

a fish-crest helmet, oblong shield, and sword.

Ludi frequently included wild animals, usually faced by condemned criminals rather than expensive gladiators. Even women fought one another, until they were barred from the activity in AD 200. Augustus had a special arena constructed to be flooded for massive mock sea battles, and his example encouraged those that succeeded him to build ever bigger and better amphitheaters, none more so than the Flavian Amphitheater—the Colosseum.

Left: The floor of the Colosseum no longer exists and the complex underworkings are revealed, where the animals and gladiators were kept and prepared for combat. Three corridors either side of the central corridor were equipped with elevator shafts at the end of the 3rd century. Only one section of the arena still has four of the five floors standing (**right**). The arches of the 2nd and 3rd floors held large statues, completing the Colosseum's magnificence.

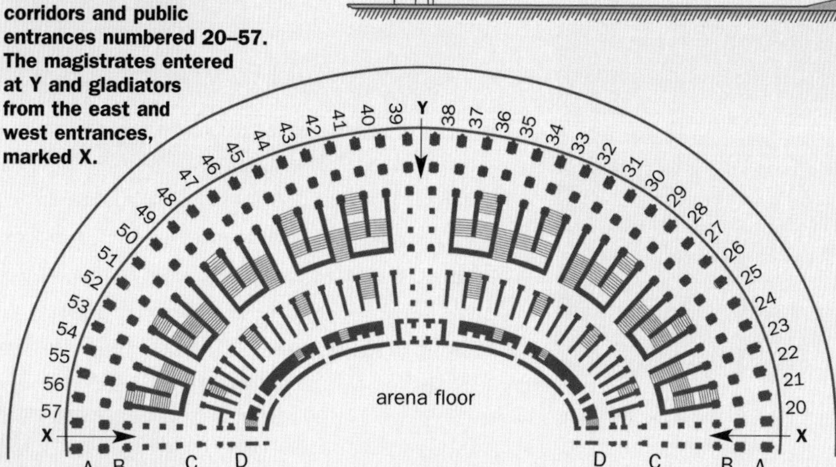

maenianum summum in ligneis
5
maenianum secundum summum
4
3
maenianum secundum immum
2
maenianum primum
senatorial
1
arena floor level
D
C
B
A

The elevation shows the five different levels of the Colosseum and connecting staircases, with the four circuit corridors (lettered). The plan below shows the north half of the Colosseum with the four circuit corridors and public entrances numbered 20–57. The magistrates entered at Y and gladiators from the east and west entrances, marked X.

Y
X
X
arena floor
A B C D
D C B A
20 21 22 23 24 25 26 27 28 29 30 31 32 33 34 35 36 37 38 39 40 41 42 43 44 45 46 47 48 49 50 51 52 53 54 55 56 57

Below: Detail of a Roman mosaic shows gladiators fighting in the amphitheater at Leptis Magna. The various weapons and armor are all accurately depicted.

Daily Life in Pompeii

On August 24, AD 79, Vesuvius erupted, killing thousands as poisonous gases sucked away the air and molten ash rained from above. The towns of Pompeii and Herculaneum were buried, but their misfortune preserved them for later generations.

Right: Bust of an adolescent from Pompeii. The tenderness of this portrait would have been enhanced by lifelike coloring, and some paint staining of the marble can still be seen.

Although there are fine examples of Roman town houses in other places—notably at Ostia—it is in Pompeii and neighboring Herculaneum that the lives of ordinary Romans can be seen, preserved by the pyroclastic wave that engulfed them. It has been estimated that at the time of the disaster Pompeii had a population of 10,000, but this would have been considerably swelled by the many visitors to the Bay of Naples area and the inhabitants of the numerous luxury villas surrounding Pompeii.

Within the town walls were a number of public buildings common to most Roman towns of its size. A forum was located in the center, there were public baths, a theater, and an amphitheater

Above: Pompeii has many marvellous examples of interior decoration, like these in the Oplonti Villa. The extent of frescos in the town suggests that only the poorest houses lacked some form of decoration.

Right: Vesuvius overshadows a street lined with houses and shops. Note the pedestrian crossings.

capable of seating 20,000. But it is among the closely packed town houses that archaeologists have uncovered the artifacts of daily life: elegant glassware, plates, cutlery, drinking vessels, pots, and pans. The secrets of cooking and plumbing are both revealed at Pompeii, with completely preserved ovens and stove tops, and the leadwork that provided Romans with their sanitary comforts. Pompeii's plumbers (workers of lead) had a flourishing trade, fashioning gutters as well as the piping to supply houses with running water from the aqueducts.

While the major urban centers of the empire disappeared under the waves of barbarian invasions of the fifth to seventh centuries, the secrets of Pompeii remained safe under their coating of volcanic ash, ready for modern historians to discover and help us a better understanding of life in the early Roman empire.

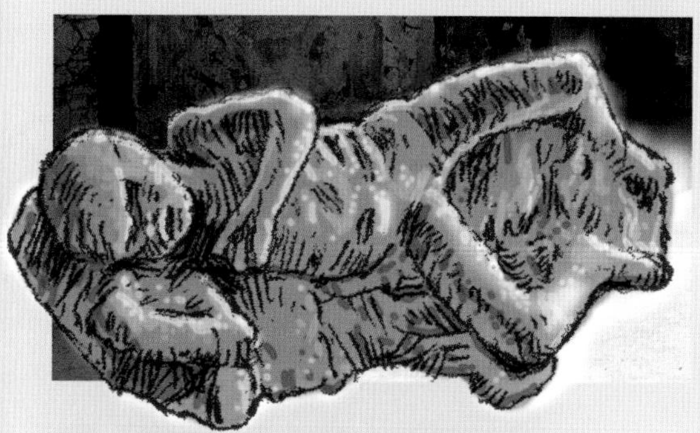

Left: A cast of a victim of the eruption—a small boy lies as he died. Many of Pompeii's citizens were entombed in the mud and ash, their bodies mummified.

Below: Atrium of the House of the Vettii. This is one of the best preserved Roman houses in the city, its interior walls adorned with many splendid frescoes.

Above: Pompeii's preservation has allowed historians to examine the lives of ordinary Romans, like Terentius Neo and his wife pictured here.

THE CIRCUS MAXIMUS

In the first century AD, the satirist Juvenal wrote, "Long ago the people shed their anxieties, ever since we do not sell our votes to anyone. For the people—who once conferred imperium, symbols of office, legions, everything—now hold themselves in check and anxiously desire only two things, the grain dole and chariot races in the Circus."

Juvenal coined the famous phrase, *panem et circenses* (bread and circuses), pointing to the political importance of chariot races in diverting energies that might otherwise have gone into rioting… as long as the grain dole was on time to make the bread. Chariot racing, not gladiatorial combat, was the most popular spectator sport in Rome.

It dates back to the city's earliest days, at least to the era of kings. The ancient Greeks also raced chariots, but there does not appear to be a link between Romans' love of the sport and the Greeks', with both cultures evidently developing their interest separately. Greek chariot races were held in hippodromes, and this continued in the east during the Roman period, while in the west races (*ludi circenses*) were held in a *circus* (ring).

By the time of the empire, racing had grown into a highly professional sport. All the jockeys belonged to *factiones* (teams), which were virtually financial corporations, like modern football teams. From the reign of Augustus there were four principal teams in Rome—the *albata* (whites), *russata* (reds), *veneta* (blues), and *prasina* (greens), identified by the colors they wore. Support for the teams was fanatical, and frequently spilled over into violence, but according to most contemporary accounts the greens and blues were usually the favorites.

As with gladiators, charioteers were usually drawn from the lower classes, freedmen, and

Below: Reconstruction of the Circus Maximus c. AD 300, seen from the northwest end. The 12 *carceres* (start gates) are at bottom left. Domitian's palace dominates the Palatine, top left. The *pulvinator* (imperial box) is on the left.

slaves. Similarly, those who had many wins became idolized by the crowd, and many earned sufficient prize money to buy their freedom and a life of luxury.

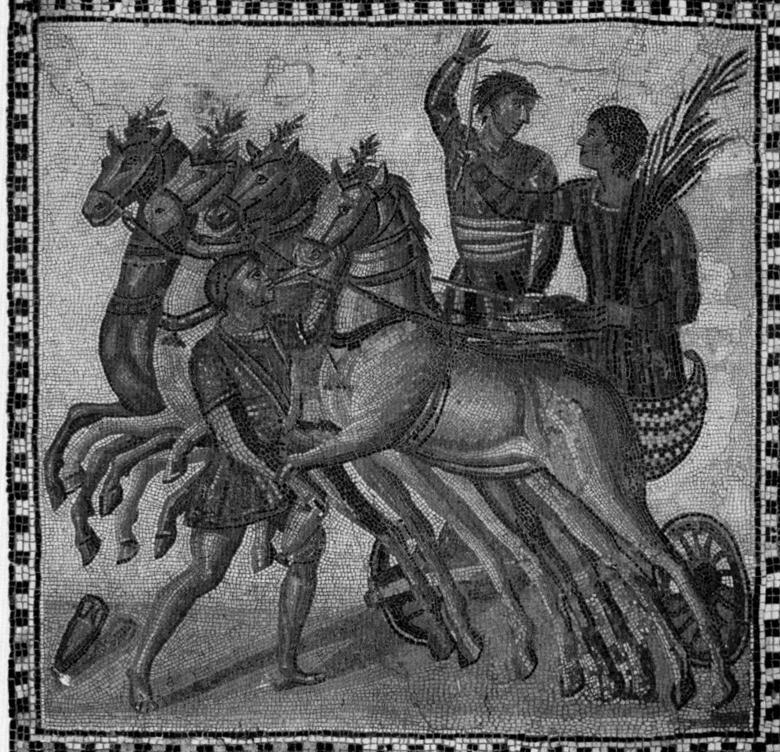

The day's program

A full day's racing usually consisted of 24 events. Each race was between a maximum of 12 chariots, with either two or, more commonly, four horses. The chariots entered the arena simultaneously from the 12 starting gates at the northern end of the circus and then raced counter-clockwise, circling the central *spina* for seven laps. Accidents, even fatalities, were commonplace and regarded as an essential part of the entertainment. At the conclusion of the games, the victors received their prizes—the victor's gold palm, crowns, and necklaces of gold.

Circuses sprang up all over the Roman world. Rome itself had three major public venues, although the Circus Flaminius in the Campus Martius had largely been built over by the time of Augustus. Caligula and Nero developed a circus on the other side of the Tiber for their own use (now the area occupied by the Vatican). But the most important was the Circus Maximus at the foot of the Palatine. Dating back to the sixth century BC, for centuries it remained a simple open area with wooden seating. By the time of Claudius it had become far grander, but it was only in the time of Trajan that it was turned into a monumental structure capable of seating an estimated 380,000 people.

Above: A mosaic shows a victorious charioteer greeted by his stable team.

Left: Only a tiny portion of the stand structure is all that is left of the Circus Maximus (marked B in the plan). Remains of Domitian's palace can be seen above.

The Circus Maximus was almost completely torn down, to use its stone in later buildings, although its shape is clearly seen in aerial photography.

Fortunately, a similar circus at Leptis Magna survived sufficiently to be able to re-create what it probably looked like during the middle to later imperial period.

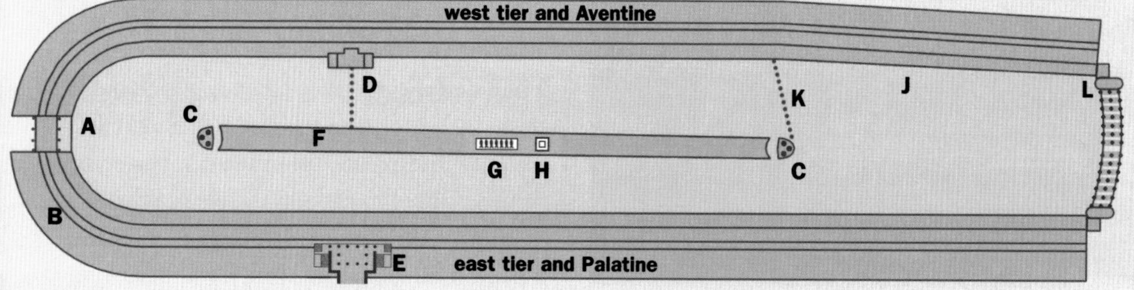
west tier and Aventine
A
B
C
D
F
G
H
K
C
J
L
E
east tier and Palatine

Key to the plan of the Circus Maximus

A Triumphal Arch of Titus
B area of remaining ruins
C *metae* (turning posts), 3 gilded bronze cones
D finish box and line
E *pulvinator* (imperial box), first built by Augustus
F 367-yard long masonry rib (*spina*) decorated by statues and trophies
G raised rack containing 7 eggs and 7 dolphins to count the race laps
H Obelisk of Rameses II (r. 13th century BC) erected by Augustus
J the right-hand lane and spina were angled to give an equal break to the start line
K *alba linea* (start line)
L 12 *carceres* (starting gates) either side of central victory arch

TRAJAN'S CAPABLE HANDS

The tenure of elderly Nerva was predictably short, lasting just two years. A liberator to the oppressed, he was nevertheless loathed by the army. Only the appointment of Trajan as his successor averted a coup.

Above: Nerva's adoption of Trajan (**right**) to succeed him above even his own relatives was a departure for Rome.

Below: Detail from Trajan's Column shows Dacian King Decabalus giving shelter to people in his fortress.

Nerva's adoption of Trajan (r.98–117) is a significant moment in Roman history, not because he was adopting a person outside his family—that had been done regularly by the Julio-Claudians—and not because he was pointing to a successor popular with the army. That, after all, was essential. What is extraordinary about Trajan is that he was not even an Italian. Born in AD 53 at the Spanish colony of Italica, Marcus Ulpius Trajanus was not unknown to Romans; he had been conferred with a consulship by Domitian in 91 and his father before him was a consul under Vespasian. Crucially, he had the support of the army, having served ten years as a tribune.

Nerva had already conferred most of the principate's powers on Trajan in 97, and 98 found him in Pannonia on the Danubian border. Being away from Rome for an inauguration would have been the undoing of any previous emperor, but conscientious, sober Trajan had the charisma to take command of the empire and finish a distant military campaign. When he finally arrived in Rome, his modest entry on foot indicated a

common touch from the first. He embraced members of the senate, instantly bridging the chasm that Domitian and many predecessors had created. His wife Plotina was equally modest. On entering the palace she said, "I enter here such a woman as I would hope to be when I depart."

Trajan did much to enhance his reputation while he was emperor. He overhauled the system of roads in Italy, built a new aqueduct, a massive forum, and shopping arcade, instituted poor relief for children, extended the numbers receiving corn aid, reduced taxes, and aimed to install worthy, honest administrators in positions of power, among them Pliny the Younger.

He enjoyed an enduring friendship with Pliny, and their correspondence, which has been preserved, has given scholars a remarkable insight into Roman rule of the era. For example, Trajan refused to endorse the persecution of Christians and actively discouraged the policy of a paper-trail denunciation that was occurring at

Right: A reconstruction shows the forums of Trajan, Augustus, Caesar, and Nerva. The Temple of Trajan can be seen at extreme left, with his column between the temple and the Basilica Ulpia.

the time. "The anonymous pamphlets which have been published must have no place in any accusation," he told Pliny.

Success set in stone

Abroad, he overturned the Augustan advice to stay within existing imperial borders and mounted campaigns in hitherto unconquered regions. His main target was Dacia, lying in modern Romania. Dacia had already faced Domitian's legions, but the outcome remained undecided. Trajan responded to some fairly low-key chest-beating by the Dacian king Decebalus with an invasion in 101, the legality and necessity of which was highly questionable.

After two campaigns, Dacia was absorbed into the empire in 106. The story of the battle is related in the magnificent spiral carvings covering Trajan's Column in Rome. Trajan inaugurated this marble masterpiece in 113 and its minute detail has enlightened subsequent generations on Roman warfare of the era. A statue of Trajan, which topped the memorial, was replaced by one of St. Peter in 1587.

Trajan incorporated several client kingdoms into the empire, including Arabia, which had previously been the domain of the Nabataeans. In 115 he turned his attentions to Parthia, a time-honored foe, successfully occupying the Parthian capital Ctesiphon. Now the empire reached it greatest extent, embracing the Mediterranean with openings on the Atlantic, the Black, Caspian, and Red seas, and the Persian Gulf. To have undertaken such extravagant campaigns indicates how he reveled in the military life.

He was immensely popular in Rome, where he was given the title Optimus Princeps (the best first man), because he increased the quality of Romans' lives while keeping war at bay in foreign parts. Trajan's reputation was perhaps saved by his death after suffering a stroke in 117, a time when Rome was facing numerous reverses as it struggled to maintain its mighty frontier. His body was cremated in Rome and the ashes interred in the base of his victory column.

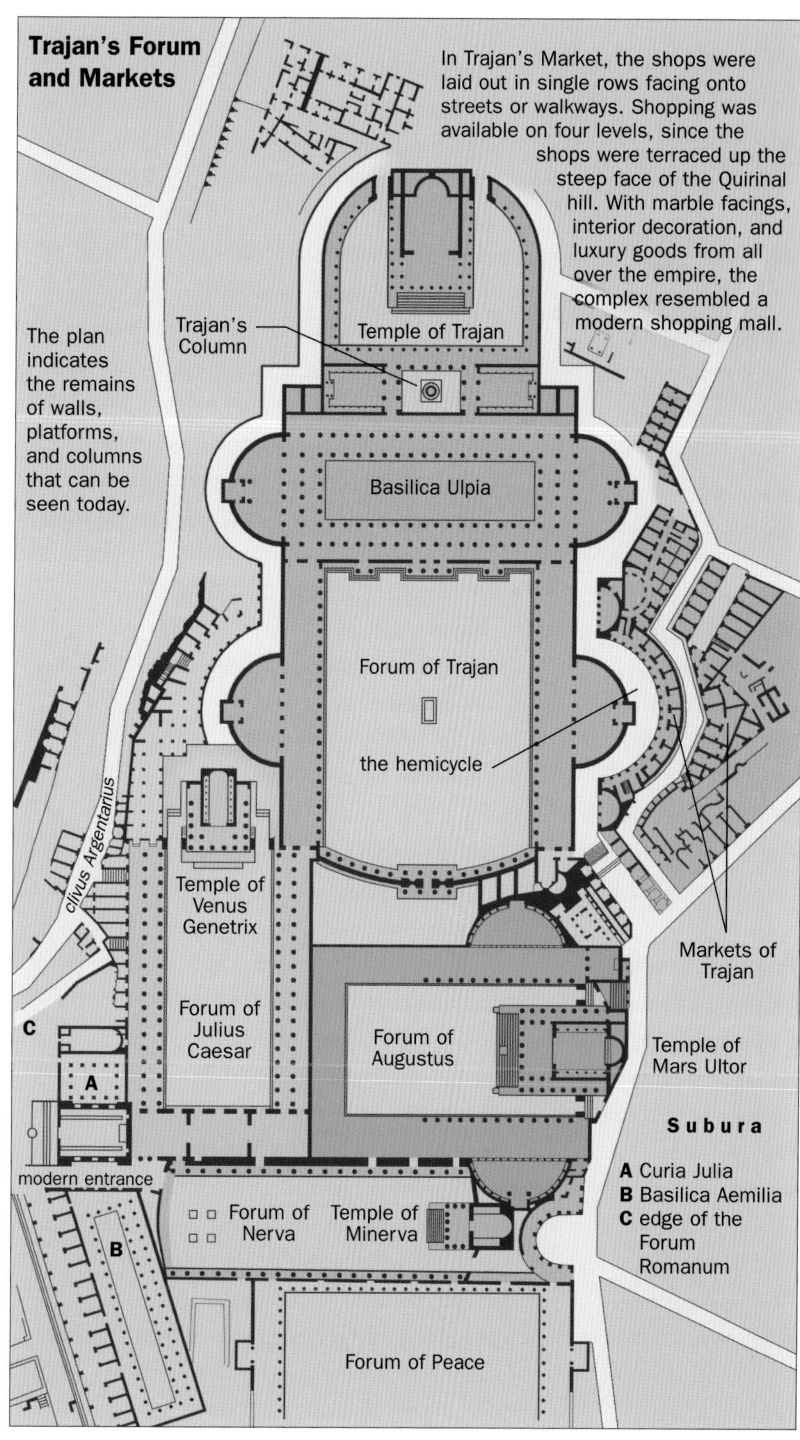
Trajan's Forum and Markets
In Trajan's Market, the shops were laid out in single rows facing onto streets or walkways. Shopping was available on four levels, since the shops were terraced up the steep face of the Quirinal hill. With marble facings, interior decoration, and luxury goods from all over the empire, the complex resembled a modern shopping mall.
The plan indicates the remains of walls, platforms, and columns that can be seen today.
Trajan's Column
Temple of Trajan
Basilica Ulpia
Forum of Trajan
the hemicycle
clivus Argentarius
Temple of Venus Genetrix
Forum of Julius Caesar
Forum of Augustus
Temple of Mars Ultor
Markets of Trajan
Subura
C
A
modern entrance
B
Forum of Nerva
Temple of Minerva
Forum of Peace
A Curia Julia
B Basilica Aemilia
C edge of the Forum Romanum

Hadrian's Consolidation

The first of the bearded emperors, Hadrian was capable but lacked the verve and vigor to become a great princeps. Tributes to his rule surviving in bricks and mortar have overshadowed the criticisms leveled against him at the time of his reign.

Publius Aelius Hadrianus (r.117–38) was born in AD 76 in Italica, Spain to a family of aspirational colonials. Hadrian was later educated in Rome, although he always spoke with a provincial accent. After his father's death Hadrian became the responsibility of fellow Spaniard and family member Trajan. The two became close, although it is by no means certain that the emperor picked Hadrian for adoption or as his successor.

Hadrian enjoyed a speedy elevation through the army ranks and choice political posts until his career stalled for a few years, possibly at a time when Trajan favored one of his rivals. Although little is known of his activities at this time, an inscription proves that he was in Athens in 112 in an official capacity. He was in command of the army in Syria when Trajan died. Thanks to the active support of Trajan's wife Plotina—who may have suppressed news of Trajan's death until the necessary adoption papers were with the senate—Hadrian was hailed Caesar. As usual, there was opposition, but even before Hadrian arrived in Rome on July 9, 118, his supporters in the senate had taken matters into their own hands and the ringleaders—four ex-consuls—had been executed.

Hadrian's policy was very different from Trajan's. Convinced that the empire had reached its viable limits, he halted expansion. The troops were recalled from the Lower Euphrates and Trajan's new Mesopotamian provinces given into the hands of client kings. In Britain he forbade any further northward advance, refused further African expansion, and made the Rhine the northern boundary in Germany.

Hadrian's aim was consolidation, chiefly by Romanizing the populations now within his sphere of power. The subtleties of the plan were not immediately obvious to hostile elements within the senate, who began planning a coup. Only the loyalty of the Praetorian Guard gave the fledgling emperor an opportunity to rule.

In response, Hadrian held an inaugural celebration, marked by a bonfire with which lists of unpaid taxes were committed to the flames. Shrewdly, he realized his priorities. The Roman aristocracy was largely ignored, while soldiers, although not fighting for the empire, were kept busy with extravagant maneuvers. He toured the provinces relentlessly, visiting the legions and leading a soldier's life. He was also interested in the welfare of his provincial subjects, and they benefited from new roads, aqueducts, bridges, temples, baths, and other civic buildings.

Above: Hadrian's lover, Antinöus, traveled widely with the emperor until his drowning in Egypt in 130. Hadrian founded a new city in his honor named Antinöopolis.

Right: Hadrian's talent for architecture and civil engineering made him a prolific and eclectic builder. His villa at Tivoli incorporated the styles of many cultures. A visit to Britain in the first years of his principate resulted in the construction of Hadrian's Wall.

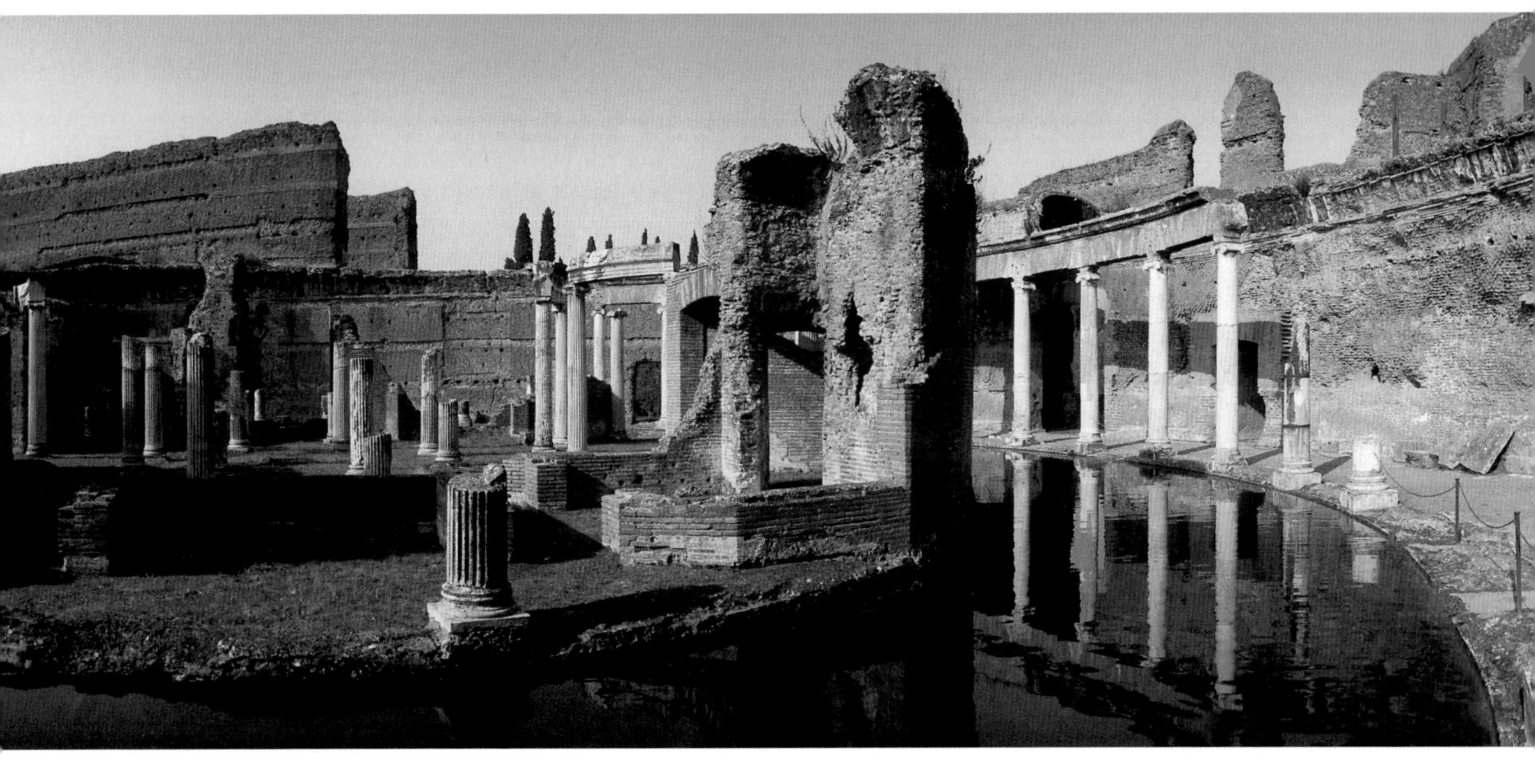

The Roman tourist

Hadrian's travels were also occasioned by his wide interest in art, literature, Greek culture—he was sufficiently vain to curl his hair with tongs in the Greek manner—and exotic sights. His behavior when traveling often resembled that of a modern tourist, visiting all the sites and monuments, climbing mountains for a view of the sunset. Hadrian, who had married Trajan's grand-niece Vibia Sabina, was blatantly homosexual and he took his lover Antinöus with him to Egypt to visit the ancient Egyptian temples. But it was here that Antinöus drowned in a swimming accident. Later, Hadrian turned his mammoth palace at Tibur (Tivoli) into a memorial for his lost lover.

Hadrian's major failure of colonial policy came about when he renamed Jerusalem Aelia Capitolina and banned Jews from entering it except on one day a year. The resulting rebellion in 132 (*see page 111*) led to much bloodshed and the final dispersion of Jews from the region. At the end of 132 he returned to Rome and seems to have given up traveling, preferring to indulge in his passion for all the arts.

During his reign, in accordance with his consolidation and defensive policies, all the major border Roman fortifications were constructed, among the best preserved of which is the wall in northern Britain that today bears his name. But he spent almost half of his reign away from Rome, and much time in Tivoli when he was in Italy. Given this and the harsh way he dealt with opposition, when he died, enfeebled by disease in 138, he had become a distant and unpopular character. His successor Antoninus Pius was far more compassionate and better liked.

Above: Ruins of the Maritime Theater in Hadrian's Villa, Tivoli. Hadrian was heavily involved in the design and building of what is more a small town than a living space. Construction started in 118, immediately after he became emperor, and was completed by 134. Hadrian's engineering skills also lent themselves to the construction of fortifications like the great wall in Britain.

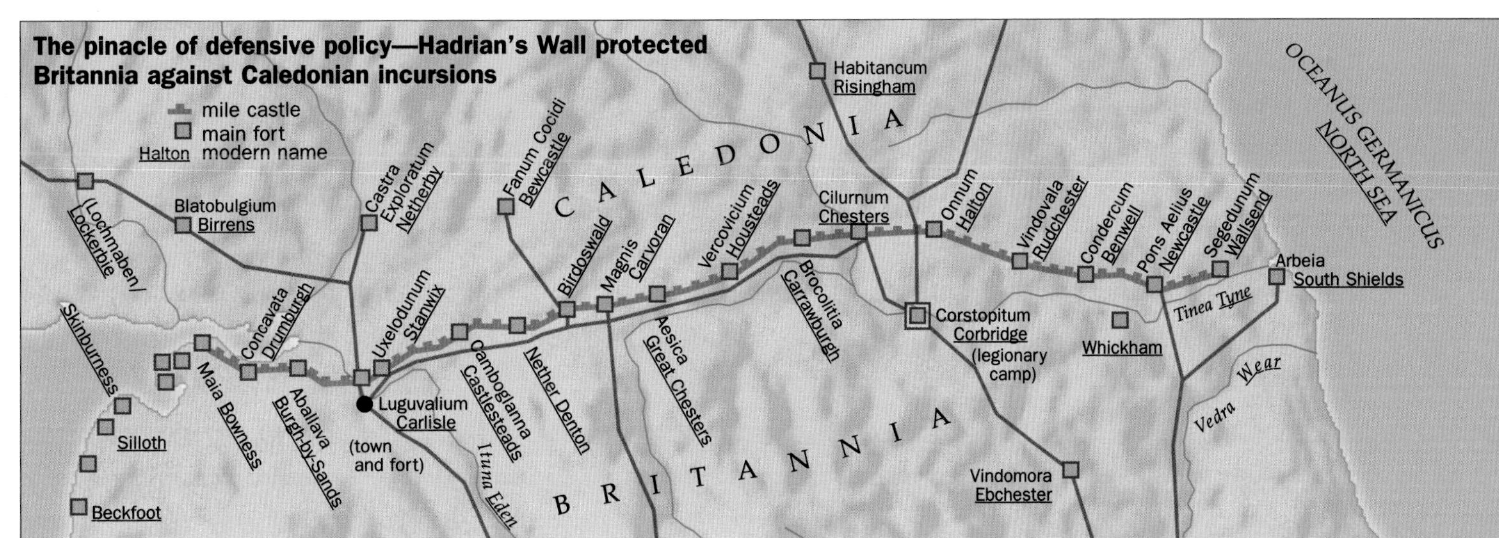
mile castle
main fort
Halton modern name
CALEDONIA
BRITANNIA
OCEANUS GERMANICUS
NORTH SEA
Habitancum
Risingham
(Lochmaben/
Lockerbie
Blatobulgium
Birrens
Castra
Exploratum
Netherby
Fanum Cocidi
Bewcastle
Cilurnum
Chesters
Onnum
Halton
Vindovala
Rudchester
Condercum
Benwell
Pons Aelius
Newcastle
Segedunum
Wallsend
Arbeia
South Shields
Birdoswald
Magnis
Carvoran
Vercovicium
Housesteads
Brocolitia
Carrawburgh
Corstopitum
Corbridge
(legionary
camp)
Whickham
Tinea Tyne
Wear
Vedra
Skinburness
Concavata
Drumburgh
Uxelodunum
Stanwix
Camboglanna
Castlesteads
Nether Denton
Aesica
Great Chesters
Maia Bowness
Aballava
Burgh-by-Sands
Luguvalium
Carlisle
(town
and fort)
Ituna Eden
Silloth
Beckfoot
Vindomora
Ebchester

The pinacle of defensive policy—Hadrian's Wall protected Britannia against Caledonian incursions

Economy of the Empire

Rome may have been a reluctant empire-builder during the republic, but now the benefits of extended territories were apparent. A new wealthy merchant class emerged and business boomed.

The Roman empire underpinned its success in the first century AD with the introduction of a stable, standard currency. Early coinage was minted in gold, silver, and copper (*see panel*) in order to pay the army. Because the legions were scattered around the provinces, Roman coinage spread far and wide, and was used instead of bartering. In this way, money was recycled and proved so successful its use extended beyond the army and embraced trade.

Coins made the collection of taxes much easier, with a few coins replacing a physical percentage of the harvest, for example. The result was a largely prosperous economy, although less scrupulous emperors tended to devalue the currency to boost their coffers. Some stresses on the system due to the inequity of coins slowly became apparent. By the time of Aurelian (r.270–75) there was a pressing need to standardize the precious metal content of coins. He founded two new Italian mints to ensure all coins met a standard. Diocletian (r.284–305) went further, by disposing of locally minted coins and creating a new gold standard.

Pottery was a vital industry. Jars, or *amphorae*, were used for storage and transport of mainstays including olive oil, wine, and cereals. Bronze-casting was the industry of Etruria and its work was exported everywhere. The iron industry was centered on Como, Sulmona, Salerno, and Puteoli, the latter also a producer of terracotta.

A broad range of craftsmen worked in Rome, attracted by the promise of new wealth. There were plumbers, blacksmiths, carpenters, wheelwrights, spinners, dyers, bootmakers, buttonmakers, architects, and more.

Wheels of trade—Roman coinage

The earliest coins of Rome were derived from a standard-weight bar of bronze known as an *as* (pl. *asses*). The initial *as* weighed a Roman pound (just under 11 $^{1}/_{2}$ ounces), but was later reduced in weight until by 217 BC an *as* weighed only 9$^{1}/_{2}$ ounces. The main gold coin of the early empire was the *aureus* (replaced by Constantine at the start of the fourth century with the *solidus*). However, the main denomination was the silver *denarius*. Both were minted under the direct control of the emperor.

Under Nero the weight and quality of the *denarius* dropped, a cost-cutting practice that continued under successive emperors. By the reign of Caracalla, the *denarius* was about 40% silver, and the new *antoninianus* was introduced, worth twice that of the *denarius*, but with only half the silver content. The *denarius* was gradually phased out. Silver *quinarii* (half *denarii*) were issued throughout the republic and became more regular under the early principate (there were also gold versions worth more).

Other silver coins included the *argenteus*, minted by Diocletian to replace the *denarius*, Constantine's *miliarense* worth $^{1}/_{8}$ of a *solidus* that replaced the *argenteus*, and *siliqua* worth $^{1}/_{24}$ of a *solidus*. Constantine also minted three smaller gold coins: the *scripulum* and *semissis* (both half a *solidus*), and the *tremissis* ($^{1}/_{3}$ of a *solidus*). The most widely circulated coin of the empire, and also the largest in size, was the bronze *sestertius*. There were other bronze or copper coins in circulation throughout the period: *quadrans*, *follis*, *centionalis*, and in the later empire too many to be indentified today by name and known only by their diameters.

Under Augustus, the currency equivalency was:

1 *aureus*	= 25 *denarii*
1 *quinarius* (gold)	= 12$^{1}/_{2}$ *denarii*
1 *quinarius* (silver)	= 8 *asses*
1 *denarius*	= 16 *asses*
1 *sestertius*	= 4 *asses*
1 *dupondius*	= 2 *asses*
1 *as*	= 4 *quadrantes*
1 *semis*	= 2 *quadrantes*
1 *quadrans*	= $^{1}/_{4}$ *as*

79	c.80	81	96	98	101	106	106
Vesuvius erupts, smothering Pompeii and Herculaneum	The Colosseum is constructed	Titus dies of the plague and is succeeded by his brother, Domitian	Nerva becomes emperor after the Praetorian Guard assassinates Domitian	Nerva dies, replaced by a Spanish general, Trajan	Trajan invades Dacia (Romania)	Romans in Asia establish the Arabian province in place of the Nabataea	Trajan defeats King Decebalus; Dacia is part of the Roman empire

Trade of all kinds

Slavery was a cornerstone of the Roman empire, humans being as much a commodity as anything craftsmen produced. The inhabitants of foreign towns were frequently sold by the thousand, the proceeds part of the booty accrued by triumphant commanders. Slave labor was exploited and, although the building projects in and around Rome were colossal, the number of workers was immense and supply was constant. This may help to explain why there were no scientific leaps during the Roman era; an abundance of manpower left no pressing need for the creation of labor-saving devices. While punishment for errant slaves was severe, cruel treatment was not encouraged in Rome. Some slaves were permitted to purchase their freedom, becoming entitled to the benefits of citizenship.

Further afield, Rome developed trading links with other countries to gain access to high-value products. Silk arriving from China in the eastern provinces was cherished among the Roman aristocracy. Spices were prized imports from India, hugely helpful in disguising the flavor of meat and fish that had been stored in a hot country without the assistance of refrigeration—one favorite dish among the Roman nobility was flamingo served with a spicy sauce. Other items from the Indian sub-continent included ivory statues (one was discovered in the ruins of Pompeii). Emeralds were imported from Scythia, perfumes from Arabia, and papyrus and glass from Egypt. In return, Roman goods, especially pottery and metalwork, were traded eastward along the Silk Road.

This trade in luxury goods was alien to the ordinary people of Rome. They were more likely to exchange livestock, cereals, vegetables, and fruits at local markets that ran on a nine-day schedule. And with unemployment always high in the city, the masses relied on the corn dole and the regular, lavish *ludi* presented in the Colosseum and Circus Maximus.

Above: The humble pottery amphora was designed for easy stacking in ship holds and on carts and was the empire's principal means of transporting foodstuffs and liquids such as wine and oil.

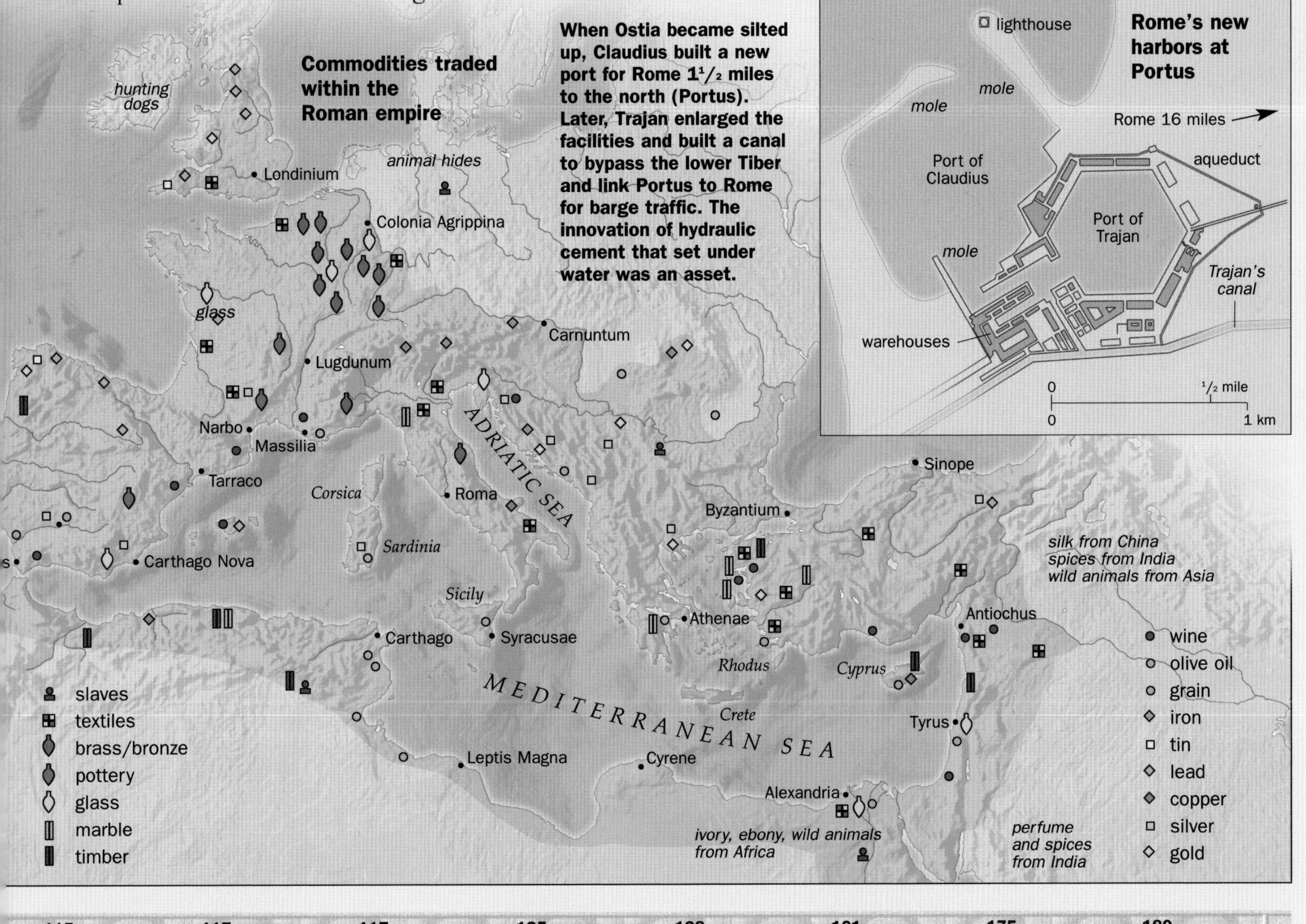
Commodities traded within the Roman empire
hunting dogs
animal hides
Londinium
Colonia Agrippina
glass
Lugdunum
Carnuntum
Narbo
Massilia
Tarraco
Corsica
Roma
ADRIATIC SEA
Sardinia
Carthago Nova
Sicily
Carthago
Syracusae
Byzantium
Sinope
Athenae
Rhodus
Cyprus
Antiochus
Crete
MEDITERRANEAN SEA
Leptis Magna
Cyrene
Tyrus
Alexandria
ivory, ebony, wild animals from Africa
perfume and spices from India
silk from China
spices from India
wild animals from Asia
slaves
textiles
brass/bronze
pottery
glass
marble
timber
wine
olive oil
grain
iron
tin
lead
copper
silver
gold
Rome's new harbors at Portus
lighthouse
mole
mole
mole
Rome 16 miles
Port of Claudius
aqueduct
Port of Trajan
Trajan's canal
warehouses
0
1/2 mile
0
1 km

When Ostia became silted up, Claudius built a new port for Rome 1½ miles to the north (Portus). Later, Trajan enlarged the facilities and built a canal to bypass the lower Tiber and link Portus to Rome for barge traffic. The innovation of hydraulic cement that set under water was an asset.

- **115** Trajan invades Parthia; Roman empire is at its greatest extent
- **117** Trajan dies at Cicilia, ending Parthia campaign; Hadrian is the new emperor
- **117** Roman forces withdraw from Armenia and Mesopotamia on Hadrian's orders
- **135** Renaming Jerusalem Aelia Capitolina results in Jewish revolt and diaspora
- **138** Antoninus Pius becomes Roman emperor on Hadrian's death
- **161** Pius is replaced by his deputy, Marcus Aurelius
- **175** Germanic invaders are driven out of the Roman empire
- **180** Marcus Aurelius is succeeded by his son, Commodus

Creating Roman Classics

The Romans left much for us to remember them by. Despite the many centuries, a legacy of painting, architecture, and literature remains intact. The skill evident in the creation of Roman artifacts and buildings is immense, even by today's standards.

Architecture took a significant leap under the Romans, largely thanks to the basic building material of concrete, usually faced with brick and sometimes marble. Roman concrete was made from an aggregate containing stone, brick, tile, or a mixture set in mortar made from water, lime, and a volcanic sand called *pozzolana*. The strength and flexibility of concrete allowed Roman architects to span ever greater spaces and, from the time of Nero onward, to form great domes.

The most famous of these, and the best preserved, is that of the Pantheon, built by Hadrian between 118 and 125 on the site of Agrippa's original in the Campus Martius. This extraordinary feat of engineering provided a dome that has a height exactly equal to its diameter. The dome's span was not surpassed until modern times, and is greater than that of St. Peter's. The Pantheon was dedicated to all the Roman gods, but its complete survival is down to the Byzantine emperor Phocas, who gave the building to Pope Boniface IV in 608 to turn it into the church of Santa Maria ad Martyres.

While the Pantheon's architect remains a mystery, his contemporary, Apollodorus of Damascus, is well known. He was responsible for Trajan's Baths, Trajan's Forum and Markets, and the masterpiece of Trajan's Column. This also survived because of the Catholic Church's intervention. It is said that Pope Gregory the Great was so moved by a scene on the column, depicting the emperor aiding the mother of a dead soldier, that he decreed Trajan to be a Christian soul and his column a Christian monument. The outer surface of

Above: Trajan's Column and, to the right, a view of the shop fronts in the hemicycle of Trajan's Market, with the ruins of his forum in front; masterpieces of Apollodorus.

Roman authors and their writings

Roman authors wrote on papyrus or waxed tablets, only fragments of which have survived the centuries, so most authors' works in Latin today are the result of copying during the medieval period, and of course much remains lost. Those who wrote more in Greek have survived better because the climate in the east was better suited to preserving papyrus manuscripts. Despite the inevitable copying errors that must have occurred, the breadth and quality of Roman texts still speaks for itself. It would take a book devoted to the subject to cover all the great Latin writers; what follows is intended to give a flavor of Roman writing. Dates given are AD unless stated.

Lucius Afranius (active c.160–20 BC) wrote plays about the upper classes (*fabulae togatae*), but little has survived, even though they were popular in the empire. Nero apparently staged one that was so realistic it required a house to be set ablaze. Appianos (Appian), who lived during Domitian's principate until c. 160, was a historian. He wrote a 24-volume history of Roman conquests from earliest times until Vespasian, of which nine books survive.

Augustus was also an author, and we know that he wrote an autobiography, epigrams, a poem, and a record of his enterprises, *Res Gestae*, the only work to survive because Tiberius had it engraved on stone tablets in many provinces. The emperor Aurelius

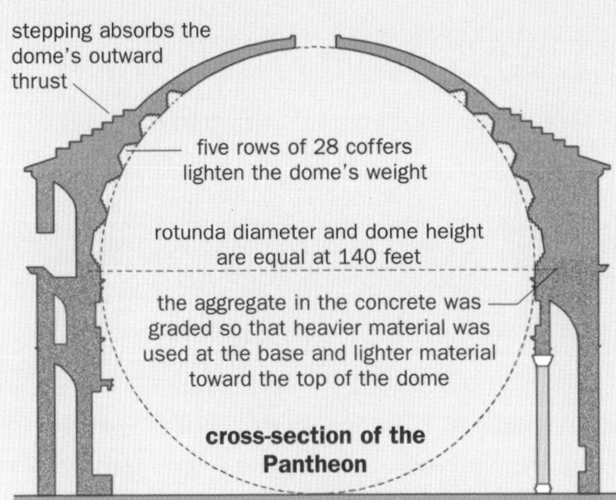
stepping absorbs the dome's outward thrust
five rows of 28 coffers lighten the dome's weight
rotunda diameter and dome height are equal at 140 feet
the aggregate in the concrete was graded so that heavier material was used at the base and lighter material toward the top of the dome
cross-section of the Pantheon

the shaft is sculpted with a continuous spiral frieze depicting scenes from the Dacian campaigns of 101 and 105. The exquisite detail (*see picture page 124*) of the sculpture provides us with the finest insights into the Roman army of the time, its arms, armor, siege weapons and tactics.

The greater space enclosed by concrete constructions led to a much greater emphasis on the interior of buildings than had been the case

M·AGRIPPA·L·F·COS·TERTIVM·FECIT

before. New concepts of decoration were needed to tie the vast elements together: free-standing

continued on next page

Above: Interior of the Pantheon. The rotunda is designed around eight load-bearing piers, with eight recesses between them alternating between rectangular and curved. The decoration is mostly from a later period. A porch supported by 16 granite columns stands in front of the rotunda (**left above**), topped by a classically Greek pediment, with a dedication to Marcus Agrippa, builder of the original Pantheon.

(r.161–80) was the last great proponent of Stoic philosophy. He wrote many formal letters as well as the 12-volume *Meditations* while on campaign on the German frontier.

Julius Caesar's *Commentaries* were memoirs about the Gallic and Civil wars. The seven books of *De Bello Gallico* (*On the Gallic War*) are the only writings to survive, but he was known for other books, including one on jokes, and poems. Cassius Dio Cocceianus (Dio Cassius, 150–235) was a historian, whose 80-volume history of Rome from Aeneas's landing in Italy to 229 (*Historiae Romanae*) survives in part. Only fragments of Cato the Elder's *Origines* survive but his *De Re Rustica* (*On Agriculture*) is the oldest surviving complete piece of Latin prose. His career has been covered elsewhere in this book, as has that of Cicero.

Galenos (Galen, 129–99) is famous for his medical treatises. Born in Pergamum, he doctored for gladiators before going to Rome and becoming physician to the emperors Marcus Aurelius, Commodus, and Septimus Severus. His surviving work became the basis of all medieval medical books.

Quintus Horatius Flaccus (Horace, 65–8 BC) was Rome's greatest poet and satirist, and all his published work has survived, due to his wide popularity. His best known works include the short poems in *Epodi*, the *Carmina* (*Odes*), *Ars Poetica* (*Art of Poetry*), and the *Carmen Saeculare* (*Secular Hymn*), a long ode written for Augustus welcoming the return of ancient

continued on next page

Below: Detail of a mosaic of the early 3rd century AD depicting Virgil writing the *Aeneid* inspired by two (unseen) muses. The mosaic was found in the remains of a Roman house in modern-day Tunisia.

sculpture, bas-reliefs, decorative as well as structural columns of colored marbles, cornice friezes, mosaic panels (*opus vermiculatum*), and paintings. Rome is famous for its legacy of mosaics. They embellished the floors and walls of civic and public buildings, as well as rich Roman homes. Hunting scenes, battles, deities, and religious symbols were all popular themes. Mosaics were also used for practical messages, such as the picture of a hound with the words *Cave canem*—beware of the dog—which appeared at or near the front door of many Roman homes.

Walls were also painted with portraits and landscapes using tempera (on dry plaster) or

Above: Livy's writings have provided us with the most detailed, and probably accurate, record of Roman history up to the time of Augustus.

continued from previous page

virtues. Horace, whose biography was written by Suetonius, had a great influence on Renaissance authors.

Decimus Junius Juvenalis (Juvenal, c.50/70–127) is known for his satires (*Saturae*) on the follies of Roman society, although little is known about the man. Like Horace, Juvenal had a strong influence on 17th-century satirists in Europe. Titus Livius (Livy, c.59 BC–AD 17) is another writer about whom little is known, but whose history is regarded as authoritative. He was author of *Ab Urbe Condita* (*From the Foundation of the City*), a massive work of Rome's history in 142 books, only 35 of which survive, although there are fragments and commentaries for most of the others.

Marcus Annaeus Lucanus (Lucan, 39–65) was educated in Rome in rhetoric and philosophy. His only surviving work is the uncompleted epic poem *De Bello Civili* (*On the Civil War*), which covers the war between Caesar and Pompey. Marcus Valerius Martialis (Martial, c.40–103) was born in Spain but wrote many of his poems in Rome. His *Liber Spectaculorum* (*Book of Spectacles*) celebrated the opening of the Colosseum. *Epigrams* consists of over 1,500 short poems realistically detailing life in Rome.

Publius Ovidius Naso (Ovid, 43 BC–AD 17) was a prolific poet whose irreverence resulted in his banishment by Augustus, probably after he published *Ars Amorata* (*Art of Love*), which deals with the strategies of seduction. Ovid continued

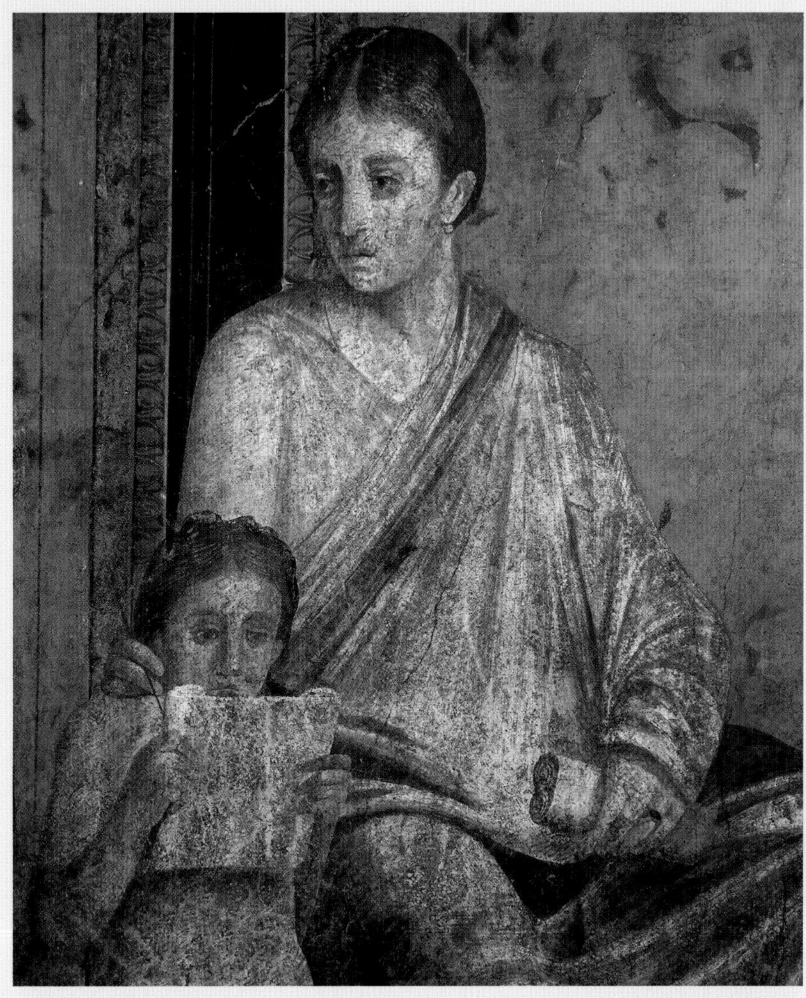

more commonly fresco, in which the pigment is applied while the plaster is still wet. A wide range of mineral and vegetable pigments was available, giving Roman paintings a vibrancy that would not be seen again until the Renaissance. Roman painters were also adepts at dealing with visual space in three dimensions, creating a sense of perspective that would also be lost with the fall of the empire for almost eight centuries.

Sculpture was widely used inside buildings and out, generally reflecting a Greek influence. Statues of deities were an important aspect of religious worship and remained in domestic shrines. While gods were made to appear perfect, those wealthy enough to commission sculptures of themselves were generally content for their physical flaws to be included in the likeness. It was especially important for emperors to have their visage set in stone. Without easily portable sculptures, their subjects would never have known what they looked like.

Three different styles of fresco work from Pompeii illustrate the naturalism that Roman artists of the 1st century AD had mastered. The mythical *Perseus Freeing Andromeda* (**far left**) presages post-Renaissance neo-classic painting, and contrasts with the intimacy of the exquisitely realized birdbath (above left) from the House of the Marine Venus. The detail of a woman and a boy (**above**) is taken from a series of frescos in the Villa of the Mysteries describing the cult of Dionysus.

to write in exile, and his numerous poems exercised a great influence on generations of Romans and post-Renaissance Europeans. Another irreverent writer fared better at first under his patron Nero. Titus Petronius Niger (Petronius the Arbiter) is famous for his *Satyricon*, only fragments of which survive. The picaresque tale of disreputable youths ends up at *Cena Trimalchio* (*Trimalchio's Dinner Party*), a display of vulgar wealth and over-eating. Petronius fell foul of Nero and was forced to commit suicide.

Gaius Suetonius Tranquillus (c.70–140) was a lawyer and author of the biographies of Julius Caesar and the first 11 emperors from Augustus to Domitian (*De Vita Caesarum*), among other works. His often acidic view of the early emperors was probably skewed in order to show how virtuous were the reigns of Trajan and Hadrian. Gaius Cornelius Tacitus (c.56–117) was another historian of the same period, and his *Historiae* makes an interesting comparison to the writing of Suetonius. His best known work was about his father-in-law Agrippa's campaigns in Britain (*De Vita Julii Agricolae*).

Publius Terentius After (Terence, c.185–159 BC) was a Carthaginian slave, later freed, who wrote comedy plays, six of which survive. The author who became so famous in his time that later his name was spoken of in reverence was Publius Vergilius Maro (Virgil, 70–19 BC). His works include the poems the *Georgics*, about farming tax, and the mammoth life of Aeneas, the *Aeneid*.

MARCUS AURELIUS, CO-RULER

The Antonine dynasty ruled over a Rome at peace with itself, while danger loomed on the frontiers. To cope with the large empire, an innovation in joint rulership proved a successful means of government.

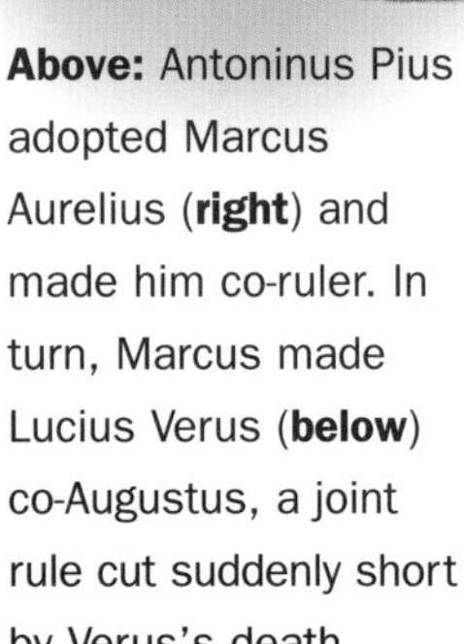

Above: Antoninus Pius adopted Marcus Aurelius (**right**) and made him co-ruler. In turn, Marcus made Lucius Verus (**below**) co-Augustus, a joint rule cut suddenly short by Verus's death.

After Hadrian's death his adopted son, Titus Aurelius Fulvus Boinonius Antoninus (r.138–61), known to history as Antoninus Pius, came to rule. Born in 86 at Lanuvium, by common consent, he was competent, calm, frugal, wise, compassionate, and his reign was tranquil. He exceeded Hadrian's frontier limits only by advancing to the Clyde-Forth line in Scotland, building there the Antonine Wall (*see map, page 101*).

When he died of natural causes, he appeared a hard act to follow. But his adopted son and successor, the 40-year-old Marcus Aurelius Verus Antoninus (r.161–80, 161–69 with Lucius Verus) was equally virtuous. He was also well versed in the role of principate, having ruled jointly with Pius for the last years of his reign.

Historian Edward Gibbon coupled Pius and Aurelius: "Their united reigns are possibly the only period in history in which the happiness of a great people was the sole object of government." The Antonine innovation of joint rulership can be viewed as a means of governing the sprawling empire by splitting responsibilities in the way the republican consuls had done, but also as a means of training a successor in the job.

On his accession, Marcus Aurelius followed his predecessor's example by adopting the youthful Lucius Ceionius Commodus (later Verus) and making him co-Augustus. In fact, Hadrian had advised Pius to adopt both Aurelius and Verus, although there is no indication that either wished them to rule together. However, the joint rule came to a sudden end after eight years when Verus died of a stroke in 169 at the age of 39.

In 177 Marcus made his own son, Lucius Aelius Aurelius Commodus, co-emperor. Marcus Aurelius had been born into a well-connected family. His route to the principate had been expedited by his marriage to Annia Galeria Faustina, Pius's daughter. She bore Aurelius eight sons and six daughters, although most died in childhood. Despite the number of pregnancies, she was accused of infidelity and may even have conspired against Aurelius, who remained devoted to her.

A Stoic leader

Marcus Aurelius is best remembered for his book, *Meditations*, a collection of notes made throughout his career, revealing a passion for Stoic philosophy, founded by Zeno in Greece, c.308 BC. Stoicism decrees that man lives with nature in accordance with a grand cosmic design. It preaches equality of man and universal brotherhood, and qualities such as modesty, sincerity, and high morals are applauded. With death, the soul rejoins the universe. Aurelius, we are told, was a solemn child who cherished the writings of the ancient philosophers, particularly Epictetus, a religious former slave.

His character appeared tailored for a peaceful

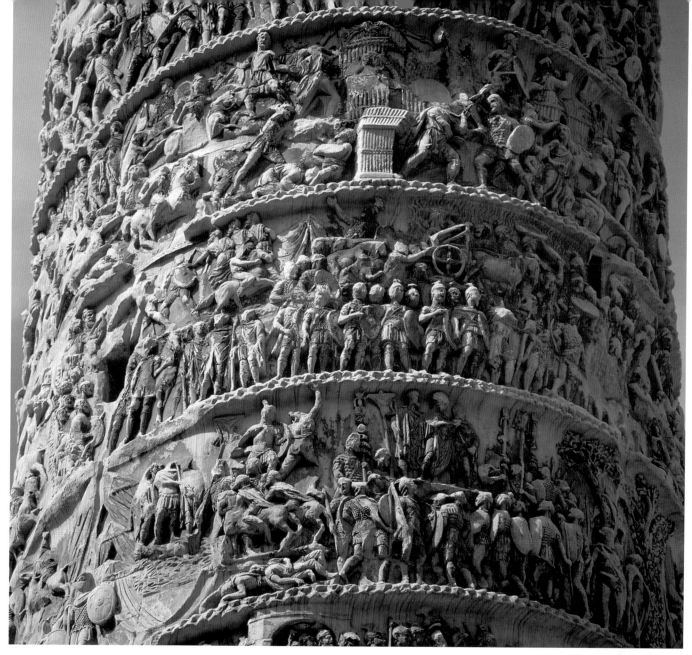

and just reign, yet driven by duty Aurelius lived a soldier's life, rather than a scholar's. Unlike Pius, Aurelius had little effect on Roman government beyond some minor modifications to the legal statutes because most of his time was absorbed with military campaigns on the empire's fringes, first in Parthia and then on the northern frontier. His *Meditations* were written on the Danube while he was involved in war against Rome's enemies, the Marcomanni and Quadi. His campaigns were recorded in a spiral frieze on a column like Trajan's.

Punishing barbarian pressure and a devastating plague epidemic convinced Marcus that the gods were punishing mankind. Perhaps by way of appeasement, he ordered a wave of persecutions against the Christians. Cassius Dio appreciated his talents: "[He] did not meet with the good fortune that he deserved, for he was not strong in body and was involved in a multitude of troubles throughout practically his entire reign. But for my part, I admire him all the more for this very reason, that amid unusual and extraordinary difficulties he both survived himself and preserved the empire."

Marcus Aurelius died on March 17, 180 at Vindobona (Vienna) of natural causes. However, fingers of suspicion were pointed at his son Commodus, who appeared all too eager to take sole control, and Commodus was a very different man to his father.

Above: The Column of Marcus Aurelius stands not far from that of Trajan, but while the latter's is an aggrandizement of conquest, Marcus's shows the defense of an empire under increasing pressure from across the Danube, a pattern that would dominate the next century.

Right: A coin bears the portrait of Annia Galeria Faustina, daughter of Antonius Pius and wife to Marcus Aurelius.

CHAPTER 9

AGE OF INSECURITY

As the second century gave way to the third, the task of governing a vast empire grew exponentially. In the next hundred years most of the emperors were self-proclaimed, often simultaneously in different provinces. The Antonine concept of joint rulers, designed to spread responsibility for managing the widespread Roman state, deteriorated into a self-seeking scramble for power. There were good men, but few and far between.

It is widely acknowledged that the business of running empires went into decline on the death of Marcus Aurelius in AD 180. According to Cassius Dio, the Severan dynasty was notably poor: "Our history and the affairs of the Romans descend from an age of gold to one of iron and rust." Still, Severus himself proved capable, but when his dynasty failed, the real power lay with the army, and its favors were often divided or quickly lost. The result was a period of chaos. Sensing Rome's weakness, her enemies gathered on all frontiers. Ironically, it was only the strength of the army, and the barbarian opponents' lack of discipline, that saved the empire from disaster.

There were other causes of dissolution, including rampant inflation and the growing dissension among Christians to accept their lot. Rome's ancient cults were unable to withstand the assault of new religious thinking, mystery cults that offered hope to a confused and frightened populace. When, at long last, a strong emperor came to power, in tidying up the mess of half a century, Diocletian tackled the problem of Christianity. Its insistence on a single god rankled his conservative attitude, and in this period what had hitherto been sporadic persecutions of Christians as convenient scapegoats became wholesale pogroms.

But for ordinary Roman citizens, Diocletian's principate provided a brief taste of how good life in the golden ages had been.

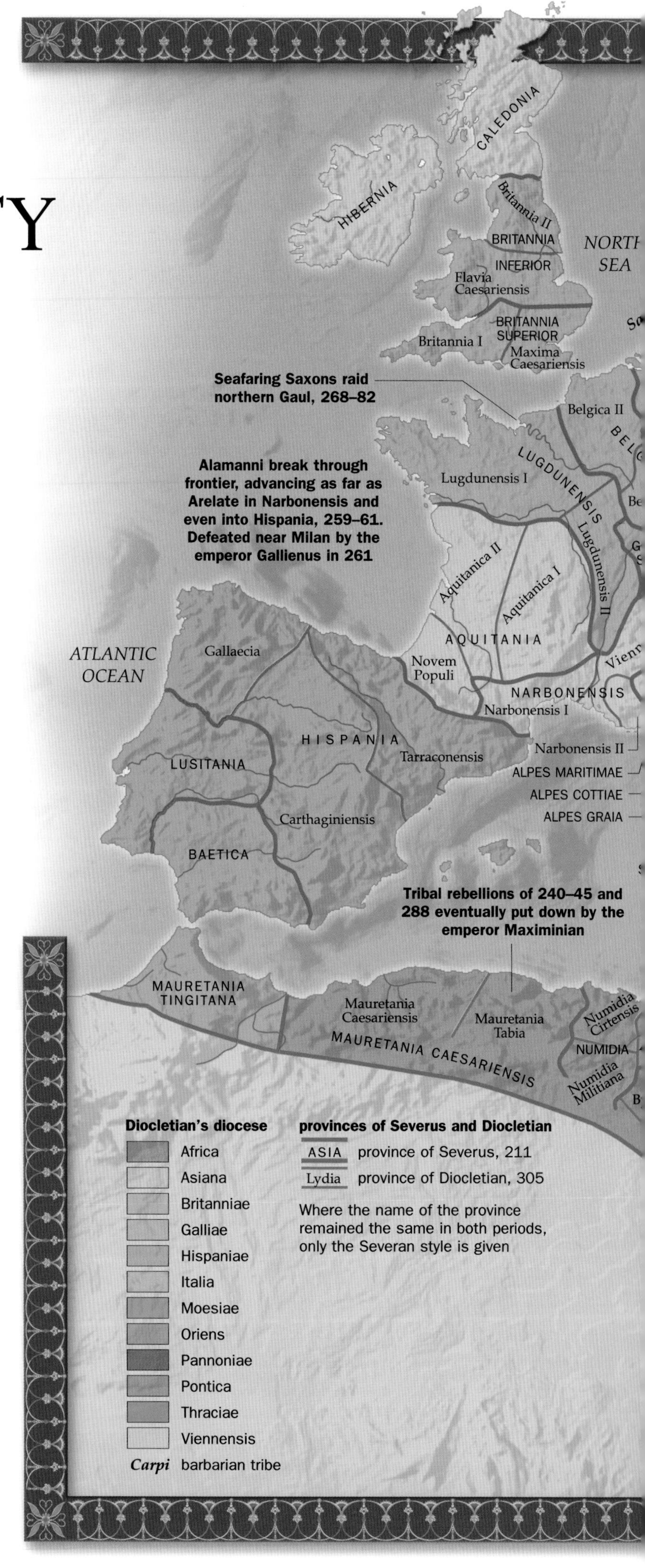

CALEDONIA
HIBERNIA
Britannia II
BRITANNIA
INFERIOR
Flavia Caesariensis
BRITANNIA
SUPERIOR
Britannia I
Maxima Caesariensis
Seafaring Saxons raid northern Gaul, 268–82
Belgica II
LUGDUNENSIS
Lugdunensis I
Alamanni break through frontier, advancing as far as Arelate in Narbonensis and even into Hispania, 259–61. Defeated near Milan by the emperor Gallienus in 261
Lugdunensis II
Aquitanica II
Aquitanica I
AQUITANIA
ATLANTIC OCEAN
Gallaecia
Novem Populi
NARBONENSIS
Narbonensis I
HISPANIA
Tarraconensis
Narbonensis II
ALPES MARITIMAE
ALPES COTTIAE
ALPES GRAIA
LUSITANIA
Carthaginiensis
BAETICA
Tribal rebellions of 240–45 and 288 eventually put down by the emperor Maximinian
MAURETANIA TINGITANA
Mauretania Caesariensis
Mauretania Tabia
MAURETANIA CAESARIENSIS
Numidia Cirtensis
NUMIDIA
Numidia Militiana
Diocletian's diocese
Africa
Asiana
Britanniae
Galliae
Hispaniae
Italia
Moesiae
Oriens
Pannoniae
Pontica
Thraciae
Viennensis
Carpi barbarian tribe
provinces of Severus and Diocletian
ASIA province of Severus, 211
Lydia province of Diocletian, 305
Where the name of the province remained the same in both periods, only the Severan style is given

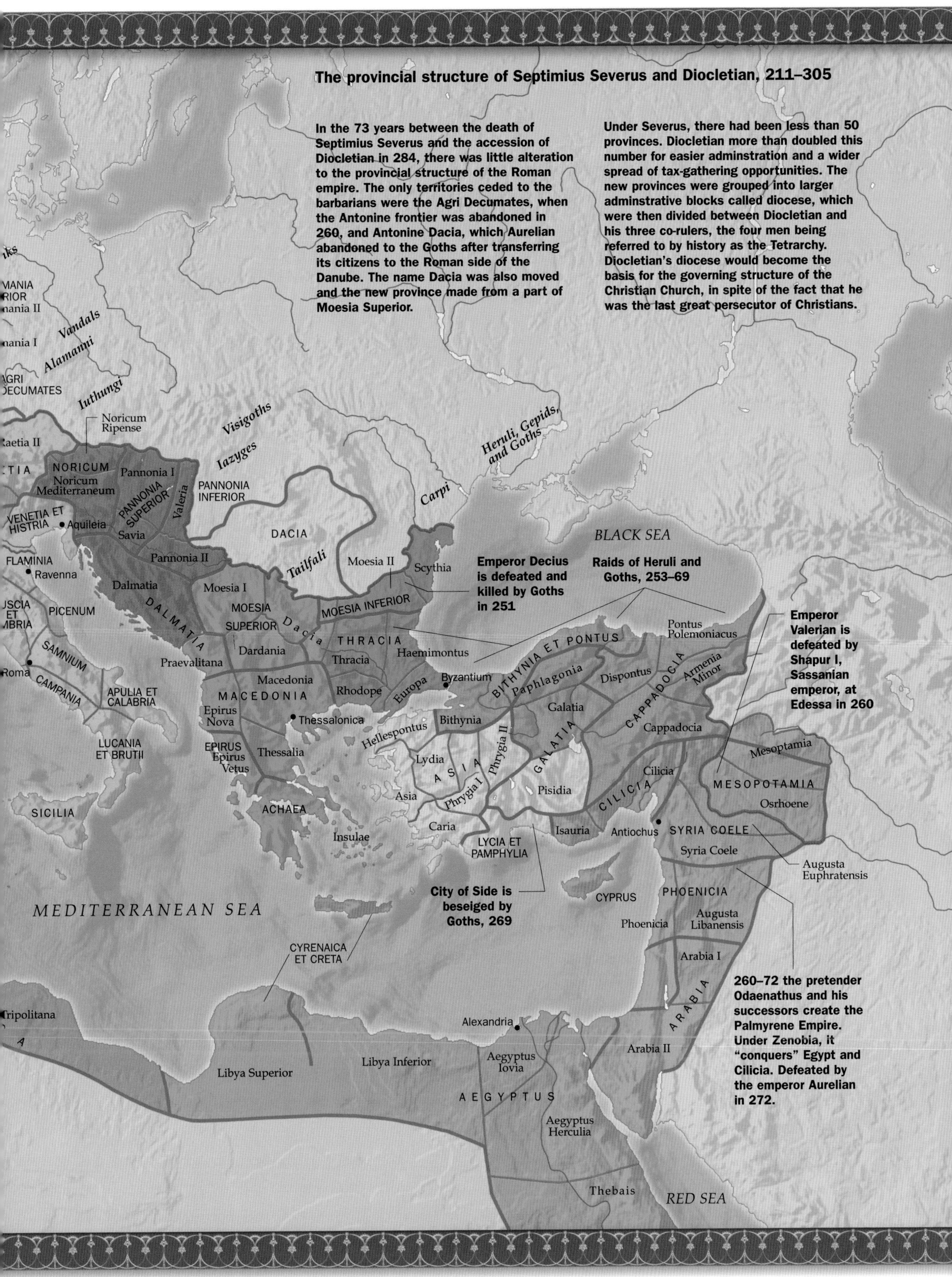
The provincial structure of Septimius Severus and Diocletian, 211–305
In the 73 years between the death of Septimius Severus and the accession of Diocletian in 284, there was little alteration to the provincial structure of the Roman empire. The only territories ceded to the barbarians were the Agri Decumates, when the Antonine frontier was abandoned in 260, and Antonine Dacia, which Aurelian abandoned to the Goths after transferring its citizens to the Roman side of the Danube. The name Dacia was also moved and the new province made from a part of Moesia Superior.
Under Severus, there had been less than 50 provinces. Diocletian more than doubled this number for easier adminstration and a wider spread of tax-gathering opportunities. The new provinces were grouped into larger adminstrative blocks called diocese, which were then divided between Diocletian and his three co-rulers, the four men being referred to by history as the Tetrarchy. Diocletian's diocese would become the basis for the governing structure of the Christian Church, in spite of the fact that he was the last great persecutor of Christians.
Vandals
Alamanni
AGRI DECUMATES
Iuthungi
Noricum Ripense
Visigoths
Iazyges
Heruli, Gepids, and Goths
NORICUM
Noricum Mediterraneum
Pannonia I
PANNONIA SUPERIOR
Valeria
PANNONIA INFERIOR
VENETIA ET HISTRIA
Aquileia
Savia
DACIA
Carpi
BLACK SEA
FLAMINIA
Ravenna
Pannonia II
Tailfali
Moesia II
Scythia
Emperor Decius is defeated and killed by Goths in 251
Raids of Heruli and Goths, 253–69
Dalmatia
Moesia I
PICENUM
DALMATIA
MOESIA SUPERIOR
Dacia
MOESIA INFERIOR
SAMNIUM
THRACIA
Haemimontus
Pontus Polemoniacus
Emperor Valerian is defeated by Shapur I, Sassanian emperor, at Edessa in 260
BITHYNIA ET PONTUS
Praevalitana
Dardania
Thracia
Roma
CAMPANIA
APULIA ET CALABRIA
Macedonia
MACEDONIA
Rhodope
Europa
Byzantium
Paphlagonia
Dispontus
Armenia Minor
CAPPADOCIA
Galatia
Epirus Nova
Thessalonica
Bithynia
Cappadocia
LUCANIA ET BRUTII
EPIRUS
Epirus Vetus
Thessalia
Hellespontus
Lydia
ASIA
Phrygia II
GALATIA
Cilicia
Mesoptamia
MESOPOTAMIA
SICILIA
ACHAEA
Asia
Phrygia I
Pisidia
CILICIA
Osrhoene
Insulae
Caria
Isauria
Antiochus
SYRIA COELE
LYCIA ET PAMPHYLIA
Syria Coele
Augusta Euphratensis
City of Side is beseiged by Goths, 269
CYPRUS
PHOENICIA
MEDITERRANEAN SEA
Phoenicia
Augusta Libanensis
CYRENAICA ET CRETA
Arabia I
260–72 the pretender Odaenathus and his successors create the Palmyrene Empire. Under Zenobia, it "conquers" Egypt and Cilicia. Defeated by the emperor Aurelian in 272.
ARABIA
Tripolitana
Alexandria
Arabia II
Libya Superior
Libya Inferior
Aegyptus Iovia
AEGYPTUS
Aegyptus Herculia
Thebais
RED SEA

Severus and Caracalla

Just a dozen years after the death of the highly respected Marcus Aurelius, the empire again faced chaos and confusion. Septimius Severus, the first Roman emperor from North Africa, seized the reigns of power to establish a new dynasty.

When Marcus Aurelius died in AD 180 he left a stable empire in the hands of his son Commodus (r.180–92). Although he was made Caesar in 166 at the age of five and co-emperor in 177, Commodus was a poor ruler. He speedily concluded a treaty with the Quadi and Marcomanni, and returned to Rome to become obsessed with his personal pleasures. Not only did he keep a harem of women and boys, but also took part in gladiatorial combats, convinced he was the embodiment of the god Hercules. His indulgences were accompanied by a viciously cruel streak, and it was this that finally encouraged senators and Praetorians to hire a professional to strangle him in his bed on New Year's Eve.

Above: Commodus was born August 31, 161 at Lanuvium, son of the great emperor Marcus Aurelius. Later in his reign of cruelty and debauchery, Commodus became insane, thought he was Hercules, and dressed for the part. He renamed Rome *colonia Commodiana* (colony of Commodus).

Commodus's death was followed by civil war, and a situation similar to that of 69 unfolded. Various legions backed their commanders, with none pre-eminent. The first of three emperors to take the throne in a period of six months was Publius Helvius Pertinax. His father had been a slave, but success as an officer under Marcus Aurelius raised him to equestrian rank and a consulship in 175. Although fair-minded, he was dead within three months, murdered by a small group of soldiers unhappy with his economic reforms.

Didius Julianus emerged as the highest bidder at 25,000 *sestertii* per man in an auction held by the Praetorians. It was an episode that did much to devalue the role of princeps. But he was not alone in making claims to the throne—no fewer than three others were preparing campaigns. In Pannonia the legions of Lucius Septimius Severus proclaimed him emperor (r.193–211). He marched swiftly on Rome, suppressed Julianus, and had the vacillating senate confirm him.

The next year he dispatched Pescennius Niger, governor of Syria, who was considered the rightful ruler by the eastern legions. The decisive battle between the two took place in modern Turkey in 194 on the same site that Alexander the Great crushed the Persians in 333 BC. Niger was chased from the battlefield and beheaded, while many of his troops fled to neighboring Parthia. Clodius Albinus, the second pretender, proclaimed himself in Britain, where he was governor. Albinus pressed down from the northwest, gathering supporters on the way, but in 196 he was defeated by Severus at Lyon. Albinus committed suicide shortly afterward.

Spoiling the recipe

The brutality continued as Severus rooted out possible opposition, killing 29 senators. In two campaigns he pursued those who supported Niger into Parthian territory, capturing the capital Ctesiphon in 197, looting the kingdom's treasures and enslaving its population. His reputation as a ruthless butcher is tempered by his architectural achievement. Severus did much to repair the damage wrought to Rome in a disastrous fire in 191 and instigated a massive building program in his birthplace, Leptis Magna, transforming the North African city into a showpiece.

His death came in England during a campaign to suppress the northern tribes. It was his intention that sons Septimius Bassianus Caracalla (r.211–17) and Lucius Septimius Geta (r.211–12), born just a year apart, should rule jointly as Antonine emperors. To establish the dynastic link, Caracalla became known as Marcus Aurelius Antoninus. However, the brothers had little Antonine love for each other and failed to heed their father's coarsely realistic recipe for success: "Agree with each other, give money to the soldiers, and scorn all other men."

Antipathy between them first led to the Palatine palace being divided, then the empire, with the eastern provinces falling to Geta and the western part together with North Africa in the realm of Caracalla. Within ten months the sibling rivals were on the verge of hostilities.

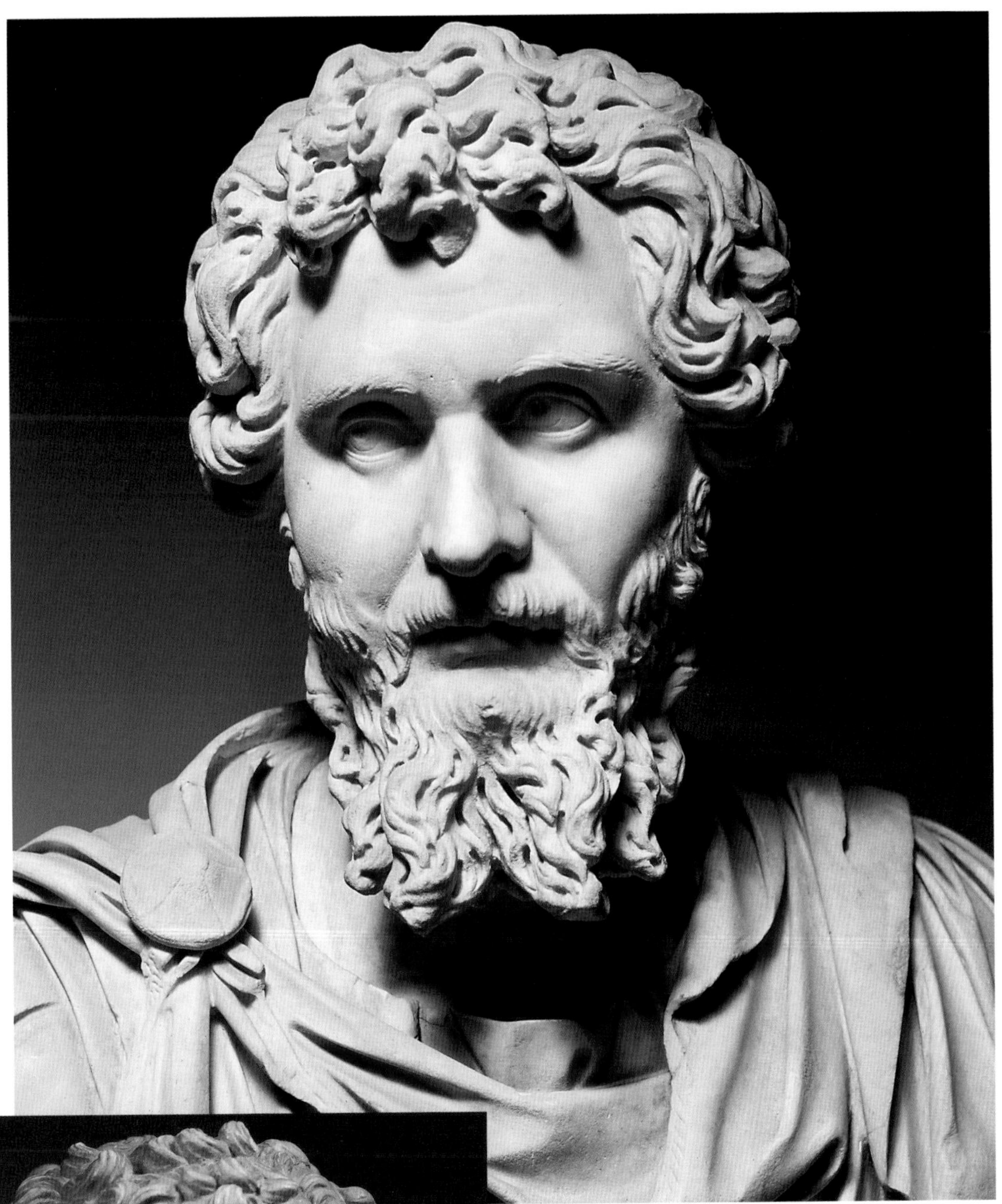

Left: When his troops proclaimed him princeps on April 13, 193, Septimius Severus put an end to the civil war and established the Severan dynasty, which encompassed five further emperors—all poor specimens, with the dubious exception of Caracalla. Severus celebrated a great triumph in 203 in Rome for his various victories, including the capture of Seleucia and Ctesiphon. His arch, which can be found at the western end of the Forum, marks a departure from classicism in Roman sculpture and architecture.

Caracalla averted open warfare by murdering his brother and purging his supporters. The bloodshed stained the rest of the reign. Caracalla spent almost no time in Rome, campaigning on the Rhine, Danube, and in Parthia. His lasting legacy is the magnificent baths in Rome named after him. When Caracalla was assassinated by an army officer between Edessa and Carrhae (Harran), there was no heir apparent.

He was replaced by Marcus Opellius Macrinus (r.217–18), a praetorian praefect, who had also planned Caracalla's murder. Born in the colony of Caesarea, North Africa in 164, Macrinus was a capable emperor, but catastrophically unpopular with the army, not least because of a humiliating defeat of Rome by Parthia during his brief rule. On the throne for just a year, he was hounded out of Rome; he and his son were later murdered.

Left: Caracalla wasted little time in ridding himself of Geta, his brother and joint emperor. Geta's name was erased from the Arch of Severus and replaced by more honorifics for his murderer. Caracalla's ambition to be a second Alexander the Great was never fulfilled, although in imitation of his hero's generosity, he granted citizenship to all free inhabitants of the Roman empire.

Public Roman Amenities

For the Romans, bathing was a luxury and a necessity. The great baths provided a convivial place to socialize, hold business meetings, read a book, take vigorous exercise, relax in beautiful gardens, and get clean.

Right: *Foricae* (public latrines) were basic facilities in baths. Of the 144 listed in Rome, few survive today and the best examples can be seen in the provinces, like this one from the Thermae of the Cyclos, Dougga, Tunisia. Latrines were flushed with waste water from the baths. The gutter in front of the seats ran with fresh water for cleaning hands and the communal cleaning sponges.

Agrippa built the first large public baths in 25 BC. A census he carried in 33 BC recorded 170 small baths in Rome; this number had grown to over 850 by the end of the fourth century. It included the 11 imperial baths (*thermae*), such as those of Trajan, Caracalla, and Diocletian. These are among the most ambitious buildings from the ancient world. The water was supplied from purpose-built aqueducts, which also served local domestic users. The Baths of Trajan were supplied by two aqueducts, the Aqua Traiana and an unnamed aqueduct that filled a great reservoir known as the Sette Sale. Caracalla's baths drew water from a specially built extension of the Aqua Marcia.

Water was stored in massive cisterns from which it could be fed to various parts of the complex. All the great *thermae* share a similarity of layout, generally first accorded to Trajan. After entering the complex free of charge (private baths charged a small entrance fee), bathers made their way through the *frigidarium* (cold room) to the *tepidarium* (warm room), off which were *apodyteria* (dressing rooms) for men and women. The *tepidarium* had no bath, but acted as a general relaxation area, often opening onto a *palaestra* (exercise area). It was also a warming preparation for the *calidarium* (hot room).

Calidariae were capable of achieving temperatures as high as 100°F and were made humid from the hot plunge pools alongside. The Romans did not use soap for washing themselves. Instead it was done by applying oils to the perspiring skin and then scraping the residue away with a *strigil* (scraper) before washing off in the hot bath. The process was completed by returning to the *frigidarium* pool for a cold plunge.

This is necessarily a simplified account. The imperial *thermae* provided space for huge numbers of people—up to 1,600 at a time in the Baths of Caracalla and twice that many in the Baths of Diocletian—so there were often several hot rooms and others for massage. Larger baths had a *laconium*, a dry room more like a modern sauna, and a *natatio* (outdoor pool). The relaxation and enjoyment available above the bath floors was not echoed alongside and beneath.

Heat to the warm and hot rooms was supplied by a hypocaust system, which introduced hot air under the floor from a *praefurnium* (furnace) that also heated the water. The floor was supported on numerous small pillars (*pilae*) around which the heated air

Below: The *pilae* supporting the bath floor above the hypocaust system are clearly visible at the Baths of Sbeitla, Tunisia, once the Roman colony of Sufetula.

Cutaway section of a hypocaust system, showing how heated air passed beneath the suspended floor and and up the walls of the *tepidarium* and *caldarium* in pottery flues called *tubuli*.

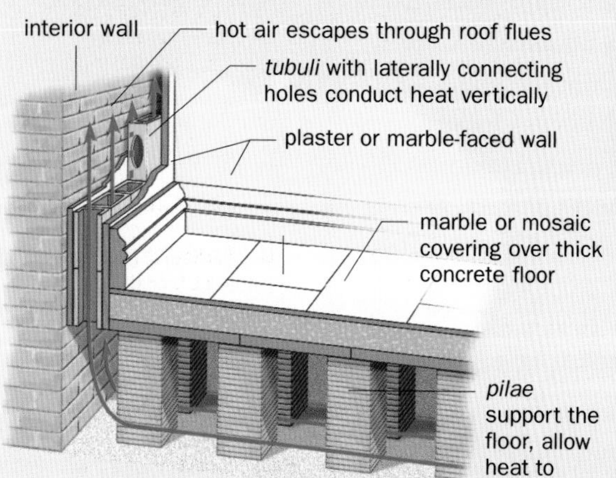
interior wall
hot air escapes through roof flues
tubuli with laterally connecting holes conduct heat vertically
plaster or marble-faced wall
marble or mosaic covering over thick concrete floor
pilae support the floor, allow heat to circulate

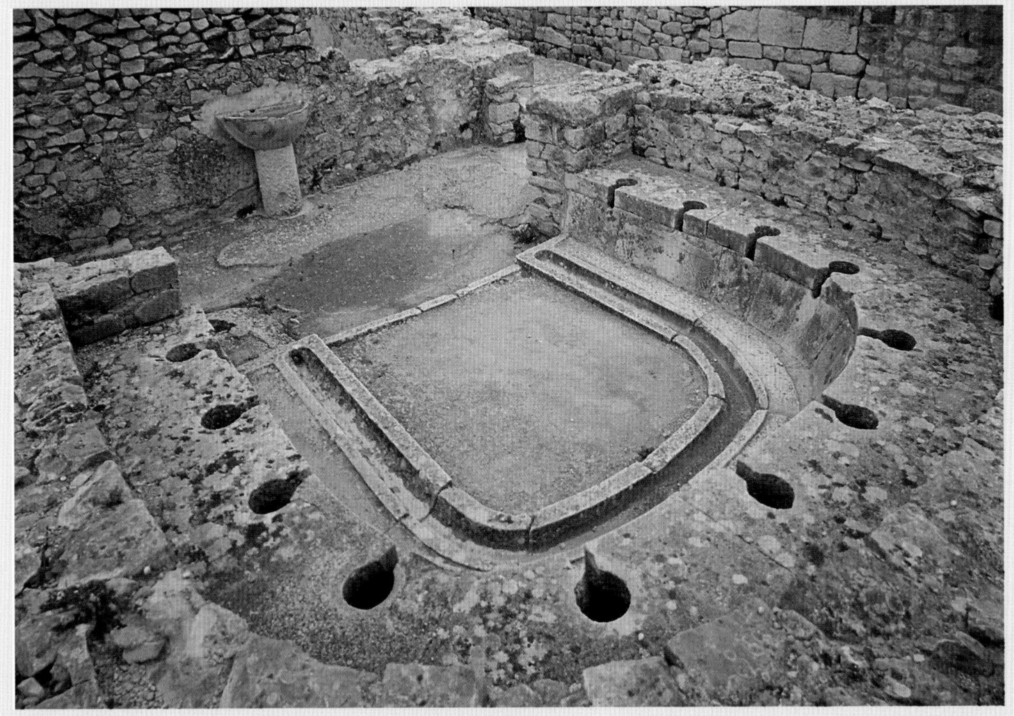

circulated. The floor needed to be thick to make it bearable to walk on, although wooden sandals were commonly supplied. The *praefurnium* was a fiercely hot, smoky environment for the slaves who stoked the fires. Some *calidariae*, such as at Ostia, were flanked by narrow passageways containing cylindrical boilers. Small holes in the passageway ceiling were the only source of light and escape for the thick smoke—it must have been a dreadful place to work.

In addition to the water features and exercise facilities, the imperial *thermae* offered beautifully arranged and tended gardens for walking and contemplation, one or two libraries (Latin and/or Greek), and sometimes a small stadium. At the Baths of Caracalla, the stadium steps are built up the sides of the cistern. With the further addition of conference and meeting rooms for hire, shops, and food stalls, the Roman baths resembled a modern leisure center complex.

Reconstruction (seen from above the cistern) and plan of the *Thermae Antoninianae* (Baths of Caracalla)

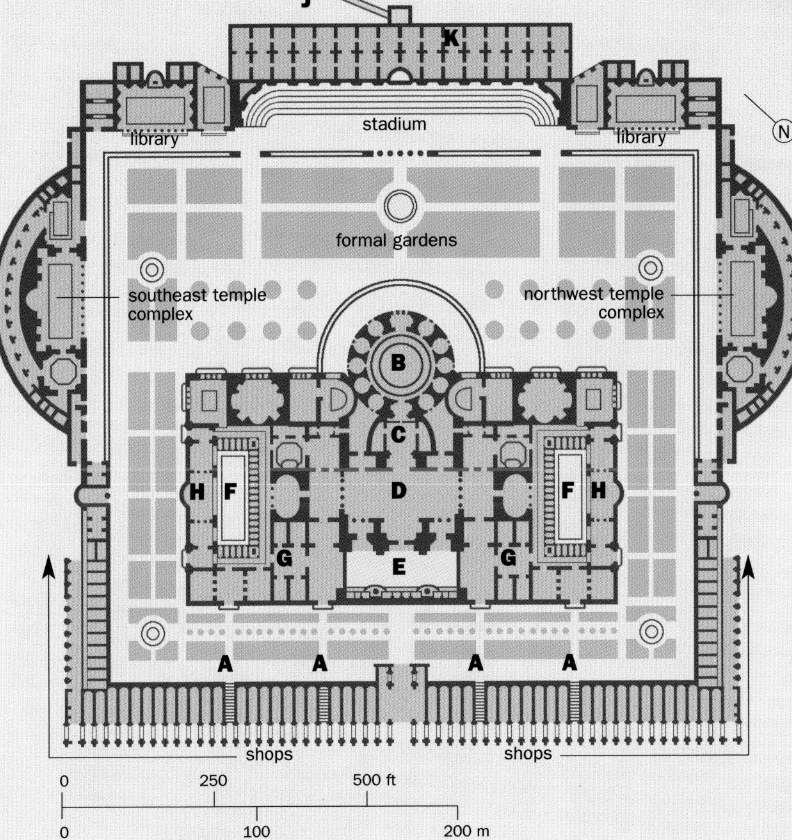

J
K
library
stadium
library
N
formal gardens
southeast temple complex
northwest temple complex
B
C
H F
D
F H
G
E
G
A
A
A
A
shops
shops
0
250
500 ft
0
100
200 m

The Baths of Caracalla, the second largest complex in Rome, were built between 212 and 219 outside the Servian Wall. The enclosure and the *thermae* themselves are bilaterally symmetrical. The outer parts contained small shops at the front and sides, six major temples in two blocks, two libraries, and a stadium built against the massive cistern.

The thermae were arranged in a line that bisected two mirrored wings containing *apodyteria*, rooms for exercise, massage, and conferences, and galleried open-air *palaestrae*.

- **A** four entrances stepped between the shops to paths leading to the four entrances, divided between men and women
- **B** *calidarium* with 12 hot plunge baths
- **C** *tepidarium*
- **D** *frigidarium*, open to (**E**) the open-air *natatio* (swimming pool)
- **F** *palaestrae* (open-air exercise areas)
- **G** *apodyteria* (dressing rooms), one for men, one for women
- **H** rooms for massage
- **J** Aqua Antoniniana, purpose-built extension of Aqua Marcia, for water supply
- **K** covered cistern with 16 compartments

Anarchy and Disorder

With the short sabbatical reign of Macrinus ended, the Severan dynasty continued, but instability crept in with the next two emperors. And after them, all semblance of Roman dignity collapsed for 50 years.

Above: Macrinus, an interloper in the Severan dynasty, was succeeded by Elagabalus, **below**, one of Rome's most exotic emperors.

Right: Maximinius I came from Thracian peasant stock, but was a successful military commander like Claudius II Gothicus (r.268–70), **far right**, who earned his cognomen from defeating the Goths in a series of battles.

Varius Avitus Bassianus Marcus Aurelius Antonius (r.218–22) was Caracalla's second cousin, but he is better known as Elagabalus, after the Syro-Phoenician sun-god El Gabal of Emessa of whom he was a priest. He may even have been Caracalla's illegitimate son. Only 15 when he came to the throne, Elagabalus was deeply committed to his god, and attempted to make everyone in Rome worship El Gabal. Promiscuous, bisexual, and fond of dressing in exotic women's clothes, Elagabalus was assassinated, along with his mother, the power behind his throne; he was just 18. Elagabalus was thought so reprehensible that the senate erased his name from official records.

His cousin Marcus Aurelius Severus Alexander (r.222–35) was acclaimed emperor, aged 14. Once again, it was a matriarch who ruled, without distinction. Alexander's cause was damaged by inconclusive military campaigns in Germany and Persia. Ultimately, the soldiers opted for another emperor and Alexander was murdered in his mother's arms, bringing the Severan line to an end.

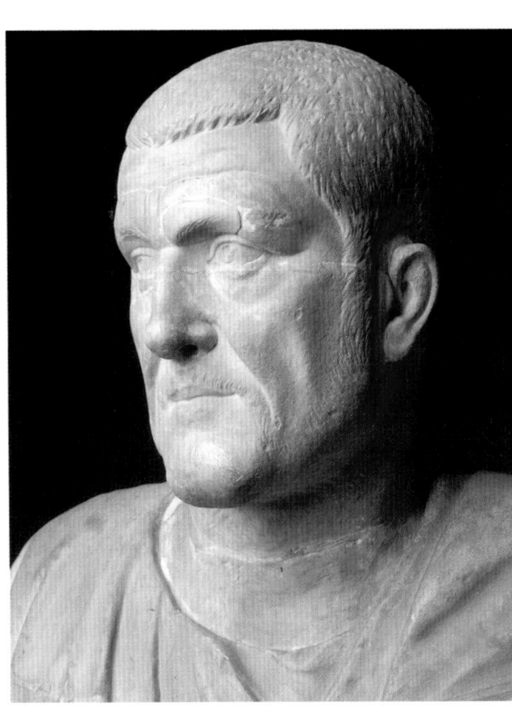

With the accession of Gaius Julius Verus Maximinus (r.235–8), the Roman empire descended into a state of continual anarchy that lasted 50 years until the accession of Diocletian. It is hard to make sense of the events of this period. The reliable chronicler Dio Cassius died in 235, and the work of contemporary historians is either suspect or only survives in fragments. In a quick-fire succession of some 20 self-claimed emperors and still more pretenders, only a few names stand out—and not always for good reasons.

Gaius Messius Quintus Decius (r.249–51), an experienced senator, became the first emperor to die bearing arms against external enemies. He fell in battle against the invading Goths on

the lower Danube, an insult later avenged by Marcus Aurelius Claudius II Gothicus in 268.

Publius Licinius Valerianus (Valerian, r.253–60) was proclaimed by his troops in Raetia, where he was governor. He marched on Rome in opposition to the emperor Marcus Aemilius Aemilian (proclaimed in the summer of 253 and assassinated by his own troops in the fall). Valerian, who made his son Gallienus his co-ruler, appeared to be a capable man, but his campaign in 260 against the new Sassanid dynasty of Persia was a disaster. He became the first Roman emperor to be captured. Valerian was never released. After his death he was skinned and paraded as a macabre trophy before visiting Romans to illustrate Persian power.

Aurelian's light in darkness

The situation on the frontiers demanded more attention than one ruler could give, which goes part of the way to explaining why so many emperors came and went, usually proclaimed close to the borders, where there were perpetual barbarian raids. The more successful were those who could contain the threat and provide a semblance of local government, regardless that a more legitimate emperor might be on the throne. A particular example is Marcus Cassianus Latinus Postumus, who rebelled against Gallienus in Gaul in 259, and set up an independent Gallic empire that lasted through four further usurpers until 270.

Publius Licinius Egnatius Gallienus (r.260–c.268), son of Valerian, was too occupied in the east and with the Danube frontier to provide security along the Rhine. He seems to have taken the realistic view that Postumus was in a better position to do so, and left the pretender to get on with it.

One light in a bleak outlook was the reign of Lucius Dimitius Aurelianus (Aurelian, r.270–75), who earned the name *Restitutor Orbis*, or restorer of the world. He combated numerous troublesome tribes on the borders before returning to Rome in triumph. Aurelian ascribed his successes to the cult of Sol Invictus—the Unconquered Sun (*see also page 149*)—that he had imported to Rome from the East. Aurelian came from humble origins but was a brilliant military commander, winning victories against Germans in the north, rebellious pretenders in the west, and Palmyrans in the east (*see following page*). His lasting legacy is the massive fortified walls he built around the expanded city of Rome, and which still stand in great part today (*see page 160*).

Despite his twin achievements of unity and security, Aurelian was murdered by conspiring officers. Of the six emperors who followed within the next decade, five were murdered and one was allegedly hit by a bolt of lightning.

Facing top: In 251 Decius became the first Roman emperor to die in battle against enemies of Rome.

Above: Aurelian gave Rome new walls and several victories, including against the Palmyran pretender Zenobia.

Below: A rock carving shows Shapur I of Persia humbling the emperors Philip (244) and Valerian (260.

THE EASTERN FRONTIER

From the time of Julius Caesar, the Parthian empire was a thorn in Rome's side. Roman emperors continued in their attempts to conquer this vital center of communications that straddled the eastern trade routes.

Facing top: The remains of the façade and open audience hall, known as the Arch of Chosroe, of the Sassanid palace of Ctesiphon, Taq-i-Kisra, Iraq. Capital of the Persian Sassanian empire, Ctesiphon was sacked several times by invading Roman armies. The palace façade has been leaning for many years, and is now supported by a great buttress.

Parthia was created within the borders of modern Iran in about 200 BC, when a rogue leader severed links with the ruling Greeks. Between the Roman empire and Parthia lay the buffer state of Armenia, sometimes a client of Rome, sometimes under Parthian occupation. Although Rome had access to greater numbers of fighting men, the battles were inevitably fought in Armenia or on Parthian soil. This gave Parthia easier access to supplies and reinforcements of fierce, effective soldiers. Parthians became famous for fielding a skilled heavy cavalry and accurate mounted archers.

Roman legions came to count the cost. In 53 BC Marcus Licinius Crassus was defeated near Carrhae. Crassus lost his life and seven legions. Mark Antony tried redressing the balance in 36 BC but suffered heavy losses. Thereafter, Rome attempted conquest of Parthia five times, but none of the campaigns was an overriding success. Trajan's sacking of Ctesiphon in AD 115 left a client king installed, but insurgents were not contained, and Hadrian soon abandoned the new provinces. Marcus Aurelius invaded following Parthian aggression in Syria but also failed to secure long-term gains.

In 195 Severus took northern Mesopotamia after defeating Pescennius Niger, his rival in the race for the throne. The resulting province was named Osrhoene. When he appreciated the divided nature of the Parthian hierarchy at the time, Severus returned, this time sacking Ctesiphon and claiming much of Mesopotamia. However, Parthian strength was disseminated into small, semi-nomadic populations that were out of Roman reach. The Parthians survived to fight another day.

Caracalla aimed to build on his father's success. In 216 he struck in Media, gaining considerable territory. However, this time the Parthians gathered for a counterattack. A year later they forced the Romans, by now under Macrinus, to come to terms.

The Parthian empire finally fell victim to another Persian clan, the Sassanids, who overwhelmed the region in 228. There was no immediate response from Rome—the empire was in the state of disorder described on the previous page.

The deeply insular Sassanid dynasty erected barriers to commercial as well as military travelers, and a series of poor quality Roman emperors found it impossible to deal with border security. Valerian's ignominus defeat in 260 at Edessa led to his capture, and the pitiless Shapur I enjoyed making the ruler of the civilized world crouch down like a footstool so the Persian could more easily mount his horse.

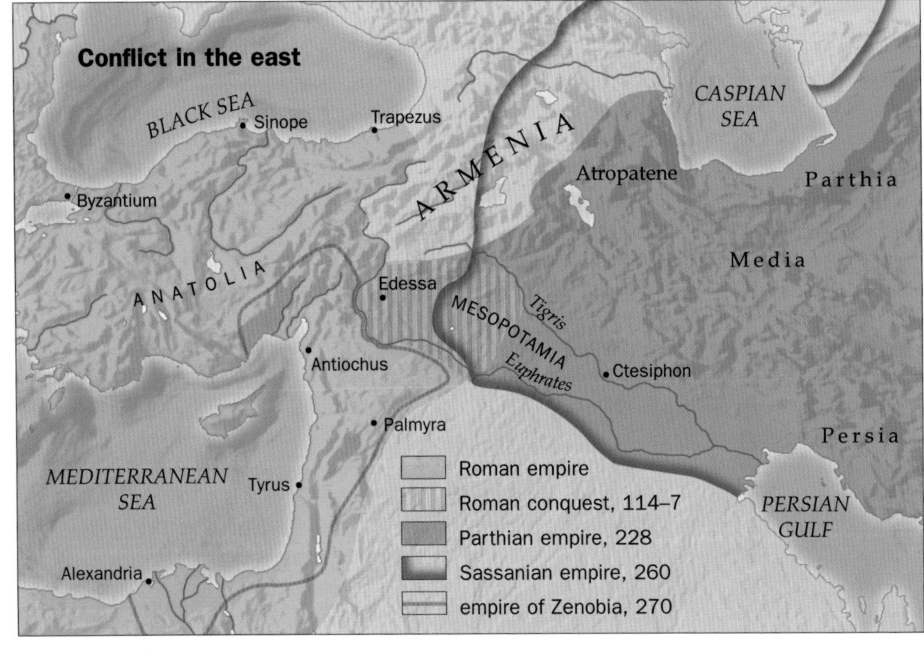
Conflict in the east
BLACK SEA
Sinope
Trapezus
ARMENIA
CASPIAN SEA
Atropatene
Parthia
Byzantium
ANATOLIA
Media
Edessa
MESOPOTAMIA
Tigris
Euphrates
Antiochus
Ctesiphon
Palmyra
Persia
MEDITERRANEAN SEA
Tyrus
PERSIAN GULF
Alexandria
Roman empire
Roman conquest, 114–7
Parthian empire, 228
Sassanian empire, 260
empire of Zenobia, 270

192–193 Commodus is assassinated; civil war between potential successors

195 Septimus Severus temporarily adds part of Parthian Mesopotamia (Iraq) to the empire

197 With the death of Clodius Albinus, Septimus Severus emerges as the new emperor

211 Severus dies in Britain; sons Caracalla and Geta are named as co-rulers

217 Caracalla is assassinated while campaigning against Parthians

218 Emperor Macrinus is driven from Rome; Elagabalus succeeds him

222 Elagabalus is assassinated, replaced by boy-emperor, Alexander Severus

251 Emperor Decius dies in battle against Goths

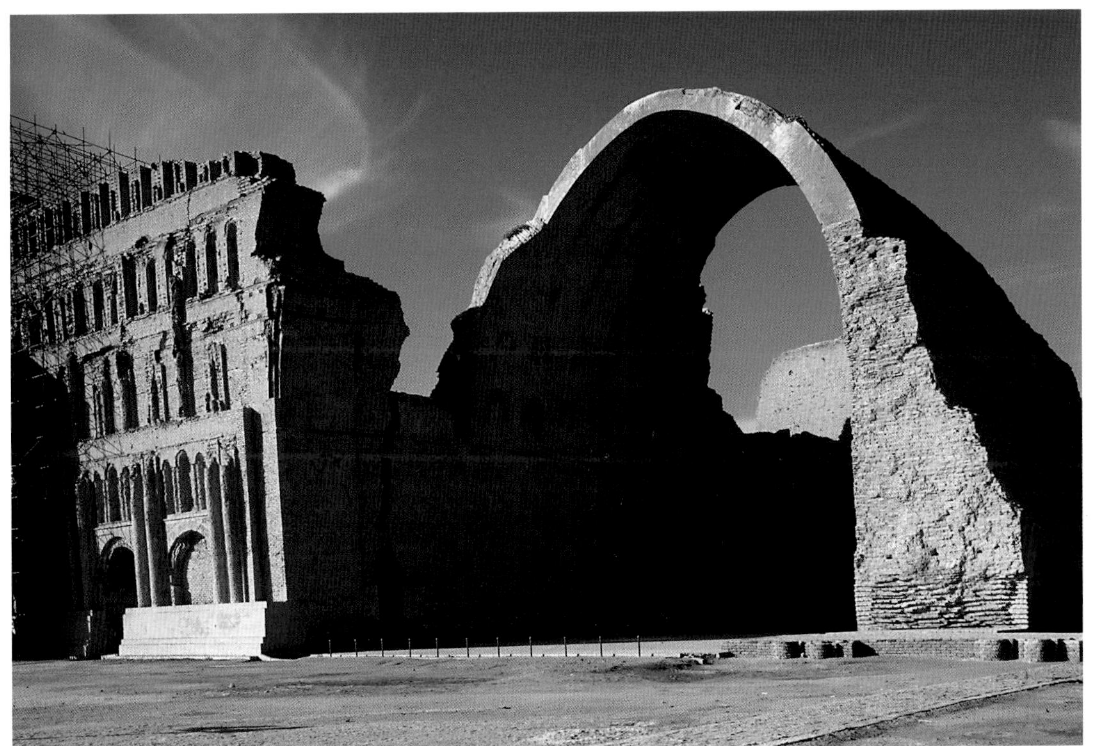

The Palmyran adventure

Palmyra was another troublespot in the later third century. A spectacular oasis lying at the center point between the Euphrates and the Mediterranean Sea, its position made the city a favored stopping point on the essential trade routes of the era. Palmyra fell under Roman control during the reign of Tiberius, although Hadrian later declared it a free city. Later still, it was freed of its tax obligations to Rome. Palmyra became a critical buffer colony between the Romans and Persians. Valerian's son Gallienus gave the governorship to the Palmyrene dynast Septimius Odaenathus.

On the pretext of securing revenge for the capture of Valerian, Odaenathus launched an assault on Persia. It was intended as the first move in a campaign of Palmyran expansion, but in 267 Odaenathus and his eldest son were murdered, probably by his wife Zenobia. She was an accomplished warrior, hunter, writer, and linguist. She assumed control of the Palmyran armies in the name of her young son, quickly organizing a campaign to further extend her territories. Palmyran forces soon overran Egypt, Syria, and part of Anatolia, carving an eastern empire for the redoubtable Zenobia. For a while she presided over a lavish court, modeled on that of Cleopatra's, where intellectuals and artists found succor. She imagined herself becoming the first empress of Rome, and even had a gold chariot made for a triumph in its streets.

But ambition tripped her after she refused to supply Rome with Egyptian grain. Rome was now under Aurelian, and the new emperor's response was to besiege Palmyra, an act met with dismay in a people weary of conflict. Aurelian told the senate: "The Roman people speak with contempt of the war I am waging against a woman. They are ignorant both of the character and the power of Zenobia. It is impossible to enumerate her war-like preparations of stones, of arrows, and every species of missile weapons.... The fear of punishment has armed her with a desperate courage."

Zenobia was finally captured and paraded through the streets of Rome in 272, after which she was permitted to marry a senator and live out her days in a villa. Alas, insurrection swiftly occurred once more in Palmyra. This time Aurelian razed the city to the ground.

Below: Septimia Zenobia ruled Palmyra through her son Vaballathus as a nominal ally of Rome. It is an indication of how the period of anarchy had affected Roman military preparedness that Zenobia, who declared herself Augusta in 271, was able to seize Egypt—Italy's granary—and hold Rome to ransom over corn supplies. Defeated by Aurelian in 272, she retired on a pension in Rome, and lived to old age.

260	272	275	284	293	297–298	301	305
Sassanids capture Valerian while the emperor is on campaign in Persia and humiliate him	Emperor Aurelian conquers Palmyra and captures Queen Zenobia	Aurelian is murdered; the following six emperors are also killed	Diocletian is made Emperor of Rome	Diocletian instates a co-ruler and both appoint a deputy (Caesar) forming the Tetrarchy	Galerius, Caesar of the East, defeats the Sassanid Persians	Diocletian issues Edict on Maximum Prices for the protection of the poor	Diocletian survives to retirement; leadership rivalries return

Diocletian's Tetrarchy

On November 20, 284 an act whose significance could not be forseen took place when in Nicomedia yet another emperor was proclaimed by his troops. But this one was different. He was Diocletian.

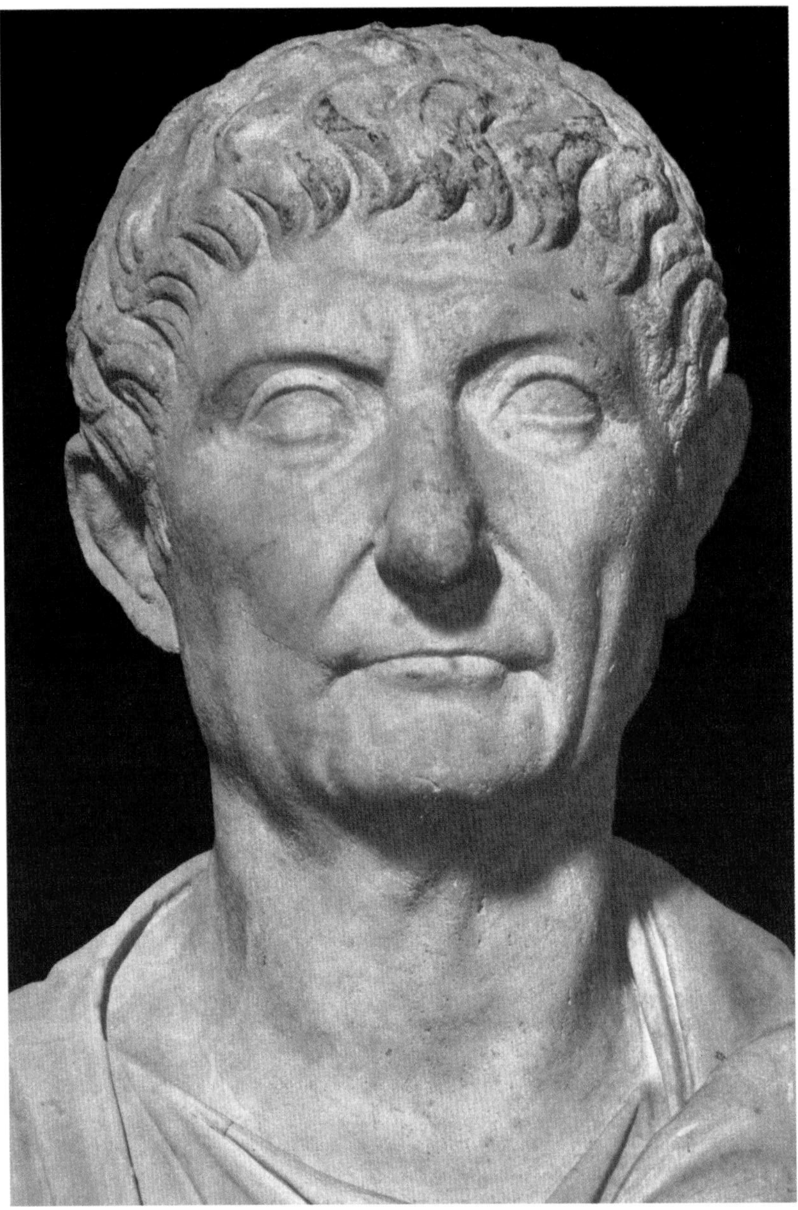

Above: Diocletian brought the period of anarchy to an end and provided Rome with wise and stable government for the first time in 50 years. Inflationary and price controls were his bequest to the empire.

The anarchic spiral halted on the accession of Gaius Aurelius Valerius Diocletianus (r.284–305). Born in 245 of humble Dalmatian stock, Diocletian rose to eminence through the ranks of the army, and enjoyed massive popularity among his Illyrian troops. The reign of brothers and current joint emperors Marcus Aurelius Carinus and Marcus Aurelius Numerianus (r.283–4) came to a violent end when Numerian was murdered by Arrius Aper, the praetorian praefect, while returning to Rome. For this act, Diocletian was said to have struck down Aper with his own hand before the assembled army when he caught him. After which, he took the Purple himself.

In the spring of 285 he defeated Carinus in Pannonia, and now held unrivaled power. Over the next 20 years a campaign of vigorous governmental reform was to create the political structure of the late Roman state. His greatest innovation was the devolution of his power to reliable colleagues. This was not an entirely new idea, but it was a legitimization of what had been happening since Antoninus Pius. In 286 he promoted as Caesar Marcus Aurelius Valerius Maximianus, another Illyrian officer. In 287 he made him co-Augustus in command of the western part of the empire, where he won victories over the German Alamanni, while Diocletian confronted the Persians in the east.

In March 293 two more Illyrians were appointed Caesars, Gaius Galerius and Flavius Valerius Constantius, who were adopted respectively by Diocletian and Maximianus. This rule of four is known to historians as the "Tetrarchy." The arrangement was cemented by inter-marriages, one consequence of which was that Constantius had to divorce his wife Helena in favor of Maximian's stepdaughter. Helena took her young son Constantine to be educated in the east.

The Tetrarchy proved to be a success. Diocletian suppressed a revolt in Egypt, Galerius defeated Gothic armies on the Danube and won a great victory over the Persians in 297–98, Constantius defeated the pretender Allectus (who had proclaimed himself over Britain and northern Gaul in 293), and Maximian put down a rebellion in Mauretania.

Christian persecution

Diocletian and his colleagues developed a fully mobile field army to complement the increasingly stagnant frontier garrisons. Contemporary critics claim he quadrupled the army's size, but doubling it seems more likely. This meant more new taxes to pay for the measures, and highlighted the problem of

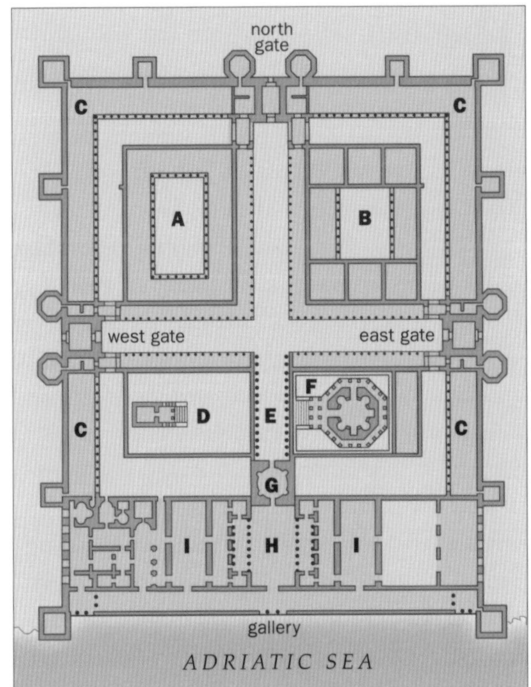
north gate
C
C
A
B
west gate
east gate
F
D
E
C
C
G
I
H
I
gallery
ADRIATIC SEA

Diocletian's palace at Split was laid out in the strict fashion of a Roman military camp, but with its fortified walls, gates, and intermediary towers, it bears a startling resemblance to a medieval castle. Ironically, for a man who persecuted Christians, Diocletian's mausoleum later became a church.

A office and workshops
B general accommodation
C multi-storied gallery over arcade
D temple of Jupiter
E peristyle
F mausoleum of Diocletian
G vestibule
H audience hall
I imperial private apartments

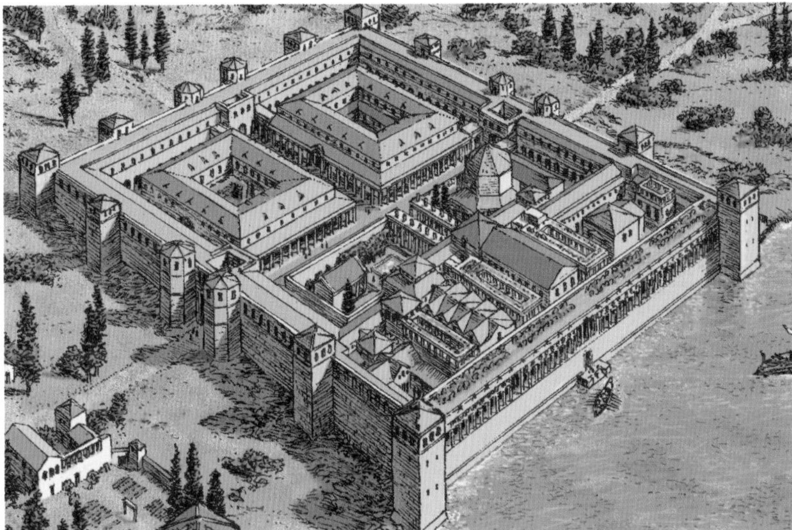

spiraling inflation that had resulted from the period of anarchy. Diocletian had new gold coins struck at a greater rate of metal purity and created a silver standard, which gradually stabilized the economy. But since copper did not hold its value as well, and copper coinage was the basis for the everyday population, the poor had to wait some time for the benefits to accrue.

To offset this, in 301 Diocletian issued his Edict on Maximum Prices for the protection of the poor. Maximum legal prices were imposed on a range of products and services, although critics said this only drove goods off the market. These measures and the increased complexity of tax legislation led to an increased bureaucracy, which became typical of the late Roman period.

In religious matters Diocletian portrayed himself and Maximianus as the sons of gods Jupiter and Hercules, reflecting resurgence in the old religion occurring at the time. He was also taken with Mithraism, especially the idea of a celebratory meal made from the sacrificed bull. Accordingly he had little sympathy for Christians. Controls he outlined for the sect were applied with violent zeal, earning Diocletian a reputation for cruelty that overshadows his exceptional energy, intelligence, and administrative genius. Christians tolerated the campaign with remarkable forbearance, impressing more people than ever before with the faith's spiritual strength.

Diocletian and Maximian retired in 305—something no other Roman emperors had managed, and entailed the promotion of the two Caesars, Constantius in the west and Galerius in the east to Augusti. Diocletian retired to his palace in Split on the Dalmatian coast, where he died peacefully six years later, having taken pride and pleasure in growing vegetables during his retirement.

Above: Reconstruction and plan of Diocletian's palace in Split, Dalmatia.

Below: A section of Diocletian's massive Edict lists maximum prices for goods and services, and tariffs for sea transportation. It was written in Greek, which was becoming the bureaucrats' language.

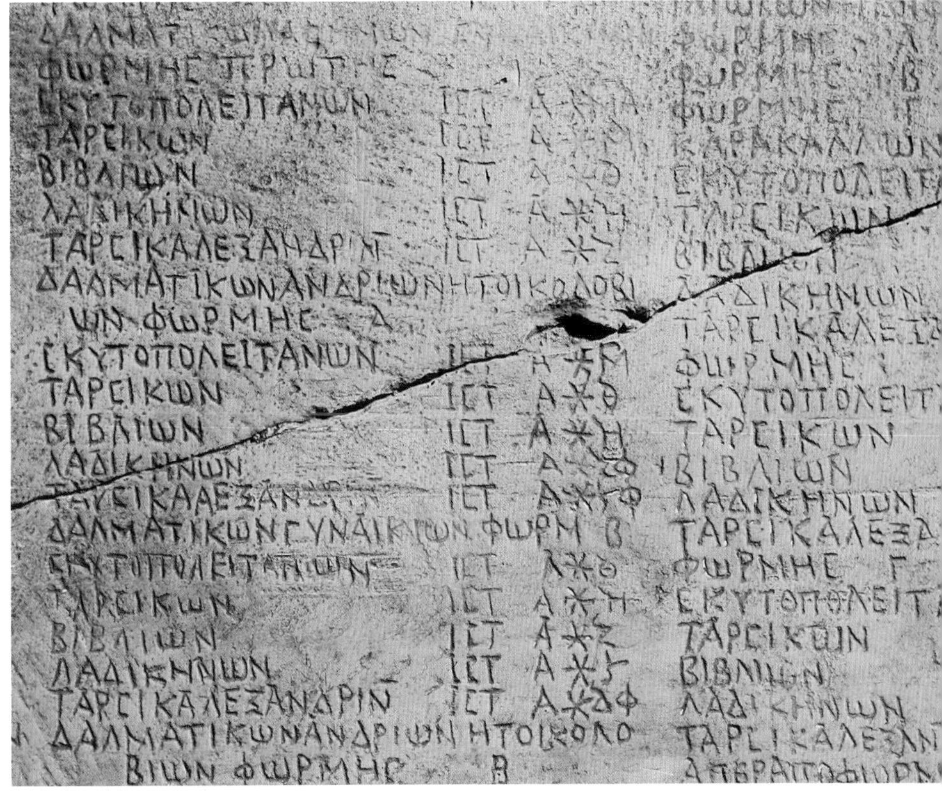

Late Roman Religion

The Roman empire had no definitive state religion; the diverse pantheon of gods were worshipped in numerous cults. During the period of anarchy and in following decades, new, exotic beliefs began circulating, offering people new attractions.

Below: Mithra, or Mithras, was an ancient Indo-Iranian god of truth and light. His cult reached Rome in the second half of the 1st century BC, but only became widespread in the imperial period. The cult appealed to merchants, soldiers, and charioteers. Even after the adoption of Christianity as the state religion, Mithra was worshipped by the majority of frontier legionaries. The charioteers dedicated a temple to him in the Circus Maximus (**right below**).

The ancient cults had concerned themselves with essentially basic issues: of man's relationship with his fellow beings, his land, his ancestors. There were few mysteries, and when there were, they involved women more than men. But in the second and third centuries AD there was a great change in Roman religious observance. Shadowy, mythical figures that once filled that void were becoming obsolete in an increasingly sophisticated Roman society. The attraction of religions that promised deeper understanding became much greater.

During the first century, the senatorial class began to adopt Greek stoicism, probably a reaction to their loss of political power under the emperors. Stoicism placed man at the center of the universe, and stoics accepted that cause had effect, that a person's misfortunes were brought about by themselves or their fellows, not as the result of a capricious god's interference.

For ordinary Romans, new forms of devotion were adopted from the influences of Egypt, Judaea, Syria, and Mesopotamia—Judaism, Christianity, the cults of Isis, Osiris, Mithraism, and Manichaeism. These mystery cults set out to explain the order of the universe and man's place in it. They offered their supplicants hope of salvation, a better life after death. They offered explanations of good and evil, suffering and wickedness, concepts in which the ancient Roman religions were uninterested.

A strength of early Roman religion lay in its creation of brotherhoods and communities among diverse populations around the empire. The minimum of personal commitment it demanded was its weakness—there were few spiritual benefits once the external necessities were met, prayer and sacrifice for example. The new cults demanded belief and faith in the message offered. They still provided a sense of brotherhood, indeed emphasized it through complex initiation ceremonies and exotic rites.

The spread and acceptance of these new cults

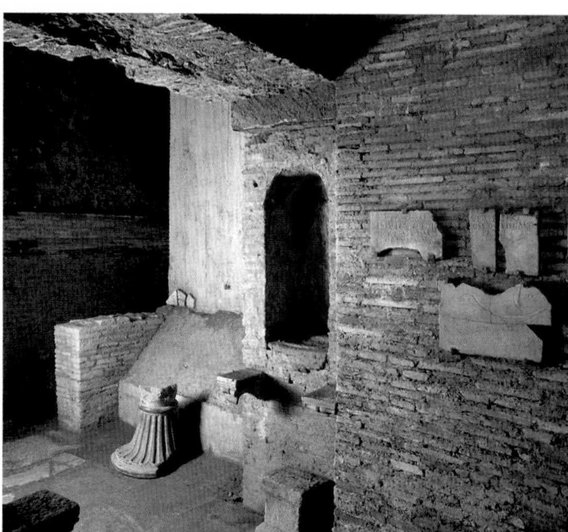

may have been due to the nature of the times—chaos and anarchy breed anxiety. However, mystery cults had already flourished in the golden ages; Isis had a temple in Rome in the first century AD, and paintings at Pompeii depict scenes from the ancient Greek Eleusinian Mysteries. It is probably better to see the rapid spread of new religious thought in terms of the

greater mobility available to people in the Roman empire.

Roots of persecution

One of the most popular new cults was Mithraism, a secret, men-only cult that nonetheless dictated a high code of personal conduct. Mithra was sent down to earth by the Zoroastrian god Ahura Mazda to struggle against evil. He was to hunt and kill a bull, from which all living things sprang. The cult held particular appeal for soldiers, and archaeological evidence of it is often found at sites once occupied by Roman legions.

The deification of emperors offered a focal point for loyalty among Roman citizens who were already wrapped up in the idea of obligation toward ancestors. Augustus eased the concept into the political arena, but he was astutely aware that deification would have to be posthumous. Many of his successors were deified while alive, at least in the sense that their staues erected in far-flung provinces were instantly worshipped. It was another potent weapon in the imperial arsenal.

From the mid-third century, emperors linked themselves to Sol Invictus, the Unconquered Sun. Aurelian established the cult in Rome and created a college to administer it. Gallienus, Diocletian, and Maximian associated themselves publicly with Sol Invictus, despite Diocletian's extreme conservatism in religious matters. It was his desire to see the old Roman religions observed that led to his persecutions of Christians and Manichees. He denounced their arrogant wickedness for preferring their own beliefs to those entrusted to mankind by the ancient gods.

For the same reasons the monotheistic Jews remained unpopular. Insistence on their own (controversial) ceremonies and celebrations earned Jews a reputation of being stubborn and even as being agitators. Tacitus, no friend of Christians or Jews, wrote that those who converted to Judaism were instructed "in contempt of the gods, in the disowning of one's fatherland, the despising of one's parents, children, brothers, and sisters." Nevertheless, some Romans sought solace in Judaism, in despair at a lack of spiritual depth in the Roman faith or the moral laxity of some cults.

Above: The largest place of worship in the Roman empire was begun by Julius Caesar at Baalbek, in modern-day Lebanon. The temple of Jupiter Heliopolitanus measures 290 by 160 feet. It was surrounded by 54 columns with a height of 70 feet, a size and magnificence designed to show that Rome's Jupiter was the chief god of many deities. The temple complex was never quite finished when 150 years of building stopped.

THE CHRISTIAN MESSAGE

Christianity was pitted against numerous other faiths in a race for hearts and minds, including Judaism. Its success lay in the speed that Christian philosophy traveled around the Roman empire, gathering converts as it went.

Although Christianity had differing ceremonies and messages, its adherents were strongly associated with the Jewish faith. Indeed, Christianity has a debt of gratitude to Jews who spread the message in those early days. Jews had introduced the notion of worshipping a single god rather than a celestial hierarchy long before the advent of Jesus, so Christianity was not absurdly radical. Significantly, Jews had set up a chain of synagogues throughout Europe, offering a series of platforms from which the Apostles could be heard.

A schism between Judaism and Christianity was nevertheless inevitable. The Jewish faith had spread across Europe centuries before the birth of Christ. It survived and thrived even in hostile locations. But its laws and customs, although less evident among those Jews living outside Palestine, were unattractively complex. By comparison, the Christian message was straightforward. While committed Jews were quick to chase the Apostles out of the synagogue, believing them to be blasphemers, the proselytes (converts or sympathizers) were prepared to listen.

Below: An early 4th-century Roman bas-relief depicts the Apostles Peter and Paul. Christian iconography became popular within years of Constantine making Christianity the Roman state religion.

Jews and Christians finally fractured in bitter disagreement over observances of Jewish law. Many Christians responded by leaving Jerusalem for other major cities, including Antioch and Ephesus, which became centers of Christian scholarship. Any temptation for the new faith to remain in Palestine was erased with the Jewish revolt of AD 66.

The primary figures in Christianity mid-millennium were the Apostles Peter and Paul. Yet even before Paul began his mission there were Christian communities across the Roman empire. No one is sure who was the first to spread the message. Undoubtedly slaves, for whom the Christian teaching held special appeal, were responsible for carrying the words of Jesus to the common man miles across the empire.

Spreading the word

Apostles, notably Paul, spoke and wrote in Greek, which was universally known in the Roman empire. There was no language barrier for the early missionaries to contend with, which strengthened the thread of unity among worshippers. Early Christians also reaped the benefits of *Pax Romana* and the Roman roads that took them quickly and safely from one key destination to the next. When merchants adopted the new faith it traveled with them into the furthest reaches of the empire and the numbers of believers mushroomed.

Both Peter and Paul are believed to have been martyred in Rome, probably during Nero's purge against Christians following the fire of Rome in AD 64. Both were inevitably drawn there as a culmination to the work begun by Jesus, for this city was the center of the civilized world. Anyone wishing to spread the word had to convince Rome if they wanted to be effective.

Within a few decades, Christians adopted Rome as the home of their faith and Church authority radiated out of the city, its claim to primacy enhanced by the martyrdoms of St. Peter and St. Paul. From Rome came the cohesion that would bind the Christian Church.

The burgeoning religion attracted the attention of wary Roman rulers but, since it did not mount a challenge to the Caesars, they did not actively oppose it. If Romans were antagonized by the proximity of Christians, it was the secret nature of their worship and beliefs that grated. Early Christian ceremonies were carried out underground in catacombs, causing those outside the faith to ponder just what went on. Rumors of incest and cannibalism abounded as the message of the Eucharist (eating bread representative of bodily flesh amid exhortations of brotherly love) was corrupted.

Attitudes like this provided Diocletian with all the ammunition he needed to begin a systematic persecution of Christians, but as history has shown, Christianity not only survived any amount of persecution but even thrived on the martyrs it created. And less than 50 years after Diocletian's abdication, Christianity became Rome's first state religion.

Below: Two nuns worship at a statue of the Virgin Mary at the Catacombs of St. Calixtus on the Appian Way, Rome. These networks of underground passages were carved from the rock, with niches along the walls for interrment.

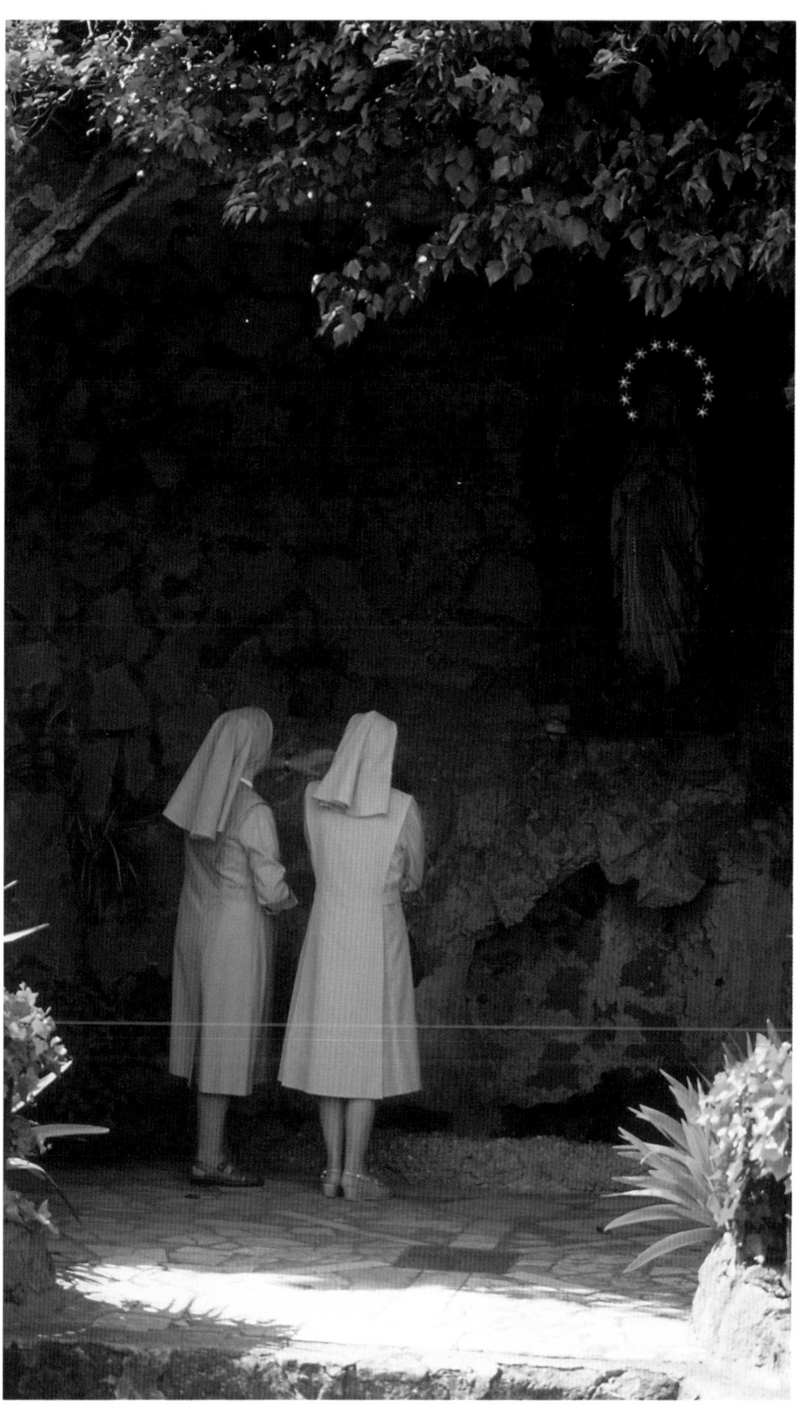

CHAPTER 10

A NEW DIRECTION

For centuries the Roman empire imposed cultural unity on disparate peoples. So when Constantine led the empire to embrace Christianity, he made sweeping changes that affected many. A Celt living in the shadow of Hadrian's Wall would become a Christian, along with an African eking out an existence on the edge of the Sahara. A Spaniard on the Atlantic shores could adopt the faith, as would the Syrians on the eastern arm of the empire. The seed, though widely scattered, brought forth a mighty harvest as the numbers of Christians grew exponentially.

Although Constantine began the process, it was Theodosius who made Christianity a legal requisite of citizens in the Roman empire, with the following pronouncement in 380: "It is our will that all the peoples we rule shall practice that religion which the divine Peter the Apostle transmitted to the Romans. We shall believe in the single Deity of the Father, the Son, and the Holy Spirit, under the concept of equal majesty and of the Holy Trinity." Thereafter, Christianity became as oppressive as any regime it had opposed.

The second vital change made by Constantine was the focus of the Roman empire. He refashioned Byzantium as a new capital in the east, renaming it Constantinople. Rome was left as a poor relation in the west. Like a clockwork toy left to wind down, the city slowly lost its impetus as investment and interest were channeled elsewhere. Once the priority of Roman emperors had been to keep the bustling city content with never-ending entertainments in the circuses and amphitheaters, and free bread from the corn dole.

In Trajan's reign the inhabitants of Rome stood at one-and-a-half million. No other city even approached this size until the 19th century. It had been the capital of the world, but those days were gone. The great city of Latin culture faded into an obscurity overshadowed by the new metropolitan centers of Ravenna, Milan, Trier, Nicomedia, and Constantinople.

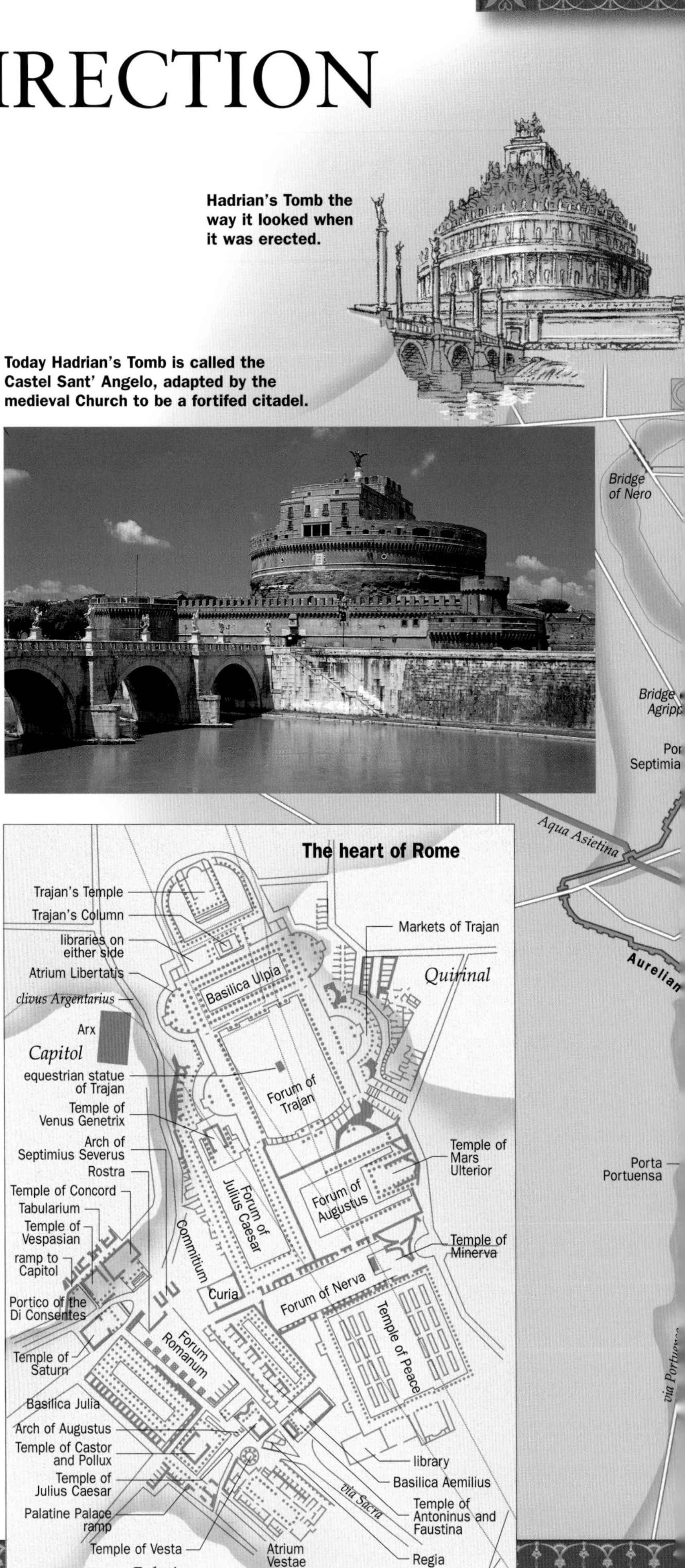
Bridge of Nero
Bridge of Agripp
Por Septimia
Aqua Asietina
Aurelian
Porta Portuensa
via Portuensis
The heart of Rome
Trajan's Temple
Trajan's Column
libraries on either side
Atrium Libertatis
clivus Argentarius
Arx
Capitol
equestrian statue of Trajan
Temple of Venus Genetrix
Arch of Septimius Severus
Rostra
Temple of Concord
Tabularium
Temple of Vespasian
ramp to Capitol
Portico of the Di Consentes
Temple of Saturn
Basilica Julia
Arch of Augustus
Temple of Castor and Pollux
Temple of Julius Caesar
Palatine Palace ramp
Temple of Vesta
Palatine
Atrium Vestae
Markets of Trajan
Quirinal
Basilica Ulpia
Forum of Trajan
Forum of Julius Caesar
Forum of Augustus
Temple of Mars Ulterior
Temple of Minerva
Comitium
Curia
Forum of Nerva
Temple of Peace
Forum Romanum
via Sacra
library
Basilica Aemilius
Temple of Antoninus and Faustina
Regia
line of the modern Imperial Way

Hadrian's Tomb the way it looked when it was erected.

Today Hadrian's Tomb is called the Castel Sant' Angelo, adapted by the medieval Church to be a fortifed citadel.

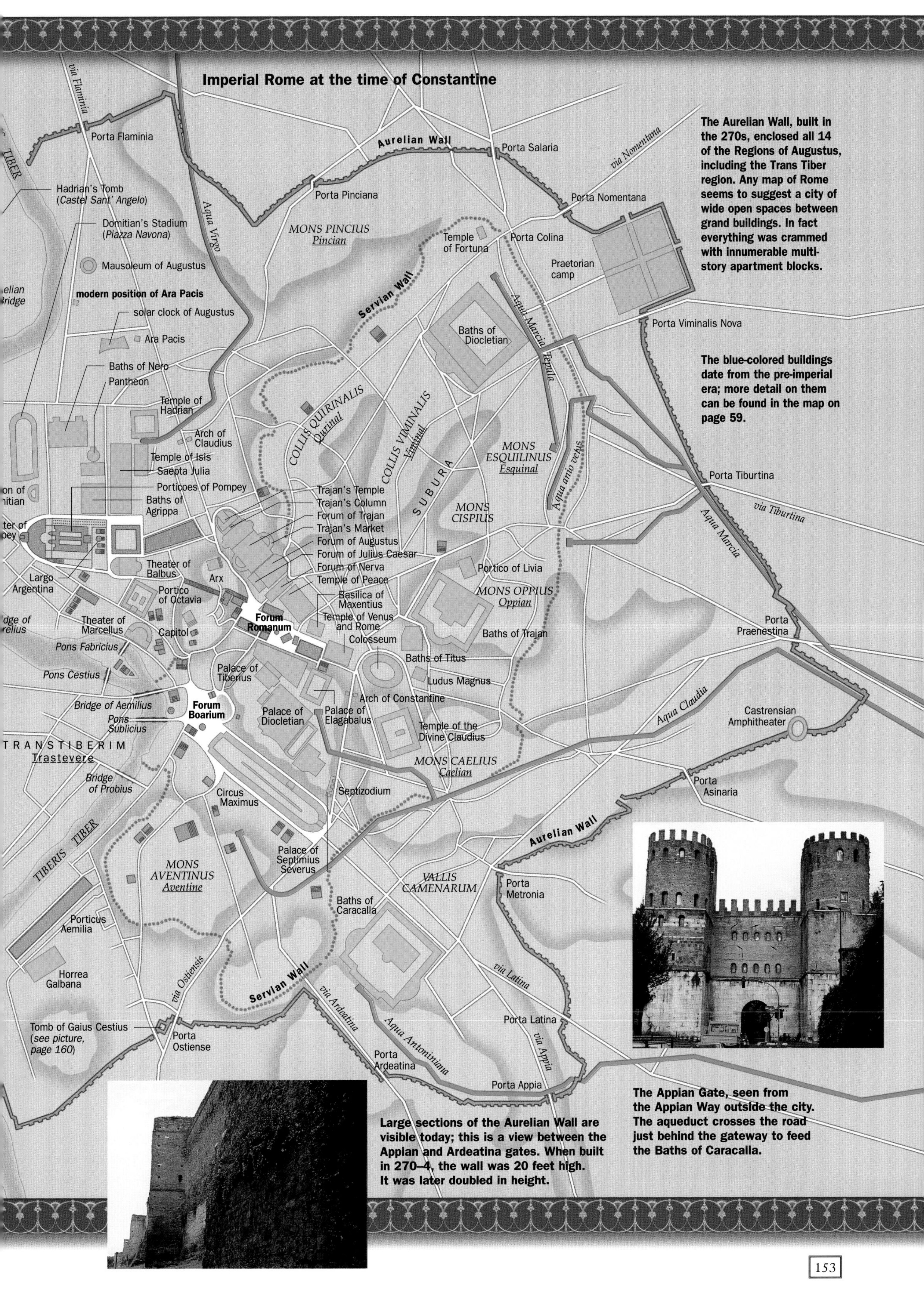
Imperial Rome at the time of Constantine
via Flaminia
Porta Flaminia
TIBER
Hadrian's Tomb (Castel Sant' Angelo)
Domitian's Stadium (Piazza Navona)
Mausoleum of Augustus
modern position of Ara Pacis
solar clock of Augustus
Ara Pacis
Baths of Nero
Pantheon
Temple of Hadrian
Arch of Claudius
Temple of Isis
Saepta Julia
Porticoes of Pompey
Baths of Agrippa
Theater of Balbus
Largo Argentina
Portico of Octavia
Theater of Marcellus
Capitol
Arx
Pons Fabricius
Pons Cestius
Bridge of Aemilius
Pons Sublicius
TRANSTIBERIM
Trastevere
Bridge of Probius
TIBERIS TIBER
Porticus Aemilia
Horrea Galbana
Tomb of Gaius Cestius (see picture, page 160)
Porta Ostiense
via Ostiensis
MONS AVENTINUS
Aventine
Servian Wall
Aqua Virgo
Aurelian Wall
Porta Pinciana
MONS PINCIUS
Pincian
Porta Salaria
via Nomentana
Porta Nomentana
Temple of Fortuna
Porta Colina
Praetorian camp
Baths of Diocletian
Aqua Marcia Tepula
Porta Viminalis Nova
COLLIS QUIRINALIS
Quirinal
COLLIS VIMINALIS
Viminal
SUBURA
MONS ESQUILINUS
Esquinal
Aqua anio vetus
Porta Tiburtina
via Tiburtina
Aqua Marcia
MONS CISPIUS
Trajan's Temple
Trajan's Column
Forum of Trajan
Trajan's Market
Forum of Augustus
Forum of Julius Caesar
Forum of Nerva
Temple of Peace
Basilica of Maxentius
Temple of Venus and Rome
Forum Romanum
Colosseum
Portico of Livia
MONS OPPIUS
Oppian
Baths of Trajan
Baths of Titus
Ludus Magnus
Palace of Tiberius
Forum Boarium
Palace of Diocletian
Palace of Elagabalus
Arch of Constantine
Temple of the Divine Claudius
MONS CAELIUS
Caelian
Septizodium
Circus Maximus
Palace of Septimius Severus
Porta Praenestina
Aqua Claudia
Castrensian Amphitheater
Porta Asinaria
VALLIS CAMENARUM
Porta Metronia
Baths of Caracalla
via Latina
via Ardeatina
Aqua Antoniniana
Porta Latina
via Appia
Porta Ardeatina
Porta Appia

The Aurelian Wall, built in the 270s, enclosed all 14 of the Regions of Augustus, including the Trans Tiber region. Any map of Rome seems to suggest a city of wide open spaces between grand buildings. In fact everything was crammed with innumerable multi-story apartment blocks.

The blue-colored buildings date from the pre-imperial era; more detail on them can be found in the map on page 59.

The Appian Gate, seen from the Appian Way outside the city. The aqueduct crosses the road just behind the gateway to feed the Baths of Caracalla.

Large sections of the Aurelian Wall are visible today; this is a view between the Appian and Ardeatina gates. When built in 270–4, the wall was 20 feet high. It was later doubled in height.

Constantine the Great

Constantine changed the course of first-millennium history. Thanks to him, the vibrant but insular religious sect of Christianity spread throughout the Roman empire, and thus became the faith that fired the civilized world.

Right: A gold *solidus* of Constantine shows the emperor in a Hellenistic style.

Above: Constantius, father of Constantine the Great, abandoned his son in childhood.

Below: Maxentius stood in Constantine's way as Augustus in the west.

The political expediencies that persuaded the ambitious Constantine to embrace Christianity are largely forgotten. Nor did his conduct in later life appear appropriate for a humble servant of Christ. But Constantine, by playing the religious card, united a fractured empire under one banner.

Flavius Valerius Constatinus (r.306–37) was born in February 285—a time when Persian armies were attacking Rome in the east, while Barbarians were battering frontiers in the west. Little is known of his childhood, although the activities of his father Constantius Chlorus ("the pale") are recorded (*see page 146*). After supporting a coup that put Diocletian in power in AD 284, Constantius became a Caesar under the co-Augustus Maximian in return for severing ties with Constantine's mother in order to marry Maximian's stepdaughter.

When Diocletian and Maximian retired in 305 the two Caesars, Galerius in the east and Constantius in the west, became joint Augusti. In turn, they were to appoint co-Caesars to continue the government of the Tetrarchy. The obvious choices were Maximian's son Maxentius and Constantius Chlorus. Yet they were passed over for the relatively unknown Maximinus Daia and Flavius Valerius Severus II. The seeds of discontent had been sown. Constantine, of course, was still in the east, and under the thumb of Galerius, an effective hostage to the good behavior of his father Constantius.

Eventually, in 305 Galerius allowed Constantine to leave and join his father, who was campaigning in Britain. In the following year Constantius died at York and the army proclaimed Constantine Augustus. He now embarked on an energetic campaign to seize control of the entire empire. His first target was the removal of Maxentius, who had proclaimed himself Augustus in Rome in 307 and eliminated Severus II. The climactic battle came in 312 at the Milvian Bridge, which takes the via Flaminia across the Tiber a few miles north of Rome. Before the action began, Constantine claimed a divine vision. He saw a fiery cross topped by the words "In this sign, conquer." After he imparted this message, the few Christians among his troops believed in the righteousness of the cause; the others keenly accepted sacred signs, even when the religion was not their own.

Shifting the capital eastward

With his invigorated troops, Constantine defeated Maxentius, who famously died by drowning after falling from the bridge. Meanwhile, Galerius had also died, leaving the east in the capable hands of Valerius Licinianus Licinius and Maximinus Daia. Needing time to consolidate his hold in Rome, Constantine negotiated a peace with his colleagues, which lasted for four years. Licinius made himself master in the east in the following year by defeating Maximinus at Tarsus.

But Constantine was restless. Raised and educated in Byzantium, he was painfully aware that the west was now eclipsed in the imperial partnership. Trade and culture buzzed in the east, as Asia grew in importance. He made his move in 324 and was victorious against Licinius on land at Hadrianople and at sea at Chrysopolis. From then until his death, he was sole ruler of the Roman empire, appointing three of his four sons as Caesars. Licinius was executed in 325 on charges of raising a rebellion.

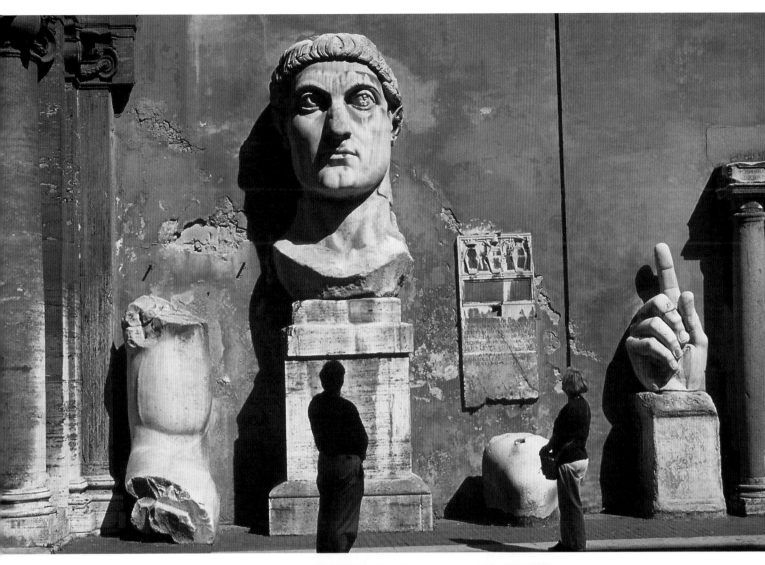

Constantine resolved to build a new capital that would ultimately signal the demise of Rome as the Mediterranean world's premier city. Although the population of Byzantium was just 50,000, compared with the one million-plus that resided in Rome, it was deemed the hub of the empire thereafter. Classical cities were raided of art treasures to adorn Byzantium, which was renamed Constantinople.

Aged 48, Constantine once again took to the saddle to fight for Rome, this time against the Goths and Samatians, but his health was fading. Knowing death was approaching, he organized his baptism, thereafter wearing saintly white garb, rather than regal purple. He was buried in Constantinople at the Church of the Apostles, causing outrage in Rome, where his body had been expected.

Above: Tourists gaze at the fragments of a colossal statue of Constantine in Rome

Left: A statue of Maximius Daia. Both these representations exhibit an interesting departure from earlier Roman portraiture, especially that of Daia. Gone is the older complexity and subtlety to be replaced by an abstract symmetry that presages the iconic Byzantine and later Gothic styles. Introspection is sacrificed for monumentalism and a rigid structure that hides character.

A Christian State

Christians were well organized and ideologically secure even before the era of Constantine. Even with his support, Christianity had to compete for hearts and minds with other, long-established religions, particularly those long beloved in the Roman empire.

Christianity was given crucial support by Constantine the Great, finally emerging as an orthodox faith rather than a radical one. For Constantine, Christianity was much more than a focal point to distinguish his rule. He summoned great theologians of the day to his court so he could listen and learn. He penned prayers and ensured that the number of copies of the Bible was swelled.

Above: Late Roman sarcophagi were often adorned with scenes from the Old and New Testaments, such as this early 4th-century example known as the Sarcophagus of Layos. Many such late Roman sarcophagi exihibit a duality, combining both pagan and Christian symbology.

As the inscription "Inspiration of the Divinity" on Constantine's triumphant arch in Rome testifies, he believed God engineered his victory in the civil war. Thereafter, Constantine increasingly considered himself God's chosen instrument. Indeed, artwork of the era reveals he viewed himself as the 13th Apostle, at the right hand of Jesus.

Undoubtedly he used religious symbolism to flatter his vanity, but this was the first time a world leader had supported a monotheistic faith. Until this era, emperors had joined the celestial ranks after their deaths through a process of deification. It probably seemed appropriate to most to place Constantine on high, even while he was living. Ironically, Constantine was also deified after his death by the senate, placing him in the ranks of pagan gods with previous emperors.

Of course, Constantine was not the first emperor to use religion to generate popular support. But after the adoption of Christianity had served him politically, Constantine continued practicing the religion when it might have seemed simpler and more fitting as a Roman ruler to revert to pagan ways. The influence of his mother Helena, a devout Christian (later made a saint), undoubtedly played a part.

The monuments he bequeathed in the name of Christianity can be seen today. In AD 313 Constantine donated imperial property at Lateran to the Bishop of Rome so a new basilica could be built. Today it is known as San Giovanni in Laterano. In Constantinople construction of the Santa Sophia began, although this grand buidling was later wiped out in a riot, to be rebuilt by Justinian.

Legally supported religion

Crucially, Constantine built the Church of the Holy Sepulcher in Jerusalem, allegedly encasing the very spot where Jesus died on the cross and the tomb in which he was laid. It has subsequently been remodeled and extended, while also becoming a bone of contention between different branches of the Christian Church.

Constantine used law to encourage Christianity. In 313 he issued the Edict of Milan, together with co-emperor Licinius, which provided for the toleration of Christian beliefs throughout the empire and the restitution of property confiscated in Diocletian's time. He went on to abolish crucifixion, began the observance of Sundays as a day of rest, and made tentative steps toward the legal suppression of paganism, although he sidestepped wholesale confrontation on that issue. However, an official visit to Rome ended in disarray when he refused to join a pagan parade. Constantine never went to Rome again.

But even Constantine's powerful personality cult was insufficient to prevent a schism in the Church. He urged that theological differences pulling the Church this way and that be resolved, for strength surely lay in unity. Senior churchmen concerned with questions of interpretation could not agree and continued the debate for centuries.

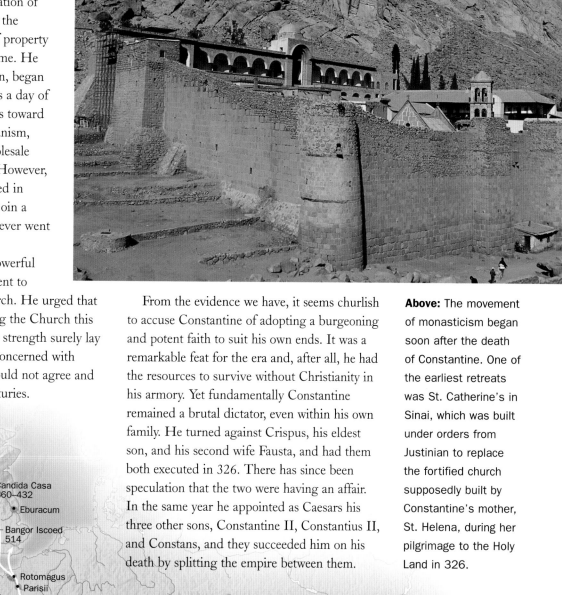

From the evidence we have, it seems churlish to accuse Constantine of adopting a burgeoning and potent faith to suit his own ends. It was a remarkable feat for the era and, after all, he had the resources to survive without Christianity in his armory. Yet fundamentally Constantine remained a brutal dictator, even within his own family. He turned against Crispus, his eldest son, and his second wife Fausta, and had them both executed in 326. There has since been speculation that the two were having an affair. In the same year he appointed as Caesars his three other sons, Constantine II, Constantius II, and Constans, and they succeeded him on his death by splitting the empire between them.

Above: The movement of monasticism began soon after the death of Constantine. One of the earliest retreats was St. Catherine's in Sinai, which was built under orders from Justinian to replace the fortified church supposedly built by Constantine's mother, St. Helena, during her pilgrimage to the Holy Land in 326.

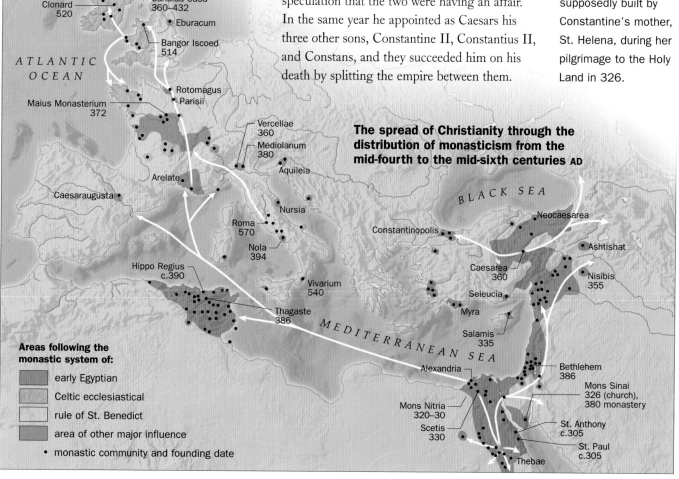

The spread of Christianity through the distribution of monasticism from the mid-fourth to the mid-sixth centuries AD

Iona 563
Clonard 520
Candida Casa 360–432
Eburacum
Bangor Iscoed 514
ATLANTIC OCEAN
Rotomagus
Parisii
Maius Monasterium 372
Vercellae 360
Mediolanum 380
Aquileia
Arelate
Caesaraugusta
Nursia
Roma 570
Nola 394
BLACK SEA
Neocaesarea
Constantinopolis
Ashtishat
Caesarea 360
Nisibis 355
Seleucia
Myra
Hippo Regius c.390
Vivarium 540
Thagaste 386
MEDITERRANEAN SEA
Salamis 335
Alexandria
Bethlehem 386
Mons Sinai 326 (church), 380 monastery
Mons Nitria 320–30
Scetis 330
St. Anthony c.305
St. Paul c.305
Thebae

Areas following the monastic system of:
early Egyptian
Celtic ecclesiastical
rule of St. Benedict
area of other major influence
• monastic community and founding date

JULIAN AND VALENTINIAN

When Constantine the Great split the empire between his three sons, it set the stage for a family struggle. First to go were Constantine's numerous half-brothers and nephews in a concerted campaign of murder that left the sons in undisputed control.

Flavius Claudius Constantinus (Constantine II) ruled over Britain, Gaul, and Spain, Flavius Julius Constantius II took control of the east, while Flavius Julius Constans held sway over Illyria and Italy. The situation did not last long. Three years after Constanine the Great's death, Constantine II was suppressed by Constans, who then ruled in the west for a further ten years. In 350 Constans fell to the military usurper Flavius Magnus Magnentius. Constantius II moved against Magnentius and defeated his forces in two battles at Mursa (351) and Mons Seleucus (352).

Constantius (r.353–61) was now sole ruler of the Roman empire. But he faced the problems that civil war had brought in its wake—renewed German hostility. Constantius realized that he needed help and unwillingly appointed his disliked nephew Julian as Caesar of Gaul and Britain in November 355. Constantius intended this as a sinecure for Julian, who was to adminster while his generals got on with the German war. However, Julian proved to be a competent general himself and, in 357, won a

Above: A *solidus* of Constantine II. Introduced by Constantine at 72 to the Roman pound of gold, the *solidus* retained the same rate for centuries.

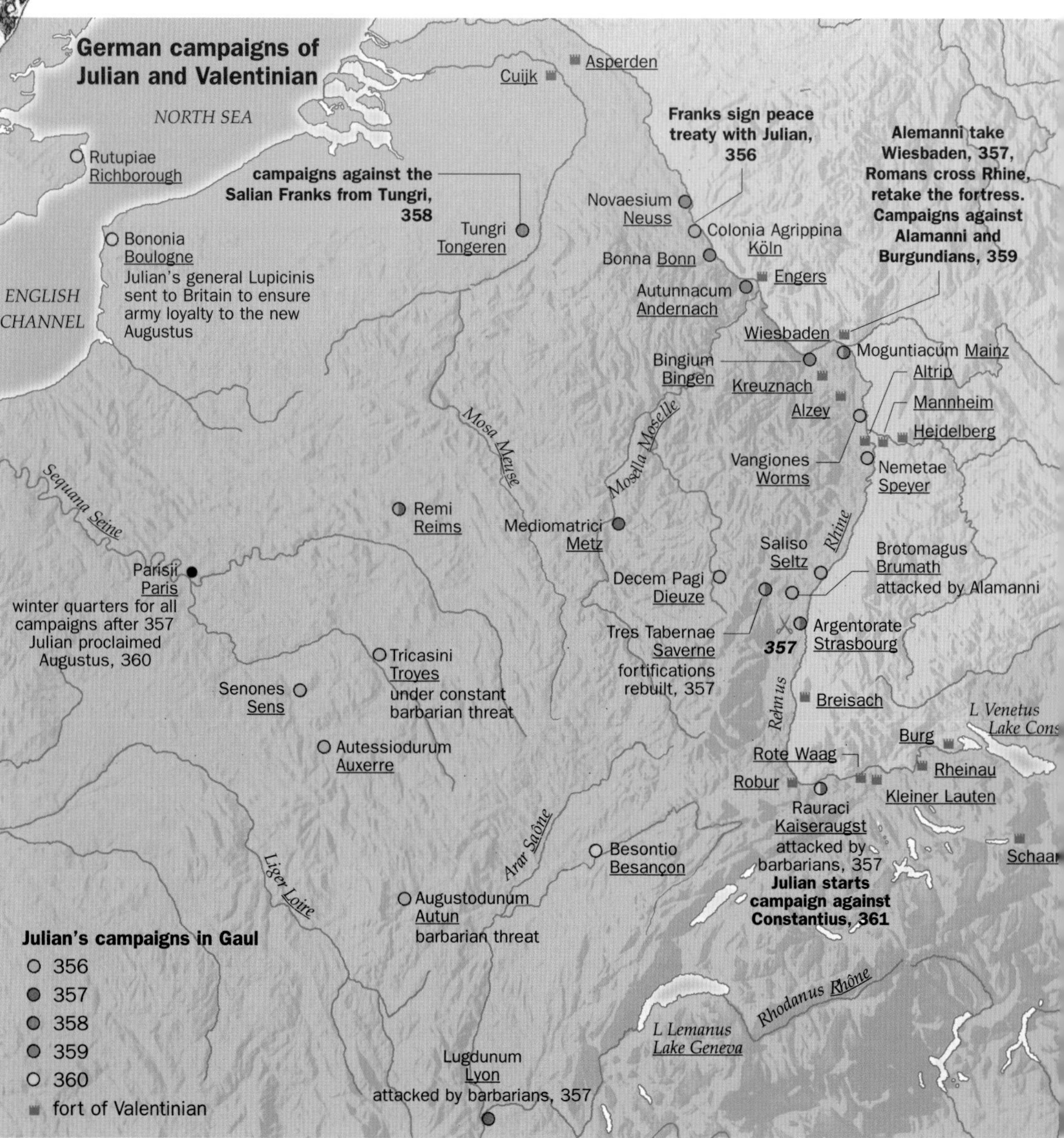
German campaigns of Julian and Valentinian
NORTH SEA
ENGLISH CHANNEL
Rutupiae Richborough
Bononia Boulogne
Julian's general Lupicinis sent to Britain to ensure army loyalty to the new Augustus
campaigns against the Salian Franks from Tungri, 358
Tungri Tongeren
Cuijk
Asperden
Franks sign peace treaty with Julian, 356
Alemanni take Wiesbaden, 357, Romans cross Rhine, retake the fortress. Campaigns against Alamanni and Burgundians, 359
Novaesium Neuss
Colonia Agrippina Köln
Bonna Bonn
Autunnacum Andernach
Engers
Wiesbaden
Moguntiacum Mainz
Bingium Bingen
Kreuznach
Alzey
Altrip
Mannheim
Heidelberg
Vangiones Worms
Nemetae Speyer
Mosa Meuse
Mosella Moselle
Sequana Seine
Remi Reims
Mediomatrici Metz
Saliso Seltz
Rhine
Brotomagus Brumath attacked by Alamanni
Decem Pagi Dieuze
Tres Tabernae Saverne fortifications rebuilt, 357
357
Argentorate Strasbourg
Parisii Paris winter quarters for all campaigns after 357 Julian proclaimed Augustus, 360
Tricasini Troyes under constant barbarian threat
Senones Sens
Autessiodurum Auxerre
Rhenus
Breisach
L. Venetus Lake Cons
Burg
Rheinau
Rote Waag
Robur
Kleiner Lauten
Rauraci Kaiseraugst attacked by barbarians, 357
Julian starts campaign against Constantius, 361
Schaa
Besontio Besançon
Arar Saône
Liger Loire
Augustodunum Autun barbarian threat
Rhodanus Rhône
L Lemanus Lake Geneva
Lugdunum Lyon attacked by barbarians, 357
Julian's campaigns in Gaul
356
357
358
359
360
fort of Valentinian

Right: For four and a half years before declaring himself Augustus, Julian waged a series of successful campaigns against the Germans. However, when he drained Gaul of troops to fight Constantius, the province became vulnerable. It was left to the reliable Valentinian to recover lost ground, building a series of forts to protect the frontier.

great victory over the Alamanii near Strasbourg.

Meanwhile, Constantius was facing an invasion of Mesopotamia. The fighting dragged on for three years, until Constantius requested reinforcements from Julian in 360. Julian's response from his base at Paris was to have himself proclaimed Augustus. In 361 he marched east to confront his uncle, and a bitter civil war was averted by the unexpected death of Constantius at the age of only 44.

An empire split

Flavius Claudius Julianus (r.361–3) is known to historians as Julian the Apostate because he reversed the progress of Christianity and reinstated the pagan gods of Rome. He saw the worship of the ancient deities as a moral and cultural renewal. Although Julian did not move against the religion in any overt way—apart from forbidding Christians to act as teachers—it is probable that this would have changed had he ruled for more than two frantic years. He was killed in battle against the Persians at Maranga on June 26, 363 during an ambitious campaign mounted from Antioch.

Julian's successor, Flavius Jovianus (Jovian) was acclaimed by the Mesopotamian troops. His task was to disentangle the army from Persia, which he did by ceding territories in northern Mesopotamia. He began the return to Constantinople, but suffocated from the fumes of an untended charcoal brazier in his bedchamber at Dadastana, having been sole emperor for only eight months.

Once again, the army in the east was stranded without a commander. However, there was no immediate threat from the appeased Persians, so time was made to call a meeting of civil officials with the senior military commanders. The result was the proclamation of another military officer, Flavius Valentinianus (r.364–375), as sole emperor. Valentinian appreciated that so much recent unrest in the empire had been caused by the lack of trust between the split rulers of east and west, but he also knew that the defense of the realm could not be undertaken by one man. He solved the dilemma by appointing his younger brother Valens as his imperial colleague.

On the face of it, the solution looked odd. Valens was not noted for any distinguished accomplishments, and in fact looked unpromising as any sort of ruler. But it made sense to Valentinian, who knew his brother's loyalty to him was unquestioned and, while Valens would never be a great general in the east, he would never pose a threat to Valentinian in the west. After the Conference of Sirmium (364/5), which legitimized the divisions of territory and administration, Valens returned to Constantinople (*see pages 164–5*) and Valentinian devoted the rest of his reign to the defense of the Rhine and, in its later years, of the Danubian frontier.

Valentinian was noted for his vigorous campaigns and defensive constructions both on the frontier and around the major centers behind. There were problems elsewhere: in Africa the Tripolitanian colonies and Mauretania suffered from tribal uprisings, suppressed by Valentinian's general Theodosius in 373–5, whose son would become the last ruler of the whole Roman empire. Valentinian died on November 17, 375 of a stroke at Brigetio on the Danube, leaving the west in the hands of his sons Flavius Gratianus (Gratian) and Flavius Valentinianus (Valentinian II).

Above: A gold *solidus* of Valentinian I. Rulers in the later 4th century reverted to a more Hellenistic appearance from those of the period of anarchy, who portrayed themselves wearing the Sun Crown—forerunner of medieval kings' crowns.

Left: Julian the Apostate appears in statues and on his coinage as the bearded philosopher-emperor. In his short reign he antagonized the huge bureaucracy by reducing its size and doing away with the elaborate ceremonial of the imperial palace. Believing that Christianity was incompatible with a love of the classics, he banned Christians from teaching.

Rome in the Fourth Century

Although Rome remained the spiritual center of Christianity, it was no longer the home of emperors, their courtiers, great statesmen, artists, writers, or philosophers. Rome's heyday was over.

The Aurelian Wall now embraced Rome, built by Emperor Aurelian (r.270–75) to fend off marauding Alamanni and Goths. Despite the absence of military builders, who were engaged on the eastern front, the work was completed in just four years; numerous homes and public buildings were obliterated in the process, older monuments were knocked down to provide stone. This indicates how urgently the task was tackled—the threat of attack was believed to be imminent. The walls were 20 feet high and 11 feet thick, with plain gateways and towers at regular intervals. At the beginning of the fifth century Emperor Honorius doubled the height of the walls and installed much grander gates to mark the main entrances to the city, still in evidence today.

Proud though it may appear, the wall was a symbol of the city's decline. Since the earliest republican days Rome had had no need of walls, safe at the heart of the empire with enormous distances separating it from the frontier troublespots.

Rome had been hard hit by imperial strategy. Diocletian's Tetrarchy undermined the city's importance. Each of the Caesars and Augusti operated from new capitals far from Rome: Treverii (present-day Trier), Mediolanum (Milan), Sirmium (Mitrovica) in Yugoslavia, and Nicomedia in modern Turkey. Although the building of Diocletian's lavish baths gave lie to the fact that Rome was neglected outright, art and architecture for the new capitals were fostered at its expense. And when Diocletian retired from public life, it was to a newly built palace in Split, rather than Rome or one of its suburbs.

Had Maxentius triumphed over Constantine it would have been different, for he chose Rome as his base. In his short reign he furnished the city with new buildings, including a circus, temple, and a magnificent basilica. Had he lived after Milvian Bridge, the focus of the empire would have remained in the west, although Christianity would not have prospered.

Below: The tomb of Gaius Cestius is one of Rome's more eccentric sights. After the conquest of Egypt in 30 BC, pyramids became popular as tombs; that of Cestius, a magistrate who died c.18 BC, is the only one remaining. Unusually, Aurelius incorporated it into the wall instead of knocking it down. It stands in a curve of the wall beside the Porta Ostiensis (gate of San Paolo).

312	312	313	324	330	337	c.340	340
Constantine sees a vision and converts to Christianity at Milvian Bridge	Constantine defeats Maxentius to become emperor in the west	Edict of Milan allows Christianity to be tolerated throughout the empire	Constantine defeats Licinius in the east, becomes emperor of entire empire	Constantine creates the eastern capital of Constantinople	The empire is divided between the three sons of Constantine	Christianity is the official religion of the Roman empire	Constantine II is defeated by his brother Constans

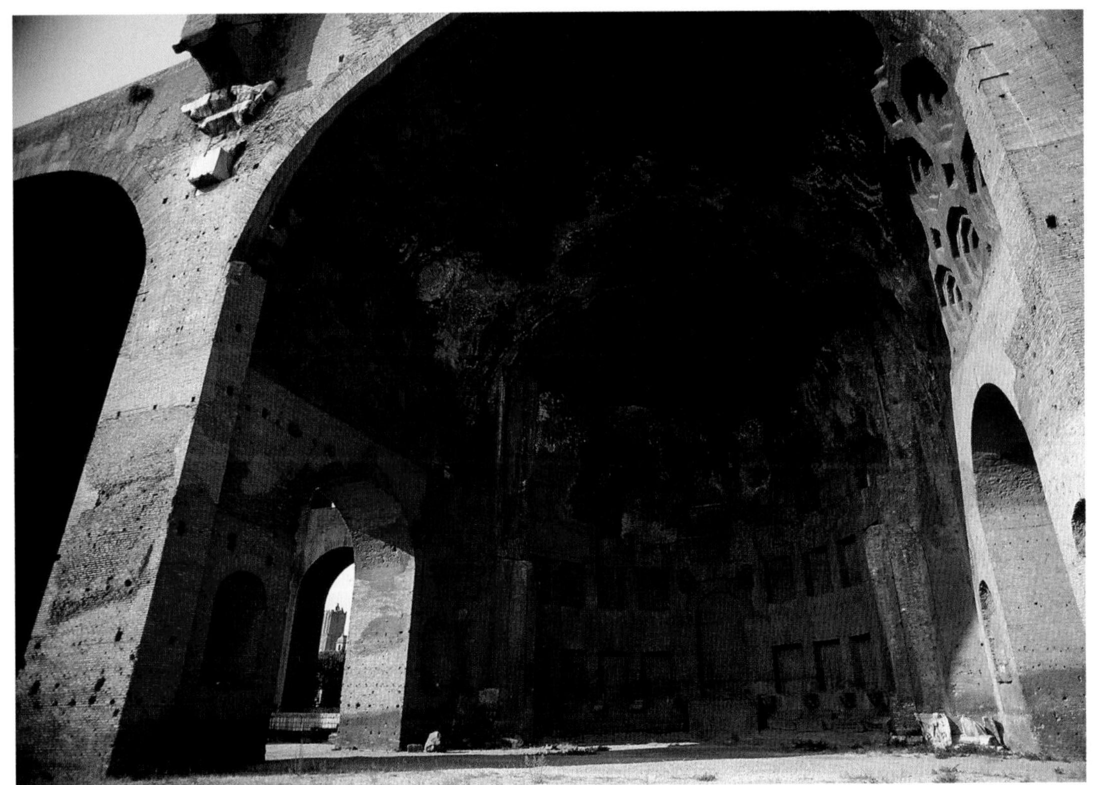

Left: The Basilica of Maxentius (or Basilica Nova) is rated as the finest monument standing on the Forum. Its massive concrete, coffered arches can only hint at its grandeur when finished (by Constantine). Today only three arches—one half of the side apses—survive, despite being turned into a church and renamed the Temple of Peace in the early 6th century by Theodoric the Ostrogoth.

Faithful to Rome

Constantine did embellish the city with his triumphal arch, largest and best preserved of the three remaining in Rome, but it was one of the last official works. Thereafter all efforts were directed at Constantinople, and it was left to the religiously zealous to fashion the face of Rome.

Constantine's mother Helena brought to Rome pieces of the true cross on which Jesus died, claiming it had miraculous life-giving properties. The veracity of such statements can never be disproved. She gave it a home by converting her palace into the Church of Santa Croce in Gerusalemme (Jerusalem). Although it stood on the outskirts of Rome, it became a center of pilgrimage.

But the religion that gave it so many grand buildings was also responsible for cultural vandalism. In 391 Theodosius ordered the closure of all pagan temples. Other pagan symbols, including the statue of Victory that had been standing in the senate since the Augustan age, were removed. Christian writers did, however, begin to illuminate the literary world. Their work endured, since papyrus was largely replaced with the more durable parchment.

Despite the confusion caused by barbarian invasions, the Roman Church held firm. Popes like Innocent I (r.401–17) laid down laws on discipline and liturgy to keep the faithful in line. Surviving letters in his hand reveal he was convinced that Rome was the natural home of the Church, and kept a watchful eye on the ambitions of the Church in Constantinople. Innocent and his successors tried to keep Rome safe from invasion while the western empire crumbled. Their efforts were not always successful.

Left: The Arch of Constantine stands beside the Colosseum at the end of the Triumphal Way. The carvings depict Constantine's victory over Maxentius at the Milvian Bridge. The arch was to be a swan song—Constantine had little interest in Rome and soon moved to Byzantium to build his new capital of Constantinopolis.

350	353	355	363	364	c.370	374	376
Magnentius kills Constans and seizes power in the west	Constantius II controls the entire empire after defeating Magnentius	Constantius appoints Juilan the Apostate as Caesar in Gaul and Britain	Emperor Julian dies in combat with Sassanids, ending his reign at two years	Valentinian is emperor in the west, while his brother Valens rules in the east	Huns stop Ostrogoth progress in the Ukraine	Alans fleeing from Huns in Russia defeat Visigoths	Valens accedes to Visigoths' request for sanctuary from Huns

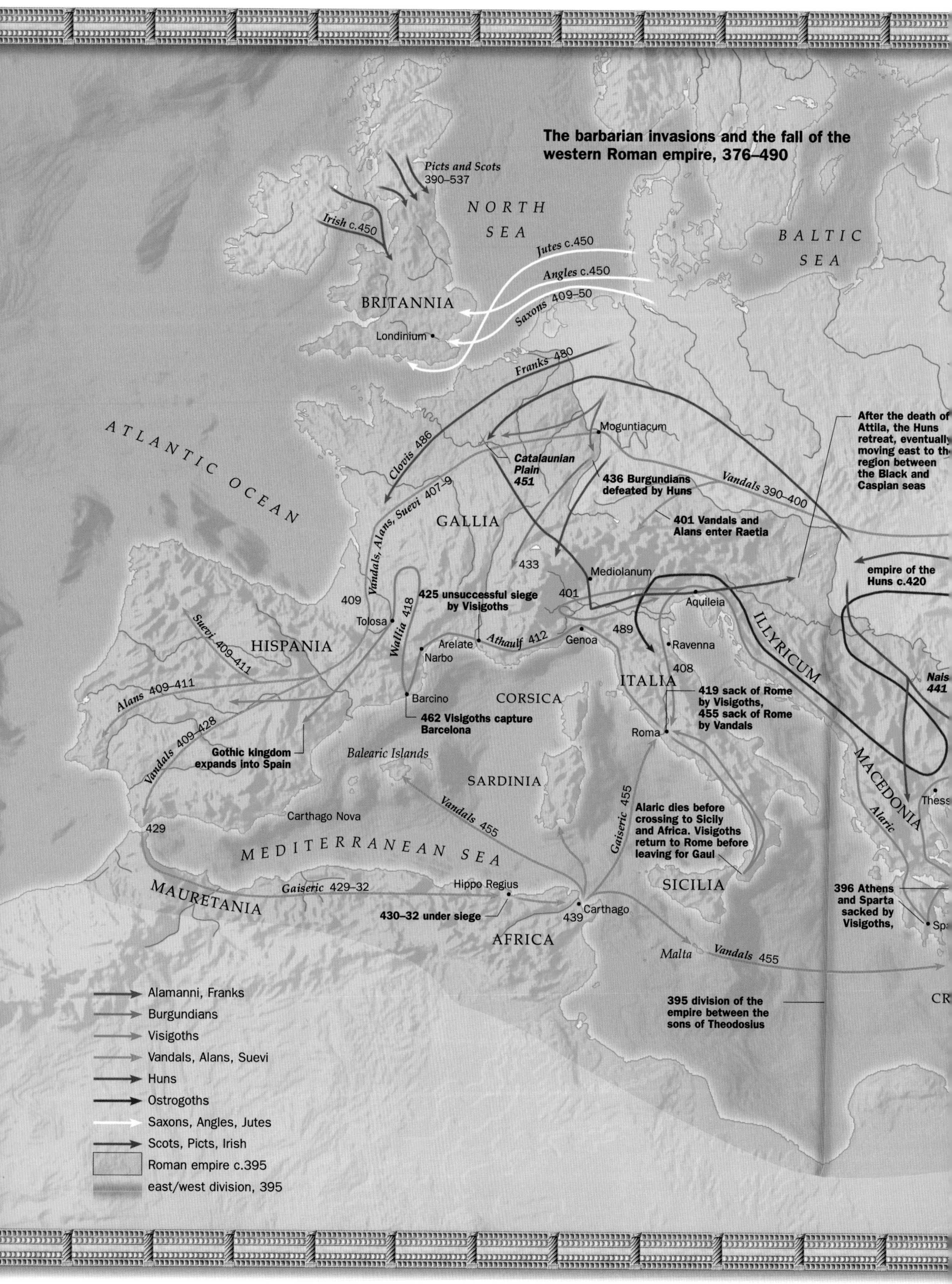
The barbarian invasions and the fall of the western Roman empire, 376–490
Picts and Scots 390–537
NORTH SEA
Irish c.450
BALTIC SEA
Jutes c.450
Angles c.450
Saxons 409–50
BRITANNIA
Londinium
Franks 480
ATLANTIC OCEAN
Clovis 486
Moguntiacum
Catalaunian Plain 451
436 Burgundians defeated by Huns
Vandals 390–400
After the death of Attila, the Huns retreat, eventually moving east to the region between the Black and Caspian seas
Vandals, Alans, Suevi 407–9
GALLIA
401 Vandals and Alans enter Raetia
433
Mediolanum
empire of the Huns c.420
409
425 unsuccessful siege by Visigoths
401
Aquileia
Tolosa
Wallia 418
Suevi 409–411
HISPANIA
Arelate
Athaulf 412
Genoa
489
Ravenna
ILLYRICUM
Narbo
408
ITALIA
Alans 409–411
Barcino
CORSICA
419 sack of Rome by Visigoths, 455 sack of Rome by Vandals
462 Visigoths capture Barcelona
Roma
Vandals 409–428
Gothic kingdom expands into Spain
Balearic Islands
SARDINIA
MACEDONIA
Vandals 455
Gaiseric 455
Alaric dies before crossing to Sicily and Africa. Visigoths return to Rome before leaving for Gaul
Carthago Nova
429
Alaric
MEDITERRANEAN SEA
MAURETANIA
Gaiseric 429–32
Hippo Regius
SICILIA
396 Athens and Sparta sacked by Visigoths,
430–32 under siege
Carthago
439
AFRICA
Malta
Vandals 455
395 division of the empire between the sons of Theodosius
Alamanni, Franks
Burgundians
Visigoths
Vandals, Alans, Suevi
Huns
Ostrogoths
Saxons, Angles, Jutes
Scots, Picts, Irish
Roman empire c.395
east/west division, 395

CHAPTER 11

COLLAPSE OF AN EMPIRE

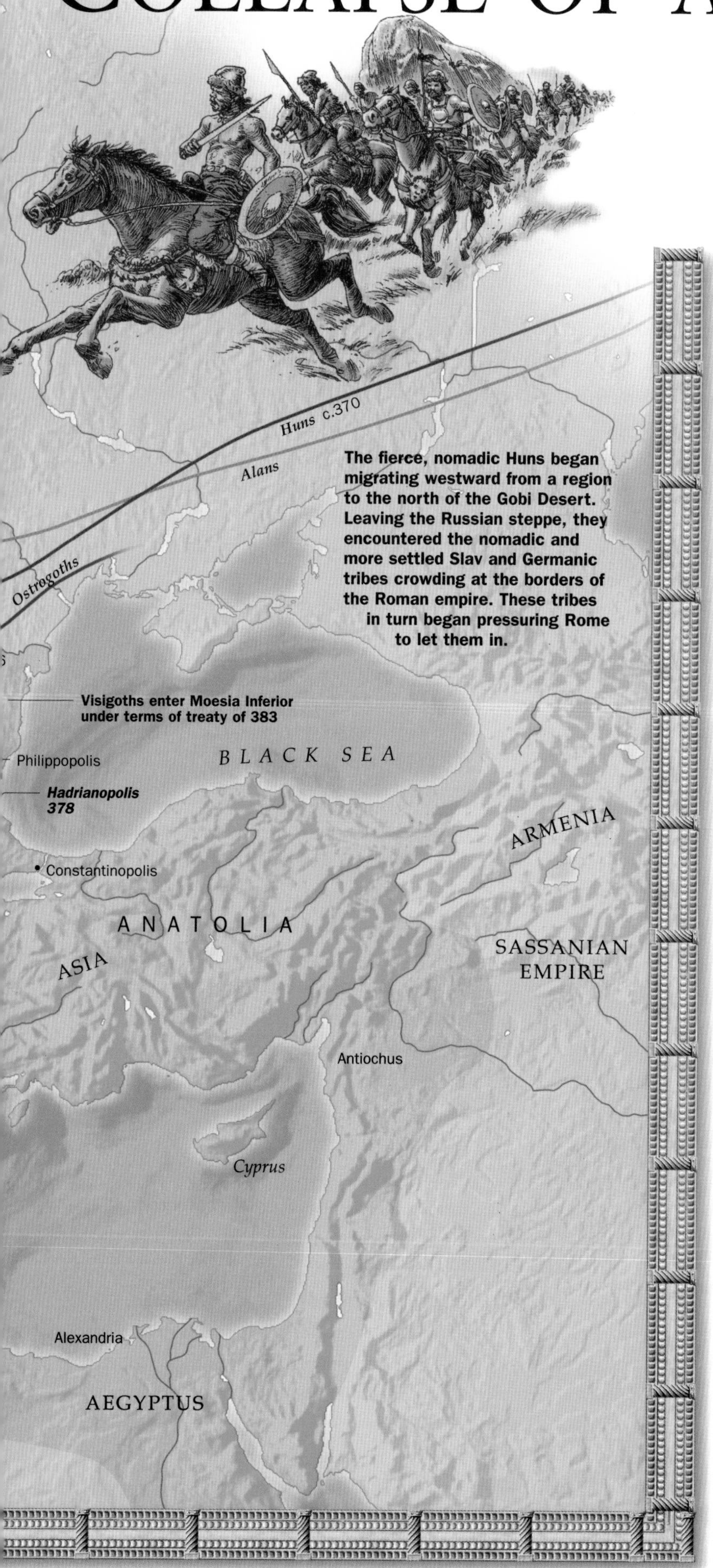
Huns c.370
Alans
Ostrogoths
The fierce, nomadic Huns began migrating westward from a region to the north of the Gobi Desert. Leaving the Russian steppe, they encountered the nomadic and more settled Slav and Germanic tribes crowding at the borders of the Roman empire. These tribes in turn began pressuring Rome to let them in.
Visigoths enter Moesia Inferior under terms of treaty of 383
Philippopolis
BLACK SEA
Hadrianopolis 378
ARMENIA
Constantinopolis
ANATOLIA
ASIA
SASSANIAN EMPIRE
Antiochus
Cyprus
Alexandria
AEGYPTUS

By the end of the fourth century AD, the Roman empire's borders had expanded to the extent that they were impossible to defend with any degree of certainty. On every frontier, barbarian tribes massed as a result of continual southward and western migrations, eagerly looking across the natural barriers of the Rhine and Danube rivers at the lush, cultivated lands of Gaul and Thrace. The six main groupings were the Ostrogoths (sometimes known as Greuthungi), Visigoths (or Tervingi), Vandals, Burgundians, Lombards, and Franks. At their backs was a terrifying new force that had swept west across the Russian steppe all the way from Mongolia—the Huns.

In the west, the late period is characterized by a series of strong military men creating and then breaking puppet emperors. Within the divided empire corruption was rife, abetted by a flow of weak rulers and an increasingly complex, self-seeking bureaucracy, both at Constantinople in the east and at either of the imperial courts of Milan or Ravenna. The military situation was worsened by poor strategic planning. Instead of holding powerful armies in reserve, perhaps to the east and west of the Alps, successive emperors strung out their forces along an impossible 4,500-mile frontier. Their reasoning was self-preservation—it was harder for ambitious generals to rebel if they first needed to assemble forces—yet the result was a war machine that clanked rather than rolled into action.

The first of the major barbarian invasions came in the east. From their heartland in the Balkans the Goths had been splitting into two as early as the third century AD. The Ostrogoths ("bright" Goths) pushed north and east into the steppelands of the Ukraine, only to be overwhelmed in 370 by the Huns. This left the Visigoth ("wise" Goths) kingdom in modern Romania dangerously exposed to the approaching Huns, and their leaders Fritigern and Alavivus appealed to Valens, emperor of the eastern Roman empire, to allow their people to find sanctuary within Roman borders.

Disaster and Division

When Valens Augustus received a desperate plea from the Visigoths in the spring of AD 376, he did not dismiss it. His reasoning underlines the dilemma both halves of the divided Roman empire faced.

Below: Valens exercised a tentative hold on the eastern empire after the death of his powerful brother Valentinian I in the west.

Above: Valens' nephew Gratian succeeded his father Valentinian in the west, but he was too young to be an effective emperor. He was murdered by the British usurper Magnus Maximus.

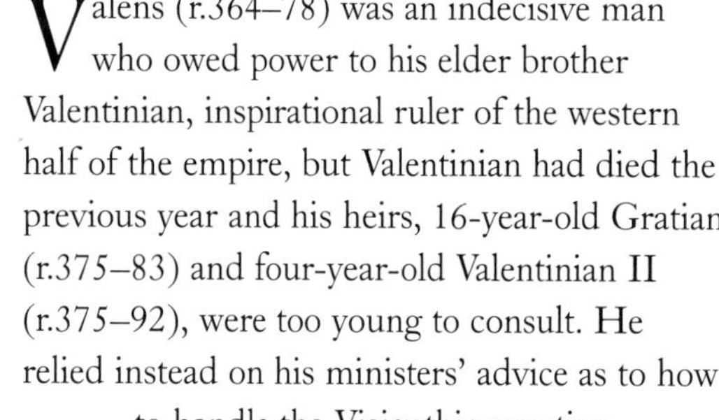

Valens (r.364–78) was an indecisive man who owed power to his elder brother Valentinian, inspirational ruler of the western half of the empire, but Valentinian had died the previous year and his heirs, 16-year-old Gratian (r.375–83) and four-year-old Valentinian II (r.375–92), were too young to consult. He relied instead on his ministers' advice as to how to handle the Visigothic question.

The court was temporarily at Antioch in Syria facing a looming war with Persia. Refusing the Visigoths would mean warring on two fronts, and his troops were not sufficient to the task and the outcome uncertain. Visigothic leaders Fritigern and Alavivus had pledged "submission" to Valen's brand of Arian Christianity and a supply of fresh recruits. Not only would they strengthen the Roman army, it would also relieve local landowners of a duty to provide troops (they could pay tax in much-needed gold instead), and the Visigoths would provide a bulwark on the borders against the Huns.

In return, the Visigoths were to be fed before wide dispersal to allotted farmlands. The Danube crossing was placed in the hands of two Roman administrators, Count Lupicinus and his associate Maximus (other names unknown). These two cared little for efficiency—their aim was to make a fast profit out of the crisis. They also underestimated the numbers of refugees and the operation's logistics. Instead of dispersal, the refugees were kept in appalling conditions close to the Danube. Their valuables were taken as payment for inadequate supplies of food and, as hunger increased, so the exploitation worsened.

However, Lupicinus proved as incompetent as he was corrupt. Having failed to disarm the Visigothic warriors, his forces were virtually annihilated by the rioting barbarians. The Visigoths then rampaged through Thrace and Moesia (modern Bulgaria). For Valens, it was the worst possible outcome. He was forced to remove troops from Armenia to the Danube and engage the invaders in skirmishes, but for two years little was achieved. In August 378 Valens himself met the Visigoths in battle at Hadrianopolis (Edirne, in European Turkey).

For Valens, it was a disaster. His scouts misinformed him of the number of the enemy, and Visigoths fell on the legions in fury. According to the contemporary historian Ammianus Marcellinus, "in the great tumult the infantry, exhausted by the efforts and the perils of the fighting, no longer able to think or plan, their spears broken, rushed recklessly with drawn swords into the dense masses of the enemy, careless of their lives now that all escape was impossible."

Settling the Visigoths

Two-thirds of the army was lost and Valens was slain in the battle. It is indicative of the chaos that no Roman survivor could say when or where the emperor died. For the Visigoths, victory was sweet but immaterial. Hopeless at siegecraft, they were repulsed at every Roman garrison they tried to take. In the crisis, Gratian recalled Flavius Theodosius, the son of his father's former general, from retirement at his home in Spain. In January 379, aged 32, Theodosius (r.379–95) was appointed Augustus in the east. In 382 he negotiated a treaty whereby the Visigoths could settle in Thrace as a Roman federate ally and be allowed to serve in the Roman army under their own tribal leaders. Peace was achieved, but it would be transitory.

Theodosius was a devout Christian, and he put an end to all forms of pagan religion in 391 and founded the orthodox Christian state, for which he earned his title "the Great." He did not remain long in Constantinople, however, because of events in the west.

Gratian, who had enjoyed one victory over an Alamanni alliance, was murdered at Lyon on the orders of the usurper Magnus Clemens

Maximus. From obscure Spanish origins, Maximus had risen to become governor of Britain, and it was there in 383 that his troops proclaimed him emperor of the west. Maximus set up court in Trier, and requested recognition from Theodosius. It was not forthcoming, so in 387 he invaded Italy. Gratian's brother and co-emperor Valentinian II fled to Theodosius for protection, and Theodosius mounted an expedition to retake Italy. Maximus was defeated and killed in 388, and Theodosius restored Valentinian to the western throne under the supervision of a Frankish general, Arbogast. Theodosius resided at Milan and Rome for three years before returning to Constantinople.

In the following year, Valentinian was found hanged, and Arbogast was elected emperor. Once again, Theodosius and his general Stilicho (*see following page*) marched on Italy and defeated Arbogast at the battle of the Frigidus river, east of Aquileia. Theodosius now settled in Milan, ruler over the whole empire. From his deathbed on January 17, 395, he formally separated the state into the eastern Roman empire ruled by his 17-year-old son Arcadius, and the western Roman empire under his second son, Honorius, aged five.

Above: Magnus Maximus, governor of Britain, aspired to the Purple and had Gratian murdered after his troops proclaimed him emperor. He succeeded in chasing Gratian's legitimate successor, Valentinian II, out of Italy before being defeated and killed by Theodosius.

Above left: The last competent ruler was Theodosius I, who ruled both halves of the empire from Milan and Constantinople. In the eastern capital, he erected an Egyptian obelisk in celebration of his many victories. This detail (**left**) from one of the reliefs on the obelisk's base depicts the emperor accepting offerings from his defeated enemies.

STILICHO AND ALARIC

The military efforts of Stilicho in the second half of the fourth and start of the fifth centuries illustrates both how much the empire now relied on non-Romans to guard its borders and the extent of growing chaos in the face of barbarian pressure.

Flavius Stilicho's father was a Vandal, which at best made him only a half-Roman. Born in AD 359, he was a talented career soldier who rose quickly through the cavalry ranks to become a trusted adviser to Theodosius and, in 384, his son-in-law by marriage to the emperor's adopted daughter, Serena. Stilicho's Germanic roots meant he was unable to aspire to the Purple, yet when Theodosius died, he appeared to hold all the right cards. He alleged that Theodosius had appointed him as protector to both Flavius Honorius (r.395–423) and Flavius Arcadius (r.395–408), giving him effective control of both empires. This was contended by Rufinus, who had been appointed guardian of Arcadius. Stilicho arranged his assassination.

Above: The gold *solidae* of Honorius (top) and Arcadius illustrate the growing differences between the western and eastern states. That of Honorius shows the emperor in familiar Greek-style profile, while that of Arcadius is now an oriental full-face pose, complete with elaborate crown.

In the west Stilicho's position had been assured by his victory over the usurper Arbogast. However, this had only been achieved with considerable help from the Visigoths, now under the leadership of King Alaric and sitting on Italy's northern border. The new federated allies had little regard for either Milan or Constantinople. Alaric showed his aggressive intentions by a series of raids deep into Italy itself (401–3). Stilicho managed to drive them back into Illyricum, but his actions appeared to be half-hearted. The Visigoths switched their attentions to the east, rampaged through Illyricum and marched on Constantinople, where Arcadius bought them off.

They continued pillaging Greece, despite another indecisive encounter with Stilicho's superior forces. Stilicho wanted to keep Alaric strong as a counterpoise to Constantinople and the Visigoths as a recruiting resource. However, in a smart move by Arcadius, Alaric was named *magister militum* (military commander) of eastern Illyricum, effectively confirming him in a position he already occupied by force. It was a move designed to keep Stilicho out of eastern affairs.

In the west problems multiplied. There were Vandal and Alan incursions south of the Danube, and a massive invasion of Italy by the pagan Ostrogoth Radagaisus in 404. Stilicho's need for more troops in Italy was urgent and he began drawing them from the hard-pressed frontiers. In 405–6 he prepared to attack the eastern empire and made an alliance with Alaric to provide military assistance. The plan was advanced and payments to the Visigoths agreed, when serious developments on the Rhine frontier caused it to be abandoned.

Above: Detail of Alaric from one of his coins. This displays all the characteristics of the simple, symmetrical gothic art style that would dominate portraiture throughout the Dark Ages. The ivory relief of Stilicho (**left**) by comparison is a recognizably Greco-Roman portrait, although it is clear that the artist has less skills than his 3rd- and 4th-century predecessors.

Below: Theodosius II (r.408–50), son of Arcadius, assisted the west in its defense and married his daughter to the western emperor Valentinian III. He died after falling from his horse.

Rome sacked

Increasing pressure from Huns on their own eastern borders forced the massed tribes of Vandals, Alans, Suevi, and Burgundians to take advantage of the particularly harsh winter of 406/7 to cross the frozen river to the west bank. At Mainz the severely weakened Roman border guard was overwhelmed and all Gaul was open for the taking. A few weeks later Constantine, Roman commander of Britain, crossed to Gaul, ostensibly to deal with the barbarian invasion. Instead, he proclaimed himself Augustus Constantine III, set up court at Arles, and soon extended his power to Spain.

Before Stilicho could engage either threat, Alaric's demands for payment for his unused services—at first refused by the senate—led to his second invasion of Italy in 408 and tied Stilicho's hands. In the east, Arcadius died in the same year, leaving the seven-year-old Theodosius II as his eastern successor. But when Stilicho again attempted to impose his authority on Constantinople, his opponents at the Milan court portrayed this as a plot to make Stilicho's son Eucherius emperor. With Honorius's agreement, Stilicho was executed. As a sequel, Roman troops began slaughtering the families of their federate German fellows who had served in Stilicho's army. These men, including recruits from Radagaisus's defeated force, saw the Visigoths as their only hope of protection. An estimated 30,000 flocked to Alaric's standard.

Alaric besieged Rome in 408 and was paid to leave. He returned in the following year and, while kept outside the Aurelian Wall, managed to set up a puppet governor. But, having failed to wring a favorable treaty out of Honorius, when he came again for the third time in 410, sympathizers within the city opened the gates. His army poured into the city, which had not been taken by a foreign foe for nealry 800 years. The three days of looting and burning was a relatively restrained affair, given the earlier Roman outrage. After that, taking Honorius's half-sister Galla Placida with him, Alaric moved toward the south of Italy and prepared to continue his campaign with an invasion of Sicily and North Africa, but died in southern Italy shortly afterward.

Church and State

Constantine the Great's conversion transformed the Christian Church in Roman society. The Edict of Milan (313) handed back all property confiscated in the years of persecution. The clergy were exempted from civic obligations and bishops received the right of civil jurisdiction, effectively making them automatic magistrates on their ordination.

However, Constantine faced serious divisions within the Church between orthodox Christianity and Arianism. Arius, an Alexandrian priest, conceived that the Trinity—Father, Son, and Holy Spirit—was a hierarchy of divine beings, with God the Father at its summit. Orthodox opinion refused to see any distinction between the three. At the Council of Nicaea (325), Constantine offered a compromise that stated the Father and Son were "consubstantial." Although he succeeded in persuading all but a few of this view, Arianism continued to be the dominant opinion of the eastern empire until Theodosius I strictly enforced orthodoxy and eliminated Arianism in the east.

It is clear that the emperors were obliged to participate in theological controversies, and even enjoyed the debate, yet this is not to imply that the emperors were ever considered as being heads of the Church. Indeed, Ambrose, the bishop of Milan, exerted such authority over Theodosius that he made the emperor perform a penance for a massacre carried out by his soldiers in Thessalonica, pictured above by Peter Paul Rubens.

Spread of the Barbarians

The breach of the Rhine frontier opened a floodgate through which poured hundreds of thousands of barbarian tribes. But this invasion was made by people whose long envy of Rome made them want the mantle of Roman civilization more than plunder.

Right: Galla Placidia, daughter of an emperor, wife of a king and an emperor, and mother of an emperor, wielded power through her weak son, Valentinian III. In older age she performed charitable works and put up public buildings. Placidia died in 450 and was buried in her mausoleum (**below**) in Ravenna.

For the decade after the death of Stilicho, the dominant Roman military leader was Flavius Constantius. The vigorous general promptly finished his predecessor's business, defeating three usurpers in rapid succession: Constantine III, executed in 411; Jovinus, who had been acclaimed by the Burgundian invaders of Gaul, executed at Narbonne in 413; and his brother Sebastianus, who had become co-emperor in 412, also executed in 413.

A fourth pretender, Maximus, had set himself up in opposition to Constantine III in Spain, but was deposed in 411 and allowed by Honorius to retire. He was executed in 422, accused of fomenting rebellion. Constantius set himself up at Arelate, and in 413 granted the Burgundians land on the west bank of the Rhine and gave them the status of allies.

After Alaric's death in 410, his successor Athaulf led the Visigoths from Italy into Gaul. They settled in Narbonensis in 414, where Athaulf married Galla Placidia, daughter of Theodosius and half-sister of Honorius, who had been taken hostage during the sack of Rome. The marriage was intended as a gesture

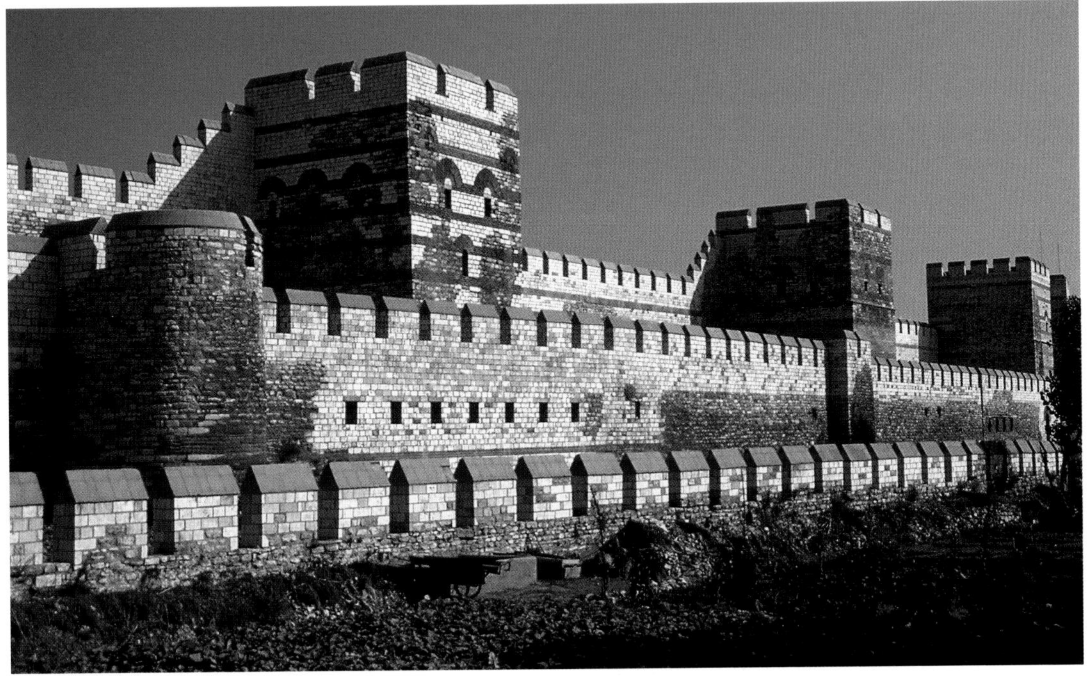

Left: The great walls that Theodosius II erected around Constantinople kept the eastern capital secure from barbarian attack, but Valentinian III only had his general Flavius Aetius for protection—and he had him executed. Under the thumb of his mother, Galla Placidia, Valentinian (**below**) was a weak ruler, but he lasted a lot longer than any of his successors.

of good faith, but Honorius refused his consent and Constantius drove the Visigoths into Spain, where Athaulf was assassinated in 415. His brother Wallia returned Placidia to the Romans in return for the right to settle in southwestern Gaul. A treaty was finally concluded in 418, and Tolosa (Toulouse) became the Visigothic capital under nominal imperial authority.

In the previous year Constantius had married Placidia, apparently against her will, although she gave him a son (Valentinian III). The marriage confirmed that Constantius was now very powerful and he was made co-emperor with Honorius on Februrary 8, 421. However, this unilateral appointment angered the eastern empire, which refused to recognize Constantius III. He prepared for war against the east but died of natural causes in Ravenna on September 2, 421.

Struggling for salvation

Soon after the death of Constantius, relations between Honorius and his dominating sister deteriorated and she fled to the east, taking the four-year-old Valentinian with her. Two years later, in 423, Honorius died of natural causes and another usurper, Johannes (other names unknown) seized the Purple. The eastern emperor, Theodosius II, intervened to restore the western dynasty, and Johannes was executed following his defeat in October 425. At the age of six, Placidia's son Placidius Valentinianus became Valentinian III. Although Placidia served as regent, few doubted that Constantinople, not Ravenna, was now the true center of Roman power.

The west was again in need of a strong military man, and found him in Flavius Aetius, a Danubian from Durostorum (Silistria in Romania). He was considered to be an expert on the Huns, having been a hostage at the Hunnish court for a period. Indeed, after Honorius's death, Aetius had led a force of Huns to attempt to block Placidia's return. But the two made their peace, and Aetius became effective commander of the Roman army. He now faced two serious threats posed by the Vandals and the Huns themeselves.

The German tribes who had crossed the Rhine in 407—Vandals, Alans, and Suevi—fanned out across Gaul, took Aquitania by 409, and crossed the Pyrenees into the urbanized homeland of the Theodosian dynasty where they soon set up competing kingdoms. In 420 the Vandal king Gunderic defeated a Romano-Gothic army and became ruler of a unified Vandal-Alan kingdom centered on southern Spain. This allowed him to take control of key ports and, more importantly, the galleys moored there.

A vast pirate fleet that assiduously raided the Balearic Islands and coastal cities now replaced Roman naval power, which for so many centuries had dominated the western Mediterranean. Their booty helped shore up the fledgling Vandal kingdom and fueled a desire for further conquest. In 429 Gunderic's successor and half-brother, the shrewd and militarily outstanding Gaiseric (or Genseric), led all 80,000 of his people across the Mediterranean to begin an assault on North Africa.

GAISERIC AND ATTILA

The beleaguered western empire faced a war on two major fronts. To the south across the Mediterranean the Vandals threatened Africa, to the north the semi-nomadic Huns massed. The vast Hunnish cavalry was the most fearsome and best organized ever encountered by imperial legions.

Inset: A coin of Gaiseric, king of the Vandals. Gaiseric was ceded much of the Roman African provinces. From his capital, the venerable Roman city of Hippo Regius (**below**), he took Carthage and then invaded Italy, capturing Rome itself.

North Aftrica was still a vital source of grain for Italy, and the Vandal invasion had to be countered. The country's semi-independent governor was Boniface. He had also opposed Placidia's return, but then made peace with the regent. However, Placidia was suspicious of his motives and, since she was equally concerned about the increasing power of Aetius, she set the two men against each other. Some accounts claim that Gaiseric was invited by Boniface as a counter to Aetius. If true, it was a foolish move—Gaiseric knew the value of the region's grain and oil markets. Boniface's troops were slaughtered on the battlefield and, by 430, the remainder of his forces fled to the fortified coastal town of Hippo Regius (now Bona).

Fear of the Vandals prompted the east to send an army to aid Aetius, but the joint army failed dismally. In 432 Boniface was killed in the fighting, and other pressures obliged the Romans to conclude a treaty. Gaiseric was granted federate status in Mauretania and Numidia, while an imperial presence was maintained at Carthage. From his capital in Hippo Regius, Gaiseric had no intention of abiding by this agreement, and in 439 he captured the rest of North Africa. The loss of Carthage was a shock to the Romans, but their hands were full elsewhere.

By the turn of the fifth century, the Huns had settled east of the Danube, particularly along the plains of Hungary. On the eastern

empire border, the Huns were appeased by tribute payments, but this changed in 434 when Attila and his elder brother Bleda became joint Hunnish rulers. Atilla soon had Bleda put to death, and as supreme leader of the Huns demanded the doubling of the subsidy to 700lb of gold each year. Theodosius II refused to pay. Attila's forces stormed across the Danube in 441. He razed major centers such as Naissus (modern Nis) and Serdica (Sofia), took Philippopolis, engaged and defeated the main imperial legions, and annihilated their remnants on the Gallipoli peninsula.

The cruelties Attila inflicted in this campaign undoubtedly fueled the way he would be demonized by Christian Romans as the Scourge of God. The slaughter in Naissus was such that years later Roman ambassadors were unable to enter the ruins for the mass of human bones and an all-pervading stink of death. Attila's peace terms of 443 trebled the annual tribute and demanded full payment of arrears.

Attila then turned his attention to the eastern Roman territories of Lower Scythia and Moesia. Again he defeated eastern empire forces, although with substantial losses, and rampaged onward through the Balkans and Greece. This time a peace treaty took three years to conclude and forced Theodosius to surrender large tranches of territory south of the Danube.

Marriage as war proposal

By now Attila's eye was turning to the western empire, with whom he had previously remained on friendly terms. His excuse for invasion came in the form of a particularly Roman scandal. In 449 Valentinian's sister Honoria was caught having an affair with her steward, who was promptly executed. She was kept in solitary confinement but, in her anger, smuggled out a ring to Attila suggesting he intervene as her champion. Attila decided that this was a marriage proposal and demanded half the western empire as dowry.

When Aetius refused it, Attila's huge army of Huns and allied Ostrogoths crossed the Rhine in 451 and swept south, sacking Mainz, Cologne, Strasbourg, Worms, Metz, Reims, Trier, and were on the verge of taking Orléans when Aetius met them. Aetius had spent months building his own anti-Hunish alliance of Romans and Visigoths and both he and Attila had recruited Burgundian, Alani, and Frankish troops. In June Aetius engaged Attila in perhaps the greatest single engagement that western Europe has ever seen. The Battle of the Catalaunian Plain (near Châlons-sur-Marne) resulted in Attila suffering his first and only reversal and, according to contemporary accounts, left more than 200,000 dead. Military strategists have criticized Aetius for allowing Attila to retreat across the Rhine, but the Romans had also taken massive losses. Perhaps Aetius felt a continued threat from the Huns would hold his Gallic alliance together.

Attila revisited Italy the following year, sacking a number of cities, including Padua, Verona, and Milan. According to some sources, only papal intervention prevented him from entering Rome itself. He was planning a further attack against Constantinople, when he died in his sleep in 453.

Left: Bonifatius, Comes Africae, was described as a strange blend of saint and medieval knight, His semi-independent control of the African granary pitched him against Galla Placidia, but his death came at the hands of Gaiseric.

Left: Attila the Hun, the Scourge of God, created havoc in both eastern and western empires. Between them, Attila and Gaiseric contributed more to the collapse of the Roman empire than any other men.

Last Emperor in the West

The western empire's later emperors were impotent and largely immaterial, as far-removed from the great Roman administrators of the past as was possible. They were puppets of their army generals, publicly paraded and ruthlessly jettisoned.

The eastern emperors Leo (**right**) and Zeno (**below**) intervened in the chaotic western politics of succession.

Theodosius I had been the last truly capable emperor (although we should not overlook the massive codification of Roman law undertaken by Theodosius II). His son Honorius (r.395–423) was incompetent, and his hand in the murder of the one outstanding general who perhaps would have loyally protected him, Flavius Stilicho, says much for his lack of wisdom. Honorius so discredited the Purple that subsequent military figures showed little interest in acquiring it, preferring to make and break emperors at will. For almost two decades from 414, power was effectively wielded by his sister, the politically astute Galla Placidia, acting as regent to Valentinian III. Valentinian's reign was, even by the late empire's standards, a tumultuous period. He became too reliant on the Roman general Flavius Aetius, who successfully demanded that Galla Placidia formally recognize him as Patrician of the western empire in 433.

Aetius's victory at the Catalaunian Plain was an unexpected boost for aristocratic morale—Aetius was, after all, a true Roman soldier rather than some barbarian upstart. However, Valentinian interpreted it as a threat to his own position. In 454 Valentinian had him executed, a deed that cost him his life six months later, when two of the general's officers took revenge. For more than two decades, Aetius had tried to check the barbarians and his assassination began the western empire's terminal decline.

The death of Valentinian prompted the ever-ambitious Gaiseric to invade Italy. His fleet landed at Ostia and captured Rome in 455. The Vandals heeded a plea from Pope Leo I to spare the inhabitants from torture or death, but Gaiseric left two weeks later having looted most of Rome's greatest treasures. The papal intervention, first with the Huns and then with the Vandals, is testament to the sway Rome's popes now held, even with Arian Christians like the Vandals.

With few exceptions, the barbarian hordes had converted to Arian Christianity. The Visigoths did so as part of their agreement with Valens, an Arian emperor (*see page 164*)—although most of their relations with Romans were made with Theodosius, a devout Catholic—but why the Vandals did so is not known. Phases of anti-Roman aggression were expressed in the persecution of Catholics, especially in Africa under Gaiseric in 430 and

From March 455 to August 476 no less than nine emperors ruled in the west, almost all of them puppets of one force or another. **Left to right:** Flavius Anicius Petronius Maximus; Marcus Maecilius Flavius Eparchius Avitus; Julius Majorianus (Marjorian); Libius Severus III; Procopius Anthemius; Anicius Olybrius; Flavius Glycerius; Flavius Julius Nepos; Romulus Augustus (Augustulus). The last was deposed by Odoacer, who made himself king (**pictured above the row**).

again under King Huneric (r.477–84). The Suevi and Burgundians remained pagan for some time, and the Franks were converted directly from paganism to Christianity at the time of King Clovis (r. c.466–511).

Return of the kings

Over the next two decades the title of emperor in the west became an absurdity. Valentinian's successor, the wealthy senator Petronius Maximus, lasted a mere 11 weeks before he was killed trying to flee Gaiseric's attack on Rome. Later that year, Avitus—a friend of the Visigoth king Theodoric II—was proclaimed Augustus in Gaul. However, he was deposed the following year by the barbarian army warlord Ricimer, himself of Gothic royal lineage. Ricimer wielded power through two puppet emperors, Marjorian (r.457–61) and Severus III (r.461–65), until it became clear that he needed eastern support from Flavius Valerius Leo I (r.457–74).

Leo's price was to name his own candidate, Anthemius (r.467–72), but the latter's campaign against the Vandals was so disastrous that Ricimer had him executed. Ricimer died the same year, shortly before the new incumbent Olybrius (r.472), which left the field to Glycerius (r.473–74), puppet-emperor of the Burgundian warlord Gundobad.

In June 474 Constantinople intervened again. The new eastern emperor, Zeno (r.474–91), sent Julius Nepos to seize control at the head of a small army in 474. A year later, Julius was overthrown in a coup by his own general, Orestes, who promptly installed his son Romulus Augustulus in 475. Known as "the little Augustus," politically speaking, Romulus was indeed so small that nobody noticed him being pushed into abdication in 476.

This was achieved by Odoacer, chieftain of the Heruli, a Germanic tribe in service to Rome as mercenaries. After defeating Orestes, Odoacer deposed Romulus. In the east, Zeno reluctantly recognized Odoacer's authority over Italy and granted him the title of patrician. The Germanic mercenary was now the king of Italy. Odoacer (r.476–493) had no need of an empty title and an empire in ruins.

INPENSAM·PATRONO·DEDERVNT

Above: A semblance of normal life in Ravenna co-existed with the political mayhem of the period. This monument in the church of San Vitale is to a ship builder called Plongidienus. Easy access to the sea for escape from barbarian raiders made Ravenna a safer capital than Milan for the later emperors.

Legions at Bay

In the half-century preceding the Vandal invasion of Africa in 429, that great bastion of Roman supremacy—the army—was challenged as never before.

Below: Late Roman infantrymen (*pedes*), while still the backbone of the army, took second place to cavalry units, and tended to be used as smaller-scale rapid deployment forces. Note the early appearance of the crossbow (bottom right).

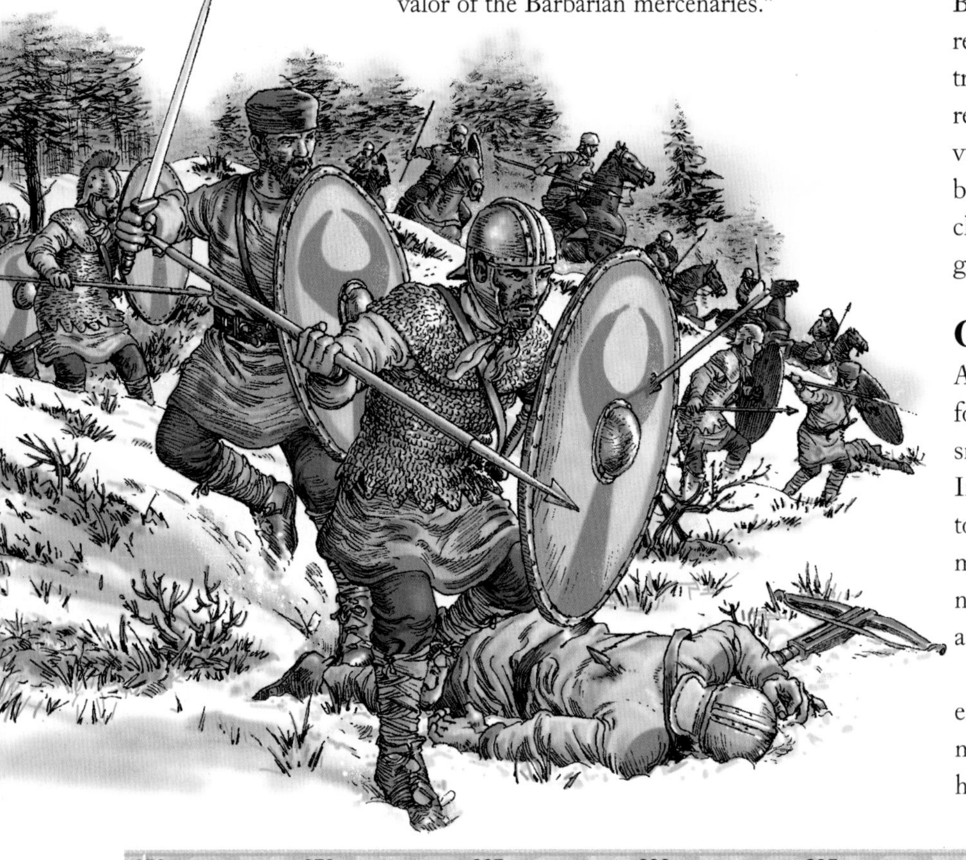

One received wisdom is that the Roman army—invincible under men like Caesar and Augustus—had become soft-bellied, packed with inferior barbarians and lacking a nationalistic fighting spirit of yore. In his *The Decline and Fall of the Roman Empire*, Gibbon observes: "The warlike states of antiquity, Greece, Macedonia, and Rome educated a race of soldiers; exercised their bodies, disciplined their courage, multiplied their forces by regular evolutions and converted the iron which they possessed into strong and serviceable weapons. But this superiority insensibly declined with their laws and manners; and the feeble policy of Constantine and his successors armed and instructed, for the ruin of the empire, the rude valor of the Barbarian mercenaries."

This portrays the late Roman army as a battlefield pushover, but the facts suggest otherwise. Valens' legions may have been annihilated at Hadrianople, but they fought well and bravely. It was Aetius, a Roman general, who masterminded the extraordinary defeat of Attila the Hun at the Catalaunian Plain. And how did the eastern empire manage to hang on for another millennium?

The truth is that change and flexibility were the army's greatest weapons, not its weaknesses. Commanders had no problem with "foreign" troops, weapons, or tactics, provided they improved performance. The real challenge was rooted in strategic change—Constantine's "feeble policy"—although this was enforced by the need to fight more and different enemies across an unfeasibly large frontier.

Before Constantine, emperors mobilized large field armies, engaged the enemy, and dispersed units back to their garrisons and frontier posts. But Constantine introduced a permanent rapid-reaction force, the *comitatenses*, comprising elite troops who could deploy at short notice. This reduced the risk of internal rebellion and allowed vulnerable borders to be quickly reinforced by battle-tested men. However, it created a two-tier class of soldier, with the *limitanei* (frontier garrisons) seen as second rate.

Crippled by neglect

As the fourth century wore on, there was a trend for both *comitatenses* and *limitanei* to split into smaller units tied to particular regions. Inevitably, they become more static and harder to move from homes and families. Assembling a mobile field army to deal with major invasions now demanded greater reliance on mercenaries and federated barbarian warlords.

Myriad other problems dogged the effectiveness of the military. Corruption was a morale-sapping issue, whether it involved buying high rank or using bribes to avoid unwanted

378	379	387	392	395	395	c.397	406–408
Roman forces led by Valens are defeated by Visigoths at Hadrianopolis	Western Emperor Gratian puts Theodosius in command of the east	Maximus drives Valentinian II from Italy but is defeated in 388 by Theodosius	Theodosius is the last emperor of both halves of the empire	Theodosius dies; Stilicho is guardian of boy-emperors Arcadius and Honorius	Stilicho defeats Visigoth leader Alaric, halting his rampage through Greece	Alaric is made Magister Militum (commander) of Eastern Illyricum, west of Macedonia	Vandals cross the Rhine and pillage Roman-held Gaul

duties. Legions were generally kept under-strength and the army's total manpower of perhaps 450,000 in the mid-fourth century must have been drastically reduced by a succession of campaigns. Apart from the Hadrianople disaster of 378, there was the ongoing trouble with Persia, endless engagements with Germanic tribes across the Rhine and Danube, and a seemingly perpetual cycle of civil war.

All this had a colateral effect on the economy as a whole. By the end of the fourth century there was a chronic shortage of agricultural workers, since the imperial court enforced a rigorous manpower tax on landowners. This in turn drove up the prices of food and supplies and encouraged corrupt government middlemen to dabble in underhand deals. The labor shortages affected all aspects of life in the late empire—even the cherished road system suffered, through a chronic lack of maintenance.

Historians can and do theorize at great length about the speed of Roman military decline. Yet occasionally the most obvious causes are neglected. Attacked on all fronts by formidable enemies, torn apart by the intrigue of senior generals, led by incompetent emperors, and hidebound by bureaucracy, the only surprise is that the eastern empire lasted as long as it did.

Below: Aerial view of Housesteads Fort and Hadrian's Wall. Once the legions had left Britain, the wall's meaning was soon lost.

408 Stilicho is executed as a result of attempts to control the eastern empire

408–410 Alaric's Goths and besiege and sack Rome

420 Eastern Emperor Theodosius II pacifies Huns with gold

420 Gunderic defeats a Romano-Gothic army and rules a Vandal-Alans kingdom in Spain

425 Eastern Emperor Theodosius II replaces Johannes with Valentinian III in the west

429 Gunderic's successor, Gaiseric, leads Vandals from Spain into Africa

430 Governor Boniface's Roman forces in Africa take refuge from Gaiseric's Vandals

431 Boniface's besieged army is liberated; a treaty is agreed with the Vandals

Byzantine Bastion

While the city of Rome paled in the fifth century, Constantinople blazed in glory. Studded with grand new edifices and underpinned by the wealth of the eastern empire, Constantinople radiated brilliance from behind splendid city walls.

Below: Symbol of Byzantine power, the great church of Hagia Sophia dominates the skyline of Constantinople (modern Istanbul). The enormous space enclosed by the dome (**right**) was once decorated with wonderful mosaics, but these were later removed. The decoration is now Islamic.

Byzantium was a compact city founded in the eighth century BC on the waterway splitting Europe from Asia. Periodically under Persian rule, it was nevertheless Greek by inclination. It attracted swift and terrible vengeance at the end of the second century AD when Byzantium backed Pescennius Niger as emperor, rather than Septimius Severus. The city's inhabitants were slaughtered and it was reduced to rubble. Severus began rebuilding the city but it remained somewhat anonymous until the time of Constantine.

Fresh from his victory against co-emperor Licinius in 324, he decided to make his base at Byzantium, reflecting a growing need to protect the eastern side of the Roman empire. Constantine was not the first to turn his back on Rome, since the city had already been deserted as the center of empire in favor of Milan in Italy, Trier in Gaul, and York in Britain.

Using wood from the forests around the Black Sea and marble from Proconeusus in the Sea of Marmara, the city mushroomed on its seven hills in a few short years. Wealthy residents had homes with ivory doors and mosaic floors, and there was conspicuous use of precious metals and gems. Its monuments were adorned with art treasures hewn from across the empire, especially from Greece.

On May 11, 330 Byzantium was officially inaugurated as Constantinopolis (Constantinople) at three times its previous size. It was orthodox Christian by faith and it was here that some of the most contentious conferences to determine the direction of the faith were held. After 381 a patriarch was installed, second only in rank to the bishop of Rome.

The language of Constantinople remained Greek, while its street map had a Roman feel. When it was founded Constantine called it New Rome; a claim also made for Antioch. But Constantinople outstripped this and every other major city in the world.

Stricken by disasters

The prime reason for its astonishing success was its impregnable peninsula site. City walls solidly constructed in the reign of Theodosius II repelled all-comers. Constantinople was so

fortunate in withstanding enemy onslaught that it became known as the God-guarded city. One of its treasures remains the Hagia Sophia. A church that formerly stood on the site was destroyed in the riots that nearly cost Justinian his throne (*see following page*). It took six years to build the spectacular replacement, which became an inspiration for architects worldwide. Alas, it fell victim to the iconoclasts, who hacked most of the beautiful mosaics from the wall during the era when puritanical beliefs prevailed. When Muslims took over there was no place for religious art so it remained grand but bare.

Constantinopolis in the time of Theodosius II

to Hadrianopolis
St. Mary in Blachernae
Palace of Blachernae
Xylokerkos Gate
River Lycus
St, Salvador in Chora
Golden Horn
St. Theodosius Gate
cistern of Aetius
cistern of Aspar
Galata
Bosphorus
army gate 5
Plateia Gate
army gate 4
St. Romanus Gate
church of Holy Apostles
Drungarii Gate
wall of Septimius Severus
column of Claudius Gothicus
moat
wall of Theodosius II
wall of Constantine
Perama Gate
Neorian Gate
aqueduct of Valens
St. Barbara's Gate
acropolis
column of Marcian
Rhegium Gate
St. Mary Chalkoprateia
Amastrianum
forum of Constantine
St. Eirene
monastery of Magnana
Forum Bovis
cistern of Mocius
forum of Arcadius
Forum Tauri
Milion
St. Sophia
Augusteion
arch of Theodosius
army gate 3
column of Constantine
St. Mary Hodegetria
column of Arcadius
St. Thomas
senate house
Selymbria Gate
St. Andrew in Krisei
baths of Xeuxippus
Bucoleon Palace
monastery of St. Menas
harbor of Theodosius
harbor of Julian
army gate 2
Pasmathia Gate
palace of Justinian
Hippodrome
martyrium of St. Carpus and St. Papylus
St. Sergius and St. Bacchus
obelisk of Theodosius
St. John Studios
army gate 1
Propontis
Sea of Marmara
Golden Gate

The hippodrome built at the behest of Septimius Severus in 200 was an integral feature of city life. It was a venue for chariot racing and public executions. Its crowds were defined by factions, with the "blues" being wealthy citizens (in the front rows) and the "greens" poorer people in the cheap seats.

The successor to Zeno, Anastasius (r.491–518), is recognized as the first Byzantine, as against eastern Roman emperor. And the end of his successor's nephew Justinian's reign is widely regarded as the end of the classical period of antiquity. Thereafter, the fates of the old western and eastern Roman empires depart of very different tracks. Constantinople continued to grow, a center of learning, culture, and increasingly oriental bureaucracy.

THE ROMAN RECONQUEST

At the beginning of the sixth century, a new Byzantine emperor dreamed of reconstituting the old Roman empire. Thanks to the brilliance of his chosen general, Belisarius, he largely succeeded.

The official date given for the fall of the western Roman empire is 476, when Odoacer deposed Romulus. Under Odoacer, senatorial administration of Rome had continued largely uninterrupted. He ordered the restoration of the Colosseum and presented entertainments there and racing in the Circus Maximus. However, the German's command of Italy from his court in Ravenna was never accepted by Zeno in Constantinople. In 488 he sent Theodoric the Great, king of the Ostrogoths, into Italy to expel Odoacer.

The war lasted until 493, when Odoacer agreed to share power, but was treacherously murdered while attanding a feast arranged by Theodoric. Theodoric made himself master of Italy and proved to be a strong and decisive leader. He successfully integrated Roman and Teutonic culture, but when he died in 526 civil unrest again erupted.

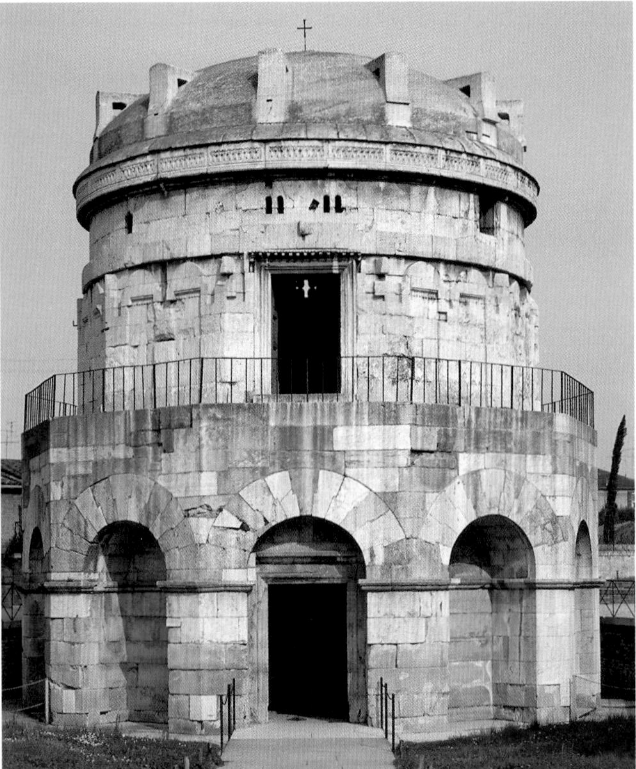

Right: The mausoleum of the Ostrogothic king Theodoric still stands in Ravenna. Its immense domed roof of Istrian stone weighs 300 tons. Images of Theodoric and his court were all erased on the orders of Justinian (**facing**), seen standing to the left of his general, Belisarius, in a mosaic from the walls of San Vitale, Ravenna. However, a portrait of Theodoric survives on one of his coins (**below**).

In the east, Emperor Justin I (r.518-27) had adopted his nephew Justinian as his son and heir. In the eyes of the aristocracy, young Justinian was an unpromising candidate. A fan of chariot racing and a frequent visitor to the hippodrome, he scandalized Constantinople when he fell in love with an actress called Theodora and married her. Justinian was elevated to Caesar in 525 and, on the death of Justin, became emperor of the Byzantine empire.

Justinian (r.527–65) forbade gaming because of its associations with blasphemy. Homosexuals were punished by the amputation of their genitals. Taxes were harsh to meet the costs of wide-ranging building projects. Fearful of assassination, he and Theodora retreated behind the palace walls, rarely to be seen by senators and subjects alike. Such was his unpopularity there was a riot in 532, with furious city folk calling for his death. Justinian prepared to flee, but his wife was made of sterner stuff and she stood firm, claiming "royalty is a good burial shroud." Fortunately, his general Belisarius was to hand. The soldiers were sent in and, at a cost of some 20,000 lives, order was restored.

A strained relationship

Belisarius had already proved his great worth in Persia, when in 530 he led the Byzantines to victory over the Sassanid Persians at Dara, followed by a peace treaty. In 533, he was placed in command of Justinian's great enterprise, the reconquest of the western Roman empire. This began by an invasion of the Vandal kingdom centered on Carthage. Ironically, by this time the Vandals wore togas and spoke Latin, unlike the residents of Constantinople. Belisarius's forces were triumphant at two battles and the lost Roman province of Africa was restored to the empire.

In 535, Belisarius invaded Ostrogothic Italy,

first capturing Sicily and then crossing into Italy. He took Naples and Rome in 536 and then moved north, taking Milan and Ravenna in 540. With the Ostrogothic kingdom under apparent Byzantine control, Belisarius returned to Constantinople to be met by a cold Justinian who had heard rumors that the Goths had offered Belisarius the crown of Italy—which were true, but the loyal general had refused it.

After an inconclusive campaign (541–2) against Khosrow I of Persia, who had broken the treaty, but then made a new one for a further five years in 545, Belisarius returned to Italy, where he found the situation had changed greatly. In 541 the Ostrogoths had elected a new leader, Totila, who had recaptured all of northern Italy and even driven the Byzantines from Rome. Belisarius took the offensive, tricked Totila into yielding Rome along the way, but then lost it again after a jealous Justinian, fearful of Belisarius's growing power, starved him of supplies and reinforcements. Belisarius was forced to go on the defensive, and in 548 he was relieved in favor of another general, Narses, who went on to complete the reconquest in 553.

Belisarius was called on again in 559, when the Bulgars crossed the Danube for the first time and raided Byzantine territory. Belisarius accepted the command, defeated the Bulgars, and drove them back across the river. It was his last victory. In 562, he stood trial on a probably trumped-up charge of corruption. Belisarius was found guilty and imprisoned, but soon after Justinian pardoned him, ordered his release, and restored him to favor at the imperial court. Justinian and Belisarius, whose sometimes strained partnership doubled the size of the empire, died within a few weeks of one another in 565.

Justinian laws

The most positive aspect of Justinian's rule was his codification of Roman law, a massive undertaking in which obsolete legislation was weeded out and new statutes drawn up by Justinian were introduced. The culmination of this work was the *codex Justinianus*, a bold attempt to give fair recourse to law for the common man.

Justinian was also deeply enmeshed in the dilemma dividing the Church at the time, revolving around the nature of Christ. He saw himself as God's regent on Earth, in charge of Church and State. Yet even from this lofty position he found himself unable to resolve the politically hazardous debate, which continued to cause serious rifts in the Church and sparked waves of persecution.

BARBARIAN SUCCESSOR STATES

When he died, Justinian was the effective ruler of more traditionally Roman territory than any of his predecessors since the end of the fourth century. Yet, inevitably, it was the barbarians who had brought down the western Roman empire who were the inheritors of a new modern Europe.

Gains made by Belisarius and Narses on behalf of Justinian were short-lived. The 20-year campaign resulted in dreadful losses on both sides. From this point, the Ostrogoths played no further role in history and were gradually absorbed into other tribes, such as the Vandals, Franks, and the Burgundians of southeast France. And then in 568 the Lombards (Langobardi, "long-beards") under King Alboin rose up from their homelands between the Danube and Adriatic and allied themselves with some 20,000 Saxons. The combined force crossed the Alps, sweeping aside ineffectual resistance from the Byzantine capital of Ravenna. They established the kingdom of Lombardy along the valley of the Po, and although they could not conquer the rest of Italy, neither could the Byzantines eject them.

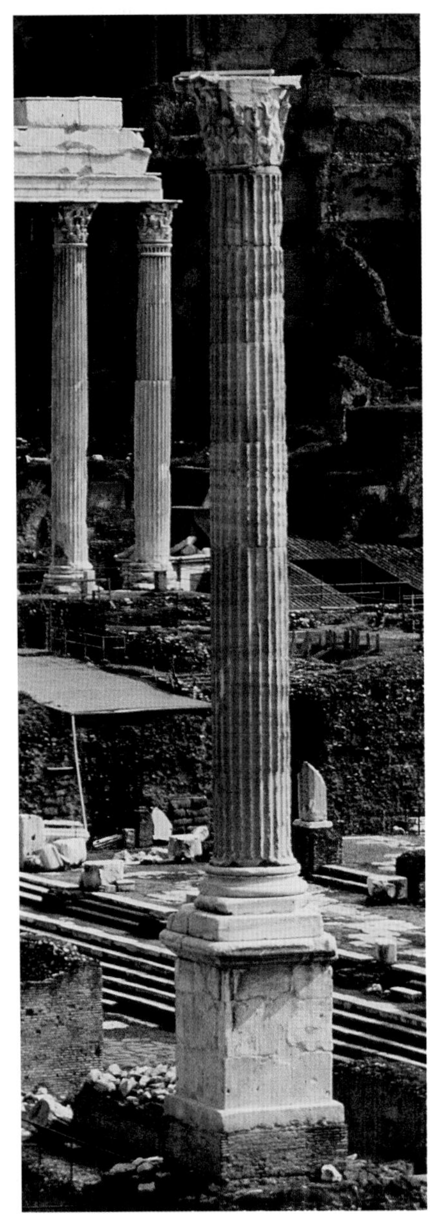

This set a framework for the region that would last 1,300 years; a motley assortment of kingdoms, principalities, duchies, semi-independent cities, and the so-called papal states (between Rome and Ravenna). Not until 1870 would Italy be unified. Lombardy lasted for two centuries but it proved unequal to the task of resisting the power of the far greater Frankish empire expanding from Gaul. In 774 it was annexed and vanished as a political entity.

The Franks created the only Roman successor state of any durability. In the mid-third century AD they were just another Germanic Rhineland tribe, but by the end of the western empire they controlled much of northern Gaul. There was some conflict between them and the rump of imperial forces, but the two sides also served as allies against the Hun empire and the Saxons. Attila's empire fell apart following his death in 453, sundered by quarreling heirs. The Huns migrated further to the east, settling between the Black and Caspian seas and ceased to be an effective force. The last Roman soldiers serving in Gaul probably entered the Salian Frankish army of Hlodwig or Chlodovech, better known to history as Clovis (r. c.466–511).

The senate vanishes

As a Roman ally, Clovis was able to exploit his status and multiply his dominions in Gaul. In 486, he defeated Syagrius, the last "Roman" governor of Gaul. The Frankish empire stretched from the Netherlands to the Pyrenees, and they subjugated the great Alamanni tribal alliance and the Burgundians. They uprooted that other old Roman enemy, the Visigoths, from their territory in Aquitaine, forcing them to retrench their kingdom in the Iberian peninsula. Here, for over 300 years, they founded a complete Visigothic kingdom, only sharing Spain with the Suevi, who founded a small kingdom in the far northwest, in Galicia, and the Alans, who settled along the valley of the Tagus.

The Franks became the backbone of the medieval period, and in 800 their great king Carolus Magnus, or Charlemagne, was crowned in Rome by Pope Leo III as Holy Roman Emperor. At the time, his scholarly adviser, Alcuin of York, wrote sadly of the city he witnessed: "Rome, once the head of the world, the world's pride, the city of gold, stands now a pitiful ruin, the wreck of its glory of old."

Roman Britannia had been emptied of legions in the years 405–10, and soon found itself at the mercy of sea-raiding Angles, Jutes, and Saxons. These raiders, pushing the Romano-Celtic tribes ever further westward, founded their own states, and so began the long history of "England."

In Italy, Justinian's reconquest was achieved at a price. Italy and Rome lay impoverished by the years of warfare, and the short-lived Byzantine occupation marks the end of the classical world. The reconquest also impacted on Byzantine resources in the east, diverting armies desperately needed along the Danube and on the Persian front. However, recovery was possible in the east, and the Byzantine empire survived Justinian for another 900 years.

In the west, Rome had become a damaged and parochical city. The senatorial class that had been its backbone for more than 1,300 years and survived the fifth-century invasions finally vanished from history at the hands of an emperor who, ironically, had wanted to restore the glory of Rome.

Left: A statue of King Clovis I in the Royal Abbey Church of St. Denis, Paris. His wife Clothilde was a Christian, and it seems he converted to her religion when he gained victory over the Alamanni after praying to the god of his wife.

Far left: The last traditional monument to be built in the Forum Romanum is the Column of Phocas (602–10), a fluted Corinthian pillar 44 feet high. It was not original. The column belonged to a temple of the early imperial era, and its base to a 4th-century building. Smaragdus, the Byzantine governor of Italy, dedicated the column to his emperor Phocas. There is little to recommend him beyond his confirmation that St. Peter's was to be head of all Churches, while the see of Constantinople was to call itself the "first of all Churches."

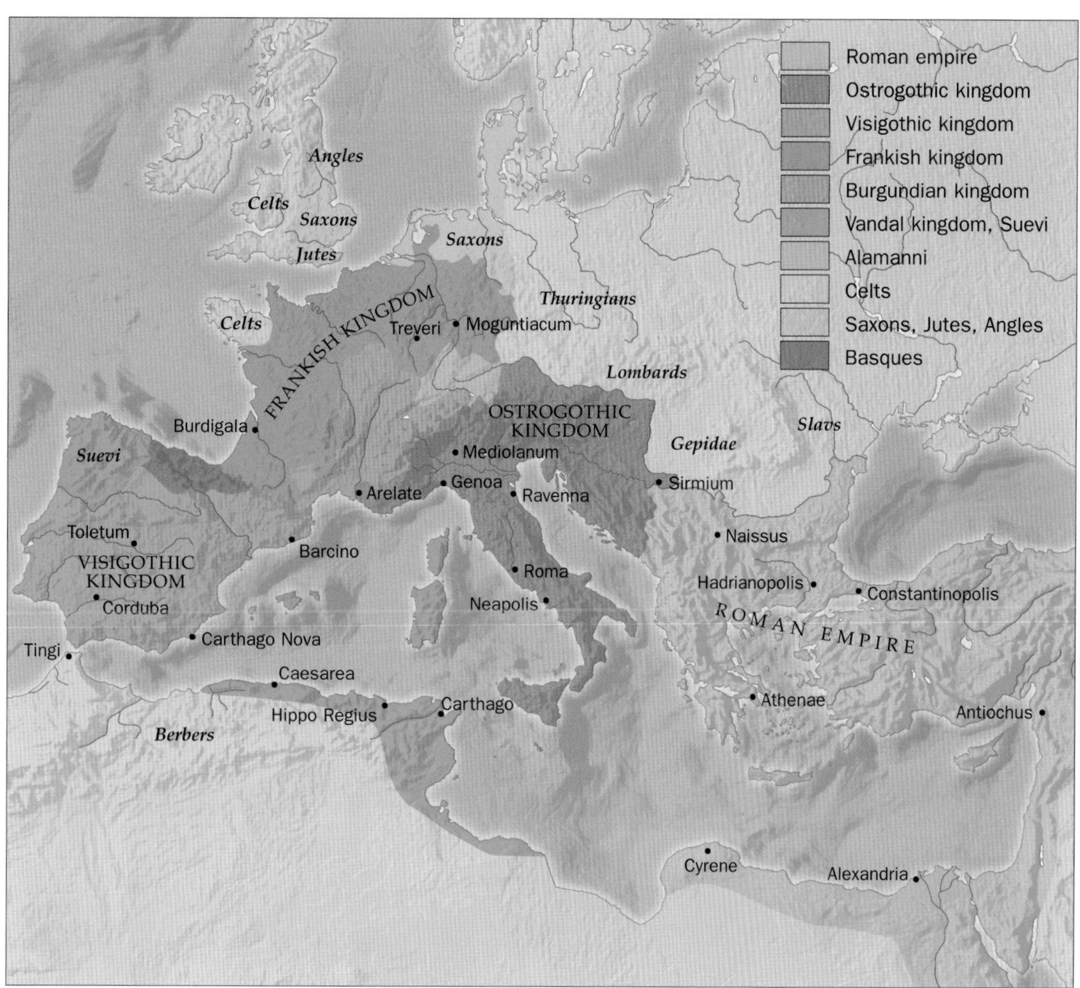
Roman empire
Ostrogothic kingdom
Visigothic kingdom
Frankish kingdom
Burgundian kingdom
Vandal kingdom, Suevi
Alamanni
Celts
Saxons, Jutes, Angles
Basques
Angles
Celts
Saxons
Jutes
Saxons
Celts
FRANKISH KINGDOM
Treveri
Moguntiacum
Thuringians
Lombards
OSTROGOTHIC KINGDOM
Mediolanum
Gepidae
Slavs
Burdigala
Suevi
Arelate
Genoa
Ravenna
Sirmium
Naissus
Toletum
Barcino
VISIGOTHIC KINGDOM
Corduba
Roma
Hadrianopolis
Constantinopolis
Neapolis
ROMAN EMPIRE
Tingi
Carthago Nova
Caesarea
Athenae
Hippo Regius
Carthago
Antiochus
Berbers
Cyrene
Alexandria

Roman Survivors

The sun set on the Roman empire in the west when Odoacer became the first barbarian king of Rome, at the expense of the juvenile emperor Romulus Augustulus. His accession marked the onset of the Dark Ages in Europe when art, education, and technology remained in the doldrums.

It was the end of an institution that had endured for centuries. Of course, the face of the Roman empire in its death throes in AD 476 was entirely different from the one known by Augustus or anyone who rose to eminence in republican Rome. The faces and places that once delineated Rome had all changed. To encapsulate the Roman empire and the bewildering ethnicity attached to it is almost impossible. Legionaries' boots had, after all, left their imprint and their progeny all over Europe.

But it is possible to make a value judgment on what the Romans left behind, for the legacy is rich. The Julian calendar introduced by Caesar continues to assure us of an ordered chronology. Numerous laws have been grafted onto original Roman statutes to help govern later generations. Latin was the universal tongue of the Middle Ages, one in which great literature and liturgy was preserved. Latin is still the most important root of the English language, along with the Indo-Germanic that arrived with the Saxons.

From the Romans we got daffodils, central heating, public baths, cooking with herbs, newspapers, regular state-organized post, and much more. Europe is strewn with fine temples, bridges, statues, and aqueducts, all monuments to the sheer magnificence of the Roman empire. They are also a significant tribute to Roman investment in the slave trade.

Determined and adaptable

The Roman genius was for engineering, but in this field as well as the arts, their other great talent came to the fore—borrowing and adaption. Roads, coins, workouts at the gymnasium, the corn dole, all second-hand ideas couched as Roman innovations. Although not all Romans thought it was good, the Romans recycled Greek ideas all the time.

Rome had its bad points too. Mortal combat in the arena, as well as an awesomely large gulf between rich and poor. Its military triumphs were tempered by phenomenal loss of life on the battlefield. But Romans had to overcome numerous difficulties, including those of defense and administration on a grand scale.

For example, their innate dislike of the sea was overwhelmed by the necessity to set sail.

Below: While monuments like the Pantheon and Trajan's Column survived the centuries of neglect, the Circus Maximus was all destroyed. Only a small fragment of the supports for the seated tiering remain at the northeastern corner, with a small Mithraic shrine underneath. Looking to the west, this is the Circus Maximus today.

south tiers, rising toward the Aventine

race track remains of spina

medieval water tower

Domitian's palace

439	443	448	451	452	454	455	475
Vandals establish a kingdom in Carthage, Africa	Romans increase their tribute to the Huns to stop their plunder of the Balkans	After successive losses in battle, the eastern empire gives territory to placate the Huns	Huns are defeated by Romans and Visigoths at Chalons	Huns plunder the cities of northern Italy; Attila dies the next year	Valentinian II has celebrated general Flavius Aetius executed	Gaiseric's Vandals from North Africa sack Rome	Orestes defeats Julius Nepos and installs Romulus Augustulus as western emperor

Those reluctant sailors embarked regardless of the weather conditions with the words of Pompey ringing in their ears: "Sailing is necessary. Living is not essential." In other words, it was doggedness that was the crucial Roman characteristic, one that ensured their survival against the odds.

In the end, pressures of economy and scale defeated Rome. The eastern arm of the Roman empire fared better, evolving into the Byzantine empire and thriving for a further millennium. But when people hark back to the good old days of the empire, they are talking about what happened in the west. As for the city itself, Rome provided generations of invaders and settlers with a treasure trove of ready-cut building materials. What the Goths and Vandals did not destroy, those that came after them tore down to make new and less grand dwellings. We are fortunate that some of Rome's greatest monuments survived because they were papally sanctified.

These and the many glorious ruins fired the imagination of the late 13th-century painters, sculptors, and architects and gave us the European Renassaince, the rebirth of culture, science, and social politics. Even so, more of the ancient remains might have been lost in recent times if it had not occurred to the Italian government that tourists would pay to see the past glories—even if much of what was left was only concreted rubble and worn down footings. Sadly, the rescue came centuries too late for edifices like the Circus Maximus and vast areas of the Palatine Palace.

Gone but not forgotten, the glories of ancient Rome were often recalled. The Holy Roman Empire, established in the tenth century and named for old Rome, was a political heavyweight in Europe for some 800 years. Mussolini, Italy's fascist dictator, reminisced about the old days and tried to recreate a similarly illustrious age as late as the 20th century. Yet none could mimic the luminous qualities of an empire that, through its accomplishments, spans the world, ancient and modern.

SERVIZIO DI INNAFFIAMENTO
SPQR

Left: It is a testament to Roman pragmatism and love of civilized comfort that the longest-lived working survivor of the archaic, republican, and imperial periods is Rome's city drainage system. The earliest sewer, the *Cloaca Maxima*, which drained the Subura district, still exists today, as do many subsidiary drains. Its exit into the Tiber between the Sublican and Aemilian bridges was only covered over by the embankment in recent times. Rome's modern manhole covers still bear the legend S.P.Q.R.—*Senatus Populusque Romanus*, meaning "the senate and the people of Rome."

palace of Septimius Severus
Palatine
remains of the Septizodium
remains of the Palatine aqueduct
Triumphal Way
Arch of Constantine

476 Romulus is pushed into abdication by Odoacer; end of the western Roman empire

486 Clovis defeats Roman governor Syagrius in Gaul; Frankish empire expands

527 Justinian becomes eastern emperor and contemplates reconquering Italy

536 Justinian's general Belisarius captures Rome

552 Byzantines gain control of southern Spain from Ostrogoths

568 Lombards under King Alboin establish the kingdom of Lombardy in Italy

663 Byzantines led by Emperor Constans II fail to drive the Lombards from central Italy

800 Charlemagne becomes emperor; beginning of the Holy Roman Empire

APPENDIX I

THE EMPERORS: AUGUSTUS TO JUSTINIAN

* joint emperor

Julio-Claudian dynasty

27 BC–AD 14 **Augustus** (Gaius Julius Caesar Octavianus)
14–37 **Tiberius** (Claudius Nero Caesar)
37–41 **Caligula** (Gaius Julius Caesar Germanicus)
41–54 **Claudius** (Tiberius Claudius Drusus)
54–68 **Nero** (Lucius Domitius Ahenobarbus, later Nero Claudius Caesar Drusus Germanicus)

Emperors of the Civil War

68–69 **Galba** (Servius Sulpicius)
69 **Otho** (M. Salvius)
69 **Vitellius** (Aulus)

Flavian, Nervo-Trajanic, and Antonine dynasties

69–79 **Vespasian** (Titus Flavius Sabinus Vespasianus)
79–81 **Titus** (Flavius Vespasianus)
81–96 **Domitian** (Titus Flavius Domitianus)
96–98 **Nerva** (M. Cocceius)
98–117 **Trajan** (M. Ulpius Traianus)
117–38 **Hadrian** (P. Aelius Hadrianus)
138–61 **Antoninus Pius** (Titus Aurelius Fulvus Boionius)
161–80 * **Marcus Aurelius** (Annius Verus, later Aurelius Antoninus, 161–69 joint with Lucius Verus)
161–69 * **Lucius Verus** (Lucius Ceionius Commodus, later Lucius Aurelius Verus)
180–92 * **Commodus** (Lucius Aelius Aurelius, later Marcus Aurelius Commodus Antoninus, co-emperor with Marcus Aurelius from 177)

Emperors of the Civil War

193 **Pertinax** (Publius Helvius)
193 **Didius Julianus** (Marcus Didius)
193 **Pescennius Niger** (Gaius)
193–97 **Clodius Albinus** (proclaimed by troops as rival to Didus Julianus, defeated by Severus)

Severan dynasty

193–211 **Septimius Severus** (Lucius)
211–17 * **Caracalla** (Septimus Bassianus, later Marcus Aurelius Antoninus)
211–12 * **Geta** (Lucius Publius Septimius)
217–18 * **Macrinus** (Marcus Opellius, later Marcus Opellius Severus Macrinus, the usurper was the first emperor not to have been a senator)
217–18 * **Diadumenian** (Marcus Opellius Diadumenianus, Caesar from 217, co-emperor with Macrinus in 218, both usurpers defeated by Elagabalus
218–22 **Elagabalus** (Varius Avitus Bassianus Marcus Aurelius Antoninus, possibly Caracalla's illegitimate son)
222–35 **Alexander Severus** (Marcus Julius Gessius Bassianus Alexianus. later Marcus Aurelius Severus Alexander)

Age of Military Anarchy

235–38 **Maximinus Thrax** (Gaius Julius Verus)
238 * **Gordian I** Africanus
238 * **Gordian II** Africanus (co-emperor with Gordian I, March 22–April 12, 238)
238 * **Balbinus** (Decimus Caelius Calvinus)
238 * **Pupienus** (Marcus Clodius, elected co-emperor by the senate with Balbinus, April 22–July 29, 238 when he was assassinated by the Praetorian Guard
238–44 **Gordian III** (Marcus Antonius Gordianus)
244–49 * **Philip the Arab** (Marcus Julius Philippus)
247–49 * **Philip II** (Marcus Julius Severus, co-emperor with his father)
249–51 * **Decius** (Gaius Messius Quintus, later Gaius Messius Quintus Traianus)
251–53 * **Trebonius** Gallus (Gaius Vibius)
251 * **Hostilian** (Gaius Valens Hostilianus Messius Quintus, Caesar from 250, co-emperor with Gallus in 251
251–53 **Volusian** (Gaius Vibius Afinius Gallus Vendumnianus Volusianus, son of Gallus)
253 **Aemilian** (Marcus Aemilius Aemilianus, proclaimed by troops against Gallus and Volusian)
253–60 * **Valerian** (Publius Licinius Valerianus, captured by Persians, date of death unknown)
253–68 * **Gallienus** (Publius Licinius Egnatius, co-emperor with father Valerian, emperor after 260)

WEST (Gallic empire of:)

259–68 **Postumus** (Marcus Cassianus Latinus, killed by troops)
268 **Laelianus** (Ulpius Cornelius, killed by Postumus)
268–69 **Marius** (Marcus Aurelius, assassinated by his soldiers)
269–70 **Victorinus** (Marcus Piavnius, assassinated by one of his officers)
270–73 **Tetricus** (Gaius Pius Esuvius, deposed and pardoned by Aurelian, died of natural causes)

EAST

260–72 Palmyrene empire of Odaenathus, Zenobia, and Vaballath

268–70 **Claudius II Gothicus Maximus** (Marcus Aurelius Valerius, died of plague)
270–75 **Aurelian** (Lucius Dimitius Aurelianus)
275–76 **Tacitus** (Marcus Claudius)
276 **Florian** (Marcus Annius Florianus, brother of Tacitus, assassinated by his soldiers)
276–82 **Probus** (Marcus Aurelius, in opposition to Florian, assassinated by mutinous soldiers)
282–83 **Carus** (Marcus Aurelius, died after being struck by lightning in Persia)
283–85 * **Carinus** (Marcus Aurelius, son of Carus, killed by his own troops battling Diocletian)

283–84 * **Numerian** (Marcus Aurelius Numerianus, brother of Carinus and co-emperor with him. Assassinated by praetorian prefect Arrius Aper

The Tetrarchy

284–305 Diocletian and Tetrarchy

WEST

287–305 **Maximian**, Augustus (Marcus Aurelius Valerius Maximianus, abdicated)

293–305 **Constantius Chlorus**, Caesar (Flavius Valerius)

305–06 **Constantius I**, Augustus

305–06 **Severus**, Caesar (Flavius Valerius)

306–07 **Severus II**, Augustus

EAST

284–305 **Diocletian**, Augustus (Gaius Aurelius Valerius Diocletianus, abdicated)

293–305 **Galerius**, Caesar (Gaius Galerius Valerius Maximianus)

305–10 **Galerius**, Augustus

305–09 **Maximinus Daia**, Caesar (Gaius Galerius Valerius Daia)

309–13 **Maximinus II**, Augustus

307–12 **Maxentius** (Marcus Aurelies Valerius, proclaimed western emperor in opposition to Severus II)

WEST

305–06 **Constantine**, Caesar (Flavius Valerius Constantinus)

306–37 **Constantine I the Great**, Augustus (co-emperor of east and west with Licinius 312–24, sole emperor 324–37)

EAST

308–24 **Licinius**, Augustus (Valerius Licinianus, co-emperor with Constantine from 312)

WEST

337–40 **Constantine II** (Flavius Claudius Constantinus, Caesar from 317–37)

337–50 **Constans** (Flavius Julius, Caesar 333–37)

EAST

337–61 **Constantius II** (Flavius Julius, sole emperor from 353 on death of Magnentius)

WEST

350–53 **Magnentius** (Flavius Magnus, proclaimed in opposition to Constans, usurper defeated by Constantius II)

355–61 **Julian** ("the Apostate," Flavius Claudius Julianus, made Caesar by Constantius)

361–63 **Julian**, Augustus (sole emperor after death of Constantius II)

363–64 **Jovian** (Flavius Jovianus, sole emperor after death of Julian)

WEST

364–75 **Valentinian I** (Flavius Valentinianus)

EAST

364–78 **Valens** (Flavius, brother of Valentinian)

WEST

375–83 **Gratian** (Flavius Gratianus)

375–92 **Valentinian II** (Flavius Valentinianus, emperor of Italy, Illyricum)

EAST

379–95 **Theodosius I the Great** (Flavius, sole emperor after death of Valentinian II)

WEST

383–88 **Magnus Maximus**, usurper (executed by Theodorius)

393–94 **Eugenius**, usurper

395–423 **Honorius** (Flavius, Stilicho regent 395–408)

409–411 **Maximus** (deposed by Honorius)

421 **Constantius III** (Flavius)

423–25 **Johannes**, usurper (executed by Theodosius)

425–55 **Valentinian III** (Placidius Valentinianus)

455 **Petronius Maximus** (Flavius Anicius)

455–56 **Avitus** (Marcus Maecilius Flavius Eparhcius)

457–61 **Majorian** (Julius Mairianus)

461–65 **Libius Severus III**

467–72 **Anthemius** (Procopius)

472 **Olybrius** (Anicius)

473–74 **Glycerius** (Flavius)

474–75 **Nepos** (Flavius Julius)

475–76 **Romulus Augustulus**

EAST

395–408 **Arcadius** (Flavius)

408–50 **Theodosius II** (Flavius)

450–57 **Marcian** (Flavius Valerius Marcianus)

457–74 * **Leo I** (Flavius Valerius)

473–74 * **Leo II** (name unknown, proclaimed co-emperor by Leo I)

474–91 * **Zeno** (originally Tarasicodissa, father of Leo II, proclaimed co-emperor by Leo II)

475–76 **Basiliscus** (name unknown, usurper when Zeno fled to Iauaria, later deposed by Zeno)

Barbarian rulers

476–93 **Odoacer**

493–526 **Theoderic**

526–34 **Athalaric**

534–36 **Theodahad**

536–40 **Witigis**

540–41 **Hildebad**

541–52 **Totila**

552–53 **Teias**

EAST

491–518 **Anastasius I**

518–27 **Justin I**

527–65 **Justinian I** (Flavius Petrus Sabbatius Justinianus)

APPENDIX II

Common Roman Names

The Romans rarely wrote out a person's full name. Since there were very few common *praenomenina* available (*see page 69*), everyone knew them and so they were commonly written as only the capital letter or an abbreviation. The list below contains the most popular.

A.	=	Aulus	N.	=	Numerius
App.	=	Appius	P.	=	Publius
D.	=	Decimus	Q.	=	Quintus
C.	=	Gaius	Ser.	=	Servius
Cn.	=	Gnaeus	Sex.	=	Sextus
K.	=	Kaeso	Sp.	=	Spurius
L.	=	Lucius	Ti.	=	Tiberius
M.	=	Marcus	T.	=	Titus

There were, of course, far more nicknames, or *cognomina* in use. These ranged from honorifics voted for military victories, such as "Africanus" or "Gothicus," to personal characteristics. Latin was a robust language and by no means were all *cognomina* flattering; some were downright rude, sarcastic, or extremely witty. The following list is not comprehensive but it does list the most common nicknames, many of which will have become familiar throughout this book.

Latin	English
Africanus	*of* Africa
Agelastus	never smiles
Ahenobarbus	red- or bronze-bearded
Albinus	white-skinned or pale
Augur	an augur, one who reads signs
Balearicus	*of the* Balearic Isles
Bambalio	(unknown)
Bestia	beast
Britannicus	*of* Britannia
Brocchus	buck-toothed
Brutus	animal stupidity
Caecus	blind
Caepio	onion vendor
Caesar	fine head of hair
Caldus	lukewarm
Calvus	bald
Caprarius	goat
Carbo	cinder, or burned out
Cato	shrewd but tightly strung
Catulus	pup, or cub
Cicero	chickpea
Cotta	splash of wine
Crassus	thick
Cunctator	one who holds back
Dalmaticus	*of* Dalmatia
Dentatus	born with teeth
Diadematus	*of a* royal headband
Dives	heavenly
Drusus	(unknown)
Eburnus	made of ivory
Fimbria	fringe of hair
Flaccus	big ears
Galba	potbelly
Germanicus	*of* Germania
Getha	from the ends of the earth
Glaucia	gray-green eyes
Gracchus	jackdaw (possibly)
Gothicus	*defeater of the* Goths
Laenas	priest's mantle
Lentulus	tardy, or slow
Lepidus	wonderful man
Limetanus	*of a* boundary
Longinus	*in the* far distance
Lucullus	small grove of trees
Macedonicus	*of* Macedonia
Mactator	slaughterman
Magnus	great
Mancinus	*of a* cripple
Margarita	pearl
Maximus	greatest
Merula	blackbird
Metellus	liberated mercenary
Mus	mouse
Nasica	nosy
Nepos	grandfather
Nerva	stringy, or tough
Numidicus	*of* Numidia
Orator	public speaker
Orestes	mother died at birth
Paullus	a trifle
Pipinna	little boy's genitals
Piso	I grind down
Pius	loyal son
Porcella	piglet
Postumus	born after father's death
Praetextatus	one who wears the toga praetexta
Pulcher	beautiful
Ravilla	talked himself hoarse
Reginus	*of a* queen
Rex	king
Rufinus	of a red-haired family
Rufus	red-haired
Ruso	hayseed, country bumpkin
Saturninus	*of* Saturn
Scaevola	left-handed
Scaurus	swollen feet
Scipio	ceremonial rod
Serranus	serrated like a saw
Siculus	*of* Sicily
Silanus	ugly flat face
Silo	flat-nosed
Stichus	slave (*stikos*, Greek)
Strabo	cross-eyed
Tubero	hump-backed, or immoral
Varro	bandy-legged
Vatia	knock-kneed
Verrucosis	wart-covered
Vopiscus	survivor of twins

Glossary

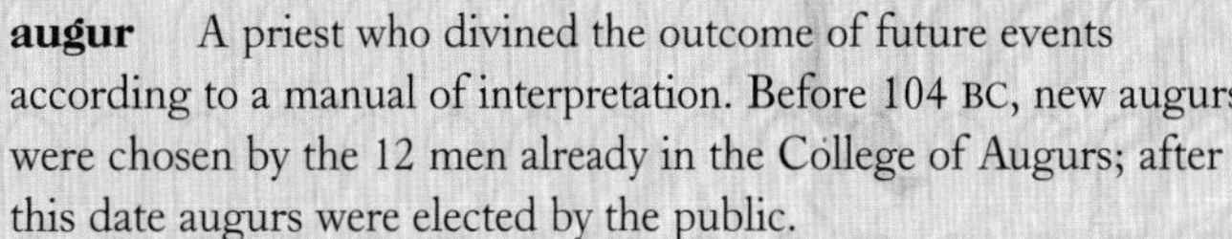

adsidui Roman citizens who owned the minimum amount of property to be classed as land-owners, members of the Fifth Class. Dispossessed of his land, an *adsidui* became a proletarian, described as *infra classem* (beneath the class).

aedile A Roman magistrate whose duties were confined to the city of Rome. There were four: two plebeian and two curule aediles. The Plebeian aediles (created 493 BC) first assisted the tribunes of the plebs in their duties and protection of plebeian rights and were elected by the Plebeian Assembly. The curule aediles (created 367 BC) were elected by the Assembly of the People to give patricians a share in the custody of public buildings and records. From the fourth century BC, all four were responsible for Rome's streets, water supply, drainage, grain dole, civic buildings, markets, and general facilities.

ager publicus Land in Roman public ownership that was usually acquired by rights of conquest or confiscated from its original owners as punishment for disloyalty. The censors leased out the land in a way that usually favored the large estate owners.

Agger Double rampart of the Servian Wall protecting Rome along the Esquiline hill.

amphora (ae) A ceramic vessel with a narrow neck above a bulbous body, with two carrying handles on the upper part, and a pointed base which allowed for secure multiple-stacking in ship holds, or wedged in sawdust or sand. Amphorae—usually holding about 5 gallons—were used for transporting wine, oil, and also solid foodstuffs: olives, dates, figs, etc.

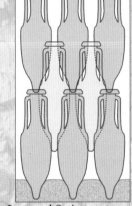

Anatolia Not a country, but the region that approximates modern Turkey from the Black Sea to the Mediterranean north to south, and from the Aegean Sea to modern Armenia, Iran, and Syria.

aqua An aqueduct, a channel for supplying water from a distant source that might be underground or carried on a bridge. By the time of the middle republic, the *aquae* were cared for by water companies hired by the censors, who charged tariffs to those connected to the supply.

aquilifer The man in a legion who carried the legion's gold eagle (earlier examples were gold and silver). He wore a wolf or lion skin as a mark of his distinction. The rank was probably created by Marius during his army reforms.

armillae Bracelets of gold or silver, which were awarded for valor to legionaries, centurions, and military tribunes.

Arx The northernmost of the rises that sit on top of the Capitoline Hill in Rome.

as The lowest-value Roman coin, made of bronze.

atrium The main reception room of a Roman house, usually located centrally, with an opening in the roof and a pool underneath. This was based on the archaic model, where the pool stored household water, but by later times had become ornamental.

auctoritas *lit.* "authority," but in Latin the word meant much more, with overtones of eminence, public leadership, and the ability to influence events through sheer personality.

augur A priest who divined the outcome of future events according to a manual of interpretation. Before 104 BC, new augurs were chosen by the 12 men already in the College of Augurs; after this date augurs were elected by the public.

basilica (ae) A large building of Greek origin to house public facilities such as banking, law courts, stores, and offices. The first, the Basilica Porcia, was built in Rome by Cato the Censor. Basilicae were usually lit by clerestory windows above, and became the standard model in the late Roman period for Christian churches.

biga A two-horse chariot.

boni *lit.* "the good men." Gaius Gracchus used the term to describe his supporters. Later it became widely used to describe ultra-conservative senators, the men whom Julius Caesar loathed.

Calabria The region of Italy that today occupies the "toe" of the country, but in ancient times described the "heel."

campus, campi A wide, flat expanse of land, sometimes marshy. The words also described a plain.

Campus Martius The flat area enclosed by a bend of the Tiber in the west, the Capitol to the south, and the Pincian hill to the north. It got its name because the army did military exercises and cadet training there, although there were also parks and market gardens along the river bank. In later imperial times, it was almost completely built over.

cella (ae) *lit.* "room." Any room in a Roman house that did not have a name describing its function (which most did), or the main space inside a temple.

censor The most senior Roman magistracy. Two were elected at the same time and held office for five years. A censor had to have been a consul previously. The censor regulated the the membership of the senate, the order of knights (*equites*), and conducted a census of Roman citizens throughout the empire. The censor lacked imperium, however, and so was not escorted by lictors.

(centurion), centurio, centuriones Regular, professional officer of Roman legions. Half were elected by the troops, the other half appointed by the election winners. The centurion was the backbone of army organization, since the senior officers were usually young aristocrats on attachment, and even the generals spent only a short time with their legions (except in times of extended warfare).

century An archaic term that applies to any gathering of 100 men (originally soldiers). By the later republican and early imperial periods, the centuries of the *comitia centuriata* contained many more than 100 men and had no military significance.

circus A place where chariot races were held, synonymous with Greek term "hippodrome." The most famous is the Circus Maximus in Rome.

(client), cliens Originally a freedman who pledged himself to his patron (*patronus*) in return for various favors, usually money or legal assistance. In his turn, a client could be a patron to his own clients, but these men were also automatically the clients of his patron. In this way a powerful Roman could build huge blocks of supporters to increase his political clout. Clashes between rival supporters frequently led to street violence. In a similar way, colonies, towns, or even allied kingdoms could be clients of Rome itself. The title "Friend and Ally of the Roman People" was a statement of clientship.

clivus A hilly street or a street on a steep incline.

cloaca (ae) A sewer or drain. Rome's system of *cloacae* were built early in the city's archaic history, although they were repeatedly enlarged and improved.

cognomen, cognomina A distinguishing nickname.
college Association of a number of men having something in common: priestly, political, religious (such as the lictors), work-related, military; there were many colleges that banded together.
comitia Any assembly gathered to deal with legislative, governmental, or electoral matters. By the late republican era there were three main assemblies. The *comitia centuriata* organized the people into the Five Classes as defined by an economic means test—from the First Class (richest) to Fifth Class (poorest). It also elected consuls every year and censors and praetors every five years. The *comitia pupuli tributa* (popular assembly) allowed participation of the patricians and met at the order of a consul or praetor in the 35 tribes into which all Roman citizens were divided. It elected the curule aediles, quaestors, and tribunes of the soldiers. The *comitia plebis tributa* (plebeian assembly) was convoked by a tribune of the *plebs* and had the right to enact laws (*plebiscitum*) and—like the other two comitia—conduct trials. It elected the plebeian *aediles* and tribunes of the *plebs.*
consul The most senior magistrate with imperium. Two were elected each year. In theory each in turn, month by month, was active while his colleague looked on. When active, the consul was said to hold the *fasces* and was accompanied by 12 lictors. In practice this was confused by the consul's military duties, especially in times of extended war, when both consuls would be in the field with their legions at the same time. There was a proper age for a consul (42), but this was increasingly ignored, as was the tradition that a consul should only serve once in his lifetime. The political route to consulship was: senator (aged 30), quaestor, and praetor. This was called the *cursus honorum* (way of honor). Although neither of the aedileships nor tribunate of the plebs was part of the *cursus honorum*, most candidates found it useful to serve in one or more capacities to attract electoral attention.
curia (ae) The most ancient Roman clan divisions, which met in a meeting hall headed by a chief elected for life called a *curio*. The word eventually came to mean the meeting hall itself rather than the meeting, but had fallen into disuse by republican times, other than for the adoption of a patrician into a plebeian family or the conferring of imperium on a senior magistrate. In these cases a *lex curiata* had to be passed by the 30 original *curiae*, represented by 30 lictors.
Curia Hostilia The senate house, thought to have been built originally by King Tullus Hostilius.
domus A city or town house as distinct from an apartment.
Domus Publicus A house owned by the state, usually given to senior priests as part of their remuneration.
emporium A large waterfront building where importers and exporters had their offices; or a whole seaport concerned with maritime trade.
fasces Originally an emblem of the Etruscan kings, these were bundles of birch rods tied with red leather thongs and carried by lictors to precede a curule magistrate. They indicated *imperium* to the man accompanied by the *lictors*. Within Rome's *pomerium*, only the rods were carried, indicating that the magistrate had the right to chastise, but outside an ax was inserted to indicate he had the right to execute offenders. A curule *aedile* had two fasces, a praetor six, a consul 12, and a dictator 24, and the appropriate number of lictors.
flame, flamines A priest who served Rome's most ancient and most Roman deities. The most senior was the *flamen Dialis*, who served Jupiter.
flumen A river.
forum An open-air meeting place. The most famous is the Forum Romanum. Other *forae* originally had specific purposes. The Forum Boarium (*boarium* means "cattle") was the meat market. A *forum castrum* was the meeting place in a Roman military camp. The Forum Frumentarium was a fruit market, Forum Holitorium a vegetable market, Forum Piscinum a fish market.
garum A food flavoring made from fermented fish viscera. It had an extremely strong taste and unpleasant smell but was highly esteemed and widely made, with the best coming from Spain.
gens, gentes A family (eg. Aemilius, Cornelius, or Julius).
hasta The pre-Marian leaf-shaped spear of the Roman infantry that went out of use in the late republican period.
head count In Latin *capite censi*, those who were too poor to belong to one of the Five Classes; also known as *proletarii*.
imperator Originally "commander-in-chief" or "general" but later used only to describe a general who won a great victory.
imperium The degree of authority invested in a curule magistrate. A man with *imperium*—it lasted for one year—could exercise the power of his office freely without objection so long as he remained within the laws governing the position. He was preceded by *lictors* bearing the *fasces*.
insula (ae) *lit.* "an island." The word described the tall apartment blocks in Rome and in other Roman cities.
iugerum, iugera The basic Roman unit of land measurement, approximately equal to half an acre.
Juno Moneta The temple standing on the Arx part of the Capitoline hill. Moneta means "warnings," probably from Juno's sacred geese that woke Romans to the Celtic attack in 387 BC. The English word "money" is derived from it because the mint was located in the temple precincts.
(legate) legatus Senior officers of a general's staff, who had to be of senatorial or consular rank to qualify.
lex, leges Latin for "law." A lex only became valid when its terms had been inscribed on bronze or stone, which is why so many, even in fragments, have survived.
lictor A public servant who accompanied a magistrate holding *imperium*. *Lictors* belonged to the College of Lictors, probably some 300 by imperial times, and carried the magistrate's *fasces*.
macellum An open-air market with booths. The forae started out this way, but were distinguished by the buildings that sprang up around them, whereas the *macellum* remained a simple space.
magistrate Elected executives of the senate and people. The hierarchy went: military tribune, quaestor, tribune of the plebs, plebeian aedile, curule aedile (the most junior with *imperium*), praetor, consul. In times of emergency the senate was allowed to appoint an extraordinary magistrate called dictator, who was indemnified for his actions when his term of six months was over.
maniple The tactical unit of a legion containing two centuries of soldiers, abandoned in the Marian reforms.
manumission Making a slave free, *lit.* "send from the hand."
minim A red pigment that triumphant generals painted on their faces, apparently to look like the terracotta statue of Jupiter Optimus Maximus.
modius, modii The Roman basic measure of grain, weighing approximately 13 pounds.
nobilis *lit.* "nobility," the term that described a man of consular rank and his descendants. It was coined by plebeians after they were permitted to the consulship to reduce the distinction of being a patrician by birth.
nomen, nomina Family name or *gens* (eg. Aemilius, Cornelius).

oppidum A Celtic (Gaulish) hill fort or fortified settlement.
ordo *lit.* "order," a social grouping with a similar family background and amount of wealth. The best known is the *Ordo Equester*, whose members were referred to as the *equites*, or knights. Originally Rome's top citizens were equipped with horses paid for by the state to be a cavalry unit. By the early republican period there were 1,800 *equites*, most buying and maintaining their own horses as a matter of civic pride. By the second century BC, this had become a social class distinction with little military connection, since Rome's cavalry was recruited from among the allies.
pantheon The array of all Roman gods.
(patron) patronus A man of rank who held the allegiance of clients in return for favors of money, legal assistance, or political promotion opportunities.
patrician The Roman aristocracy of the archaic period. They lost their special rights as plebeian power increased, and by the later republic were frequently impoverished. This was the case with one of the most ancient family, the Julians, by the time Julius Caesar was rising to power.
phalerus, phalerae Ornamented disks of silver or gold originally worn by knights as insignia. During the republican era they were awarded to cavalrymen as awards for valor, and later to legionaries as well. Infantrymen wore them on the leather straps worn over the mail shirt.
pilaster A half-column or half-pillar attached to a wall, more for decorative purposes than structural.
pilum, pilae The Roman infantry spear introduced by Marius with a barbed iron head. A weakness where the shaft joined the head meant it would break on contact, rendering the weapon useless to the enemy but easily repairable by Roman armorers.
plebeian, plebs Roman citizens of one of the Five Classes who were not of patrician rank. Originally the plebs were forbidden election to any magisterial post, but this changed rapidly during the republican period until plebs occupied almost all senior posts.
plebiscitum A law enacted in the plebeian assembly, which had the same force of law as a *lex* passed by the *comitia centuriata*. Originally a plebiscite was separately distinguished from a law, but later the two merged in the records, and all were called a *lex*.
pomerium The sacred boundary of the city of Rome. In the religious sense, Rome existed within the boundary and everything outside it was Roman territory. The *pomerium* is said to have been created by King Servius Tullus, but it did not exactly follow the course of the Servian Wall. The *pomerium* could only be enlarged by a man who substantially increased the size of Roman territory, and it was enlarged considerably by Augustus.
pontifex A priest, which may have been derived from the notion that a *pontifex* was a bridge builder—bridges being considered structures with magical or mysterious properties.
Pontifex Maximus The most senior of all Roman priests, who supervised the members of the various priestly colleges. The ancient kings held the title Rex Sacorum (holy king). Despite the universal loathing of the kings, the young republic kept the title because it was sacred, but created the Pontifex Maximus to be superior. The Pontifex Maximus was elected, which made him a statesman and head of the state religion.
porta A gate.
(portico) porticus A colonnade with a roof above, either as a straight arcade or enclosing a square (*peristylus*). Porticoes were frequently used as places of business and for meetings of the senate.
praefectus fabrum *lit.* "the prefect of making" (quartermaster in modern parlance). He was responsible for every aspect of supplying and maintaining the Roman armies, although usually a civilian not a soldier. Like his modern counterpart he was able to enrich himself through the rich contracts he handled.
praenomen, praenomina The first or given name of a Roman man. There were not many in use, which complicates distinguishing between members of the same *gens* or family, hence the importance of the *cognomen* or nickname.
praetor The second most senior rung on the *cursus honorum* of magistrates (see *consul*). Originally, it was the highest rank until the republic introduced the consuls. At first there were two, the *praetor urbanus*, responsible for Rome itself, and the *praetor peregrinus*, who looked after everything outside the pomerium. With acquisition of overseas territories, the number increased to four and then six *praetors*. A praetor was responsible for litigation and judicial matters.
Praetorian Guard Originally a bodyguard for a *praetor*, but later a separate arm of the military devoted to the safe-keeping of an emperor and his family. The Praetorians were responsible for the making and breaking of many emperors.
princeps The "first citizen," a title assumed by Augustus. Previously, the Princeps Senatus was the chosen leader of the senate, but in the imperial period the simpler *princeps* was used to describe the emperor, hence the use of the word "principate" to describe an imperial reign. The modern word "prince" is derived from it.
quadriga A four-horse chariot.
quaestor Lowest rung on the *cursus honorum* (see *consul*), and generally a fiscal role (treasury, port customs, provincial finances).
res publica *lit.* "thing" or "affair of the public." The republic is a government that constitutes the people as a whole and describes the Roman constitution after the abolition of the kings.
saepta *lit.* "sheepfold," which describes the way the open space on the Campus Martius was divided by temporary fences so that the Five Classes could vote in their centuries at an assembly. Later, buildings such as the Saepta Julia borrowed the term.
toga Made from a single piece of lightweight woolen cloth, only a full citizen of Rome was permitted to wear the toga. Its extreme length (about 15 feet) and the complex of folds it created when draped makes it unlikely that a togate man wore anything else under it. There were several types of toga: *toga alba*, ordinary white garment; *toga candida*, specially whitened to look smart when canvassing for election; *toga picta*, all purple for triumphing generals; *toga praetexta*, purple-bordered for curule magistrates; *toga pulla*, black mourning toga; *toga trabea*, particolored in strips for augurs; *toga virilis*, toga of manhood, actually a *toga alba*.
tribunus Originally a man representing one of the Roman tribus, or tribes. Later, it came to mean an official representing the interests of certain political groups.
triclinium *lit.* "three couches," or the dining room, so called because Roman meals were eaten reclining on three couches arranged in a U-shape. When women were permitted to dine with men, they sat on low stools in the center of the U. Several diners could be seated on the broad, long couches.
vexillum Flag or banner
via A road or main highway.

INDEX